D0225321

HISTORY OF EDUCATION AND CULTURE IN AMERICA

Second Edition

Library - St. Joseph's College
222 Clinton Avenue
Brooklyn, N.Y. 11205

H. Warren Button
State University of New York at Buffalo

Eugene F. Provenzo, Jr.
University of Miami

Prentice Hall, *Englewood Cliffs, New Jersey 07632*

Library of Congress Cataloging-in-Publication Data

Button, H. Warren.
  History of education and culture in America.

  Bibliography.
  Includes index.
  1. Education—United States—History. 2. Schools—
United States—History. 3. United States—Civilization.
I. Provenzo, Eugene F. II. Title
LA205.B86 1988   370'.973   88-5834
ISBN 0-13-390162-9

Editorial/production supervision: Mary A. Bardoni and Cyndy Rymer
Cover design: Ben Santora
Manufacturing buyer: Peter Havens

© 1989, 1983 by Prentice-Hall, Inc.
A Division of Simon & Schuster
Englewood Cliffs, New Jersey 07632

All rights reserved. No part of this book may be
reproduced, in any form or by any means,
without permission in writing from the publisher.

Printed in the United States of America

10 9 8 7 6 5 4 3 2 1

ISBN 0-13-390162-9

Prentice-Hall International (UK) Limited, *London*
Prentice-Hall of Australia Pty. Limited, *Sydney*
Prentice-Hall Canada Inc., *Toronto*
Prentice-Hall Hispanoamericana, S.A., *Mexico*
Prentice-Hall of India Private Limited, *New Delhi*
Prentice-Hall of Japan, Inc., *Tokyo*
Simon & Schuster Asia Pte. Ltd., *Singapore*
Editora Prentice-Hall do Brasil, Ltda., *Rio de Janeiro*

To Raymond E. Callahan

CONTENTS

122574

PREFACE

CHANGES SINCE THE LAST EDITION

This edition of *History of Education and Culture in America* has been changed, and we hope improved, in several ways. Shifts in American culture now seem more apparent, and to have occurred more rapidly. It is now to be argued that our values and moods have shifted and that what was once seen as admirable self-reliance evolved into money-making, status-seeking utilitarianism, and to narcissism and "expressive individualism."

It is far more clear now that the United States's role as manufacturer and producer of raw materials has declined. Ours is now primarily a service and information processing economy. New technologies, especially the computer and television, seem likely to have as great an effect as did the invention of movable type.

Schools' efforts to achieve equality have paused, if they have not ended, and it is possible to assess tentatively their successes and limits. The active search in the schools and elsewhere for individual freedom has been muted. We are now near the end of eight years of a conservative presidency. Schools, which were called on to do more, are now called on to do less, but to do that better, to achieve "excellence."

We have attempted to take into account the most important recent scholarship, most notably that on the nature of progressivism and on present society and culture. We have profited from reviewers' constructive comments and have corrected minor errors that have come to our attention. The Introduction has been rewritten. A background section, "Years of Turmoil," and a brief history of computers has been added, at the cost of minor deletions elsewhere. Descriptions of the schooling of women, blacks, and Native Americans have been redistributed to provide for them a more nearly satisfactory context. For errors of fact or interpretation that have been introduced in the revision, H. Warren Button accepts responsibility.

ACKNOWLEDGMENTS

Our first obligation is to our students collectively, who provided the impetus for this book. Among them we are especially obligated to Phyllis McGruder Chase, Truman Beckley Brown, Concepcion Garcia, Thomas A. Michalski, William Bonds Thomas, and Chokesui Ahagon. We have also been aided by several graduate assistants, especially John C. Ramsay and Elizabeth Graham. Our colleagues have also been most helpful, among them Maxine Seller, who read the manuscript in its entirety, and Robert S. Harnack, Gail P. Kelly, and Melvin J. Tucker, who reviewed portions of it. Our special thanks are due to William E. Eaton, Robert Kottkamp, Wayne Urban, Donald R. Warren, and Arthur Wirth. Our wives, Lee and Asterie, read carefully, criticized constructively, vastly encouraged, and showed the greatest forbearance. The flaws and errors of this book are our own.

In revising we were aided by William E. Eaton and Edgar Z. Friedenberg.

INTRODUCTION

WHY HISTORY?

Teachers and other professional educators need to know the histories of the institutions that educate and of their roles within them.* Without knowledge of their pasts, of how they have come to be and how they have changed or have failed to change, these institutions and roles cannot be understood and, therefore, cannot be intelligently improved.

For improving schooling, we believe that history can explain something of the present, how we have gotten where we are. It can generate hypotheses that partly account for schools' obstinate, perverse, adamantine resistance to change.

Debates on the quality of schooling are again loud and strident. Dozens of proposals have appeared. Some hold promise. Some are perennial and have in the past failed. Some are reactionary. Most of these proposals will be seen more clearly in the light of the past.

In these ways history of education has immediate usefulness, utility value. Beyond immediate usefulness, history has other values. It provides a sense of

*The Introduction is in part an adaptation of H. Warren Button, "Creating More Useable Pasts: History in the Study of Education," *Educational Researcher*, VIII (June, 1979), pp. 3-9.

continuity, of "community remembered,"** a feeling of being a part of one of the greatest of American enterprises, granting the enterprise has been only partly successful. Knowing of our collective past, although certainly we cannot approve of all that has been undertaken or done, provides a sense of professional and personal identity.

WHAT IS HISTORY OF EDUCATION?

At the beginning of a book, its subject and its purposes should be made clear. By *education* we mean all efforts to produce learning. One of our main concerns is with the institutions in which education has taken place. Of course the schools are such institutions. But the family has also been an educating institution, and a much more important one. Other educating institutions include churches, libraries, newspapers, and more recently motion pictures, radio, and television. Schools are the foremost professional concern of most of us, but schools have always existed with other educating institutions and in a broader cultural context. We are also concerned with the roles in educational institutions. Naturally, we have not been able to follow in detail all these institutions and roles.

The word *history* has at least three meanings. In the sense we will usually use it, *history* is the story and description of the past. The story should tell about what happened and how it happened and to whom it happened. But the historian's account should do more than that. It should also explain the story, telling why events and actions have taken place, and the effects they have had. This book was not written, as some others have been, to demonstrate a social theory. We are interested in social theories, but as ways to explain, not as theories to be historically demonstrated.

History can also mean the past itself. But there is no way in which all the events that have taken place can be recovered and documented, or that any event can be described completely. As a perhaps not too trivial example, it is impossible for any of us to recount all the events in our personal lives during, say, a week ago last Thursday. Not only is it impossible, but if it were possible, it would be meaningless, cluttered, and obscured by inconsequentials. Our story will be as faithful to the past as possible, but it will not be the past itself in unrecoverable entirety.

A third meaning of *history* implies that fate has foreordained events and made them inevitable. That meaning we do not accept.

As in every discipline and specialty, there have been changes in the ways in which history of education has been seen and written about. When, nearly a hundred years ago, history of education first appeared in teacher preparation curricula, it was history of schools. Although that now seems quite inadequate, it should not seem surprising. American historians then were writing about the history of govern-

---

**For citations, see "Bibliography, Sources, and Notes," pp. 335–359. The last three words of each quotation are given, followed by its source.

ment as an institution. The most prominent of historians of education was Ellwood P. Cubberley, who was primarily interested in the further development of schools.

By the 1950s it was becoming clear that history of education of this sort had several shortcomings. First, there was its concentration on public schools, on their spread and growth, as if nothing else had mattered and as if they had been entirely uninfluenced by other institutions or events of their times. Moreover, it did not tell of their shortcomings and failures to serve either their clients the pupils or the society of which the schools were a part. At best this was uninformed and unreflective. At worst it was dishonest.

One of these shortcomings, history of education's narrow focus upon the schools, was the subject of essays by Barnard Bailyn and Lawrence Cremin. Bailyn, writing about pre-Revolutionary War history of education, and Cremin, writing about history of education more generally, argued that *education* should be defined more broadly, that a variety of institutions educated, and that all of them fell within the proper scope of historians of education.

The second difficulty, the overly-optimistic, ever-triumphant note of history of education as Cubberley had written it, was addressed by historians who are referred to as *revisionists*. The most prominent of these historians has been Michael L. Katz. The revisionists' view has been and is that society in the United States has been from its beginnings dominated by the rich and powerful and the middle class, and that schools from their beginnings have served to maintain the status quo, to prevent change, to assure the submission of workers and the lower class. The revisionists feel, to paraphrase Horace Mann, that it is not by chance that the schooling of the poor has been poor schooling, that the children of the poor have been routed into schooling that would perpetuate their poverty, or have been dropped out of school entirely. The schools, the revisionists argue, have been used to indoctrinate rather than to inform. We feel that the revisionist historians have been in many respects correct. But to describe the schools as always oppressive is as inadequate as to describe them as always beneficial and triumphant.

We see a third difficulty in history of education as it is generally written. Far too often history of education is presented as a dry and earnest thing, and an impersonal thing, as if no teacher, pupil, parent, or onlooker had been a human being. History of education should not be written as if no human, feeling and alive and with human frailties, had ever taken part in it.

HOW? WHY?

The explaining of causes and effects of events is less simple than it at first seems. We feel, as many other historians do, that human nature, culture, and society are far too complex to allow us to explain, as a physicist might, by the use of a simple and elegant law. Every important development in education seems to come from a combination of causes. The following are some of these (not necessarily in order of their importance): culture, the customs and habits of the time; underlying values as to what is good and what is important; the nature and growth (or stagnation) of our economy; ideas, both as to the nature of the individual and of society; and technology, from the invention of printing to the introduction of the computer.

WHO?

One older way of thinking about the causes of events is what has been called the "great man theory," the conviction that history as a story is the biographies of a few great men (and perhaps women) whose thoughts, words, and deeds have determined the shape of things. Obviously there have been highly important reformers and thinkers, and their works and thoughts have played important parts in shaping the world. We shall try to summarize their actions and describe their thoughts. However, great reformers and thinkers have not been the sole causes of change in society and culture, and often have not been the most important. For us, it is at least as important to tell of how it seemed at the time to those who were alive then. We are interested in the everyday lives of those who have taught, and of those who have been taught.

WHEN?

History is a story that has no natural starting point, except with the dawn of mankind or Adam and Eve. The story we will tell begins with a prologue, a description of the sources of American culture in the England of Shakespeare and Elizabeth I. The more remote sources of our culture are in medieval or even classical times, but we will not describe them here. To begin to understand the culture of the United States, we must understand how it was formed, and to understand the schools we must first understand the culture in which they have existed, and of which they have been a part.

Part One
BEGINNINGS

Education and schools are parts of a wider culture and society. Therefore the history of education, or even the history of schools only, must be written against the background of a history of culture and society. Since the roots of American education are English, this brief description begins with England and then follows the growth and change of the colonies.

The 1500s had been times of change for Europe. The New World and voyages to the East had yielded rich and splendid cargoes of gold and silver, silk, and spices. The revival of trade circulated the new wealth throughout Europe. Intellectual riches came from the rediscovery and reexamination of writings and manuscripts from classical Rome and Greece. It was the time of the Renaissance, of the rebirth or reawakening of the traditions of classical literature, art, and architecture. The scholars known as *humanists* who led this revival saw themselves as taking up the pursuit of knowledge where it had been interrupted by barbarians a thousand years before. The works of the classical authors existed only in hand-written manuscripts until about 1500, when they were printed with the use of movable type, which aided the humanists and increased their influence.

In the 1500s other men had looked at the decadent Church and protested. Protestants believed the Church must be returned to its essentials, to its original simplicity. The Church's accumulations of fifteen hundred years—the elaborate ceremonials and rituals, its riches and wordliness—must be discarded. Protestantism, of course, was a cause to which men dedicated their lives and for which some suffered death. By the early 1600s there were many Protestants in England. The most important of them were the Puritans, whose purpose was to purify the Church of England, not to replace it. They relied first on the Bible, "the word of God," which by then had by then been translated into English and printed.

In England, with the death of Elizabeth I in 1603, an age of exuberance was coming to an end. A great age of seamanship and discovery, typified by the explorer Sir Francis Drake, was over. The splendid flowering of English literature and drama, at its height in William Shakespeare's plays, was also coming to an end. The 1600s in England were less colorful than the Elizabethan era, less remarkable for art than for science, and most remarkable for religious disputes and revolution inspired by religion. By 1600, the middle class was, as a result of peace, prosperity, and trade, much more numerous than before and had an increased influence in politics. The middle-class merchants and craftsmen and landowners accumulated wealth and, as Puritans, power enough by the 1640s to challenge—and execute—a king.

When Columbus searched for a shorter way to the Far East, his voyage joined together the fates and futures of Europe and the Americas. In South and Central America the Spanish found empires to conquer and riches to loot. For them the land farther north was less promising. There were no gold mines or riches to seize. The eastern shoreline of North America stretched for 2,000 miles and more, northward and eastward. It was indented and broken in many places by river mouths and other safe harbors. The climate was temperate in most places. The Native Americans, misnamed *Indians*, belonged to hundreds of tribes with almost as many different languages. In general, they had little in common with one another and did not unite to resist the settlement of their lands by the early colonists. The existence of numerous rivers and harbors, of a moderate climate, and natives unorganized for resistance, made North America splendid for colonization, if not for immediate exploitation. The Atlantic seaboard, a narrow strip along bays and navigable rivers, was the location of the first settlements. It was also the area in which nearly all settlers lived until after the Revolution.

The establishment of the colonies followed a fairly general pattern. The first step was the organization of a *company*, a group of adventurers or investors. It was desirable, if not absolutely necessary, to have a charter—a license to occupy a part of the land. An expedition was organized and ships contracted. The voyage itself was hazardous and trying—the Pilgrims' six-week passage from old England to New England, for example, was not long by the standards of the times. In the early colonies there were "starving years," the interval between arrival and the harvesting of food enough for survival. Only after these stages could a colony prosper and grow. There were always risks and often failures, especially for the earliest colonies. It is to be understood that there were exceptions to the general pattern of settlement. Plymouth Colony was established in a place where the Pilgrims did not have charter rights to settle. Rhode Island and Connecticut were begun without sea voyage, by men and women who came by land from Massachusetts. There was no "starving time," or famine, in Boston.

Many different motives led to the establishment of the colonies. No colony was begun for a single reason. Some colonies were established primarily for trade and profit. Other colonies, most notably Massachusetts, were founded in the hope of establishing godly and perfect societies, religious utopias based upon their interpretation of the Bible. Still other colonies were intended to serve as refuges for those persecuted for their religious faith. Nearly all the colonists expected to better themselves in material ways. Some expected riches.

Virginia is a good example of a colony founded in hopes of profit. The London Company was incorporated to colonize. Stock was sold. A board of directors was named. A charter from the king was secured for colonization along the southern Atlantic coast and west to the "South Sea." The expedition was organized in London—badly organized, as it turned out. The leaders were ineffectual, the men "disordered persons . . . profane . . . riotous . . . diseased . . . crazed . . ." (also sick, starved, regimented, and seeking a new life). During their twenty-week voyage in 1606-07, 16 of the 120 men died, and only 53 lived through the first winter. The colony survived largely because of the leadership of Captain John Smith; corn was planted, and peace made with the Indians. Contrary to initial hopes, there was no gold to be found. The "South Sea" remained undiscovered. Trade with the Indians was not very profitable, and in addition they resisted Christianization and sometimes bloodily and violently attacked the colonists. It would be several years before the Virginia colony was secure and before the planting of tobacco would lead to more general prosperity.

By 1648, there were fifteen thousand settlers on small farms along the branching bays of eastern, tidewater, Virginia. Gardening and farming, hunting and fishing provided plentiful food. Most of the land was forest. Houses were still small, and planters worked their corn and tobacco fields with their "servants," men and women who had indentured themselves—or contracted—to work five years, more or less, to pay for their ocean crossing. Only a few blacks had been brought over, and there were no slavery laws in Virginia during its first fifty years. These would come later. The early Virginians were members of the Church of England, but Puritan in sentiment. Churches were built soon after the settlers arrived; church attendance was required, and idleness, gambling, and working on Sundays were forbidden. The impressive plantation houses of Virginia would not be built until the 1700s, but the founders of some of Virginia's most famed families, Byrd, Lee, and Carter for instance, were already in the process of establishing themselves.

Massachusetts was the most important colony of god-seeking utopians, although the settlers also hoped for prosperity. Indeed, they held that "stewardship," the accumulation and care of wealth was in itself a sign of grace. Unlike the Virginians, they came in part because the English government in the 1630s frowned increasingly upon Puritan beliefs.

The most important group of Puritan settlers arrived in 1630. Under the leadership of Governor John Winthrop they brought with them their company's charter and were its officers, as well as the leaders of the colony's government. More than a thousand men, women, and children arrived aboard seventeen ships. Boston and seven other towns were established.

In spite of Winthrop's hopes and plans, Boston did not remain a "city of God," if it ever was. Perhaps the hopes and lives of the Puritans are most fairly represented by the smaller towns. Dedham, a few miles south of Boston, serves as an example. The founding families of Dedham had come from a number of places in England; they had found that they shared a common faith. The town was founded in 1636, at which time a government made up of the settlers was formed. House lots around a square, a *common*, were allocated, and outlying fields assigned in proportion to the size and wealth of families. After long discussion and prayer, the congregation agreed to a church "covenant," and a minister was recruited. Disputes were to be settled as among brothers. There are virtually no instances from this period of the prosecution of court trials or suits. To live in Dedham was to live in a godly place. It was to live in peace and tranquility, in families, houses, and a village such as those known in England. For forty years Dedham was in a modest way a working utopia.

In Boston many of those who came were "strangers," not members of the Puritan Congregational Churches. Often Puritans' sons and daughters failed to have the experience of being born again, a condition for church membership. Before 1700 the better-off merchants were accumulating more wealth. The poor remained poor. Concern had developed over the increasing number of unmarried mothers. There had been an attempt to open a brothel in the city. Even more distressful, those in control of Boston found themselves threatened by those with democratic tendencies. The Puritan hopes of a religious utopia had failed. Bostonians were interested in trade and other matters as well as in the church. Even at the expense of utopianism, they were prudent men and women, intent on living by the laws of England so as to protect their charter and rights. Successful "stewardship" increased the difference between rich and poor. (A famous historian has said that America has been the *dis*proving ground of utopias. But Americans have always had a fondness for utopias, John Winthrop's and others since.)

Pennsylvania is representative of the colonies established as refuge. Its founder, William Penn, was a devout Quaker, or Friend, and a firm believer in freedom in Christian worship. The Quakers were the most extreme Protestant group to emerge from the late 1600s. For them, repentance and truth were dependent upon the individual. The church was not necessary for salvation. Penn himself had been imprisoned several times in England. Quakers there were prohibited from holding office and even from attending universities. Penn's colony was to be a refuge for not only the Quakers, but also for the members of other faiths.

Pennsylvania's charter was secured from the king of England as payment for the king's debt to Penn's father. Pennsylvania's *Frame of Government* explicitly provided for freedom of worship. Philadelphia ("City of Friends") was established in 1682. The Quakers welcomed to the city many German Mennonites, also religious refugees. Except for the New York Dutch, the Mennonites were the first large non-English–speaking group in the colonies. Pennsylvania land was fertile and cheap, and although established late, became one of the largest and most prosperous of the English colonies.

The other colonies were in some ways like Virginia, Massachusetts, and Pennsylvania. Like the Virginians, Marylanders sought profit from the raising of tobacco. Carolinians later had the same goal and raised rice and indigo. Rhode Island, Connecticut, and later New Hampshire were offshoots of Puritan Massachusetts. Maryland, settled earlier, had been in part intended as a haven for Catholics. Georgia, last of the original thirteen colonies to be settled, was also to be a refuge, though for people who were poor rather than discriminated against on grounds of religion.

In the 160 years before independence, feelings about religion weakened, and churches of many kinds appeared in most of the colonies. In the middle 1700s religious enthusiasm grew during the "Great Awakening," which was partly a reaction to *rationalism,* the cold and impersonal scientific logic that was gaining support.

In those 160 years the colonies' population grew to three million. Puritans and planters and Quakers were joined by tens of thousands of German Protestants and Scotch-Irish Presbyterians, as well as by growing numbers of blacks. There were at least a few men and women from every kingdom in Christendom. Prosperous port cities, like the smaller cities in England, developed, although nearly everyone (nineteen out of twenty) still lived on farms or in villages.

In some colonies, growth after the first years was natural. Families were larger, especially beginning in the later 1700s. Fewer babies died. Individuals lived longer. Once the hazards of the sea crossings were overcome, the colonies had a "healthy clime" as compared with England. Pennsylvania and the other colonies grew by immigration also. The Germans continued to come, and Mennonites and members of many sects established communities of their own. The Presbyterian "Scotch-Irish" of northern Ireland were driven from their homes by failures of crops, by English trade and manufacturing restrictions, and by poverty. There were unwelcome English restrictions upon Presbyterian churches.

Many of Pennsylvania's immigrants came as contract laborers, *indentured servants.* Most indentured themselves because they had no money to pay for the sea crossing, but the signing of indentures seems to have been common because a "master" could give guidance in one's first years in the New World. Before 1776, the population of Pennsylvania had spilled southwestward, into the Senandoah Valley of Virginia and onto the Piedmont—the uplands—of the Carolinas, and even into northeastern Georgia.

The need in tidewater South for workers led to employing indentured servants there, too. As an added incentive, those who brought indentured servants were granted land, fifty acres for each servant. By the middle 1700s, indentured servants were harder to obtain. More slaves were introduced into the colonies. Most had been kidnapped or bought from villages in West Africa. Blacks were first introduced into America at Jamestown in 1619, but it was only later that the English-speaking American colonies became an important market for slaves. (There would be slaves, though in smaller numbers, in all the other colonies.)

Long before 1776, differences in wealth and power in the colonies increased. To have wealth was to gain wealth, of course. Some New England merchants who had come from London, or had relatives there, had credit. In Virginia the cost of a plantation also came from the profits of importing goods and exporting tobacco. Other plantations were bought from the earnings of doctors and lawyers, and occasionally of ministers—*parsons*. Sometimes marriage to a rich widow provided capital. In the 1700s, a few families in Virginia were "well-off," though not nearly as rich as the richest Englishmen. They owned handsome houses, shares in ships, iron furnaces and forges, and thousands and sometimes tens of thousands of acres of land. While much forested land was kept in reserve to replace worn-out fields, other land was bought for investment or speculation. The children of wealthy planters, automatically entitled to special consideration because of their families, were "aristocrats."

Yet wealth was not the norm. Most colonists in the North and South were of the "middling sort." In most instances they were farmers, but they also were skilled and semiskilled workers, and their families. The social structures of the colonies were relatively open. Although most families did not, it was possible for the poor to become rich. For the Pepperells of Maine, two generations was needed, as was the case for the Byrds of Virginia. Accumulation of wealth was possible within one's own lifetime. One early Massachusetts governor, Sir William Phips, for example, had started life as an orphan and shepherd. What most often happened was that a former indentured servant became the owner of a farm, or the son of a "middling" sea captain or small trader became a merchant. Downward movement came less often. For the slave, of course, there was only the smallest mobility at most, from field hand to plantation craftsman. Being freed was rare.

What men wrote in the 1600s often seems strange now. It is confusing to read their writings with sprinklings of references to the Bible and now-forgotten authors and Latin quotations. In contrast, what was written in the later 1700s now often seems clearer, more straightforward and modern, to our minds perhaps more logical. We understand with less difficulty what a John Adams or a Thomas Jefferson or a Benjamin Franklin said. Their language is plain to us. The "provincials," those who lived in the colonies in the fifty years or so before the Revolution, were practical persons. They were materialistic—as many of us are—and wanted to better themselves and to own more. Provincial Americans belonged to any of a number of churches, or none. They were not much interested in an idea that seemed to have no immediate use. They were violently anti-Catholic and suspicious of "Papists." To Englishmen, Protestant since the reign of Henry VIII, "Papists" were the enemy. They were prejudiced against Jews, though those prejudices were weaker than they had been, and weaker than they would become. Blacks were despised. The provincial Americans could wait for rewards. "A penny saved is a penny earned," Ben Franklin wrote.

Society and culture in America would change. Not all the colonists in 1776 saw themselves as Americans. Some saw themselves as loyal Englishmen away from home. Others thought of themselves as "Bay Staters," Virginians, or whatever, and would for long to come. Still, the pattern of society, culture, and nation had been set. Chapter 1 describes schooling and education during roughly the first hundred years—the Colonial era. Chapter 2 deals with Provincial America until the time of the Revolution.

Chapter One
EUROPE
AND COLONIAL SOURCES

Although the early colonization of North America was also undertaken by the Spanish, French, Dutch, and even the Swedes, the English settlers played decisive roles in laying the foundations for American culture and education. Yet the English settlers were also European in their traditions and outlook. This being the case, it is in the context of a wider European cultural heritage and tradition that an analysis of American education must begin.

The development of preuniversity schooling had been somewhat erratic in England during the Middle Ages. Most schools were connected with cathedrals, although some were under the control of other church organizations. The schools were intended primarily for the education of the clergy. (*Clerical* now has two meanings, "office work" and "of the clergy." The meanings were once identical.) Schools were generally subject to the supervision and control of the Church, which not only licensed the school masters, but also dictated methods of instruction and the subject matter to be taught.

A child in England during the 1500s learned to read by one of several means. Children might be taught to read by a local priest or in a "reading school" that was sometimes combined with a Latin grammar school. For boys, other opportunities for elementary schooling were provided by "song schools" supported by churches and cathedrals to train boys as choristers. In addition to musical training, pupils

FIGURE 1-1   Allegorical representation of the progress of education from the 1508 Basel edition of *Margarita Philosophica* of Gregory de Reisch. Wisdom holds in her hand a hornbook. The youth, having mastered the hornbook, will advance toward the temple of knowledge. Wisdom holds the key to the temple, in which are included authors such as Donatus, Priscian, Aristotle, and Boethius. Reprinted in Ellwood P. Cubberley, *Syllabus of Lectures on History of Education* (New York: Macmillan, 1902), p. 85.

in the song schools were taught reading and writing, and occasionally the rudiments of Latin.

The Latin grammar schools were not, as our modern use of "grammar school" implies, elementary schools. Instead, they had as their purpose the teaching of Latin grammar and language. Their origin lay in the educational principles of classical antiquity. The schools were almost entirely dependent upon ancient Roman texts as the basis for their curriculum. Students memorized grammatical rules and examples from the works of ancient authors such as Donatus and Priscian, or from medieval grammarians such as Alexander de Villedieu. After they had a command of the rudiments of Latin grammar, the students would read introductory texts, such as Aesop's *Fables* and Cato's *Disticha*, which was a collection of maxims in verse. They also read more advanced Latin works such as the poems of Terence, the rhetorician Cicero, the history of Sallust, and Ovid and Virgil. Early Christian authors such as Prudentius and Boethius were frequently read also.

Significantly, the Latin grammar school students did not study complete works, but only extracts taken from various authors. Instruction was exclusively oral. Typically, the master would read aloud from a hand-written manuscript. After explaining the content he would have students repeat the information to him. Most learning and teaching was, therefore, by recitation. Speaking Latin was emphasized as much as reading or writing it.

The curriculum in medieval Latin grammar schools was generally limited. Although examples for instruction in Latin were based primarily on the works of ancient authors, the Latin that was taught was for use in the church and in other formal situations was of a practical sort, closely linked to the vernacular. There was little attention to or appreciation for the subtleties and sophistication of Latin as a language.

Despite dependence upon ancient sources, medieval grammar schools largely rejected the cultures and traditions of antiquity. Greek, which had been particularly important in ancient schools, was totally neglected. The adoption and use of classical Latin authors was subordinated by the church to sacred learning.

By 1600 a number of remarkable changes had taken place in the Latin grammar schools in England. Humanism (emphatically Christian and not secular) changed the curriculum. Printed school books changed ways of instruction. The growth of the middle class in England changed the nature and aims of the boys who were Latin grammar school students.

Renaissance humanists believed that learning and education provided the keys to human affairs and advocated the revival of ancient Roman and Greek literature and education. The humanists spurned the utilitarian Latin of the Middle Ages and instead adopted as models the elegance of Cicero and other authors of Rome in the age of Emperor Augustus. The study of the Greek language was revived and the works of Plato and Aristotle and other ancient Greek authors were reexamined. In England, the attempt to revive classical texts and methods of instruction was led by the humanist scholars William Grocyn, John Colet, Desiderius Erasmus, and Thomas More. Excepting More, each of these men had studied on the Continent, and each of them was thoroughly imbued with the philosophical ideas and beliefs of antiquity.

While the humanists were interested in the philosophies and literature of the ancients, they were at the same time Christians and concerned with the reform of the church. In England, John Colet and others strongly criticized the corruption of the English clergy and called for the return to a simpler form of apostolic Christianity. On the Continent, Dutch-born Desiderius Erasmus emphasized the duty of parents to provide their children with a proper Christian education. Both Colet and Erasmus, and many others as well, felt that only through the careful study and reinterpretation of ancient Christian texts could the true intent and purpose of the church fathers be understood, and be fulfilled. At the same time, the study of classical Roman authors would provide models of language and citizenship.

The principal source of guidance for the humanists in reviving the educational philosophy of the ancients was the Roman rhetorician Quintilian's work, the *Institutio Oratoria*, from the middle of the fourth century. Quintilian's aim was to outline the training necessary to produce an educated citizen. During the Middle Ages, the work was only available in a very fragmented form. It was rediscovered in its entirety in 1416, by the Florentine humanist Poggio. The *Institutio* was used extensively by the humanists during the first half of the sixteenth century to define the philosophy and curriculum of the English and continental Latin grammar schools.

In their use of the educational methods outlined by Quintilian, the humanists were attempting to recreate the pedagogical system of the ancient Romans. They created something quite different. What they brought about was a new synthesis, one which combined the educational theories of the ancients with the educational practices of the later Middle Ages and the early Renaissance.

In the Middle Ages, formal education and a knowledge of Medieval Latin had served the needs of priests and other clergymen. In the 1600s formal learning had become valuable in careers not only in the Church but in government or in commerce as well. As trade and wealth grew, the number of middle-class merchants and craftsmen increased. To them, Latin grammar school education for their sons was increasingly valuable.

In 1483 John Anwykill, a master of the Magdalen College School at Oxford, had published a grammar and later published a phrase book with translations into English of excerpts of Terence. By 1500 John Holt had published the elementary instructional text *Lac Puerorum*, which included woodcuts intended to help students learn declensions. By 1600 the boys in Latin grammar schools were fully supplied with school books.

The Renaissance English Latin grammar school traces its origins to the Cathedral School at St. Paul's in London. In the twelfth century a school had been founded in conjunction with the cathedral. By the beginning of the Renaissance, however, it was no longer in existence. The school was refounded in 1509 by John Colet. Instead of placing the school under the control of the cathedral, Colet and his supporters established as lay trustee the London guild of mercers (cloth merchants). When he established the school, Colet was neither concerned with educating the clergy nor the nobility, nor with sons of members of the guilds. Schooling was to be for the sons of the general citizenry.

In 1512, Colet appointed William Lily as first master. With Erasmus, Lily was largely responsible for drawing up the curriculum of the school. The spirit of this curriculum and the school in general is clearly outlined in the statutes for the school written by Colet in 1518. Under "What Shall Be Taught," Colet wrote that he hoped that the students would always be taught

> . . . in good literature both Latin and Greek, and good authors such as have the very Roman elegance joined with wisdom, especially Christian authors that wrote their wisdom with clean and chaster Latin either in verse or in prose, for my intent is by this school specially to increase knowledge and worshipping of God and Our Lord Christ Jesus and good Christian life and manners in the children.

Unfortunately, the original curriculum from St. Paul's does not survive. William Lily, in his *Carmen de Morbuis*, which he prefixed to his Latin grammar, mentioned that Virgil, Terence, and Cicero were the most important authors to be read by the schoolboys. A subsequent curriculum outlined by Cardinal Woolsey in 1528 for his school at Ipswich, England and almost surely derived from the course of study at St. Paul's, was based exclusively on pagan authors. In the third form* Aesop and Terence were to be read, in the fourth form Virgil, in the fifth form Cicero, in the sixth form Sallust or Caesar, in the seventh form Horace and Ovid, and in the eighth form a general selection of ancients. Essentially the same curriculum could be seen in other English grammar schools during the late sixteenth and early seventeenth centuries.

Authors read in conjunction with the humanist curriculum, and included in the Renaissance grammar schools, were not much different from those studied during the Middle Ages. Humanists made their most important departure from the medieval educational tradition by developing authoritative texts, as well as fully reestablishing the Classical curriculum in its entirety—in particular the study of Greek.

English and continental humanists also created much that was new. Erasmus formulated a series of elementary exercises in Latin during the late 1490s, while he was a theology student. In its earliest version, the work consisted of simple idioms, phrases, and examples of dialogue. Expanded during his first visit to England, these exercises were eventually published in 1518 under the title of *Colloquies*. With his other major pedagogical works, *De Copia* and *Adages*, the *Colloquies* represented the continuation of the classical Latin tradition infused with the spirit of the Renaissance humanists. This spirit survived the English Reformation. When the appropriation of church property by Henry VIII ended support for church-operated Latin grammar schools, new schools supported by cities, guilds, private gifts, and inheritances took their place.

The spirit of the Renaissance also revitalized Oxford and Cambridge Universities, offshoots of the University of Paris, which had originally been founded in the thirteenth century. Erasmus, the greatest of the humanists, visited Colet at Oxford and taught at Cambridge. English universities were centers of "puritanism," which

---

Form in Latin grammar schools meant "class" or "grade." The usage may have come from an older meaning of form, bench.

attempted to reform the Church of England. Puritanism was strong in Cambridge, and strongest in its Emmanuel College.

The importance of the work of the humanists for the development of education in early colonial America was not only that they shaped the education of many of the original settlers. They also provided important models that would be used in the establishment of colonial schools. Puritanism was important in a different way, in that it led to a concern for religion and salvation which also shaped the lives of the first Americans. Yet, despite the fact that the early settlers brought with them much of the European and English school tradition, as well as religious conviction, the new land worked important changes—ones that would bring about a new synthesis and ultimately a distinctively American culture and system of education.

COLONIAL BEGINNINGS

Colonial children received their first education at home, as American children still do. The church played a far greater part in the child's education than churches generally do now. The most important part of vocational training was by apprenticeship. A child who went to school went to any variety of them. Schools in the colonies appeared early: "reading" or primary schools; for boys, "Latin grammar," special-purpose, secondary schools; and in New England, Harvard College. Although settlers of New England were more interested than those of some other colonies in schooling for their children, we cannot assume that all New Englanders were well schooled or that no Southerner was.

There is much we do not know about colonial education. Records have been lost or destroyed, or never existed. Some parts of colonial education have not been studied in detail. There are many variations in colonial American education, ones highly different from our own experiences; it is only in the last hundred years that American schools have been organized into a single pattern. Any generalizations we can make here about colonial education will have many exceptions. The reader must see the history of colonial education as tentative, more tentative than most history. One additional caution should be noted: Teachers' and prospective teachers' first professional concern in education is with the schools. But schools were clearly not the first concern of the colonials. One of the more useful general conclusions from the history of education is that schooling has continuously and vastly increased in scope and function during the last 350 years.

Underlying any type of education are the assumptions of the parent or teacher about the nature of children and the type of education that is appropriate for them. Such beliefs play a critical role in shaping the educational system and schooling. The range of views of children in colonial America is shown in the following verses. The first was written by Anne Bradstreet, poet in Massachusetts in the mid-1600s. The second, somewhat earlier, is by the father of John Winthrop on the birth of his son:

Stained by birth from Adam's sinful fact,
Thence I began to sin as soon as act:
A perverse.will, a love of what's forbid,
A serpent's sting in pleasing face lay hid.

Welcome sweet babe thou are unto thy parents dear
Whose hearts thou has filled with joy, as well
    that doth appear.

Bradstreet and Winthrop were Puritans. Bradstreet wrote as a Calvinist, as many Puritans were from the time of the colonies' establishment. For one of that "authoritarian temperament," Philip Greven has written that

> . . . family government was authoritarian and rigorously repressive. Parental authority was absolute, and exercised without check or control. . . . Obedience and submission were the only acceptable responses for children.

This was the temperament which followed logically from the views of John Calvin. Calvin, who was a Swiss reformer and theologian of the mid-1500s, had most convincingly preached that mankind, including babies and children, were damned and depraved, stained by the original sin of Adam. As the *New England Primer* put it, "In Adam's Fall/We sinned all".

But other parents were, as Winthrop's father had been, "authoritative" rather than "authoritarian." They were, as Greven has written, ". . . respectful toward legitimate and essential authority within the family, yet aware of the need to limit the exercise of authority within certain established boundaries." Children were reasoned with, not ordered about. They were to be treated leniently if possible. They were to be loved and were seen as being essentially good.

Bradstreet and Winthrop demonstrated the extremes; the way most parents felt was probably somewhere in between. Bradstreet, in another mood, wrote tenderly of her own children. What the "real" nature of the child is would often be discussed in the times that would follow. (Greven has also written about a third temperament and of education for the "genteel," which will appear later in this book.)

Most of what children learn during their first years is from their parents and families. We learn our native language that way, as well as motives and habits. This is what sociologists call "primary socialization." How we have been socialized depends upon the customs and beliefs, the personalities and temperaments of our parents. Beyond Greven's work we have incomplete information about primary socialization in colonial families. We know that in some ways it was quite different from the socialization that recent generations have experienced. Greven points out that babyhood, or at least its outward signs, lasted longer then; boys and girls alike wore babies' clothes, long dresses and aprons, until they were five or six. At the same time, adulthood came sooner after childhood; there was not the long period in between that we call adolescence. We can be sure, too, that children became

Library - St. Joseph's College
222 Clinton Avenue
Brooklyn, N.Y. 11205

Words of five Syllables.

A-bo-mi-na-ble	ad-mi-ra-ti-on
Be-ne-dic-ti-on	be-ne-fi-ci-al
Ce-le-bra-ti-on	con-fo-la-ti-on
De-cla-ra-ti-on	de-di-ca-ti-on
E-du-ca-ti-on	ex-hor-ta-ti-on
For-ni-ca-ti-on	fer-men-ta-ti-on
Ge-ne-ra-ti-on	ge-ne-ro-fi-ty

Words of fix Syllables.

A-bo-mi-na-ti-on	Gra-ti-fi-ca-ti-on
Be-ne-fi-ci-al-ly	Hu-mi-li-a-ti-on
Con-ti-nu-a-ti-on	I-ma-gi-na-ti-on
De-ter-mi-na-ti-on	Mor-ti-fi-ca-ti-on
E-di-fi-ca-ti-on	Pu-ri-fi-ca-ti-on
Fa-mi-li-a-ri-ty	Qua-li-fi-ca-ti-on

A Leffon for Children.

Pray to God.	Call no ill names.
Love God.	Ufe no ill words.
Fear God.	Tell no lies.
Serve God.	Hate Lies.
Take not God's	Speak the Truth.
Name in vain.	Spend your Time well.
Do not Swear.	Love your School.
Do not Steal.	Mind your Book.
Cheat not in your play.	Strive to learn.
Play not with bad boys.	Be not a Dunce.

A. In A D A M's Fall
We finned all.

B. Heaven to find,
The Bible Mind.

C. Chrift crucify'd
For finners dy'd.

D. The Deluge drown'd
The Earth around.

E. E L I J A H hid
By Ravens fed.

F. The judgment made
F E L I X afraid.

FIGURE 1-2 Facing pages from a 1777 edition of *The New England Primer* printed by Edward Draper in Boston.

familiar with death sooner then than children now. The colonists multiplied and were healthier than the English, but one infant in four or one in five died. Perhaps because the probability of a baby's death was too great to risk much love, parents may have somewhat withheld love from young children.

It has been thought that colonial families were "extended" families and that children and their parents shared their home with grandparents, uncles, aunts, and other relatives, and often with servants. However, several recent studies have shown that this was not usually true and that most households were "nuclear," consisting of only father, mother, and children. In Plymouth Colony and Bristol, Rhode Island, there were most often families of parents and four children, and probably families elsewhere were roughly the same size then; later there would be more children. In one important way childhood was different from that of our own time, since children then were an economic help instead of an economic burden. Even a small child could help in the garden or the kitchen.

Beyond infancy and primary socialization, children learned by helping in kitchens, gardens, fields, and orchards. Cows were to be milked and pastured, pigs fattened and slaughtered. Butter was churned and soap boiled, fruit dried, and meat salted and cured. Girls were taught to cook, to spin flax and wool, and to weave. Boys learned to provide food and shelter. The colonial child who learned to read was as likely to be taught reading at home as by going to school.

The Protestant churches, and particularly the New England Puritan churches—later called *Congregational Churches* because the congregation controlled them—existed primarily to teach. The central feature of the church service, Sunday morning and Sunday afternoon, was the lengthy sermon, intended to explain and to provide examples of evil and righteousness. The colonials believed that each man and woman and child was responsible for his or her own salvation and that knowledge of the Bible and of religious principles were necessities for salvation. The largest Massachusetts churches, which employed two ministers, called the second one the *teacher*. (The word *teacher* was not often used in any other way in colonial America.) The minister or teacher was to "catechize" the children, that is, teach by asking questions for which answers were to be memorized. Each church, often each congregation, had its own catechism or statement of faith. The Church of England was less intent on this than many others, but its *Book of Common Prayer* of the mid-1700s directed that the assistant minister should

> Diligently upon Sundays and Holy Days, or on some other occasions, openly in his Church, instruct or examine so many Children of his Parish, sent unto him, as he shall think convenient, in some part of this Catechism.

Upon one feature of learning parents, ministers, and school masters agreed: To learn was to learn to say.

Most colonial and provincial men were farmers, but a few men and a very few women became craftspersons. As had been the case in England, the crafts were learned by apprenticeship, by working with and for a master craftsman, by example and practice. A boy or very occasionally a girl was apprenticed by contract. Perhaps in return for a payment by the apprentice's family and always in return for the boy's work for several years, masters guaranteed they would teach the "art and mysteries" of their particular craft and often guaranteed that the apprentice would be taught to read as well. The master was to feed and clothe the apprentice and also to see that the apprentice received proper religious instruction. The master became a substitute father; one way to provide for an orphan was to apprentice, to "put out," a boy or girl. Paul Revere served an apprenticeship as a silversmith. Benjamin Franklin was apprenticed to his brother who was a printer, but ran away, a fairly common occurrence. Girls were occasionally apprenticed, to learn bonnet-making for instance, or to become more expert spinners or weavers. Even law and medicine were often learned through an arrangement something like an apprenticeship. A would-be lawyer "read" with a practicing lawyer. A physician-to-be "attended" a physician. A very few school masters served apprenticeships, although that was certainly unusual.

At school or at home the child learned to read by roughly the same process by which many of us today learn. First the letters, capital and lowercase. It was more complicated then, with Roman, *Italic*, and 𝔊𝔬𝔱𝔥𝔦𝔠 typefaces. Then there were syllables and their sounds, in one primer *ab, ac*, and so on to *zy*. Third, there were words, short ones first, and then sentences, adages, or Bible verses. The idea of reading instruction at home is one that we are not used to now, but it was common in the 1600s and 1700s. If not at home, the child might learn at a *dame* or *reading* school, usually paid for by tuition, occasionally by taxes.

The schooling of the Puritan girl generally went no further than teaching her to read so that she could know the Scriptures. Beyond that, schooling was useless or even harmful. Women were thought to be readily corrupted. The account in Genesis of Eve's tempting Adam with an apple and leading him into original sin was a constant reminder of the belief that women were inferior to men. Pressure upon women not to engage in intellectual pursuits seems to have been common. Anne Bradstreet wrote

> I am obnoxious to each carping tongue
> Who says my hand better a needle fits
> A poet's pen all scorn I should thus wrong,
> For such despite they cast on female wits:
> If what I do prove well, it won't advance,
> They'll say its stol'n, or else it was by chance.

It has been argued that schools were established in the New England colonies to subject all children to "the creed of the Puritan sect." The statute most often quoted, and perhaps the most important, is the Massachusetts Act of 1647. Its opening paragraph reads

> It being one chief project of that old deluder, Satan, to keep from the knowl-
> edge of the Scriptures, as in former times keeping them in an unknown

tongue, so in these later times by persuading from the use of tongues, so that at least the true sense and meaning of the original might be clouded with false glosses of saint-seeming-deceivers, and that learning may not be buried in the graves of our forefathers in church and commonwealth, the Lord assisting our endeavours.

The act then mandated the establishment of reading schools in all towns of fifty or more families and of grammar schools in towns of one hundred or more families. The act was sometimes obeyed, sometimes flouted.

The act may be read literally, of course. But Morison argues that the preamble was written "to add a religious sanction to social obligation." This seems more persuasive when early acts in the other colonies are considered.

New Haven, 1642: "for the better training up of the youth of this town, that through God's blessings they may be fitted for public service thereafter, either in church or in commonwealth. . . ."

Connecticut, 1650: "Forasmuch as the good education of children is a singular behooval and benefit to our commonwealth. . . ."

Plymouth Colony, 1677: "Forasmuch as the maintenance of good literature does tend to the advancement of the prosperity and flourishing state of societies and republics. . . ."

The teaching of religion, of the Bible, of catechisms, was important. But it was not the single concern of the colonists.

In Virginia the establishment of schools was more difficult than in New England because settlers did not live in compact settlements, but instead lived on farms and plantations spread along river banks. Still, there seem to have been reading schools there by 1640. Probably many of them were taught by part-time "school" dames and masters in their own houses. Others were taught by ministers of the Church of England.

In Philadelphia the first school master was Enoch Flower, who had had twenty years' experience teaching in England and who was authorized to collect tuition for teaching reading, writing, and accounting. The best remembered of the earliest Pennsylvania reading masters was Francis Daniel Pastorious, a German Mennonite Protestant. He was far from a typical reading master. He used German, Latin, and English fluently. He had earned a Ph.D. in Germany and had written several books. He was an important leader of the Pennsylvania German community, serving as a town clerk, justice of the peace, and representative to the Pennsylvania assembly. Just before 1700 he was teaching a school in the attic or loft of the Quaker meeting house in Philadelphia. Later he taught in Germantown. Judging from the *New Primer* that he wrote, he taught the letters, then syllables, then words, then reading, with other material—weights, distances—as an afterthought. The *New Primer's* mnemonic rhyme for remembering the alphabet is a good example of "authoritative" non-Calvinistic temperament, and is quite different from that in the *New England Primer:*

All Blessings Come Down Even From God; His Infinite Kindness Love & Mercy, Now, of Old & Perpetually, Quicketh Refresh and Strengthen True Upright Willing Xians & Young Zealots.

But the *New Primer* lists alphabetically eighty-odd sins, from adultery to youthful lusts.

In colonial America the intermediate school, for boys only, was the Latin grammar school, both for general education and as preparation for college. What was to become the Boston Latin Grammar School was established in April 1635, when the town decided that "our brother Philemon Pormont, shall be entreated to become schoolmaster, for the teaching and nurturing of children with us." By 1647 eight Latin grammar schools had been established in Massachusetts, supported, as Latin grammar schools had been in England, by taxes, gifts, endowments, and tuition in varying proportions. A "free" Latin grammar school was established in New Haven in 1642, after Ezekiel Cheever, the most famous of the New England Latin masters, had taught there privately for some years. A Latin grammar school was also established in Hartford in the same year. In Rhode Island a Latin grammar school had probably been established as early as 1640. In Virginia two Latin grammar schools were endowed by inheritance and established, the Symes School before 1647 and the Eaton School after 1659.

From about 1640 to 1659, there was a Catholic Latin grammar school in Maryland, for "either Protestants or Catholics," taught by Ralph Crouch, who had been a Jesuit novice and eventually became a Jesuit priest. A "large and stately mansion" probably served as Crouch's residence, student living space, and schoolroom. There were short-lived Catholic schools in New York and Maryland about 1680, but until then Crouch's school was the only Catholic Latin grammar school in the English-speaking colonies.

Fter God had carried us safe to *New-England*, and wee had builded our houses, provided necessaries for our liveli-hood, rear'd convenient places for Gods worship, and setled the Civill Government: One of the next things we longed for, and looked after was to advance *Learning*, and perpetuate it to Posterity; dreading to leave an illiterate Ministery to the Churches, when our present Ministers shall lie in the Dust. And as wee were thinking and consulting how to effect this great Work; it pleased God to stir up the heart of one Mr. *Harvard* (a godly Gentleman, and a lover of Learning, there living amongst us) to give the one halfe of his Estate (it being in all about 1700. l.) towards the erecting of a Colledge, and all his Library: after him another gave 300. l. others after them cast in more, and the publique hand of the State added the rest : the Colledge was, by common consent, appointed to be at *Cambridge*, (a place very pleasant and accommodate and is called (according to the name of the first founder) *Harvard Colledge*.

FIGURE 1-3 Text describing the founding of Harvard University from "New England's First Fruits, 1643," p. 12. Reprinted in *Quinquennial Catalogue of the Officers and Graduates, 1636-1920* (Cambridge, Mass.: Harvard University, 1922), p. 5.

FIGURE 1-4

A nineteenth century illustration of the Boston Latin Grammar School originally included in Barnard's *American Journal of Education* and reprinted in Ellwood P. Cubberley, *The History of Education* (Boston: Houghton Mifflin, 1920), p. 362.

A Latin grammar school was established in Philadelphia in 1689. Its first master was George Keith, a friend of Governor William Penn and Quaker founder George Fox. Keith had been a tutor and a school master. A speaker, apologist, and missionary for the Quakers, or Friends, he had been imprisoned in Scotland and England for his religious beliefs half a dozen times. His assistant was Thomas Makin, who later became master of the school. Evidence seems to suggest that Makin taught arithmetic as well as Latin.*

The influence of the Classical literary and educational tradition on the curriculum of these early Latin grammar schools was great. Unfortunately, no direct complete records of what was taught survives from these early schools. There is a surviving outline of curriculum of the Boston Latin Grammar Schools from 1712. From it, as well as booksellers' records, personal accounts, diaries, and personal recollections from the later 1600s, we can reconstruct a typical curriculum for the Latin grammar schools.

Besides such works as the "accidence" or beginning Latin grammar book, there were in the first three years texts such as the *Disticha* of Cato, Corderius' *Colloquies*, and *Aesop's Fables*. In the fourth year Erasmus' *Colloquies* and Ovid's *de Tristibus* were studied, and the reading of *Aesop's Fables* continued. In the fifth year Erasmus' *Colloquies* was completed and Ovid's *Metamorpheses* begun. Numerous other Latin authors were studied in the sixth and seventh years, and the students were introduced to Greek. There is no evidence that study of a catechism was part of the Boston Latin School curriculum, but it certainly was a part of curricula elsewhere in New England.

Essentially, what was studied in the Boston Latin Grammar School was the same curriculum as that studied in the English Renaissance grammar schools such as

---

*In 1733 Makin's brief obituary appeared in a Philadelphia newspaper: "On Monday Evening last, Mr. Thomas Makin fell off a wharf into the Delaware [River], and before he could be taken out again, was drowned. He was an ancient man, and formerly lived well in this city, teaching a considerable school; but of late years he was reduced to poverty." *Pennsylvania Gazette*, November 29, 1733. Quoted from James Pyle Wickersham, *A History of Education in Pennsylvania* (Lancaster, Pa.: Inquirer, 1885), p. 43.

St. Paul's, which John Colet had reformed 130 years before. Boston Latin's long-time master, Ezekiel Cheever, had attended St. Paul's.

That the Latin grammar school curriculum had not changed in more than a century seems paradoxical. Although religion was the primary concern of the Puritans, it was not a first concern at Boston Latin. On a new frontier, certainly, there was more useful knowledge than Latin. There are two solutions to the paradox. The first is to note mitigating circumstances, Latin was necessary for theology, for medicine, and for foreign correspondence, and it did provide a key to classical literary masterpieces. The second solution of the paradox seems to us to be more generally satisfactory. Schools, that argument goes, do not answer only to the social and cultural needs of the moment. Schools—masters, texts, scholars; and later, teachers, administrators, and school boards—are in themselves social institutions, with customs and conventionalities of their own. They may have not, for good or bad, answered to the felt needs of the moment. We shall see again and again the seeming contradiction between curricula and social needs.

We know about a few Latin grammar schoolmasters: about Elijah Corlet, because his small stone schoolhouse was in Cambridge, Massachusetts, and served as a preparatory school for Harvard; about Ezekiel Cheever, whose extraordinarily long career seemed at his death and afterward a splendid example of devotion to the teaching of young scholars in Boston. Of most masters we know nothing at all.

Master Elijah Corlet (1610–1687) had been a student at Oxford. His reputation as master was already good in 1643, when an early favorable report, *New England's First Fruits*, said that his school was

> . . . a fair [faultless] Grammar school for the training up of young scholars, and fitting them for *Academic Learning*, that . . . they may be received into the College. . . . Master *Corlet* is the master, who has very well proved himself for his abilities [,] dexterity, painstaking in teaching of youth under him.

Elijah Corlet's scholars were ambitious boys and youths of Cambridge. A number of boys from other New England towns were sent to Cambridge to benefit from Master Corlet's instruction. His school prepared thirty of Harvard's graduates, a quarter of the total, in the mid-1600s. Corlet was supported—probably rather badly—by tuition, some paid in farm products; gifts, occasional grudging payments from the town, and a grant of land. He was one of the longest-lived, best known, and presumably most capable of the Latin masters.

Ezekiel Cheever (1614–1708) had at the time of his death been a New England schoolmaster for seventy-one years. Born in London, son of a shopkeeper selling cloth (or, some say, a spinner), he had attended St. Paul's school, which John Colet had reformed more than a hundred years before. Cheever studied at Emanuel College, Cambridge, the favorite college of the English Puritans.

He had come to New England in 1637, perhaps on the same ship as Corlet. Cheever taught at New Haven, at first in his house and then as master of the "free" school there. In 1649 he became the master of the endowed Latin grammar school at Ipswich in northeastern Massachusetts; when Anne Bradstreet's family moved on, one of her sons stayed behind to study with Cheever. One of Cheever's own sons subsequently played a small part in the witchcraft trials in nearby Salem. In 1660, Cheever moved to Charlestown, and in 1671, to Boston, where he was master of the Latin Grammar School for the thirty-seven years remaining before his death. Like Corlet, Cheever was an ideal—and idealized—colonial master, a master for a long career instead of merely in passing; diligent; industrious; dedicated; regular in attendance (colonial schools were open six days a week year around); godly. Unlike Corlet, Cheever was well paid. One of the most prominent ministers of New England said at one point that "Tis Corlet's pains, and Cheever's, we must own. / That thou, New England, art not Sycthia [barbaric] grown." Many others have agreed.

The earliest masters of the smaller towns were a varied group. In Dedham, 16 miles south of Boston, there were nine masters between 1644 and 1672, teaching English, writing, Latin grammar, and arithmetic to boys. One started to teach at twenty, another at sixty. Four had attended college. One, Michael Metcalfe, had been trained as a weaver's apprentice in England before being forced into exile. "Enemies conspired against me to take away my life, and sometimes, to avoid their hands, my wife did hide me in the roof of the house, covering me with straw." (Eight Metcalfes taught in Dedham in the following 250 years.) Two of the masters later became ministers; one stayed on as a respected farmer. The first masters of New Haven, Dorchester, and even Boston showed the same range of education and usually, the same brief service as masters.

The peak of formal schooling in the colonies in the 1600s was Harvard College. It was patterned upon European colleges, in particular upon Emanuel College, Cambridge University. In turn Harvard has been a model for many colleges and universities in America.

Harvard was established in 1636, only a year after the establishment of the Boston Latin Grammar School. The Massachusetts legislature voted £400 for a college.* It was established at Newtowne, which was speedily renamed Cambridge. The following fall John Harvard, a recently arrived Puritan minister, died, leaving half his estate and all his library to the college, which was then named in his honor. The establishment of Harvard in a primitive land was a remarkable accomplishment. Yet it was consistent with the experience and intellectual ambitions of the Puritans. By 1640 135 university graduates and former students had come to New England. As historian Lawrence Cremin wrote, ". . . higher learning had been a salient feature of the puritan experience in England, and it remained so in New England."

The first reason for Harvard's establishment was to provide education for the ministry. As *New England's First Fruits* (1643) put it,

> After God had carried us safe to *New England*, and we had built our houses, provided necessaries for our livelyhood, reared convenient places for God's worship, and settled the civil government; One of the next things we longed

*£ = pound, English unit of currency, now about $1.80 U.S., formerly much more.

for, and looked after was to advance *learning* and perpetuate it to posterity; dreading to become an illiterate ministry in the Churches, when our present ministry shall lie in the dust.

But the preparation of ministers was not the only purpose of Harvard. Half of its graduates in the 1600s became ministers but half did not, and some had no intention of becoming ministers. The Harvard charter of 1650 said the purpose of the college was "the advancement of all good literature, arts, and sciences." The study of divinity had only a small place in Harvard's curriculum.

In 1638 Harvard's first president, Nathaniel Eaton, taught Harvard's first classes. Eaton seemed well qualified. But the students (who lived in the college from the start) were served moldy bread, spoiled beef—or no beef—and sour beer—or no beer. Students were whipped, and Eaton was dismissed when it was charged that he had beaten his assistant with a walnut club "big enough to have killed a horse." Classes were suspended.

In 1640 Henry Dunster was named president. He was thirty-one then and had just arrived in New England. A Cambridge graduate, he had been a school master and a *curate*, or an assistant minister. Until 1643 he taught all the classes. At that time two "tutors" were appointed to help him. For fourteen years he delivered lectures and raised money for the new college. He also managed a printing press his wife had inherited; printing as well as schooling was important in New England then. When he resigned in 1654, after disagreement with students and with Harvard's board of overseers, college customs and rules had been established, and Harvard would continue.

Three years was required for a degree while Dunster was president of Harvard. For admission as a student, reading, writing, and speaking of Latin and a rudimental knowledge of Greek was required. Teaching was in Latin. Students studied logic, rhetoric, ethics, physics, metaphysics, and on Saturday morning Hebrew. The study of divinity was via catechisms, questions and answers memorized.

Harvard's enrollment was between twenty and fifty. The average age of new students was less than sixteen; they were ranked in class according to their scholarship.* Students were the sons of fathers of the better sort; colony officials, physicians, large landowners, or ministers. Craftsmen's sons sometimes attended; although a few scholarships were available, there were almost no sons of small farmers. Students' surviving notebooks and personal libraries show that the reading of some of them went far beyond textbooks, and that there were pranks and riots, no doubt entertaining.

This, then, was the general pattern of schooling in the 1600s: reading learned at home or in a reading school; for a few boys there was as long as six or seven years of study in a Latin grammar school; and for a very few, college study at Harvard. But the general pattern was often violated. Some boys, and a few girls, learned from parents, masters, or tutors what other boys learned in Latin grammar schools. Some

---

*Not until the 1700s were class rankings based upon the social eminence of students' families. The practice was abandoned in 1770.

children never learned to read at all, since school attendance was not compulsory and parents did not or could not instruct them. Some Latin grammar schools also accepted reading pupils. At the end of the 1600s, some boys were sent to "writing" school. By the early 1700s, others studied in schools in Boston that were conducted by masters who were paid tuition and who taught a welter of subjects: mathematics (for surveying or navigation), French, Greek, and even needlepoint and fencing. Newspaper advertisements published in Boston from the beginning of the eighteenth century include many announcements of masters teaching bookkeeping, surveying, navigation, and languages for commerce.

Aside from the variations in schooling in the English-speaking colonies, there were also Dutch, German, and even Swedish and French schools. The Dutch schools, of course, were in New Netherland, which had been established in 1624 by the Dutch West India Company as a fur trading post and supply base for Dutch traders. The first reading school opened in New Amsterdam (New York City) in 1638. By 1664, when New Netherland was surrendered to the English and became New York, there were eleven reading schools in the colony. A Latin school was operated for a year or two. Schooling in New Netherland resembled schooling in New England, but there were important differences. Schools in New Netherland were established by and under the control of the Dutch West India Company, which paid masters. Masters were selected and licensed by a committee in Holland, comprised of the Amsterdam Dutch Reformed Church ministers. The reading master in New Netherland was to assist the minister. One master's contract called for him to clean the church, ring the church bell, read parts of the Sunday church services and substitute for the minister in his absence, teach the catechism, serve as the church messenger, and dig the graves.

The first New Amsterdam reading master was Adam Roelansen, whose life and teaching in New Amsterdam have been carefully investigated. His was not a particularly inspiring life. He was named as defendant in at least three civil suits and was charged with slander and attempted rape; he was convicted of the latter.

In Pennsylvania, schools were generally established by churches. German churches established German schools, but most of their growth was in the 1700s and we will return to them. New Sweden, in the valley of the Delaware River, may have had a reading school. If so, it was closed in 1655, when the Dutch took over New Sweden as the English would take over New Netherland. An attempt to revive the Swedish schools in the early 1700s was not successful. Among the New Netherlanders were French Huguenots. Their schools were, naturally, taught in French.

One of the purposes of the first English colonists had been to Christianize the Indians. The Royal Charter for Virginia began with an expression of concern for Christianizing Indians who "as yet live in darkness and miserable ignorance of the true knowledge and worship of God." English hopes of Christianizing and "civilizing" were far from the interest of most Indians. In 1622, "Henrico College" was being built for the instruction of Indians and a "rector" had been named. Then, as part of a large-scale and well-planned attack, the Indians butchered the workers and their families. A report to the Virginia Company in London said that "the way of conquering them is much more easy than that of civilizing them and Christianizing them." For two hundred years Indians would be taught so that their souls might be saved.

About the Indians themselves it is difficult to generalize. Indian cultures varied enormously. There were both warlike and peaceful tribes; tribes quick to accept change, and tribes quick to reject it; and differences in values and in social organization, which were as great. There were hundreds of tribes and nearly as many languages. Far westward, Spanish soldiers and priests were already conquering the land and beginning the Christianization and subjugation of Indians there. Indians who were to be converted needed to know the Bible (and so needed to read) or the Mass. To be within reach of the Protestant meeting hall or the Catholic chapel or church, it was necessary for Indians to be sedentary farmers rather than nomadic hunters. For some Indians a change in religion meant the dismemberment of their culture; it is said that the Pueblo Revolt against the Spaniards in 1680 (successful for eighteen years) resulted from that realization. Beyond conversion, missionaries also had cultural preferences. Spaniards tried to recreate medieval monastery life, with servants, gardens, and farms. New England missionaries favored recreated New England towns.

The most famous Puritan missionary to the Indians, John Eliot, said he found it "most necessary to carry on civility with religion." Being a good Christian was reading the Bible, farming instead of hunting, living in a village, attending church, and wearing cloth instead of skin clothes. Eliot spent forty-four years as minister of a church in Roxbury, Massachusetts, and in preaching to the local Algonquin Indians. He translated catechisms, the psalms, and finally the Bible into the local Indian language. A few Indians heard Eliot's sermons in their language and became Christians. At Natick, adjacent to Dedham, an Indian village was established. Homes and a meeting house were built; the meeting house also housed the school for reading, of English as well as the Algonquin language. Thirteen other "praying Indian" villages were established with Eliot's help, and with financial support of the first missionary society in England, the New England Society for the Propagation of the Gospel. On Nantucket Island, off the coast of Massachusetts, three generations of the Mayhew family were also missionaries to the Indians. There were others, of course. John Cheever, one of Ezekiel's sons, was for twenty-three years missionary to the Indians of Plymouth Colony. There is no record of his success.

The Indian boys New England missionaries hoped to train as ministers were sent to Elijah Corlet's Latin grammar school in Cambridge, and if they lived, to Harvard. As students they progressed well enough. At the commencement of 1659, Harvard's president said they "gave good satisfaction . . . considering their growth in the Latin tongue." But the Indian scholars died of consumption and "hectic fevers" thought (correctly enough) to have been brought about by the changes in their diet, clothing, and way of life. (Indians, it seems reasonable to say after three hundred years of experience in their schooling, do not do well outside the context of their tribal culture, unless they have fully accepted, and been fully accepted by, American culture. But the death rates were appalling.) Of the twenty Indian boys sent to Master Corlet, two survived to complete the work for their bachelor's degrees at Harvard. One, Joel Iacoomis, suffered a grim fate. Before commencement he visited his relatives, and while returning to Cambridge he was shipwrecked on Nantucket Island. He was drowned or, it was said, he was "murdered by some wicked Indians."

CONCLUSION

Education in colonial America does not clearly demonstrate the origins of American public schools, as historians once thought. It does, however, provide a basis for making several informative generalizations about education.

Considering American Indians and missionaries, one might begin to see that it would be difficult for missionaries, even if they wanted to, to change religion without changing schooling, or to change religion without changing a culture. The experience of the Indians in Elijah Corlet's school and at Harvard might illustrate one of the hazards of removing children or youths from their native environments and cultures simply for the sake of schooling.

More widely, one might see that some societies and cultures, such as those of the colonies, operate and survive well enough without extensive systems of schooling. More schooling may—but possibly may not—be necessary in a highly technological culture.

The schools of Colonial America had limited purposes and small numbers of pupils. The balance of this text about the history of American education will address many matters, but always with increasing responsibilities assigned to the schools, and increased time spent in schooling and the resources used for it.

Schools do not automatically shape themselves to the needs of a society, nor do they teach everything they are intended to teach. Schools are partly independent organizations, following their own customs and conventions. The "paradox" separating what a school teaches and what a society appears to need is a consequence of the partial independence of schools. The colonial masters had roles very much different from those of present teachers. *Teach* was a verb and not a noun.

In Colonial America there was every possible precedent for financing schools, all that had been employed in England—tuition, tax, gift, endowment, and land rent, singly or in any combination. Patterns of control varied as greatly. Schools were controlled by town meetings, by trustees or *feoffes*, by committees, by those paying tuitions, or by the masters themselves. The analysis of control is complicated because the colonials did not make the same clear distinction we make between "public" and "private." They spoke of "free" schools, but sometimes meant that admission to them was "free" in that any qualified student could attend, and sometimes to mean that the schools were free, without charge, for students whose parents could not afford to pay.

The schools of the colonials might have served as precedents for anything—or nothing.

Chapter Two
CULTURE AND SCHOOLING BEFORE THE REVOLUTION

In the 1600s, colonists most often thought and acted like Englishmen or other Europeans away from home. The social and cultural history of the colonies in the 1600s is largely the history of the transportation of a culture and society and of schools.

In the 1700s, until the eve of the Revolution, those who lived in what would become the United States still thought of themselves as loyally English, but no longer as Englishmen away from home. They lived in one of the parts of England, in its transoceanic "provinces," as other Englishmen lived in Kent or Cornwall. The provincials' way of speech, thought, and behavior were already distinctive. The social and cultural history of America in the 1700s is largely a history of a transmuted, changed society and culture, and of its schools.

Schools changed with their environment, often lagging behind, but occasionally leading the changes. Growing cities, because of the variety of their residents and simply because of their size, made available to parents living in them a number of schools to choose from. In the middle colonies, particularly in Pennsylvania, the convention of many church-related schools, together with the many churches, led to diversity of schools. However, because of distances, there were fewer choices for any one child's schooling. In New England, schooling tended to be more practical. District schools and traveling schools added to convenience but had their educational drawbacks. Nevertheless, literacy was more general. In Virginia and in the rest of the South, self-supported masters and Church of England ministers operated schools, and there were tutors and an occasional "governess." School learning seemed to be increasing there also. In provincial America, a new and American school, the academy, made its appearance. Few slaves and blacks were taught to read, but a few schools demonstrated that they could be taught. Several new colleges were established, most for religious reasons.

The period of provincial America ended with the Revolution, which had primarily political causes, and as immediate outcomes few other than political effects. Its later influence would be more profound.

BECOMING AMERICA

Perhaps American practicality, the search for solutions to everyday problems, came from living in a new environment with new problems. Whether because of their environment or not, provincial Americans wanted and needed practical answers immediately. A tale by Benjamin Franklin demonstrates the concern and response:

A militia chaplain told Franklin the men would not attend prayer meetings. Franklin, although not himself a praying man, had a suggestion. "It is perhaps below the dignity of your profession to act as steward of the rum; but if you were only to distribute it out after prayers, you would have them all around you." Franklin said that "never were prayers more generally and punctually attended."

Practicality was a state of mind. Rationalism was a way of thought. It was based on the belief that the truth, often "self-evident truth," could only be discovered from that seen or experienced and must be developed by rational analysis. Rationalism was an extension of scholarly humanism. It was—and is—the basis of scientific thought. Among the scientists of provincial America was Benjamin Franklin, inventor of the lightning rod and Franklin stove. (Franklin comes to mind in every connection. He was almost the spirit of provincial America.) In a way Franklin's friend John Bartram was as typical as a scientist. He collected plants from Florida to the Ohio Valley to Nova Scotia. He was a "naturalist" or "natural philosopher" who observed, collected, and classified rather than experimented.

In political thought American rationalism took a turn backward, away from the English royalists' arguments of the 1700s and back to the 1600s, the English period of the Glorious Revolution, when "republican" thought had been strongest there. The English Whigs who sympathized with American revolutionaries were in an important way reactionary. In political matters the most highly thought-of philosopher was John Locke (1632-1704), who, in his *Treatises on Government*, had argued that government was a "social contract." To this line of thought John Adams and Thomas Jefferson adhered, no matter how strong their disagreements on many other matters:

We hold these truths to be self-evident, that all men are created equal; that they are endowed by their creator with certain inalienable rights; that among these are life, liberty, and the pursuit of happiness. . . .

The number of provincial Americans grew from 250,000 in 1700 to 3 million at the beginning of the Revolution. There were many immigrants, but families were larger, too. As Franklin noted, provincial American men and women married younger, because it was not too difficult to support a family. Families were larger than they are today because children were most often an economic asset and because brides were usually younger. The Biblical advice to "be fruitful and multiply" was followed. The effect upon family life has not, as far as we know, been studied. A provincial woman commented in her diary: "I have often thought that women who live to get over the time of child-bearing . . . experience more comfort and satisfaction than at any other periods of their lives."

Most provincial Americans were of the "middling sort," and others of the "better sort." By the mid-1700s there were in America social graduations and social class structures. Compared with Europe then or with the United States in the 1800s, there were only a few rich and a few poor, but their numbers had increased. Since a community, or indeed an entire province, could accumulate wealth, most families in it could become more prosperous. As well as can be judged, this was the general pattern. The indentured servant or other immigrant could and very often did become a farm owner. The son of a middling sort of merchant sometimes became wealthy. But it is necessary to add quickly that in the older and more heavily farmed areas, there was less mobility and people became poorer more often than wealthier.

There were few Africans in the colonies of the 1600s. The colonists had brought with them from Europe their racial prejudices, but until the late 1600s slavery had not been institutionalized, which is to say that laws had not been enacted until then to protect slaves' owners. In the middle and late 1700s, it was more and more difficult for planters in the South to get indentured servants from Europe. Therefore, with reluctance, they purchased slaves. The black population of the United States had reached a half million by 1776.

In Virginia and in Maryland, an aristocracy, a class made up of people whose high social position had been determined by the circumstances of their birth or marriage, had taken shape. The most prominent Virginia families—for instance, the Carters, the Smiths, and the Byrds—were rich by American standards. Their social position could not be rivaled. There were many Virginian planters, merchants, and craftsmen of the middling sort, but the aristocrats set the tone and, largely, ruled. A similar but somewhat later aristocracy appeared in South Carolina. The large landowners of New York had aristocratic positions in their society. In Boston, and to a lesser extent in the other large seaport cities, there were merchant aristocrats.

There had always been violations of the old Puritan standards, both because Puritans had human weaknesses and because many of the colonists had not been Puritans. But in the mid-1700s, the old standards seemed to have been lost. Even in Boston there were far too few church pews to accommodate the Bostonians if they had all elected in a given Sunday to go to church, which of course they did not. In the cities there were taverns, brothels, and theaters. Some merchants were more interested in profits than in salvation. Perhaps the cities in part reflected the easy moral codes of England at the time.

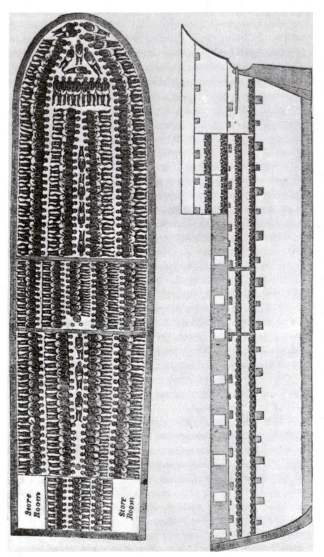

FIGURE 2-1 Illustration showing the decks of a slave ship. Taken from W.O. Blake, *The History of Slavery and the Slave Trade, Ancient and Modern* (Columbus, Ohio: Printed by H. Miller, 1862), pp. 304-305.

On the frontier, behavior was largely unrestricted by social conventions; even where it had been strongest, the moral codes were breaking down. In New England there were still two-hour-long Sabbath sermons and the old droning psalms, but many had fallen away to other churches, and most did not belong to any church. There were many signs of this falling away. For example, babies born less than nine months after marriage had once been rare and scandalous, but, by the mid-1700s, became commonplace. When one New Englander, recently a bride, gave birth to a child seven and a half months after marriage, her church refused even to censure her. Bundling—sleeping fully clothed in the same bed by an engaged couple—was not a completely innocuous custom by former Puritan standards of behavior, but the old social norms had faded.

The Puritan faith was also being supplanted. The Church of England had established a congregation in Boston in 1689. Unitarian convictions—that there should be complete religious freedom and that none of the theologies or catechisms of the conventional churches were essential to Christianity—appeared. Beyond this, even, was *deism*, the belief in a God who had created the universe and the natural laws that governed it but who would not intervene. "God the great clockmaker," a phrase stated somewhat irreverently, indicated a vision of God that originated from a scientific view.

Before 1750, there had been a revolution, or a counterrevolution, in religion. It seemed to be a reaction against the commonplace abandonment of the old faith and morality, against the increasing instability of society, and against rationalism, deism, and worldliness, and the broadening and dilution of old faiths. Called the *Great Awakening*, it spread through all the major denominations. In New England its strongest spokesman was Jonathan Edwards, a Yale graduate and a Congregational minister. The term "Great Awakening" was, as a matter of fact, his. More than any other person, he was famed for his preaching of hellfire and damnation. For him salvation might come only through a return to strict Calvinism, with its original sin and predestination. In the Dutch Reformed Church the first awakener was Theodore Frelinghausen, a New Jersey pastor, who had come from Holland in 1714. He preached in English, contrary to the custom of his church. As did the other evangelists of the Great Awakening, he appealed by emotion, fervor aroused to encourage salvation. In his efforts he was joined a few years later by Gilbert Tennant, a Presbyterian. Another of the successful evangelical preachers was George Whitefield, who made nine tours of America between 1739 and 1771.

By 1750, the first wave of the Great Awakening was past, although there would be further instances of it in the South in the next few years, and a tide of "New Reawakening" would appear in the 1800s. Perhaps it led to feeling rather than thought in religion, and to a certain kind of equalitarianism in which all men and women were equally damned. For those converted or at least apprehensive, the Great Awakening turned religion into a central concern, a concern that would effect schooling.

PROVINCIAL SCHOOLING:
THE CITIES

Our society was shaped on the frontier, historians argue. On the other hand, the intellectual and institutional parts of our history have more often been shaped in our cities. Many of the developments of schools in the 1700s took place in the cities. The largest cities were Boston, population 16,000; Philadelphia, 13,000 and rapidly growing; and New York, 11,000. Each of the largest cities, and some not so large, offered many choices in schooling; their very size made the alternatives possible.

Patterns of schools and schooling were generally similar in the largest cities. In Philadelphia some boys studied at the Quaker Latin grammar school. At one time or another in the 1700s, schools were operated by several churches: the Church of England, German Reformed, Moravian, Lutheran, and Baptist. Most schools in the cities were, however, private, operated by their masters. A white boy in a large city could be sent to school to learn any subjects his parents thought fitting, if they could pay for it and if he could be spared from work. Even if a boy could not be spared from work or was an apprentice, there were master-operated night schools that he could attend. At its best, schooling in the largest provincial cities was purchased in a free market. An outstanding master earned twice as much as a carpenter and lived comfortably. For the pupil of parents of limited means, there were other masters whose fees were lower. For girls there were fewer possibilities even in the big cities, but many of the private schoolmasters and schoolmistresses, "school dames," accepted them at beginning schools. There were schools that would accept girls who were to study English, or Latin, or feminine and ladylike accomplishments—as examples, needlework, singing, or playing the harpsichord or spinet. Between 1740 and 1776, there are records of about 130 schoolmasters and mistresses in Philadelphia. Of course, not all of them were teaching at any one time, but there were surely others of whom there is no record. We cannot estimate the average length of a child's schooling because school and class sizes cannot be estimated. We do know that nearly all men and most women in Pennsylvania could write their names and that there were three newspapers in Philadelphia, and libraries.

In New York and Boston there were also free markets in schooling. There were newspapers there, and they were read as eagerly as in Philadelphia. In New York the Church of England's Society for the Propagation of the Gospel operated several free schools for the poor, including one for blacks, and the Dutch schools, by then supported by the Dutch Reformed Church, were still open. Private masters taught in Boston, too, supporting themselves by tuition. A second Latin grammar school had been established, and the town of Boston also supported three writing schools, primarily for teaching boys to write the clear legible script expected of clerks and useful to others, and arithmetic. One writing master was John Tileston, who had turned to teaching because his hand was so seriously burned when he was a child that he could only hold a pen or a penknife in it. Tileston was one of the very few masters who had been trained by apprenticeship. He would not retire until 1819, after having taught for seventy years.

PROVINCIAL SCHOOLING: PENNSYLVANIA

In the Pennsylvania of farms and small villages there were schools established by and connected with each of the English-speaking churches. The Quakers', or Friends', schools were under the direction of the "weekly meetings," local congregations. They appointed schoolmasters and schoolmistresses to teach pupils "to read the Holy Scriptures and other English books, and to write and cast accounts [,] so far as to understand some necessary rules of arithmetic." There were also schools of the Church of England and of the Presbyterian Church and even the Roman Catholic Church.

The Church of England was aided in the mid-Atlantic colonies and in the South by the Society for the Propagation of the Gospel in Foreign Parts—the S.P.G. Founded in England in 1701, it established in the following seventy-five years, 170 missions and appointed eighty schoolmasters in America. One of its aims was to convert or reconvert provincials to the Church of England. (A second aim was to Christianize Indians, in which it was not successful. Its third aim, the Christianization of blacks, will be discussed later in this text.)

The Germans in Pennsylvania were bound together by their language and their churches; a distinctive cultural minority, the Pennsylvania "Dutch" (*Deutsch* translates as German) still exist in the United States and Canada, and there are still schools of some of the Pennsylvania German denominations. The first German schools in Pennsylvania had been established by the Mennonites. The Mennonite Church splintered in Switzerland, producing several sects, including the Amish. Further divisions took place in America. There were also German Lutheran and Reformed Churches, the German Roman Catholic Church, Schweckenfelders, Dunkers, and Ephrata Hermits.* Like the English-speaking churches, the larger German churches established schools.

The first Moravians, persecuted members of a German sect that was opposed to both Catholicism and Lutheranism, came to Pennsylvania in 1740, after an earlier settlement in Georgia had failed. They believed in communal settlements, a kind of Christian socialism. They also believed in communal schools. Children were to board there. Parents were not to visit and not to send expensive gifts. The first Moravian communal school was opened in 1742 by Nicholas Ludwig, Graf (Count) Zinzendorf und Pottendorf. After he had returned to Europe to share his

---

*Cremin also mentions Labadists, New Born, New Mooners, Separatists, Zion's Brueder, Ronsdorfer, Inspired, Gichtelians, Depellians, and Mountain Men.

faith there, several other communal schools were established. Indians were sometimes pupils there; the Moravians saw missionary work as most important.

The best remembered of the German schoolmasters of the 1700s is Christopher Dock, who taught near Philadelphia and in small settlements, from 1718 until 1771. He was the author of *Schulordnung* (1770), on teaching. Dock was a Mennonite (though not all his pupils were) who was interested first in teaching piety, morality, and manners. Second, he taught reading, starting as usual with a rhymed alphabet. Third, he taught writing. Arithmetic in his school was perfunctory, intended as far as one can tell to help a pupil find a psalm or other Bible passage, or a hymn to be sung. Tradition says Dock died in prayer in his school at the end of a day. From the *Schulordnung*, one would conclude that Dock was a gentle teacher, nearer to Greven's description of "authoritative" than of "authoritarian." Whipping a child was only the last resort for Dock. But Calvinism and its sternness was not unknown in the German schools. By 1740, the German Reformed Church schools were using the *New England Primer* translated almost word for word.

The Scotch-Irish lost their cultural identity soon. Their language, English, did not set them apart. Neither did their church, since there were English and Scotch Presbyterians too. More often than the Germans, they settled on the frontier, where cultural differences and church denominations were easily blurred.

The Presbyterians, whether from North Ireland or not, brought with them a concern for schooling, much like that of the Puritans nearly a century earlier. In the Presbyterian reading schools there was the usual course of study: reading, catechisms, Bible, and, as time allowed, writing and a little arithmetic. If the Scotch-Irish were settling on the raw frontier, a school might wait a little. But the schools were not far behind the frontier, occasionally not far enough. In the summer of 1764, Master Enoch Brown and nine of his pupils were killed and scalped in their schoolhouse at the foot of the Blue Ridge Mountains. A tenth was scalped but survived. One was "truant" and probably lived because of his truancy. Others were absent because of "hot weather and seasonal duties"—it was at the height of the harvest.

In Pennsylvania the parochial schools, those connected with churches, became a tradition, as did diversity in education. That tradition would long survive and, indeed, survives in some places still. Parochial schools and diversity would later postpone the establishment of public schools. Within limits this also held true for schooling in the other middle colonies, New York, New Jersey, and Delaware.

PROVINCIAL SCHOOLING: MASSACHUSETTS

There were general similarities, too, in New England schooling. Massachusetts's was as near to typical as any. A representative town is Dedham, although, of course, schooling in each New England town differed in detail. The settlements in Dedham had spread—its population had grown to 750 by 1700, and 1900 by 1765. In the first half of the 1700s, Dedham's Latin grammar school had continued, and the town employed a year-round Latin and English schoolmaster. Between 1700 and the 1750s, the Dedham masters were young men, nearly all of them Harvard graduates and awaiting calls to the ministry. Because many families moved beyond walking distance from the schoolhouse, Dedham arranged for the master to teach in various locations in the town for a few weeks at a time. This was a "traveling school," which had made its first appearance in New England before 1700, and was for a time commonplace.

In the 1750s, the traveling school was replaced by four schools, which came to be controlled by the different sections of the town. These were "district schools," locally controlled, of which much more was to be heard. Their beginning pupils studied English, and the advanced ones, Latin. Teaching in Dedham was no longer a year-round occupation, since all the Latin and English schools then met in the winter at the same time. Masters came and went more quickly. In the 1750s, only half of Dedham's masters were college graduates; in the 1760s, only a third. In the 1750s, women began to teach in Dedham, as much as a hundred years after school dames had first been employed elsewhere in New England. In Dedham, women first taught in summertime reading schools and were first paid from money bequeathed for schooling expenses. Most men who had lived in Dedham had been literate from the beginning, at least literate enough to sign their names. By 1760, only one out of five women signed by mark, an *x*.* The women of Dedham were literate far more often than formerly. At school and with the help of tutors, boys still learned Latin. Between 1760 and 1783, eighteen of Dedham's young men graduated from Harvard.

We have scraps of information about some provincial New England masters because they were later famous or because they were quaint. The letters of future president John Adams, who taught in Worcester in western Massachusetts, 1755–58, after graduating from Harvard, have been published. He wrote to friends about his pupils, sometimes annoyed, sometimes amused and fanciful. "[L]ittle runtlings, just capable of lisping A B C, and troubling the master." ". . . My little school, like the great world, is made up of prigs, politicians, devines, . . . fops, buffons, fiddlers, sycophants, fools, coxcombs, chimney-sweepers." His oldest scholars were learning Latin. During those three years Adams read, dined, and talked with the leading citizens and learned law.

PROVINCIAL SCHOOLING: THE SOUTH

The clergy of the Church of England, private schoolmasters, and plantation tutors played important parts in schooling in the South. The Church of England was the established (that is, tax-supported) church of the region, as the Congregational

*Standards for estimating literacy have shifted from time to time, generally upward. A signature is not a good test of literacy. An otherwise illiterate person may have learned to sign his or her name. Some provincials could read but not write. Poor people do not and did not usually sign legal documents; therefore the sample was not representative. However, one study has demonstrated that if and when people sign their names, people can also read.

Church was in most of New England. However, there were always too few capable dedicated Church of England ministers. Their parishes were large, and they were expected to visit church members as well as conduct services. As their time and resources allowed, they were to catechize and teach. Although they normally went from catechism to Book of Common Prayer and Bible, their teaching occasionally included Latin.

Since the mid-1600s, there had been private masters in the South. At their least, they were not much better scholars than their students and were poorly paid. Devereaux Jarrett, orphaned son of a Virginia carpenter, read "indifferently" and his handwriting was a "sorry scrowl" when he began to teach at nineteen.

> [T]hat I might appear more than common in a strange place, and be counted somebody, I got me an old wig, which, perhaps cast off by the master, had become the property of his slave, and from the slave it was conveyed to me. But people are not obliged, you know, to ask how I came by it.

In his first year of teaching, Jarrett earned only one-sixth as much as a carpenter would have. He caught malaria, but was well pleased recalling that he had been able to buy on credit two fine shirts.

From 1758 until 1773 Donald Robertson, capable and prosperous, a Scotch university man, was master of his own private school in Virginia. From his school he earned on the average £90 a year, nearly twice a carpenter's wages; he also had a farm.* About half his students studied English, the other half Latin, for which the tuition was twice as much. The students were boys, except for Miss Patsy Throckmorton in early 1761. (Girls did not go to private schools as a rule, but more often than not learned how to read.) Robertson had an average of thirty pupils. About half of his students were with him for a year or less, and only one in twenty for more than five years. Most of his students had learned to read before they came, and some went to other schools. The notebook of James Madison, a better student, has extensive notes on Socrates and Plato, and on Locke and more recent philosophy. It would be interesting to see the notebook of, say, Tommie Broadus, who spent six years instead of the usual two or three studying English.

The children of some middling well-off planters, as well as those of the wealthy, were tutored. It has been said that their tutors were often indentured servants, but that may have been first said in spite. One tutor, John Harrower, was an indentured servant. He had sailed and walked from the north of Scotland to the south of England without finding employment or profit, and in 1774, "reduced to the last shilling," he had signed an indenture. Landed at Fredericksburg, Virginia, his contract was sold to Colonel William Daingerfield of Belvedira plantation, and as Daingerfield's servant, he taught the colonel's three sons. "His elder son Edwin, ten years of age, entered into two syllables in the spelling book. His second son Bathurst, six years of age, in the alphabet. William, his third son, four years of age, does not know the letters." Daingerfield helped Harrower find additional tuition-

---

*£ = pound, an English unit of currency, in 1988 about $1.50; formerly much more.

paying students. The colonel was generous and friendly, although Mrs. Daingerfield disliked Harrower's Scotch way of speaking and his punishment of her children. Harrower was not well schooled, and even his spelling showed his Scotch burr. He seems to have been a thoughtful and religious man, although he was drunk with Colonel Daingerfield on Christmas Day 1775—Harrower, because he was homesick for his wife and children, and Daingerfield, because his tenants had not paid their past-due rent.

Philip Vickers Fithian was employed in the fall of 1773 to be for a year the tutor for Colonel and Mrs. Robert Carter of Nomoni Hall, a plantation a few miles from Belvedira. The Carters were a rich aristocratic family, and the upbringing and education of their children seems representative of those of the aristocratic and wealthy. Fithian was a graduate of Princeton and was preparing to become a Presbyterian minister. (Fifthian and Harrower apparently never heard of each other.) A few weeks after his arrival Fifthian wrote to a friend,

> I began to teach his [Colonel Carter's] children on the first of November. He has two sons, and one nephew; the oldest son is turned seventeen, and is reading Sallust [a favorite Latin author] and the Greek grammar; the others are about fourteen, and in English grammar and arithmetic. He has besides five daughters which I am to teach English, the eldest is turned of fifteen, and is reading the *Spectator* [an English magazine, the standard of graceful English]; she is employed two days every week learning to play the piano-forte and harpsichord. The others are smaller, and learning to read and spell. Mr. Carter is one of the chancellors of the upper court [council, upperhouse] at Williamsburg [capital of Virginia], and possessed of as great . . . fortune as any man in Virginia.

Fithian, presumably having been raised in an "authoritative" or "moderate" family, was unaccustomed to the aristocratic way of child rearing. The children of the Carters were raised by slaves (and tutors) as much as by their parents. Slave women often served as wet nurses for the children of southern aristocrats. By Fithian's standards the Carter children were "indulged"—spoiled. Schooling was canceled or postponed for pleasure: horse races, balls and parties, cock fights, and boat races. Girls were expected to learn to play the piano and guitar and to learn to dance with style and grace. The children of the Carters were being prepared to be gentlemen and ladies.

There were variations, naturally, in the education of aristocrats and gentility. There might be servants in the place of slaves. Occasionally there was a governess in place of a tutor; Fithian mentioned several times governess Sally Panton, recently arrived from London. Sometimes boys—and, less often, girls—were sent away to school. Occasionally a son or daughter was returned to England for school, although not as often as has been traditionally said. But in sum, the sons and daughters of aristocrats were being educated to become aristocrats.

Taking them together, the well-off, the middling, and the poorer sort of Virginians and Southerners generally were better schooled than they had been a century earlier, if not quite as well schooled as New Englanders. Virginians in the oldest, eastern part of the state were generally literate. Between 1763 and 1771, in Elizabeth City County, nine white men out of ten and two out of three white women could sign their names; in the 1600s, only one woman in three had been able to write her name. Many children still learned to read at home, and apprentices learned from their masters, but in 1745, at least five men and a woman taught in the county—a master at Symes or Eaton School, the Church of England minister, and private masters or tutors. The role of the school was less important than in New England, but as in New England, men and women were better educated than a hundred years before. In Virginia and in the rest of the South, there was less schooling in the up-country frontiers, but New England and Pennsylvania had their less well-schooled frontiers, too.

SCHOOLING FOR BLACKS:
THE FIRST PRECEDENTS

Nearly all the half million blacks in America in 1776 were slaves. Few of them could read, and fewer still could write. Most of those who did learn, as poetess Phyllis Wheatley did in Boston, were taught outside schools. Schools and schooling for blacks, when they did exist, usually resulted from efforts of churches, particularly those of the Church of England and the Quakers.

The Church of England's Society for the Propagation of the Gospel (S.P.G.) provided support for many of the Church of England efforts to Christianize blacks and for that purpose to teach them to read. In New York City it supported the school of Elias Neau, begun in 1704. Neau taught school three nights a week, for blacks and also for Indians and whites. He sometimes had more than a hundred pupils. When he died in 1722, other missionaries continued his school.

According to one account the Church of England's Charleston, South Carolina, school for blacks, which was established in 1743, followed a straightforward plan. Two slaves, Harry and Andrew, were purchased. They built the schoolhouse and then were taught to teach reading, which they did for some years. The more usual plan, of course, was for a white missionary or schoolmaster to teach, as in a school founded in Philadelphia in 1743. One of the less formal schools for blacks was established by The Reverend Jonathan Boucher, who was also rector of a parish and master of a school for better-off boys and managed his own plantation. With the support of another English society, the Associates of John Bray, he preached to, converted, and baptized slaves. To aid in Christian instruction, Boucher "set up two or three serious and sensible black men as schoolmasters to teach the children around them merely to read in their leisure hours." Perhaps that not unjustly sums up the view of the Church of England: blacks had souls; therefore, blacks should be converted; therefore, it would be valuable for them to read; but worldly matters were not interfered with in any way. Some slave owners wanted assurance that Christianizing their slaves would not interfere with their ownership. Laws, for instance one passed in South Carolina in 1711, insured that even if slaves had been converted to Christianity, their conditions of bondage were not in any way affected.

Colonial slave owners gave little further thought to schooling for slaves, but their learning became a crucial part of the economy of the Southern plantation. Carl Bridenbaugh's *Colonial Craftsmen* has described numerous slave artisans in the later 1700s. Occupying the position of journeymen, usually having learned their craft from white craftsmen, slave artisans were plantation sawyers, carpenters, coopers, blacksmiths, farriers, and coachmen, and in the planters' houses they were cooks, maids, and even butlers. Slave artisans also worked in Charleston, South Carolina; Philadelphia; New York; and other cities. Often the slave artisan was seen by free white craftsmen as an unfair source of competition.

The Quakers, starting with their founder George Fox, found slavery morally evil. Quakers in Pennsylvania were discouraged and later forbidden to own slaves and may have established a school for blacks as early as 1700. Other black children were taught with white children in the Quaker schools. The best remembered and most important Quaker school for blacks was the one founded in Philadelphia in 1770 by Anthony Benezet.

Benezet was a refugee French Protestant, as Neau was. Like Corlet and Cheever, Benezet had been a master throughout his career. Benezet had taught in Germantown (where Pastorous had taught), then in the Friend's English School (where the first master had been Enoch Flower), and had been master of a Quaker school for girls. He was a saintly man, gentle and charitable. More important, he believed that blacks were "generously sensible, humane, and sociable, and that their capacity is as good, and as capable of improvement as that of white people." What was most important was that Anthony Benezet, with fellow Quaker John Woolman, were the first American abolitionists. The Church of England had hoped to save souls. To put it simply, Benezet and his fellow abolitionist Quakers aimed to save men and women.

An "African School" was proposed to the Quaker monthly meeting in Philadelphia by Benezet in 1770, when he was master of a school for "indigent" (poor) girls. The proposal was approved. From 1782 until his death in 1786 after the Revolution, he was master of the Philadelphia African School. Much of his estate was willed to the school. It thrived, and the Quakers opened other "African" schools. While he was master of the African School, Benezet was one of the most determined spokesmen for abolition, speaking not only to Americans but also across the Atlantic.

SCHOOLING NATIVE AMERICANS: INDIANS

Schooling for Indians had been from the first intended to Christianize and "civilize" them. Some teaching missionaries realized that in some ways religion was dependent upon a way of life, so that it too must be changed. It is also true that missionaries had the encouraging, and as yet unexamined, belief that their own way of life was better. Further, schooling would serve (even if not so intended) to teach and maintain the subservience of the Indians. Understandably, Indians often rejected missionary schooling. It was said that in 1744 the Iroquois were invited to send their sons to William and Mary College. They declined, saying,

> We know that you highly esteem the kind of learning taught in those Colleges. . . . We are convinc'd, therefore, that you mean to do us Good. . . . But . . . our ideas of this kind of Education happen to be not the same with yours. . . . Several of our young People were . . . brought up at the Colleges of the Northern Provinces; . . . they were bad Runners, ignorant of every means of living in the Woods, knew neither how to Build a Cabin, take a Deer, or kill an Enemy, spoke our language imperfectly, were therefore good for nothing. . . . [I]f the gentlemen of Virginia will send us a Dozen of their Sons, we will instruct them in all we know, and make Men of them.

The Virginians declined the Iroquois offer, of course.

This incident, a parable about appropriate and inappropriate education and one of Benjamin Franklin's favorite tales, was at least partly fictional. It does emphasize one of the most important issues arising from attempts to educate Native Americans, or Indians. In general, attempts to "civilize" and Christianize Indians were failures.

AN AMERICAN SCHOOL: THE ACADEMY

Historically, the new kind of school, the academy, is associated with the name of Benjamin Franklin of Philadelphia, although it is not clear that the idea of the academy was wholly originated by him. John Milton had proposed a plan for a type of academy as early as the 1640s. Before discussing Milton's contribution, however, it is best to say what an academy was and what it would become: an *academy* was a secondary school, not usually a preparatory school for college. It was privately controlled and privately financed, by tuition and gifts, but also often by public funds. Many academies were affiliated with churches, but most were "public" in the sense that any student who could pay tuition could attend, regardless of church membership. Most academies offered a wide range of studies—some people said too wide. But even to a definition this broad, there are exceptions. A few academies offered college-level instruction. A few continued the old Latin grammar school curriculum and eventually became college preparatory schools. Some academies were controlled by a state or the national government, as West Point and Annapolis are (though, of course, they are no longer secondary schools).

In 1749, Franklin published a pamphlet, *Proposals Relating to the Education of Youth in Pennsylvania.* In the academy he proposed, youth was to be instructed in ". . . those things that are likely to be *most useful* and *most ornamental*, regard being had to the several professions for which they are intended." The charter for the academy, granted a few months later, specified that it was to teach

... the Latin and Greek languages, the English tongue, grammatically and as a language, ... French, German, and Spanish ... history, geography, chronology, logic and rhetoric, writing, arithmetic, algebra ... natural and mechanic philosophy [science], drawing ... and every other useful part of learning.

It was a long way from the Latin and Greek of the Latin grammar school.

In the proposal Franklin most often cited John Milton, who had also proposed a type of academy in his *Tractate on Education* in 1644; John Locke, who had died in 1714 but was still the most often quoted philosopher in provincial America; Charles Rollin and George Turnbull, then well known; and others. At the very least, Franklin contributed a synthesis that was a good match for the provincial experience. Before briefly describing the short and unsuccessful history of Franklin's Academy of Pennsylvania, some other sources of the academies need to be examined.

The inspiration for academies in America, it has sometimes been said, was the dissenters' academies in England, schools for the education of young men not allowed to attend Cambridge or Oxford in the 1700s because they were not members in good standing of the Church of England. However, there was a great deal of variety among the dissenters' academies, and so collectively they could not have had influence. If the American provincial academies were influenced by *an* English academy, the academy at Northampton may have had more influence than any other. The language of instruction there was English, and the variety of subjects taught was similar to that taught later in American academies. Master Philip Doddridge of Northampton did correspond with several Americans, but it is not clear how much he influenced them.

It has also been argued that academies followed the examples set by American Presbyterians. They established schools because it was necessary for "New Side" evangelical Presbyterians, who were very much influenced by the Great Awakening, to provide training for new ministers. It followed that the "Old Side" Presbyterians also needed to train ministers of their conviction. It is surely true that a number of Presbyterian ministers did establish schools. The most famous of them was the "Log College," which had been established in 1727 by William Tennant, father of evangelist Gilbert Tennant. The schools of the Presbyterians were called *academies* and began early in the 1700s.

Thus, it might be said that the academy was another invention of Benjamin Franklin's, or that the academies were inspired by one in England, or that the needs of the Presbyterian Church had led to the academies. Perhaps more important than any of this was the trend toward practicality in provincial American schooling. As an example, within a few years James Maury, Virginia parson-schoolmaster wrote that a student should "be chiefly employed in studies which will be useful to him in approaching the active scenes of life. . . . [He] ought to be instructed as soon as possible in the most necessary branches of useful, practical knowledge." No matter how complicated the history of the invention or introduction of the academy, it is entirely clear that it was the product of its times. Distinctly American academies would be established by the thousands in the 1800s and would be the most important kind of American secondary school until the rise of the high school toward the end of the 1800s.

The Academy of Philadelphia opened in 1751. Franklin thought it a failure because its "English school" became not much more than preparation for its "Latin school," and the Latin master was in charge of the Academy. The Academy's first English master, David Dove, a portly and voluble man, had come to Philadelphia in 1750. His teaching in the Academy of Pennsylvania gained Franklin's approval, because he admired Dove's student's elocution. Out of school Dove was a political caricaturist and writer of pamphlets, a "sarcastic and ill-tempered doggerelizer, who was but ironically *Dove*, for his temper was that of a hawk, and his pen the beak of a falcon pouncing upon his prey." It is fitting that a caricature is the surviving picture of him. He wrote supporting Franklin and his friends, changed sides, wrote against them, and attacked both sides on one issue or another. Dove insisted on also teaching at his own private school, to the objection of the Academy's trustees, and resigned or was discharged in 1753. Thereafter he kept private schools in and near Philadelphia.

"COLLEGE ENTHUSIASM"

Harvard had been established in 1636 and, after a false start, reopened in 1640. For sixty years it was the only college in the English colonies. The second college was William and Mary in Williamsburg, the capital of colonial Virginia, and was chartered by the King in 1693. The charter cost two years of effort by Commissary (bishop's representative) James Blair. Like Harvard, its first stated purpose was to provide ministers for the colony. As did Harvard, it provided a part of the formal education of many other students. William and Mary's Latin grammar school opened in the 1690s, and its first permanent buildings were completed in 1699. Students did not graduate from the college of William and Mary until the early 1700s.

The third American college, Yale (to use the name by which it is now known) was chartered by the legislature of Connecticut in 1701. It was established because leaders of Connecticut felt the need for a college and because conservative ministers in Massachusetts felt that Harvard was already too liberal and too much under the influence of unitarians. Yale was at Killingsworth and Saybrook, Connecticut, before it moved to New Haven in 1716. As Harvard had been, it was named for an early benefactor.

Frederick Rudolph, in *The American College and University*, points out the similarities among the first three colonial colleges. As had Harvard's founders, William and Mary's and Yale's founders declared that their colleges would train ministers. All three colleges were governed by their presidents and a board of outside laymen and ministers serving as trustees. The long-time English tradition had been government by faculty, but the lack of a strong and permanent faculty had made that impossible. The conventional American pattern of control of colleges is

FIGURE 2-2
David Dove, first English master of the Academy of Philadelphia. The contemporary sketch by Benjamin West, one of the most prominent American artists of the time, captures Dove's petulance. Joseph Jackson, "A Philadelphia Schoolmaster of the Eighteenth Century," *Pennsylvania Magazine of History and Biography*, 35 (1911), p. 314.

the one that was first introduced at these earliest American colleges. The first three colleges were partly supported by taxes, but the other pre-Revolutionary colleges were not.

The fourth American college, Princeton, was not chartered until forty-five years after Yale. Princeton was the first of the colleges to be founded as a result of the Great Awakening. The colleges coming out of the Great Awakening were controversial, and governmental aid could not be obtained for them. Princeton was the college of the evangelistic—"New Side"—Presbyterians, some of whose education had been at the "Log College" of William Tennant.

Within the thirty years remaining before the Revolution, five more colleges were established. To use present-day names, they were Brown, Columbia, Dartmouth, Rutgers, and the University of Pennsylvania, all the result of what Yale President Ezra Stiles called "college enthusiasm." Except for the University of

Pennsylvania, the new colleges were intended to educate ministers and other young men in the new or "reawakened" denominations. All of these colleges were small. Even Harvard and Yale had no more than one or two hundred students.

The colleges faced contradictions that would continue after the Revolution. One of these contradictions was the need for tuition to meet expenses, and hence the need to attract as many students as possible. While the colleges could and did demand that professors and tutors be of their faith, there were no religious tests for students; the need for students made such qualifications impractical. For chartering and survival there was need for wide support. Although Eleazar Wheelock had intended Dartmouth College for Indians, to receive a charter and to attract donations, it was necessary that the college have a more general attractiveness and admit other students.

There was a conflict in curriculum, too. Although most of the colleges had been intended to strengthen faith, the science of the 1700s, coming more than anywhere else from the Scottish universities, was introduced into the course of study. At Yale in the mid-1700s, students studied algebra, geometry, and calculus. Copernican astronomy, which placed the sun instead of the earth at the center of the universe, was introduced. At William and Mary a professor of "natural philosophy," William Small, was appointed in 1758. There would later be a long and heated conflict between science and religion, but it did not arise as long as science was seen as evidence of God's handiwork.

At the time when academies with more practical and general sources were beginning to be established, the first professional courses were being offered in American colleges. George Wythe was professor of law at William and Mary, and his students included Thomas Jefferson. Medicine was taught at the University of Pennsylvania starting in 1765 and at Columbia (then called King's College) in 1767. Students there could study anatomy, physiology, and chemistry, as well as applied medicine.

At some of the colleges, particularly Harvard, Brown, and Columbia, students were early and loud advocates of revolution against England. At the first commencement at Brown University in 1767, for instance, there was a debate on "whether British America can under present circumstances consistent with good policy, affect to become an independent state."

THE REVOLUTION

There have been many explanations for the causes of the American Revolution. The central issue—the most important cause of the American Revolution and the one that is most crucial in determining its immediate effect—was political. The Colonists' collective political experiences had for 150 years been different from people of mother country England. The fundamental issue underlying the Revolution was independence, freedom from what was seen as the tyranny of King George III and Parliament. Only a few leaders wanted to change society or to distribute wealth, as the French and Russian revolutionaries would. The immediate outcome of the Revolution was independence because most of the Revolutionary leaders had intended no more than that.

The political and ideological battles that led to the Revolution were sometimes fought in colonial assemblies and by speechmakers. But most often they were fought in newspapers and pamphlets, by writers and editors. They were effectively fought and followed with great interest because before the beginning of the Revolution most men knew how to read. Since most men and women had been taught to read in schools, the schools contributed indirectly, but nonetheless significantly, to the coming of the Revolution. Perhaps the strong pro-Revolutionary convictions on the college campuses also speeded the coming of the Revolution.

Not all Americans supported the Revolution. Perhaps one-third of them favored it, one-fouth of them opposed it, and the rest were onlookers. A few schools were destroyed, as Rutgers was when British Colonel John G. Simcoe burned its building. Others were closed, as the Boston Latin School and John Tileston's writing school were. Some schools, such as Dartmouth College, continued undisturbed except for the usual wartime effects of inflation and shortages.

The Revolution wrecked lives and made careers, and divided the families of schoolmasters as well as others. The experiences of John Lovell, master of the Boston Latin School, and of his son James Lovell, usher (assistant master) at the school, are examples of schoolmasters caught up in these kinds of events.

John Lovell (1710-1784), A.B. Harvard 1728, had been master of the Boston Latin School since 1734, as the successor of Nathaniel Williams, who had followed Ezekiel Cheever. Loyalist (Tory) students remembered him as gentle. The Revolutionaries (Whigs) remembered him as a flogging despot. A portrait of John Lovell still exists, a picture of a well-fed, smug-looking man wearing an Eastern turban, a fad of the time. One of his former students reported shuddering when he looked at the painting. John Lovell believed in loyalty—loyalty to England. When the British evacuated Boston in 1776, John Lovell went to Halifax with them as a refugee.

James Lovell had been usher of the Boston Latin School for fifteen years and a strict disciplinarian in school. He supported his wife and five sons on a modest salary of £60 a year and what he could earn by teaching arithmetic before school and teaching French at night. In the pockets of a Revolutionary leader killed at Bunker Hill, the British found letters implicating the younger Lovell as a revolutionary. On the strength of these letters, the British troops clapped Lovell in jail. Young Lovell shared as a prisoner his father's voyage to Nova Scotia. He was later freed as part of a prisoner exchange and became a member of the Continental Congress, a man of some political power. Old John Lovell died in Halifax, leaving behind him relics of a prosperous past, "a mahogany desk . . . tea table . . . two china punch bowls," and the household furnishings of a poor man, "one pair blankets . . . one small copper tea kettle (old)." Young Lovell, the revolutionary, lived on—a citizen and official of the new American republic.

The last major campaign of the Revolution ended with the surrender of a British army at Yorktown in 1781. The peace treaty was signed two years later. Then, in the words of a patriot, it was "time to begin again."

FIGURE 2-3 Portrait of John Lovell based on a painting by Nathaniel Smibert. From Justin Winsor, ed., *The Memorial History of Boston*, Vol. 2 (Boston: James R. Osgood and Company, 1881). p. 401.

CONCLUSION

The history of education in the colonies was at first the history of the "transit," or transportation, of a culture across the Atlantic, and its transplanting into the wilderness. Later, perhaps from roughly the time of Ezekiel Cheever's death in 1708, education and schooling evolved as American culture and society evolved. As Lawrence Cremin has written, education during the provincial period was popularized. It provided an opportunity for learning that would be more easily attained, more appropriate in subject, and more directly controlled by the public. At the same time, the role of the schools was increasing. Children learned to read in schools more often, rather than at home. Parts of the knowledge needed for trades and professions were taught increasingly in school rather than by apprenticeship.

Schools were influenced by a changing way of thought, less devout and less theological, more logical and more scientific. Some schools were also influenced by the Great Awakening, which was in part the reaction to the new rationalism. As American culture drifted toward materialism, the schools shifted, belatedly, toward a material emphasis. As America's first cities grew and became more prosperous, the varieties of education available within them grew. When schools are private enterprises, they follow the same patterns of growth and change as do other small enterprises.

At the same time, the colleges affected the professions of law and medicine, making the equivalent of apprenticeship less important. Schooling also changed the social standing of the student. As Philip Fithian wrote to a friend, a college degree from Princeton was as good in Virginia—as far as social standing was concerned—as £10,000.

The Revolution interrupted schooling, but did not immediately change it.

Part Two
AGE OF THE
COMMON MAN

The Corliss steam engine was the largest in the world, forty feet high and weighing 700 tons. With 2500 horsepower at thirty-six revolutions per minute, it provided power for Machinery Hall, a 1,400-foot-long building, quite appropriately designed by railway engineers, which was part of the 1876 Philadelphia Centennial Exhibition. At the height of the Industrial Revolution, machines were a most important attraction at the Centennial Exhibition, though one could see there what one wished to see: machinery, paintings, Japanese bronzes and lacquerware, even a display of false teeth. Two conclusions were certain: In its first hundred years the United States had become a great power, and Americans in 1876 lived in a world in which machines had become overwhelmingly important.

The United States and its culture had changed in many ways. Values and beliefs had shifted. Socially, America was more varied and more complex, with a much larger population. The economy had grown prodigiously. The United States had been enlarged geographically, too. Its western border, once the Mississippi River, was in 1876 the Pacific Ocean. Ways of travel had changed. Trails had been replaced by highways and canals. Canoes and flat-bottomed barges had been replaced by steamboats. Railroads moved products and people more quickly and inexpensively. America manufactured goods instead of only selling raw materials and buying

FIGURE II-1
The Corliss Engine at the Philadelphia Centennial Exhibition of
1876 was the symbol of power
and progress. The Bettman
Archive.

manufactured products. The American political system had changed: nearly every American man was entitled to vote. A system of schooling—tax supported, state controlled, and available for nearly every child—had been developed. Generals, explorers, businesspeople, statesmen, inventors—many, perhaps all, Americans—had contributed to progress.

It is a temptation to search for the mainspring, the driving force, for American change. There have been compelling arguments that the changes in America have come first from cultural values, social dynamics, the West and free land, efficient transportation, the American Industrial Revolution, a republican form of government, or even from distinctive American patterns of schooling. However, a search for the driving force in American history will almost certainly be unsuccessful. Progress, or change, came from interaction of all these factors.

The culture of a time and place is never uniform or monolithic; there are always dissenting views and deviant behaviors. Here, only general features can be sketched: the work ethic, the romanticism, the faiths and reformers of the time.

The "Protestant ethic"—the concept was German sociologist and historian Max Weber's—was and is a set of convictions and habits. Tomorrow is more important than today. To save is better than to spend. To be rich is to be righteous. To work is better than to rest. Your fate is in your hands, and you are responsible for it. These beliefs were not new, of course. Benjamin Franklin's *Poor Richard's Almanac* had stated them in pithy little sayings. The Protestant ethic is still important. (Critics say schools depend upon it too much, and so penalize pupils who do not share it.) The Protestant ethic seems to have been most pervasive in America in the early and mid-nineteenth century. Americans were inventors. (Abraham Lincoln patented a strange device to enable steamboats to walk over mud banks.) They looked to each person to reform himself or herself. (Solitary confinement cells in prisons were to aid the convict in doing so.) Americans were industrious. On the farm or in the shop or factory, they worked long hours, longer than before, much longer than today.

Americans of this period were, more than before or most times since, "romantics." They turned away from what seemed to them to be the limits of classical and conventional learning; in philosophy, this was a basis for *transcendentalists*, the most famous of whom was Ralph Waldo Emerson. They emphasized the virtues of the individual and the evils of society. In education romantics thought of the child as a garden plant, to be cared for and cultivated so that it would develop, grow, unfold, and bloom. For the romantics, feeling was more important than thought; grown men and women read Johann Goethe's *Sorrows of Werther* and wept at the hero's death by his own hand. It was the fate of man, or woman, to be isolated, alone; Lord Byron, poet, revolutionary, convention flouter was an influential man, a hero. Edgar Allen Poe not only wrote as a romantic but seemed to live as one.

Admiration for classical heroes and classical architecture continued and in some ways increased after the Revolution. Thomas Jefferson's architectural design for the University of Virginia was neoclassical. Admiration was reflected in place names, too: Cincinnati, Ohio; Syracuse, New York—or even Hannibal, Missouri, the setting for *The Adventures of Tom Sawyer* and boyhood home of its author, Mark Twain.

During the same time the romantics rediscovered nonclassical history, architecture, and art. One of the authors much admired and much read by Americans was Scotsman Sir Walter Scott. Many of his high romantic novels had historical, nonclassical settings. *Ivanhoe*, perhaps most loved of them, was set in early medieval England. There had been a revival of Gothic architecture in England. Churches and schools and other American public buildings were built in that style in America. Many American homes were adaptations in wood, "carpenter Gothic" and "steamboat Gothic." Some survive and are cherished. American Gothic was followed by designs inspired by Italian villas, Swiss chalets, and, at the extreme, Egyptian tombs and mosques of India. There were also American romantic painters, members of the "Hudson River School," glorifiers of nature.

This was also a period of reform. Our first interest here is in school reformers and reforms, but there were other reformers and other causes. The most important of these reformers were abolitionists; their cause was to end slavery. American abolition may have had its beginnings with the efforts of schoolmaster Anthony

Benezet. In 1807, Congress ended by statute the legal importation of slaves. The American Colonization Society was founded ten years later to send blacks back to Africa; the intent was charitable (if racist); the practice, wholly impractical. Among abolitionists, William Lloyd Garrison was one of the most influential and determined abolitionist spokespersons. He established an abolitionist newspaper, the *Liberator*, in 1831. He wrote about abolition,

> On this subject I do not wish to think, or speak, or write with moderation. . . .
> I am in earnest—I will not equivocate—I will not excuse—and I will not retreat
> a single inch. And I will be heard.

The *Liberator* undertook, with some success, to convert Northerners to abolitionism. Another abolitionist, Eijah Lovejoy, was killed in Alton, Illinois, when his newspaper office was mobbed in 1837; he became the abolitionists' first martyr. One of the abolitionist heroines was Harriet Tubman, an escaped slave who aided other slaves to escape northward. Far more famous were the characters of *Uncle Tom's Cabin*, the best-selling antislavery novel that appeared in 1852. "Uncle Tom," the name of a "good darky" who "knew his place," would become an insulting term.

Most Southerners, though not all of them, were antiabolitionist. Slavery was a part of the Southerner's idealized way of life. Slavery was profitable in work-demanding cotton, sugar cane, and tobacco fields. In parts of the South black slaves were much more numerous than were whites. A few white refugees from Haiti settled in the South, and Southerners knew of the deaths of two thousand whites at the hands of black Haitian revolutionaries. Southerners were alarmed by Nat Turner's Rebellion in Virginia in 1831 and by other slave uprisings. Finally, there was John Brown's 1859 attempt at Harper's Ferry, Virginia, to start a general insurrection of slaves. After seventeen deaths Brown was captured by troops under the command of Colonel Robert E. Lee and hanged. The abolitionists had another and greater martyr: "John Brown's body lies moldering in the grave / But his soul goes marching on. . . ."

The most important reformers of the times were the abolitionists, and those in which we are primarily interested were school reformers. It is not to be forgotten that this was the time of many reformers and would-be reforms. One of them, "temperance," which later became prohibition, was the basis for the Eighteenth Amendment. It serves as one of the best examples of ill-considered and unsuccessful reform. Some other causes have devotees still. "Women's suffrage" was devoted to securing voting, property, and other rights for women. Other projected reforms seem less important, although they have their ardent supporters now: vegetarianism, the prevention of cruelty to animals, and suppression of the use of tobacco. Dr. Sylvester Graham, an important supporter of abolition, was also a devoted vegetarian and the developer of unbolted whole wheat flour. We use his name when we speak of *Graham crackers*.

In the late 1700s, detached and logical ways of thinking about religion and about God had led to deism and to outright atheism. In the 1800s, there was renewed commitment and warmth of faith for the churches and for religion. In long-settled places there was propriety and faith and weekly attendance at services in churches that were as impressive as they could be made to be. Nearer the frontier there was less propriety. Religion and faith there were strengthened by traveling preachers, many of them Methodists, and days-long camp meetings. The society, culture, and the schools of the time must always be seen against this background.

New churches and sects appeared. Unitarianism, the faith and conviction of liberal gentlemen and ladies, began with a somewhat mystical reformulation by William Ellery Channing, initially while he was a tutor in Richmond, Virginia. Other churches and sects were further from conventionality. One group, the Millerites, believed that the end of the world would come on March 21, 1843, and made every preparation for that event. Other sects established religious utopias: the "Shakers," founded in 1774, who forbade marriage and sexual intercourse; the Oneida community, along somewhat different lines; the Amana community in Iowa. The names of the latter two are still familiar. The most nearly successful of the religious communities was, of course, Salt Lake City, established in 1847 by the Mormons.

There were also nonreligious, shorter-lived utopias. There were more than thirty "phalansteries," rural communes. The most famous of them was Brook Farm, near Boston. Many prominent transcendentalists came there during its short existence. New Harmony, Indiana, established in 1825 by Robert Owen, is particularly interesting because of its socialistic principles and its Pestalozzian schools.

The United States' population grew from 5 million in 1800, to 39 million in 1870. By 1870, there were great cities. The population of New York was 800,000; that of Philadelphia, 500,000. After an ebb tide, immigrants were flooding in again, from Ireland and Germany. Regional differences had increased. Southerners, with their "unique institution" of slavery, Western farmers, and Eastern city dwellers and factory workers had different views and spoke in different accents. America had become much more diverse as well as larger.

In 1800, there had been only a few Americans west of the Appalachians. By 1840, they were settling in Iowa. In 1849, the Gold Rush brought 80,000 men and some women to California, which became a state the next year. In the 1870s, homesteaders were establishing themselves in sod cabins in the Dakotas and Montana. Unsettled land, free or cheap, was the most important attraction of the West, far more important than gold. The West was the country of the common man, the location of purest democracy. The rich generally did not go west, and new Western fortunes would usually take decades to accumulate. Cowboys, gold prospectors, embattled Indians, hardrock miners, and sod-breaking farmers would become a part of America lore.

After the War of 1812, American cities resumed their rapid growth. Cities were ports then, where farm and natural products—cotton, wheat, fish, pitch pine— were gathered for shipment by sea and where finished and tropical products—cloth, tools, guns, coffee, sugar—were sold by merchants. Shipping itself and buying and selling were the sources of merchants' growing wealth. The *transportation revolu-*

tion was a necessary preliminary to the growth of manufacturing and of inland cities. Between 1815 and the Civil War, transportation was revolutionized by the building of turnpikes, canals, railroads, and steamboats. Larger sailing ships, and later, propeller-driven iron steamships, appeared on the Atlantic Ocean. In 1861, a telegraph line replaced the pony express. Even the transportation of information had been revolutionized. Most important, freight rates declined by three-fourths or more. For the first time it was feasible to ship farm products—for instance, wheat—from the Ohio valley to the eastern seacoast. The cost of shipping manufactured products west also declined, of course.

By 1825, the cities of the Ohio and Mississippi Rivers—for instance, Cincinnati, Pittsburgh, Saint Louis—and the Great Lakes—Buffalo, Detroit, Chicago—had begun their most rapid growth. Typically, they also had industries, processing farm and raw products. Cincinnati was "Porkopolis," where hogs were slaughtered and pork cured for shipment. Pittsburgh, although like the others at first a trading city, produced iron and glassware. Buffalo was the eastern terminal of Great Lakes shipping, where wheat was unloaded from lake boats, and where much of it was milled into flour before it was shipped farther eastward.

Some other early manufacturing was located in the cities, too, because transportation was good there and workers were available, and because the cities themselves were markets. Fortunes were made in cities, or at least displayed there by the building of mansions, by elaborate furnishings for them, by the finery of wives' clothing, by an elaborate way of life. Cities were centers of cultural life. Painters and writers found patrons in the cities. The largest audiences for theatre and music were in the cities. There was not only great wealth and comparative sophistication there, but also extreme and commonplace poverty. Living costs seem low to us—in 1851, a New York City family of five could live on $10.37 a week—but wages were lower still, and being "out of work" was too common. In 1846, one person in seven in New York City was a pauper. Houses were overcrowded, airless, lightless, unsanitary. Crime and illness in the cities were distressingly commonplace. Many of the new immigrants lived there, not much more comfortably than in the old land.

Between the War of 1812 and the Civil War, 5 million immigrants came to the United States. The most common reason for coming to America was hope of economic gain. Immigrants came also because of their religious or political beliefs. About two million of the immigrants were from Ireland. For reasons we do not entirely understand, population had increased in Ireland, as it had in the rest of Europe. The cost of food had risen. In Ireland, farm landlords, who were greedy or at least opportunistic, evicted tenants or raised land rents. A million Irish children, women, and men starved to death when the Irish potato blight struck in the late 1840s. Irish newcomers settled in the largest seaport cities, New York, Boston, and Philadelphia. They were not welcome. They were "Papists," Roman Catholics, "Clodhoppers," reputedly often drunk, surely underemployed or unemployed. The life expectancy of an Irish child born in Boston in the 1850s was six years.

Germans also immigrated in large numbers. Before the Civil War many were Protestants, troubled by interference with their churches. In 1831, three thousand members of a Hamburg, Germany, Lutheran church came together to Buffalo. German Catholics and German Jews immigrated also. A few of the Germans were "48ers," liberal or even radical exiles. Smaller numbers of immigrants came from Norway and Sweden and other European countries. Thousands of Chinese laborers were brought to the Pacific Coast. Some immigrants who were skilled workers quickly found jobs and enjoyed at least some prosperity. Many of the immigrants settled on farms in the West or became farmhands there. Others found jobs in the first mills and factories. On the West Coast, laborers recruited in China provided the heavy labor for the building of railroads. In the Lowell, Massachusetts, cotton spinning and weaving mills, Irish families replaced the first mill "operatives." girls and women from farming New England. Lowell was the first American industrial city. Water power was plentiful there, and transportation good. A number of cotton spinning and weaving mills were built there, starting in 1846.

Most of the new immigrants settled in Philadelphia, Boston, New York, and other northern cities. Relatively few settled in the South. By 1860, only 500,000 immigrants lived below the Mason-Dixon line. Only New Orleans had a substantial immigrant population. By the time of the Civil War, New York, Milwaukee, St. Louis, Chicago, and other big cities had foreign populations that outnumbered those of American birth.

Although the Industrial Revolution in England had been underway since at least 1750, it did not take place in the United States until much later. The process of industrialization was long and complicated. It was necessary to develop or borrow designs for the machines that would replace skilled labor—the designs for the first power looms, in Rhode Island in 1811, were more stolen than borrowed. It was necessary to provide power for the machines, first from water wheels and water turbines, later from steam engines, which provided most of the power after 1870. For factories to be profitable, it was necessary to develop at least a rudimentary management system. For manufactured goods a mass market was necessary: the transportation revolution had aided in that.

Industrialization had its price. It tended to concentrate wealth and power. Workers were exploited; working hours were long; the pay, low. It made it more difficult for skilled craftsmen to maintain themselves. It was expensive for our environment. Industrialization did result, however, in America being less dependent upon foreign manufactured products. Products generally were less expensive. A clock, after clockmaking had been industrialized, cost $2. Farming, also, had been revolutionized by machines performing tasks that men had formerly done. Productivity increased and with it, the standard of living.

Wars had social, cultural, and political consequences of their own. Even the War of 1812, embarrassing and at most indecisive, had its consequences. It led to a shift of capital from shipping to manufacturing, hurrying the American Industrial Revolution. The headlong attack by Andrew Jackson on the Indians of Florida had a consequence, easing the acquisition of Florida by the United States. The hero of the Battle of New Orleans, Andrew Jackson, became the hero of the common man and two-term president.

The Mexican War produced more glory, though its ends were more venal. Texas and the Southwest were added to American territory. Another military hero, Zachary Taylor, was elected to the presidency.

However, no American war has had greater social consequences than did the Civil War. The causes of the war, remote and immediate, have been the subject of many books. The war itself has been the subject of many more. Occasionally a school figured directly in the fighting. For instance, the southern students of Virginia Military Institute, as the "Cadet Corps," fought in the Battle of New Market. Eight student cadets were killed then. The record of the 33rd Illinois Infantry is less distinguished, but is was a school regiment. Most of its recruits were from the Illinois normal school, and the principal of the school was the regiment's colonel. In 1862, the end came to a Kirksville, Missouri, academy, when a battery of field artillery galloped up and unlimbered its guns on the lawn. But those are mere details, three among many. The consequences of the war concern us here. The first human consequence was the death of hundreds of thousands of soldiers, North and South, black and white. The first social consequence was the freeing of the slaves. Abolitionists melted away, their cause triumphant. They believed that slavery was immoral and evil: Most of them did not believe that whites and blacks were equals or should be treated as equals. Of course, for blacks, freedom was only the beginning. Economically, the South was devasted, and it would be the end of the century before it recovered. In the North there were new fortunes. All these would affect schools and education. Once more a military hero, U.S. Grant, became president.

In 1876, American wealth was growing fast, but the distance between the rich and the poor was greater. Businessmen had built large-scale enterprises, but it was difficult to organize worker unions. There were mansions in the cities, but also crowded, dirty, damp, airless flats in crime-ridden slums, where death rates were high. For good or for bad, city governments were often controlled by political bosses and their machines. Americans were prejudiced against Catholics, against Jews, against foreigners, and white prejudice against blacks was still strong. In the North there had been and would be race riots. General Sheridan had repeated that "the only good Indian is a dead Indian." In the summer of the Philadelphia Exposition, 1876, General George A. Custer made his last stand at Little Big Horn. Custer, dead, was a hero. It would be a long time before white Americans would begin to feel that what Custer had attempted was wrong in principle. In 1876, there would be doubts about the honesty of the national government. General Orville Babcock, President Grant's personal secretary, was implicated in a distillers' tax avoidance deception. Secretary of War William W. Belknap resigned rather than face impeachment for selling Indian trading posts. Nevertheless, President Grant, with Emperor Dom Pedro II of Brazil and many other dignitaries, was present at the opening of the Philadelphia Centennial Exhibition.

Chapter Three
SCHOOLING IN
THE NEW REPUBLIC

As a rule, successful revolutionists have drastically changed patterns of schooling. The American revolutionists were an exception. They had no wish to change the schooling or the nature of their fellow citizens. They wished to preserve rather than to change. Except for independence from English king and English Parliament, few had any intent to change. Consequently, they made no effort to.

In the fifty years after the Revolution the schools did of course change. Part of the change was due to the "republican spirit" that appeared during the American Revolution and during the French Revolution a few years later. The "republican spirit" led to new views of human nature, of society, of government, and of the contributions to be made by schooling. Thomas Jefferson developed a social philosophy that was both representative and influential in his times, and proposals for schooling that followed from it. His unsuccessful bill in 1779 for the establishment of common schools anticipated in many ways the forms common schools would take fifty years later. He founded the University of Virginia, a fragment of the public school system he had first envisioned.

During those fifty years new kinds of schools appeared. One of the new kinds of school was a Pestalozzian school in 1825 in the short-lived utopia of New Harmony, Indiana, and is further discussed later in this chapter. Another new kind of school was the monitorial, or Lancastrian, school, which was widely popular where the poor, particularly the urban poor, were numerous, and where resources for schooling were small. The monitorial school is also discussed later in this chapter. Academies, which had first appeared before the Revolution, were established by the hundreds, and even by the thousands. Dozens of new colleges were established.

For the "common" or "district" schools, new school texts reflecting the "republican spirit," and voicing the new nationalism—but the old religious values—appeared quickly. Noah Webster's *A Grammatical Institute of the English Language, Part I*, later editions of which were to become famous as the "Blue-back Speller", was the first published in 1783, only two years after the British capitulated. Jeddidiah Morse's *Geography Made Easy* appeared the next year.

FIGURE 3-1 Frontispiece and title page from Noah Webster's "Blue-back Speller." In the frontispiece, the Ancient Greek goddess of wisdom Minerva is pointing the child towards the temple at the rear of the illustration in which are enshrined Knowledge and Wisdom.

Both these texts, and others, deliberately tried to educate their readers in a political and value system that was consciously "American."

The development of thought and the evolution of schools required time. At the end of the Revolution not much was changed. Of course, some Loyalist masters had fled, but others resumed teaching. For Robert Proud of Philadelphia, "revolt, rebellion, and destruction, under the name and pretense of Liberty" were "popular and disagreeable objects." He spent the years of the Revolution in seclusion, but in 1780, returned as master of the Friends Latin school.

In New York, as Carl Kaestle described it, there were still schools supported by churches. Perhaps thirty masters operated their own private for-profit schools, and there were dames' reading schools. As before the Revolution, schooling was offered in something like a free market. Parents chose what schooling seemed best from what schooling they could afford. For the poor—and in the cities the poor were becoming more numerous—there were only the church schools. Often there was no schooling at all. The monitorial schools would not appear in the cities until twenty years later.

In the South, education changed relatively little after the Revolution. John Davis, who had served in the British navy and who had learned "passable" Latin and French, spent four years, 1798-1802, traveling and teaching in the South. Not as well qualified as Philip Fithian, he lived and taught in circumstances less opulent than Fithian's. He lived with a family in their log house on a new plantation in South Carolina and taught the family's children. At other times he was treated with disdain. Toward the end of his stay in America, he taught, very much as John Harrower had, in a school in Virginia only thirty miles from where Harrower had taught.

Even after new kinds of schools and education were appearing, older ways of schooling survived. In 1831, Abigail Mason of Salem, Massachusetts, went to Virginia to be the governess of Robert Temple's family on their plantation near Richmond. Teaching the Temple children, her life was probably not much different from that of a governess Philip Fithian had known fifty years earlier on the eve of the Revolution.

THOMAS JEFFERSON AND BENJAMIN RUSH, THEORISTS

While the decades following the Revolution saw a continued decline in the importance of the study of Latin in the schools, the vision of education as a moral enterprise was maintained. Noah Webster's intention was probably not much different from most educators' when he declared in the introduction to his spelling book that its purpose was to help teachers instill their students with ". . .the first rudiments of the language, some just ideas of religion, morals and domestic economy."

Undoubtedly the most important characteristic that emerged in the educational practice and thought following the Revolution was a deliberate cultural nationalism. The new nation's political and social values emphasized the worth of governments based upon the principles of a classical republican ideology. The disorder of the Revolution and the preceding colonial rule would be corrected by the proper implementation of a democratic republic, in which a virtuous citizenry through the help of government would establish a new social order.

Opinions varied then as to specific characteristics that the new republic would have. Essentially what was conceived was a system of government whose strength was lodged in a largely agrarian population of independent landholders. The republican philosophy required participation in government by its landowning citizenry freed from monarchial rule. Property ownership was a critical qualification for participating in politics. Aristocracies and inherited status were largely rejected in favor of the natural leadership of talented men. Ideally, though the enactment of republican principles of government, cultural unity could be achieved—one that would provide the nation with a basis for its identity. Education was to play an important role in the establishment of this democratic republican consciousness.

Thomas Jefferson, best known of the early republican educational theorists, was born at Shadwell, Virginia, on April 13, 1743. His father, Peter, although not of a particularly distinguished family, was nevertheless a member of Virginia's landed gentry. His marriage in 1739 to Jane Randolph linked him to one of Virginia's most important families and placed him and his children in a prominent position in local society. At the time of his death, when his son Thomas was fifteen, Peter Jefferson owned more than sixty slaves and between seven and ten thousand acres of land.

Jefferson's early years were probably typical for the son of a successful Virginia planter, although the closeness of his home, Shadwell, to the frontier may have exposed him to influences that were more democratic than those of the older and more traditional tidewater region of Virginia. After having learned to read and to do basic arithmetic, Jefferson was sent at the age of nine to a school conducted by the Reverend William Douglas. Besides religious instruction, Jefferson also received training in French, Latin, and Greek.

Starting when he was fourteen, Jefferson attended a school under the direction of the Reverend James Maury. Maury was a much more sophisticated scholar than was Douglas and provided Jefferson with a thorough grounding in the Greek and Latin classics and in contemporary literature. Maury, as has been said, was an early advocate of utilitarian schooling rather than pure classical preparation. Jefferson studied with Maury for two years and then entered the College of William and Mary.

At William and Mary, Jefferson came largely under the influence of William Small, the single lay member of the faculty. According to Jefferson, Small was a man knowledgeable in most areas of science, of a liberal disposition, and a gentleman. It was from Small that Jefferson received his first systematic introduction to science, philosophy, and social theory.

Jefferson began to read law while still a student at William and Mary and practiced law until shortly before the outbreak of the Revolution. It was as a lawyer that he first put forward ideas about education. Asked to accept a cousin as an apprentice, Jefferson declined, explaining that he did not have the time to train an apprentice adequately. He wrote that most lawyers had a tendency to require apprentices to do their work for them and usually did not provide them with adequate time for their studies.

Jefferson was elected to the Virginia House of Burgesses in December 1768. His involvement in politics would continue until his death more than fifty years later. So too would his interest in education. In 1779, Jefferson put forward in the House of Burgesses a systematic plan for public education in Virginia entitled "A Bill for the More General Diffusion of Knowledge." In the bill, Jefferson outlined a system of schooling that would support his more general political and social philosophy.

According to Jefferson, a democratic society needed an educational system that would provide its citizens with the understanding and knowledge necessary for them to not only be able to pursue their own personal happiness, but also to fulfill their obligations and duties as citizens. Education would also provide the training that would allow those with unusual talents to assume roles as leaders of the culture.

Jefferson's bill of 1779 proposed that a natural aristocracy be identified by means of the educational system, one which would supplement rather than supersede the existing aristocracy based upon birth and wealth. Jefferson proposed to do this by means of a three-tiered school system that would provide a free general education for the entire population, but would also select and train for positions of leadership those individuals of superior intelligence and virtue.

Jefferson's plan would have established a school program that operated in two distinct manners. For the general citizenry, a system of instruction was to be established that would provide them with three years of free schooling. Beyond basic instruction in reading, writing, and arithmetic, each individual would be provided with a general background in the principles of democratic government.

The second phase of Jefferson's educational program was to be implemented by means of a system of twenty Latin grammar schools, which were to be established throughout the Commonwealth of Virginia. Those who wished to pay the necessary tuition could send their children to these schools at their discretion. In addition, a set of examiners would visit the elementary schools throughout the commonwealth and provide scholarships to a limited number of the community's most talented boys. As Jefferson outlined his proposal,

> Of the boys thus sent in one year, trial is to be made at the grammar schools one or two years, and the best genius of the whole selected, and continued six years, best geniuses will be raked from the rubbish annually, and be instructed at the public expense, so far as the grammar schools go. At the end of six years' instruction, one half are to be discontinued (from among whom the grammar schools will probably be supplied with future masters); and the other half, who are to be chosen for the superiority of their parts and dispositions, are to be sent and continued three years in the study of such sciences as they choose, at William and Mary College.

Jefferson felt his plan would provide basic instruction in reading, writing, and arithmetic for every male citizen, as well as more specialized training for those individuals of unusual ability. In addition, a basic uniform political education would be provided to the entire citizenry. Significantly, Jefferson opposed religious indoctrination by the schools. He felt that in a republic individuals should not have imposed upon them any type of instruction that would be contrary to their personal religious creeds.

Although Jefferson advocated the separation of church and state, he realized that it would be virtually impossible to eliminate all religious functions from the schools. In the general education bill that he proposed to the Virginia legislature in 1817, for example, Jefferson argued that the educational system should simply be required not to threaten through compulsory religious instruction the religious freedom of any group attending the schools. According to his proposal, no religious rite or instruction could be required of a student attending the public schools, clergymen would be excluded from administrative positions in the schools, and the establishment of a professorship of divinity at the University of Virginia would be prohibited.

To some extent Jefferson's views were a compromise with existing religious authority and tradition. Commonly held religious holidays by the various religious groups within Virginia could be observed by both the public schools and university; religious materials and issues could be studied at the university if they were placed in a literary or philosophical context. Thus students in philosophy could study the implications underlying religious belief, or Biblical languages such as Hebrew or Greek, but not specific views concerning religion. Religion could be dealt with by reason, not dogmatically.

Jefferson failed to convince the members of the Virginia House of Burgesses of the need for a uniform system of public elementary schools. Cost and class interests undoubtedly encouraged the bill's defeat. It was not until the mid-1830s that widespread support for public schools of the scope and impact Jefferson proposed was to develop throughout the United States.

Jefferson is perhaps the only major theorist to have put forward his ideas on education during the Revolution. In the decades following the Revolution, numerous other theorists presented specific proposals concerning the type of educational system that would be most suitable for the new republic. Among the most important of these theorists was Benjamin Rush.

Rush was a signer of the Declaration of Independence and early established himself as one of the leading intellectual figures of the new nation. Rush was the best-known physician of his period. Having graduated from Princeton University in 1760, he had studied medicine at the College of Philadelphia and at the University of Edinburgh, which at the time was probably the most sophisticated center of political, philosophical, and social thought in Europe, as well as a major center for the study of medicine.

Rush was acutely aware of the significance of education in the promotion of the newly achieved republican system of government. As he wrote in a letter in 1786,

> We have changed our forms of government, but it remains yet to effect a change in our principles, opinions and manners so as to accommodate them to the forms of government we have adapted. This is the most difficult part of the business of the patriots and legislators of our country.

Rush argued that the educational system established during the colonial period encouraged diversity. Through the establishment of a uniform system of education —one which included the establishment of a federal or national university—Rush hoped to create an essentially homogeneous population that would be particularly well suited to a uniform and peaceful system of government.

Unlike Jefferson, who was strongly opposed to the inclusion of religion in education, Rush felt that it should be an important subject in any system of public schools. According to him, by being exposed to the principles of Christianity, society was assured that the individual would posses those virtues that were most desirable for the citizen of a republic. Rush felt a Christian could not fail to be a good republican citizen since

> . . . every precept of the Gospel indicates those degrees of humility, self-denial, and brotherly kindness which are directly opposed to the pride of monarchy and the pageantry of a court.

Rush's vision of the republic was clearly one of a Christian commonwealth.

Rush was interested in the proper education of women. As a result of Enlightenment debates on the rationality and educability of women, there had been increased interest in the matter in the later 1700s. Jean-Jacques Rousseau's *Sophia,* his companion work to *Emile*, had outlined in detail the possibilities and limitations of education for women. In 1787 Rush, in his essay "Thoughts upon Female Education," maintained that the education of an American woman should be quite different from that of an English woman. Rush wrote that the American should have a good knowledge of English, that she should learn to read and to write clearly and to keep accounts. An acquaintanceship with geography and history would also be helpful. She should in instructed in the basics of Christianity but also in music and dancing.

Much more radical theories concerning women emerged in England. Among the most interesting of them were those of Mary Wollstonecraft's. Wollstonecraft had been born in Ireland in 1759. Self-educated, a radical thinker in her time, she protested the low status and limited opportunities for women. She did not hesitate to violate convention. At thirty-three she lived in France with an American, Gilbert Impay, and gave birth to a daughter. Later, as wife of English philosopher William Godwin, she would die giving birth to her daughter, Mary. (Mary would later write the novel *Frankenstein* and marry the great English poet Percy Bysshe Shelley.)

Thoughts on the Education of Daughters, published in 1787 (the year of Rush's essay) was in many respects typical of pedagogical and childrearing manuals written then. The primary purpose of girls' education, she wrote, was to prepare them for their roles as wives and mothers. Her *Vindication of the Rights of Man* (1790) was a rebuttal of Edmund Burke's criticisms of the French revolution.

Wollstonecraft wrote then in the belief that new and just system of government was being created in France. But Talleyrand proposed a system of national education that excluded women, and she realized that the rights of men proclaimed by the French Revolution would apply only to men. Shortly afterward she published *A Vindication of the Rights of Women*, the most important statement in the 1700s concerning the rights of women.

She wrote that sexual tyranny was no different from political tyranny. Admitting that most activities of women were domestic, she argued that women must be their husbands' intellectual companions and that they should be capable of supporting themselves if necessary. To do so, education was imperative. She called for a system of nationally supported elementary schools and equal schooling for all girls and all boys. Expectations for women and for men would be equal. What Wollstonecraft envisioned was a society in which qualities of individuals, rather than their sex, would determine what they would do and how they would be treated. When she wrote, Mary Wollstonecraft's ideas were radical departures from the accepted wisdom.

Rush, as well as contemporaries of his such as Noah Webster and Jedidiah Morse, were strongly opposed to any foreign involvement in the education of American citizens. This was clearly part of a larger movement to define and establish a national identity and tradition independent from that of Europe, and England in particular. The threat posed by the failure to establish an independent cultural identity seemed serious. In England, Lord Sheffield published a pamphlet declaring that cut off from the political and cultural influence of England, the American political experiment would fail..

Nationalists in all sections of the culture emerged to support the development of a specifically American consciousness. Artists such as Charles Wilson Peale began to paint works with specifically patriotic themes, while Joel Barlow composed an epic patriotic poem, *Columbiad*. They were clearly self-conscious in their nationalism. Despite their limitations, they were part of an attempt to solve the problem of establishing a distinctive national identity.

ROBERT OWEN, JOSEPH NEEF, AND FRIENDS: UTOPIANS

Robert Owne was, like Jefferson, a social theorist. As they did for Jefferson, schools played an important part in his theories. Jefferson had envisioned a farming society, but Owen an industrial one. Owen was born in Wales in 1771. He was himself a successful and prosperous industrialist, manager, and partner in British cotton mills. As a reformer and utopian, he was a forerunner of the socialists.

The "infant schools" Owen established in New Lanark, Scotland, and New Harmony, Indiana, were loosely based on the work of Swiss educator Johann Heinrich Pestalozzi. Pestalozzi had been born in Zurich, Switzerland, in 1746, the son of a lower-middle-class family. Having tried careers in the ministry, the law,

FIGURE 3-2
Johann Heinrich Pestalozzi (1764-1827). His school at Yverdon, Switzerland and his book *Leonard and Gertrude* greatly influenced Robert Owen and William Maclure, Friederich Froebel, and American reformers. Barnard's *American Journal of Education*, 4 (1858).

and farming, he gradually turned to education. Strongly influenced by the work of the French philosopher Jean-Jacques Rousseau (1712-1778), Pestalozzi argued that men are born neither good nor evil but instead, are shaped by the environments in which they live. The idea of providing children with healthy and supportive environments, which would allow them to develop their personalities and characters to the fullest extent, was to be the basis of Pestalozzi's educational system.

Profoundly disturbed by the apparent distingration of Swiss peasant society and family life taking place as a result of the rapid growth of cities and towns, Pestalozzi became concerned with reestablishing the importance of the family as a unit, and of using education as a means of developing an understanding of the world, through the use of object lessons whose applicability to real life situations would immediately be evident. Both these ideas were developed by Pestalozzi in his book *Leonard and Gertrude*, which was first published in 1781. Written in the form of a novel, *Leonard and Gertrude* was loosely based on the story of a Swiss peasant woman's struggle to reform her alcoholic husband and educate her own children and the children of her village. Although not formally trained as a teacher, Gertrude, the heroine of the book, had an instinctive ability to instruct children. Warm and loving, she developed a curriculum for the children that emphasized things with which they were already familiar from their homes. Pestalozzi, for example, explained how the instruction Gertrude gave the children to whom she was teaching arithmetic

. . . was intimately connected with the realities of life. She taught them to count the number of steps from one end of the room to the other, and two of the rows of five panes each, in one of the windows, gave her an opportunity to unfold the decimal relations of numbers. She also made them count their threads while spinning, and the number of turns on the wheel, when they wound the yarn onto the skeins. Above all, in every occupation of life she taught them an accurate and intelligent observation of common objects and the forces of nature.

Appealing to the senses rather than simply to reason, Gertrude's system emphasized the natural goodness and curiosity of the child. By emphasizing the importance to the learning process of love and the idea of practical and object lessons, Pestalozzi radically departed from rigid authoritarian modes of education, emphasizing obedience and rote memorization, that were then common in Europe.

Owen first became interested in education as a way of improving the conditions of workers in his factories. Indeed, he is best known as an early socialist. Interested in further developing his investments. Owen, together with his business partners, acquired the New Lanark cotton mills in Scotland in 1799, and proceeded to develop a community around the mills which for the period was a model of social and industrial organization.

Owen did not believe that industry should be a specialized activity separated from agriculture, but that the two should be carefully integrated. In this sense, Owen was repudiating the dichotomy between the city and the countryside that was to become a major issue in Europe and America during the nineteenth century. It was Owen's intention to establish industry in a rural setting under ideal conditions that would eventually not only lead to improved working conditions for laborers, but also lay the foundations of a new moral and social order.

Owen was particularly concerned with the welfare of children in the programs that he established at New Lanark. Child labor was widely used in factories in England during the late eighteenth and early nineteenth centuries. When Owen first arrived at New Lanark, the working conditions of children in factories horrified him. Such conditions were typical in England during the period. In his autobiography Robert Dale Owen, Robert Owen's son, recalled his experiences when he was fourteen and his father took him on a tour of various British mills:

> The facts we collected seemed to me terrible almost beyond belief. Not in exceptional cases, but as a rule, we found children of ten years old worked regularly fourteen hours a day, with but half an hour's interval for the midday meal, which was eaten in the factory. . . . In some large factories, from one-fourth to one-fifth of the children were cripples or otherwise deformed, or permanently injured by excessive toil, sometimes by brutal abuse. The younger children seldom held out more than three or four years without serious illness, often ending in death.

Robert Owen set out to eliminate conditions such as these. In doing so, education was to play a crucial role in his reforms.

Owen believed that education was the cause of most good and evil, misery and happiness found in the world. At New Lanark he radically improved working conditions for children in his factories and developed an exemplary educational program for them. His ideas concerning education were clearly rooted in the belief that individuals were primarily shaped by their environment and that, given a decent education and living conditions, "the good" would predominate. In this sense, Owen saw education as being a critically important means for achieving the reform of society.

In 1824 Owen came to the United States and purchased from a communal religious group called the Rappites thirty thousand acres of land in Indiana, along the lower Wabash River. Owen's purchase included the village of Harmony. Quickly renamed New Harmony, the village became the center of a major utopian experiment. At Owen's invitation, more than eight hundred people settled there by the following year to create a "New Moral World" in the wilderness. Among the basic programs set up by Owen and his followers, the system of schools was undoubtedly the most successful. Owen's educational efforts at New Harmony were largely supported by the work of William Maclure and Joseph Neef.

Owen met Maclure at New Lanark in the summer of 1824. In many respects their careers closely paralleled one another. Maclure was born in Scotland in 1763. Like Owen, he had made a fortune in business and then turned to other interests. Coming to the United States during the late 1790s, Maclure began pioneer studies in the field of geology and minerology. Within a few years he established, both in the United States and in Europe, a reputation as an important scientist.

Maclure also became concerned with education. In 1805, he visited Pestalozzi's school in Yverdon, Switzerland, and quickly became a supporter of Pestalozzi's system of education. Wishing to establish a Pestalozzian school in the United States, Maclure asked Pestalozzi to suggest someone who could set up such a program. The Swiss educator suggested Joseph Neef as a candidate. Meeting with Neef, who was then living in Paris, Maclure was impressed by him and his ideas and agreed to support him in the establishment of a Pestalozzian school in the United States.

Maclure financed Neef for two years while he learned English. Some time about 1808, a Pestalozzian school was established by Neef near Philadelphia, the first such school in the United States. After a few years the school was transferred to Delaware County, Pennsylvania, where it was eventually forced to close because of objections by the local community to Neef's atheism. Giving up teaching, Neef moved to Louisville, Kentucky, and took up farming.

Despite the failure of the school under Neef's supervision, Maclure continued to support various educational experiments. In 1819, he went to Spain and attempted to establish a school based upon the educational ideas of Pestalozzi and Philip Emanuel von Fellenberg (1771-1844), an early advocate of agricultural and trade education. In addition Maclure was involved in the support of Pestalozzian schools in Paris under the direction of Guillaume Sylvan Casmir Phiquepal d'Arusmont and the Madame Marie Duclos Fretageot. The Spanish educational experiment ended in 1823, when the French army entered Spain and brought to an end the liberal Spanish rule under which Maclure had established the school. Forced to flee, Maclure made his way to Ireland and then England, and finally to Scotland and New Lanark, where he met Owen.

By then Fretageot and Phiquepal d'Arusmont had with Maclure's help transferred their activities to Philadelphia, where they operated a Pestalozzian school. After some hesitation, Maclure agreed to go to New Harmony with Owen and direct the utopian colony's schools, Significantly, Maclure had complete control of the educational experiment. Neef, Fretageot, and Phiquepal d'Arusmont worked with him. The school opened in 1826.

In many respects the immigrant and higher schools established at New Harmony represented a continuation of the Pestalozzian programs begun by Owen at New Lanark. One fundamental concept was that of free public education for all members of the community. Classes included both sexes. Emphasis was placed upon "object methods" of instruction. Whenever possible, visible concrete examples were presented to the children. Geometry was taught by means of a machine called a *trigonometer* and arithmetic by a kind of abacus. Natural history was studied by direct observation, while geography was learned by having students make their own maps and globes.

Drawing and music were important parts of the school curriculum, as was gymnastics. Language training was provided by bringing together children of different language backgrounds to teach one another. Central to the curriculum was the program in trade education, which was the first of its type in the United States. Included in the program was instruction in engraving and printing, as well as in other manual arts.

The educational experiment at New Harmony was short-lived. Almost from the start, Owen and Maclure disagreed about the school and its operation. Maclure envisaged the schools as being centers for scientific study, in which the students and their teachers would systematically pursue new fields of inquiry. Owen increasingly saw the schools as centers that would draw the members of the community together by cultivating in them similar dispositions and beliefs. By the spring of 1827, these differences were of little meaning, since the utopian experiment had come totally to an end. The schools in various forms continued for some time afterward.

Although largely a failure, the educational experiment undertaken by Maclure and Owen at New Harmony was to anticipate many of the major trends and reforms that took place in American education during the nineteenth century. The emphasis upon Pestalozzian principles of instruction, the attempt to use education as a vehicle for reforming the society, the idea of the school as a social center, as well as the emphasis upon industrial or trade education, are all issues that were to figure prominently in the educational programs and reforms of the middle and late nineteenth century.

In varying forms Pestalozzi's ideas were popularized by many individuals. Samuel Wilderspoon, at first a master and then agent of the London Infant School

Society, did much to promote "infant schools" in England. They were for a time popular in the United States, in a not very Pestalozzian form that brings to mind today's nursery schools, and they probably served the same general functions.

ROBERT RAIKES, JOSEPH LANCASTER, AND ANDREW BELL: CHARITY AND UTILITY

Two other new kinds of school, the Sunday school and the monitorial school, appeared. Both, but particularly the monitorial school, were important because they established or strengthened conventions of thought about schooling. Both Sunday and monitorial schools were first popular in Great Britain. England's industrial revolution was well underway. As a result, the poor in the cities had become more numerous and more conspicuous. In England, too, it was a time of political and social reform. Despite its political independence the United States had not yet achieved complete intellectual independence and often adopted English precedents.

The Sunday school was popularized in England after 1780 by Robert Raikes, a newspaper publisher and editor in Gloucester. A rather natural development, Sunday schools had been organized by some revivalists of the Great Awakening in England and in the American colonies. Their increased popularity in England was from Raikes's efforts, as well as from greater concern for the needs of the poor. Usually the Sunday schools were in cities, although there are records of Sunday schools outside them. It was said that in 1821 there were 430,000 Sunday school pupils in England. Sunday schools eventually appeared in every American state. There were 5,000 Sunday school pupils in Boston and nearly 600 in Salem, Massachusetts. To demonstrate their learning, the Salem pupils recited Bible verses—one pupil learned sixteen hundred of them—and gave answers to questions about the Bible. In the United States the American Sunday-School Union supported the development of Sunday schools. It also influenced the direction of their development, so that they would come to be exclusively concerned with religion and would become the kind of Sunday school some of us or our parents remember from childhood.

The first assumption about Sunday school pupils was that they were in ignorance of Christianity and therefore in danger of damnation. The primary purpose of the Sunday school was to teach religion. In some Sunday schools the Bible was the only textbook. Teaching for salvation was already a very old idea, as was reading for salvation. Second, the Sunday schools were for poor children and teaching was a form of charity to the poor. Sunday school teachers were usually volunteers, charitable young Christians who contributed their Sundays—except for the time of church service—to good works for the poor.

Of a different nature was the monitorial or Lancastrian school first developed by Andrew Bell and Joseph Lancaster. Bell organized a prototype school in Madras, India. Lancaster's monitorial school in London was the first to gain wide attention.

Later there were hot debates as to the originator of the monitorial system. In America Joseph Lancaster, Quaker schoolmaster, was far more influential than was Andrew Bell, Church of England clergyman. Bell and Lancaster would be fascinating subjects for psychohistorians.

Andrew Bell (1753-1832) was a tutor in Virginia from 1774 until 1781, a contemporary of Philip Fithian. In Virginia, Bell saved £350. He would always know the value of money. Back in England, he was ordained by the Church of England and in 1787 was in Madras, India. He was appointed to serve in, was paid for nine concurrent posts there, and saved £3,000 a year. In 1797, after he returned to England, he wrote and published *An Experiment in Education. . .* , describing the school he had superintended in Madras. In England he spoke and wrote in behalf of his system of schooling. He again had concurrent well-paying posts. Near the end of his life he was unable to speak, whether for physical or psychological causes. An avaricious man, most of his fortune of £250,000 ($800,000) was left, paradoxically, to support his system of charity schools.

Joseph Lancaster (1778-1838), son of a sieve maker, was born and grew up in Southark, a worker's part of London across the Thames River from the old city. Lancaster became a Quaker and a reformer. In 1798, he opened a school in Southark for poor boys, where pupils, "monitors," taught younger pupils. His school was admired and supported by many, including King George III. He described his system, by then fully developed, in 1805, in *Improvements in Education. . . .* Lancaster's biographer said that as a teacher Lancaster had "zeal, self-confidence, ingenuity. . . , intuitive insight into the nature of children, and ardent love for them, and rare power of managing them." Lancaster was a compelling speaker. One of his extracurricular passions was spending, as Bell's was saving. Lancaster spent his money, his schools' money, his benefactors' money. His coach drawn by four horses was a substantial extravagance. Eventually he was imprisoned for his debts. Lancaster also seems to have been a practicing sadist. This might have been suspected from the bizarre school punishments he devised: yokes, shackles, sewing boys into blankets, and pupils in baskets hauled to the ceiling. A letter published in 1977 is persuasive.* Debts, and sadistic tendencies, drove him to America, where his "system" was already known and honored. He lived and organized schools in Philadelphia. When his reputation overtook him, he went to Baltimore to establish a "Lancastrian Institute" there. In 1825, he was invited to Caracas, Venezuela, by Simon Bolivar, but $20,000 for the establishment of schools somehow disappeared before the schools materialized, and Lancaster returned to the United States. In New York City, he was struck and killed by a runaway team and coach.

The central feature of the monitorial school was having pupils, serving as "monitors," teach less advanced pupils. Of course, this had been done previously (and would be done later), but not as systematically. So that monitors might instruct, it was necessary to divide lessons, and knowledge, into small bits. For

---

*H. R. deS. Honey, *Tom Brown's Universe: The Development of the English Public School in the Nineteenth Century* (New York: Quadrangle/New York Times, 1977). pp. 202-03.

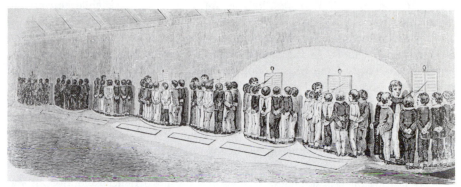

FIGURE 3-3   A monitorial school in operation, from a manual published by the British and Foreign School Society. Reprinted in Paul Monroe, ed., *A Cyclopedia of Education,* Vol. 4 (New York: Macmillan, 1913), pp. 296–97.

example, the first step taken was to teach the beginning pupil—most often a boy—the letters of the alphabet. This was reduced to teaching first the "perpendicular" letters, **I, H, T, L, E, F, i, l.** The "triangular" letters, **A, V, W,** and so on, followed, and then the "circular" ones.* Pupils learned to read from wall charts or book pages, a page at a time. The pupils competed for prizes: badges, medals, candy. In that way, a monitorial school was like a mammoth never-ending spelling bee. A monitor heard the recitals. A monitor tested and promoted the pupils. A monitor took attendance.

In New York City the Free School Society, later called the Public School Society, adopted monitorial instruction. The Public School Society was a charitable, nonprofit organization, receiving state and city appropriations to provide schooling. Between 1805 and 1853, the Society would provide schooling for a half million New York City boys and girls. As Michael Katz has pointed out, the Free School Society was an example of a "corporate volunteeristic" organization, one alternative to public school organization as we know it. Corporate volunteerism in New York City provided cheap schooling, without administrative costs. Of course, with this kind of organization middle-class benefactors controlled the schooling of the children of the poor. It was called "benevolent despotism" by an earlier historian.

The Public School Society adopted the monitorial system because, as John Griscom wrote, of *"1st Cheapness, 2nd Large Number."* Griscom, a hawk-nosed, slope-shouldered Quaker, established a successful monitorial "high school" in New York City, a combined primary, elementary, and secondary school. Monitorial schools appeared in Detroit; Springfield, Massachusetts; Saint Louis; Buffalo; and other cities. The African School of New York City also adopted the monitorial

---

*Lancaster's schools did teach reading and writing concurrently, an exception to then usual procedures.

system. One-third of New York City's eighteen hundred black children were enrolled there.

It is worth considering the assumptions, explicit and implicit, that supported the monitorial schools. As the Sunday schools were, the monitorial schools were primarily for the children of the poor. In New York City in 1823, the cost of a year's instruction of a pupil in monitorial school was only $1.80. As in the Sunday schools, the teaching of Christian beliefs and morals was important. Lancaster insisted that there be religious instruction and that it be nondenominational. (The latter was an important disagreement with Andrew Bell, who insisted that the doctrines of the Church of England be taught.) As most monitorial schools did, the New York African school started the day with readings from the Bible.

If instruction was to be given by young and inexperienced monitors, it was necessary that what was to be learned be split into small segments. From one point of view this was (and is) logical enough. As Griscom saw it, even scientific knowledge was of unrelated facts—"pyroligneous acid" did not prevent the spread of yellow fever, iodine was helpful in the treating of goiter. From an opposing view, saying that knowledge and learning are nearly endlessly divisible is like maintaining that a cathedral is a high pile of rocks or that a sonata is played by depressing the keys of a piano three thousand times.

More conspicuous was the analogy of the school as machine. If, as the deists argued, God could be "the great Clock-maker," it was commendable for a school to be a "perfect machine" and for teaching to be mechanical and endlessly repetitive, as the motion of a clock pendulum was. Monitorial schooling was "a new machine of immense power, parallel and rival to . . . the greatest of modern acquisitions to mechanical operation." To another writer, "every boy seems to be the cog of a wheel—the whole school a perfect machine."

Beyond the analogy of the school as machine was the analogy of the school as factory. One of the Bell's supporters wrote that "the principle of schools and manufactories is the same. The grand principle . . . is the division of labour applied to intellectual processes." These lines of thought were predictable enough. In one way they were efforts to develop and apply a science of education, to make schooling orderly and its outcomes logical, rational, and predictable. Before more than a few dozen Americans worked in factories, many Americans had heard of factories and anticipated them with pleasure. Teachers were sometimes referred to as *operatives*. Governor DeWitt Clinton of New York saw the monitorial school as a labor-saving machine. The machine analogy and the factory analogy would be important. As Karl Kaestle wrote, Lancaster caught the spirit of a new technological age and applied it to the problem of mass education. Our schools have not escaped the preoccupation with classification and output that began with the monitorial movement, for we still live in an industrialized age.

By 1830, enthusiasm for monitorial schools had ebbed, although they would persist or reappear when there was not money for other forms of instruction.

DISTRICT SCHOOLS: SCHOOLBOOKS

While the new kinds of schools appeared, older kinds survived. In Massachusetts and Connecticut, state laws, though somewhat less stringent from the colonial ones, perpetuated the town and district schools. District schools were established in New York state and in the Western areas in which New Englanders settled. However, other patterns of school funding and control persisted. Even where there were district or town schools many children were sent to private ones. As late as 1825, the New York Public School Society found nearly four hundred private schools in New York City. In Pennsylvania schooling continued to be primarily the responsibility of churches anxious to perpetuate and spread their theologies and faiths. Farther south, schooling was a private responsibility, and the schools were generally private.

The proprietary, or entrepreneurial, school had the simplest form of payment for and control of schooling. Alonzo Potter quotes the recollections of an early nineteenth-century Kentuckian:

> The applicant for a school would draw an article of agreement, stating what branches (subjects) he was able to teach, and for what rates of compensation. The paper was passed around from house to house for signatures, and subscriptions partly payable in money and partly payable in "produce." The tuition of the children of the poor was paid customarily by the public-spirited individuals of comfortable fortune.

As before the Revolution, schools were supported by every conceivable means. There were gifts and endowments, "rate-bills" or tuition tax, charges for firewood, and state "permanent funds" paying interest to the schools. In New York state there was an attempt to support public schools by lotteries.

Although the idea of establishing a federally supported university failed to be adopted in the Constitutional Convention, support for the establishment of schools at the elementary level and secondary level was provided by the federal government through the Ordinances of 1785 and 1787. The Land Ordinance of 1785 outlined the procedures under which western frontier lands were to be surveyed. The new land was to be divided by surveyors into six-mile-square townships. Each township was divided into one-mile-square (640-acre) sections, and section 16, near the center of each township, was to be reserved for the public schools. If school lands were sold, receipts were to be invested or spent for the public schools. (New England colonials had made roughly the same provisions.) The Ordinance of 1787 confirmed this policy. "Religion, morality, and knowledge, being necessary for good government and the happiness of mankind, schools and means of education shall forever be encouraged."

The land grants to states and territories were the first federal aid to education. A very few of the Land Ordinance school lands were kept by school systems; usually they were sold. Unfortunately, money received for them was not always used for the intended purpose. In Illinois, for example, the capital and interest from the sale of the school lands was allowed to accumulate in a school fund. During the early 1830s, the bulk of these funds, more than $100,000, was channeled by various means into programs for the building of canals and railroads. Similar actions took place in other states.

The published recollections of pupils in the first republican years are usually negative. Sixty years later Nathan Hedges remembered without pleasure attending school near Morristown, New Jersey:

> The first [school there] I attended was taught by a cruel old man, by the name of Blair, usually known as "Clubber Blair." The [school] house was new, about sixteen feet square; had a writing table on one side, fast to the wall, for the larger pupils; all others were seated on benches made of slabs. The only books used in spelling and reading were Dilworth's Spelling book and the Testament. I have no recollection of an arithmetic [book] in the school. Geography and grammar were not even thought of. To spell, to write, to read in the Testament, and to work the four elementary rules of arithmetic, comprised the whole scope, aim, and object of the school. . . I well remember that when I could not multiply by even one figure, he would give me a sum in multiplication, with four figures for a multiplier, and from day to day would pound my bare feet with his hickory club for not doing the sum correctly. He furnished no help, no instruction, no kind of encouragement to a beginner, but relied on the severity of his punishment.

Hedges did concede that other district school teachers were "more qualified and more humane."

We should keep in mind that many of the recollections of those early republican schools were printed a half century later to show how much the schools had improved. It is possible, also, to find a scattering of recollections of men and women who had enjoyed attending district schools. However that may be, financial support was certainly meager. School terms were usually short. The status of teachers was low. Many district schools were open for only a few weeks during the winter. In others there was also a summer term for the smaller children who were not needed on farms between planting and harvest time. Only a few schools in the cities and in the most prosperous towns still stayed open through the year. Colonial times' scattering of well-paid masters nearly disappeared, except perhaps for men teaching in the academies. Elsewhere, *master* was giving way to *teacher*, more humble, more pious, with greater hoped-for dedication, and lower wages.

Pupils in the district schools and in those similar to them provided their own schoolbooks. They used books that their families had or that their families preferred. Each pupil was heard individually, coming forward to "toe the line" painted on the school house floor and to recite. Each pupil proceeded at his or her own pace. There were no classes. The district schools were not "graded." A capable pupil could proceed without waiting, and at least in principle, a less capable pupil

FIGURE 3-4 A district school in Connecticut illustrated in *The Malte-Brun School Geography*. Reprinted in Clifton Johnson, *Old-Time Schools and Schoolbooks* (New York: Macmillan, 1904). p. 116.

was spared embarrassment. On the other hand, a busy teacher with a big "school"— many pupils—might be able to devote only a few minutes daily to each child.

In general, to learn was to memorize, still. In the *American Spelling Book* there were "Familiar Lessons." This is a part of one of them:

> Henry, tell me the number of days in a year. Three hundred and sixty-five.— How many weeks in a year? Fifty two.—How many days in a week? Seven— What are they called? . . .

For somewhat older pupils, Nathaniel Dwight's *System of the Geography of the World* (first edition, 1795) was in question-and-answer form from beginning to end. It could be mastered only by memorizing.

The most plentiful evidence of the content of instruction in this period is in surviving school books. School textbooks have always been important determinants of what has been taught. They were especially important when teachers were ill-prepared, and emphasis was on memorization, rote learning. Hundreds of school texts were published, some in dozens of editions. They were read and studied by rich and poor, and often by the old as well as the young. Noah Webster's spelling book, first titled *A Grammatical Institute of the English Language, Part I*, was first published in 1783. In 1816, Webster claimed, probably without great exaggeration, that more than three million copies of his spelling book had been printed.

It is true that there are limits to discovering what was taught from what old texts said. Some subjects, most obviously writing, or penmanship, were usually taught without a printed text. Some books, for example, *Aesop's Fables*, were used as schoolbooks although they were not so intended. At least some teachers taught mathematics from notes rather than from books. Some schoolbooks were used in a variety of schools; common or district schools, academies, and private schools. But even taking into account these limits, schoolbooks determined much of the curriculum. School textbooks presented a consistent set of values and beliefs. They reached large, geographically dispersed, and culturally diverse audiences. The texts that appeared after the Revolution were one of the beginnings in American culture of mass political and cultural education.

As before, schooling started with the teaching of reading. New editions of the *New England Primer* continued to appear, but there were changes. An engraving of King George II was retitled George Washington. The alphabet rhymes were changed. For instance, the earlier "Queen Esther comes in royal State, / To save the Jews from dismal fate" was replaced by "Queens and kings / Are gaudy things." There were many new primers, including *The Boston Primer, New York Primer, American Primer, Columbian Primer, The Evangelical Primer* (almost entirely religious in content), and *The Franklin Primer*. Lessons, as in the Colonial period, began with reading: first letters, then syllables, then words.

Next, the schools taught writing and spelling. "Correct" spelling would be far more important in the 1800s. Thomas Dilworth's *A New Guide to the English Tongue*, a British spelling, grammar, and reading book popular since the 1750s, was replaced by Noah Webster's speller, with reading lessons but without grammar. American speech, as Noah Webster maintained, was no longer identical to British speech, and American spelling should therefore be different. Originally titled *A Grammatical Institute of the English Language, Part I*, Webster's speller was later *The American Spelling Book*, and after 1829, the *Elementary Spelling Book*. Often called the "Blue-Back Speller," tens of millions of copies were sold in the 1800s and into the 1900s. An 1817 edition, after preliminaries, presented the alphabet from *a* to *z* and *&*. It proceeded with one-syllable words, plurals, two-syllable words, and so on. It also included selections for reading. A typical selection was the fable of "The Boy That Stole Apples," taken word for word from Robert Dodsley's *Select Fables of Esop and Other Fabulists* (1761), first included by Webster in the 1787 edition of his spelling book.

The Boy That Stole Apples

An old Man found a rude Boy upon one of his trees stealing Apples, and desired him to come down; but the young Sauce-box told him plainly he would not. Won't you? said the old Man, then I will fetch you down, so he pulled up some tufts of Grass, and threw at him; but this only made the Youngster laugh, to think that the Old Man should pretend to beat him down from the tree with grass only.

Well, well, said the old Man, if neither words nor grass will do, I must try what virtue there is in stones; which soon made the young Chap hasten down from the tree and beg the old Man's pardon.

MORAL: If good words and gentle means will not reclaim the wicked, they must be dealt with in a more severe manner.*

Interestingly, the fable "Of the Boy That Stole Apples" was included in numerous schoolbooks published in the nineteenth century. It may have been the source of Theodore Roosevelt's famous statement concerning American foreign policy of "speaking softly and carrying a big stick."

The American Spelling Book concluded with a list of place names, ". . . The

---

*_American Spelling Book_ was unremittingly masculine. *Boy* and *man* appear fifteen times as often as *girl*. *Woman* is not mentioned.

History of the THRIFTY AND UNTHRIFTY," and "A Moral Catechism" in question-and-answer form. Webster's spellers were not unusual in this respect. The *United States' Spelling Book*, widely used in the West, included the story of the New Testament and numerous maxims: "A bad life will make a bad end." Spelling books were intended to teach more than spelling. They were to teach reading and dashes of geography and grammar. More generally, they emphasized piety, morality, and patriotism.

Many arithmetic books were in use, according to one source at least sixty-five of them. The most popular arithmetic books seem to have been Englishman Thomas Dilworth's *The Schoolmaster's Assistant* (1773), Nicholas Pike's *New and Complete System of Arithmetic* (1788), and Nathan Daboll's *School Master's Assistant* (1800). The books began with the rudiments of arithmetic and continued through the "rule of three" (direct and inverse proportion) and square roots. To learn arithmetic was to learn "rules" for every occasion. The assumption was that pupils could read, read well. Daboll wrote that addition is "putting together of several smaller numbers of the same denomination into one larger." Pupil sometimes compiled simplified versions, presumably dictated by teachers. Arithmetic books dealt with many units of measurement: currency in cents and shillings; weight in grams and pennyweights, drams and ounces; cloth in nails and ells; distances in fathoms and hands; land in poles and roods; liquid in anchors and runlets, firkins, and hogsheads; and in dry measure, pottles and pecks. Even in arithmetic, patriotism could be reflected: "Washington was born in the year of our Lord 1732: He was 67 years old when he died: in what year of our Lord did he die?"

A greater variety of schoolbooks was needed because a greater variety of subjects was taught in common schools and in the academies. "The young masters and ladies throughout the United States" to whom Jedidiah Morse dedicated his geography books were to learn in greater detail about the United States. America's orators-to-be needed material for the practice of elocution. If history was to be taught, a history of the United States was called for, although this was a while in being developed.

Beyond the primer, reading lessons in spellers, and the Bible, reading in school was often intended to serve as preparation for elocution or public speaking. Americans spoke rather than wrote, listened rather than read. "Great Orations"—speeches in legislative halls, arguments before the bar, platform addresses, and sermons—were, as Daniel J. Boorstin has observed, the American media. Among the most successful of the early compilers of readers was Caleb Bingham, himself a professional elocutionist (and one-time usher to John Tileston, Boston writing master). About 600,000 copies of his *American Preceptor* were sold. A 1799 edition of *American Preceptor* has 228 pages and 100 selections from speeches, the Bible, sermons, poetry, and short stories. It begins with "General Directions for Reading and Speaking" by Hugh Blair, Edinburgh professor of rhetoric. Perhaps a dozen selections were by Americans. Selections in *American Preceptor* and other reading and elocution books often dealt with conventional virtues. The anonymous editor of the *Columbian Reader* (3rd edition, 1815) wrote that "*In making selections for the following pages, an uniform preference has been given to such pieces as were calculated to instill into the minds of youth the principles of virtue and morality"* There were admonitions about the virtue or vice of disrespect, charity, forgiveness, industriousness, superstition, benevolence, generosity, argumentativeness, cheerfulness, modesty, integrity, candor, ingratitutde, and liberality.

Patriotism was also an occasional topic. Bingham included an elegy to Columbia, which began

> Columbia, Columbia, to glory arise;
> The queen of the world and the child of the skies;
> Thy genius commands thee; with rapture behold,
> While ages on ages thy splendors unfold.

Ten years later, a selection in Asa Lyman's *American Reader* described the death of George Washington.

> Thus on the fourteenth of December, 1799, in the sixty-eighth year of his age, died the father of his country, "the man, first in war, first in peace, and first in the hearts of his fellow citizens." This event spread gloom over the country, and the tears of America proclaimed the services and virtues of the hero and sage, and exhibited a people not insensible to his worth.

The *American Preceptor* and the others were eventually overtaken in sales by a three-book series edited by Lindley Murray, a New York loyalist living in England.

As an example of often-displayed nationalism, Jedidiah Morse wrote about more recent immigrants that

> The time, however, is anticipated, when all improper distinctions shall be abolished; and when all the languages, manners, customs, political and religious sentiments of the mixed mass of people which inhabit the United States, shall come to be assimilated, as that all nominal distinctions shall be lost in the general and honourable name of Americans.

Like most of the textbook writers, Morse was a New Englander, and reflected his background. "New England has a very healthy climate. It is estimated that about one in seven of the inhabitants live to the age of seventy years; about one in thirteen or fourteen to eighty years and upwards." Morse seemed to feel that slavery was an evil. Of the Virginia planters he said,

> Labor is carried on almost wholly by slaves; who, in many of the countries, are much more numerous than the whites. Great numbers of the white inhabitants are thus exposed to habits of idleness, and to the manifold evils and vices which always accompany it.

Proslavery Southerners, of course, objected to such passages, as well as to Northern authors of schoolbooks about the South and its culture in general. In 1795, Virginia jurist St. George Tucker published a pamphlet objecting to Morse's description of the Southern States. According to Tucker, not only were Morse's physical descriptions of the South inaccurate, but also his interpretations of southern life misrepresented and distorted the culture as it actually was.

Even so, Morse was not immune to the charms of parts of the South. Of Charleston, South Carolina, he said,

> And in no part of America are the social blessings enjoyed more rationally and liberally, than in Charleston. Unaffected hospitality, affability, ease in manners and address, and a disposition to make their guests welcome, easy and pleased with themselves, are characteristics of the respectable people in Charleston.

There are many other geography books, nearly fifty others published before 1840. Among the more popular works were Nathaniel Dwight's *System of Geography of the World* (1795), more than two hundred pages of unbroken questions and answers, a catechism of geography to read, to memorize, and to recite. J. A. Cummings's *Introduction to Ancient and Modern geography* (1813) also included a geological section and an introduction to spherical geometry. Cummings, following the example of Oliver Goldsmith, was careful to make comparisons and show connections between countries, for instance in commerce. Cummings published a short, eighty-three page version, *First Lessons in Geography and Astronomy*, in 1818.

There were fewer schoolbooks for other subjects that were usually taught in academies rather than in common schools. *Cheever's Accidence, a Short Introduction to the Latin Tongue*, was still in use. *American Latin Grammar*, compiled by Edward Rigg, had been published by 1780, and was in its eighth edition in 1793. Science books were unusual, but *Conversations on Chemistry*, by Jane Marcet, a British author, appeared in the United States in several editions starting in 1809. A simplified and shortened version of Goldsmith's *Natural History*, edited by Mrs. M. Pilkington, was printed in Philadelphia in 1810.

Schoolbooks reflected the biases, and even the personalities, of their authors. They also reflected, more generally, the biases of the new nation's culture. They both shaped and were shaped by curriculum. For good or for bad, a national elementary curriculum was appearing. The curricula of the academies, to which we now turn, were much more varied.

ACADEMIES AND COLLEGES

The most rapidly multiplying form of school in the United States, 1781–1825, was the academy, the origins of which have been described in Chapter 2. Their speedy multiplication began after, or even during, the Revolution. Latin grammar schools were converted into academies or replaced by them. (One of the few Latin grammar schools that did survive was the Boston Latin School, the first to have been founded in the colonies.) The academies also supplanted in large part the earlier entrepreneurial or private venture schools. Academies were established in the North, the South, and the West. There were probably more than a hundred academies by 1800, and more than a thousand by 1830.

The academy, ideally, was incorporated and was charted by the state. It was a legal entity under the control of its board of trustees. In general, this was the same as the legal procedure for establishment of a college. A charter testified legitimacy, and incorporation had the advantage of giving an academy a continued existence, or at least the possibility of continued existence, after the departure of a popular "preceptor," "principal," or "president." However, most academies operated without the formality of a charter. Ideally, an academy had an endowment that would produce revenue to supplement tuition, but most academies did not. Academies had a variety of names: *seminaries* for boys or girls, *institutes, collegiate institutes*, or even *colleges*. The names of individual academies ranged from re-sonant to rustic—*Liberty Hall* in Virginia; *Eel River Seminary* in Indiana. A few of the early academies were Latin grammar schools in all but name, and continued the traditional classical curriculum. Phillips Andover, which had opened in 1778, later offered other courses, perhaps "for the great end and real business of life," as its charter said. However, it continued the classical subjects and served as a prepara-tory school. More than eighty years later one of its first pupils, Josiah Quincy, wrote

> The course of studies and text-books I do not believe I can from memory exactly recapitulate; I cannot, however, be far out of the way in stating that "Cheever's Accidence" was our first book; the second, "Corderius;" the third, "Neops;" then, if I mistake not, came "Virgil." . . .Our studies in Greek were slight and superficial . . . a thorough ability to construe the four Gospels were all required of us to enter the college. . . .
>   Of "methods and discipline," . . . I can only say that the former was strict and exact, and the latter severe.

Other academies, most of them, were intended to be terminal institutions, serving as alternatives to college rather than as preparation for them.

The academies' pupils were young and old. At Phillips Andover, Josiah Quincy, aged six, was seated next to James Anderson, aged thirty. Many other academies had preparatory departments teaching the elementary subjects. A few academies had students studying college-level subjects. The academies were pri-marily schools for middle-class and well-off pupils. Samuel Phillips, Jr., was bene-factor of Phillips Andover and also of Phillips Exeter Academy. At one point he wrote that ". . . certainly the happiness of such a child [a rich child] is of as great consequence as that of a poor child, his opportunity of doing good much greater." However, tuitions were within the means of middle-class parents, and some academies made loans to poor students and found them work to pay their expenses. The academy students included at least some of the poor as well as many of the middle class and some of the sons and daughters of the well-to-do.

The pre-Revolutionary precedents for secondary schooling for girls were slender indeed. Academies for girls, and academies that admitted girls as well as boys, were an important departure, following from the "republican spirit." Before 1790, there were at least four short-lived private schools for girls in New England. The course of study in Jedidiah Morse's school in New Haven appeared in a public announcement: ". . . Reading, Arithmetic, English Grammar, Geography, Composition." It might have been the course for a boys' academy except for the addition of ". . . the different branches of Needle Work," and because Latin was not offered. In 1787, John Poor established an academy in Philadelphia for ". . . instruction of young ladies in Reading, Writing, Arithmetic, English Grammar, Composition, Rhetoric, and Geography."

Miss Sarah Pierce's Litchfield Female Academy was successful and well documented. (Some students in their twenties were not "girls." A ten-year-old pupil was too young to be called a "lady.") Miss Pierce (1767–1852) was described as "a small woman, slender and fragile," "a woman of more than ordinary talent," with "fair complexion and blue eyes." It was said that in 1792, when she started to teach in Litchfield, Connecticut, she and two or three students met in the dining room of her home. After her school had grown, a schoolhouse was provided.

> Her school house was a small building of only one room, probably not exceeding 30 ft. by 70, with small closets at each end, one large enough to hold a piano, the other used for bonnets and over garments. The plainest pine desks, long plank benches, a small table and an elevated teacher's chair, constituted the whole furniture.

The number of students increased to nearly 140 "females" from nearly every state and from Canada. It was said that one girl had ridden horseback 150 miles to attend. Since there were no dormitories, students boarded with approved families, as at most academies. A student neatly paraphrased the rules:

> Been neat in your chambers? Combed your hair? Cleaned your teeth? Left anything out of place? Been present at table? At family prayers? Been to bed at the proper time? Rose in season? Studied two hours without speaking? Disturbed others? Been angry? Been impolite? Told an untruth? Wasted time in school? Mis-spent the Sabbath? Read in the Scriptures. . . .

In 1833, room and board was $1.75 or $2.00 a week, perhaps higher than at most places. Tuition that year was $6.75 a quarter, half again what it had been thirty years earlier. In 1821, students studied arithmetic, grammar, geography, history, natural science, and chemistry. Miss Pierce's brother-in-law taught writing. For extra tuition girls could study music, painting, or French. In 1835, girls between eight and fourteen who were studying French could room and board with a Mrs. Gimbrede, since "she loves young girls . . . the only way to learn to speak French well [is] to live in a French family."

The renowned law school conducted by Judge Tapping Reeve was also in

Litchfield. The law students attended balls given by the academy girls and in turn organized balls for them, sometimes in the dance hall at the tavern. Only academy students who were sixteen or older were permitted to attend the law students' balls. Nevertheless, Juliana McLachlan, "beautiful and a belle," was at fifteen the bride of a law student. There were also academy plays in which law students as well as academy students took parts. Attendance at Sunday church was required, and sermons heard there were matters of interest. Miss Pierce's Academy was exceptional, since most of the first academies for girls and women were, like other academies, short-lived and transitory. However, innovationists and reformers had established that girls and women should be educated in academies. As early as 1808 and as far off as Ste. Genevieve, Missouri, an academy at least planned a "female department." Long before Miss Pierce retired in 1833, there were many academies for women and girls, and still more admitted them.

Although the course of study at Miss Pierce's school was like that of other academies, the purpose of Litchfield Female Academy was also different in a quite fundamental way. As Miss Pierce's nephew, and successor as principal, said in his farewell address:

> Our object has been, not to make learned ladies, or skillful metaphysical reasoners, or deep read scholars in physical science: there is a more useful, tho' less exalted and less brilliant station that woman must occupy, there are duties of incalculable importance that she must perform: that station is home; these duties, are the alleviation of the trials of her parents; the soothing of the labours & fatigues of her partner; & the education for time and eternity of the next generation of immortal beings. . . .

The speaker was expressing the usual view of education for women. Even liberal thinkers advocated schooling for girls so that they would be good daughters and become good wives and mothers.

Noah Webster, far better known for his "Blue-Back Speller," wrote in 1804 about his ideal young woman, calling her "Sophia." Webster described a virtuous woman who had learned to obey and serve in her parents' and later in her husband's household. As Webster explained,

> Without much knowledge of the world, she is attentive, obliging, and graceful in all she does. A good disposition does more for her than much art does for others. She possesses a degree of politeness which, void of ceremony, precedes from a desire to please, and which consequently never fails to please.

Perhaps the academies of The Reverend Joseph Emerson at Byfield and later at Saugus, Massachusetts, were exceptions among girls' and women's academies. Several of his students would become academy teachers. One of them, Zilpah Grant, became principal of a female academy in Londonderry, New Hampshire, and then at Ipswich, Massachusetts, from 1828 until 1837. Students at Ipswich Academy would become in turn principals of other academies for girls.

The first women's colleges were begun as the Troy (New York) Seminary in 1821 and Mt. Holyoke (Massachusetts) Seminary in 1836. The Troy Seminary was founded by Emma Willard, who had taught at several schools before she opened her own school in 1814. Believing, as Wollstonecraft did, that women were entitled to the same educational opportunities as men, she acted upon her beliefs by teaching her students philosophy, mathematics, and other subjects normally only taught to men. In 1819, she proposed that the New York State Legislature sponsor the establishment of a female seminary, which would be a model for similar schools throughout the country.

In her proposal Willard presented four areas of instruction: religious and moral training, literary training, domestic training, and ornamental instruction. The proposed curriculum and stated purposes of the seminary recall Miss Pierce's Litchfield Female Academy. The primary purpose of educating women was to be a means of preparing them for family duties.

Religious and moral training for Willard meant instruction in Christianity. In her rationale for the literary training of young women, she argued that they should be familiar with the operations of the mind. As she explained,

> The chief use to which the philosophy of mind can be applied, is to regulate education by its rules. The ductile mind of the child is instructed to the mother; and she ought to have every possible assistance, in acquiring a knowledge of this noble material, on which it is her business to operate, that she may best understand how to mold it to its most excellent form.

Domestic training was intended to provide young women with the skills necessary "to make either good wives, good mothers, or good mistresses of families." Drawing, painting, elegant penmanship, music and "the grace of motion" would provide ornamental skills. One is struck by the apparent contradiction between intent and means. The proposal did not receive support in the New York legislature.

However, upon the invitation of the city of Troy, Willard established a female seminary there. Its curriculum included history, geography, chemistry, and mathematics. Many students were trained as teachers. "If the women were properly fitted by instruction, they would be likely to teach children better than the other sex; they could afford to do it cheaper. . ." she wrote.

Mary Lyon had attended Byfield Academy and then taught with Zilpah Grant at Ipswich Female Academy. (Grant was in ill health; otherwise, she might have been the college founder.) Lyon's intent was to set up a college-level school that would attract the daughters of the well-to-do but also young women of moderate financial means.

Lyon strongly emphasized religion as a part of the school's training. Domestic skills were not formally taught, but the students were expected to perform domestic activities as part of their normal activities. Lyon's curriculum was patterned after Amherst College's. A sophisticated curriculum, it included subjects such as mathematics and chemistry. Students were to attend the school for three years. The school had laboratory facilities and a library.

Despite the efforts of Willard and Lyon, the general acceptance of higher, and even secondary, education for women was gradual during the nineteenth century. Women were simply not seen by many as needing schooling. In a satirical article in the Springfield, Massachusetts, *Republican and Journal*, March 14, 1835, the establishment of a proposed college for women in Lexington, Kentucky, was discussed. The author suggested that the college seriously consider awarding the degrees of M.P.M. (Mistress of Pudding Making), M.D.N. (Mistress of the Darning Needle), and so on.

Instruction at some men's colleges had been interrupted by the Revolution, of course. Yale's faculty and students had been driven from New Haven by fear of starvation. Rutgers's only building was burned by British raiders. William and Mary's building, near Yorktown, became quarters for French soldiers, who set fire to it accidentally. When college instruction was resumed, it followed the older pattern in most ways. Fascination with the French and their revolution did lead to the introduction of French in a few of the colleges.

The founding of new colleges, the "college enthusiasm," resumed after the Revolution, and by 1800, there were perhaps twenty-five colleges in the United States. Most of them were in the old Northeast, but at least half a dozen were in the South: North Carolina, Georgia, Tennessee, and Vermont established colleges and funded them in a modest sort of way. A few of the new colleges were in the West, near the frontier. Transylvania (in English, "beyond the forest") in Lexington, Kentucky, lost six of its original trustees in Indian wars.

Historians disagree as to the causes for the new colleges' establishment; piety or pride, parochialism or profit. Piety may have led to colleges; several of their presidents said their first purpose was to strengthen and extend faith, piety, and prayer. Contrarily, it has been argued that college supporters (and academy supporters, starting with Samuel Phillips, Jr.) acted to add to their status in their communities. It has been argued that colleges were established because college students would bring money with them. The issue is open, and the histories of some of the early colleges would support each of these theses. It seems to us that piety was more frequent than pride or avarice, although they were not mutually exclusive.

It was often said that the first purpose of the colleges was to preserve and strengthen morality and Christian faith and to aid in strengthening character. As a Yale alumnus said,

> . . . although I did not, perhaps, profit as much as I ought, by the strict lessons of precision and morality which I received in my Connecticut Alma Mater, yet it is impossible that a youth brought up . . . under the eye of the venerable Timothy Dwight, should not have been in some degree moulded and impressed by the circumstances in which his ductile youth was passed.

College presidents were nearly always ministers, and nearly all the early colleges (including those that were state supported and called "universities") were affiliated with a church denomination. School days began and sometimes ended with prayers in the college chapel, at which attendance was required.

Boys attended colleges, too, because of the lingering tradition that a gentleman should have a "liberal" education or, less and less often, because they were to become ministers, lawyers, or physicians. A college education was not needed even for teaching in an academy. Yale, the largest of the colleges, had no more that 250 students. No more than 1 boy in 200 attended college, including the occasional American who studied in Europe.

Unlike the academies, the colleges usually had dormitories and "commons" (for everyone) dining halls, survivals from colonial and earlier English traditions. All the college students were male, and, except for one in hundreds, white, and no older than high school students are now. At the end of the 1700s, they considered themselves to be atheists or deists, as was then the fashion. Dartmouth and some of the new small colleges admitted poor boys and men, and so aided mobility from the farm to the pulpit. On the other hand, the colleges were the scenes of student riots, disruptions, and town and gown fights, and there is some evidence suggesting that even the small old colleges did not effect long-time changes in students' values.

In 1800, there were no electives; all courses were required for graduation. The college course was primarily the classical one, to which a mathematics course, one year, once a week for an hour or so, had been added. Only a few colleges offered a course in "natural history" (roughly, general science) then, although in the next twenty years natural history courses would be added by most of the colleges, and some of them would also offer chemistry.

That colleges in the United States were so long in including more than a few snippets of science in their curricula seems strange. One of the thrusts of the Enlightenment was scientific. Before 1800, universities in Germany had professors in natural sciences or in the segments of it that would become scientific disciplines. In 1816, nineteen of thirty-three professors at the University of Edinburgh in Scotland taught medicine or one of the sciences. Americans knew of and admired the University of Edinburgh, and more of them seem to have attended it then than any other European university.

There are several plausible reasons for the colleges' delay. The pattern of organization of the colleges, with each entering class typically taught by the same tutor for three or four years, did not lend itself to specialization. Nearly all the colleges were poor, sometimes on the brink of bankruptcy, and science professors and their expensive demonstration equipment and laboratories were beyond the colleges' means. The colleges saw themselves as just that, and not as universities. Few of them had professional schools, and none offered other graduate study. They did not support scholarship or research. Finally, industry and technology did not depend much then upon the "pure" mathematical or experimental sciences, and would not for most of another hundred years. Although one might have expected it to be, the objection to science was not religious. The most devout were sure that science would serve to demonstrate the handiwork and glory of God.

CONCLUSION

For many historians of education the period between the Revolution and the "Common School Revival" about forty years later has been a sort of prelude to school history, neither important nor interesting, and for some, negligible. To overlook that time is, of course, to overlook the republican educational theorist Thomas Jefferson and his contemporaries interested in education. The school in New Harmony, Indiana, was the first systematic, wholehearted application in the United States of the school theory and practice of the leading educationist of his day, Johann Pestalozzi. In a way as important, if less elegant and elevated, the monitorial schools of Joseph Lancaster and Andrew Bell strengthened the concept of the pupil as recipient of charity, and added to education the anology of school as machine or as factory. Those, too, would have many consequences that have not ended. The organization of "common" schools into state, county, and city systems had not begun, but a tradition of elementary school curriculum was set, which in some ways still survives. The academies are of interest as an educational expression of their times, because they are the only American mode of schooling that has approached extinction, as one of the ancestors of the public high school and because, for reasons good or bad, there are at least some signs of their revival. The colleges of that time are not (fortunately) the colleges of our time, but corporately and spiritually they are ancestors of today's colleges and universities.

Theorists, romantic Pestalozzians' schools, machinelike monitorial schools, hetrodox academies, and devout and pious colleges all set the stage, making up their times and shaping our own.

Chapter Four
THE RISE OF THE COMMON SCHOOLS

Between the 1820s and the end of the Civil War, schooling had become an increasingly important factor in American culture. By the 1830s, in industrializing states of the Northeast such as Massachusetts, New York, and Pennsylvania, wide-ranging programs had been enacted to introduce free universal public schooling at the elementary level. Known as the *Common School Movement*, this effort to provide mass popular education for all white citizens spread rapidly throughout the nation. In spirit, the Common School Movement recalled Thomas Jefferson's fundamental belief that a democratic government depended upon an educated citizenry.

The causes for the emergence of the Common School Movement are complex. As Lawrence Cremin and others have pointed out, the decades preceeding the 1830s saw a number of critical changes take place in American culture, which were to have a major impact on education. An increasing democratization of politics developed during the Jacksonian period. Social equality emerged as an increasingly important issue. The rise of the "Common Man" accompanied the development of a coherent nationalism.

Historians have tended to look upon the Common School Movement in wholly positive terms. The traditional wisdom has been that by providing free universal elementary education, the common schools were important vehicles of social reform that provided opportunities for newly arrived immigrants and the poor to improve the conditions of their lives and those of their children. Led by idealistic and humanitarian intellectuals, an enlightened working class was able to overcome the narrow interests of not only the wealthy elite population, but also the conservative religious groups within the culture.

This essentially idealistic interpretation of the origins of the Common School Movement has been seriously questioned since the late 1960s by the writings of revisionist historians such as Clarence Karier, Joel Spring, Walter Feinberg, Michael Katz, Samuel Bowles, Herbert Gintis, and others. According to Katz, who has particularly focused on the Common School Movement in his work,

> . . . the extension and reform of education in the mid-nineteenth century were not a potpourri of democracy, rationalism and humanitarianism. They were the attempt of a coalition of the social leaders, status-anxious parents, and status hungry educators to impose educational innovations, each for their own reasons, upon a reluctant community.

Katz's research, usually organizational and structural analysis, is a powerful reinterpretation of the traditional role of schooling in American culture.

In this and the chapters that follow, the reader will find much explained by the revisionist interpretations of Katz and others. Other interpretations will be drawn upon as well. Education and schooling in America presents the historian with a number of paradoxes. Beginning during the Revolution, education was seen as being a means of reforming the culture through its children. As Donald Warren has explained in his study on the United States Office of Education,

> Education, as formulated during the country's beginning years, represented a national, as over against a sectional, concern and a chance for achieving nationhood. Talk about education braved unsettling realities; it endured, not because schools fulfilled the high expectations, but inexplicably because they did not. American education, as both process and institution, has never escaped the reformist role in which it was cast in the republic's first days.

As the revisionists have pointed out, in examining the history of American schooling, it is clear that schools have tended more often than not to reinforce and support the status quo. The schools have consistently voiced rhetoric emphasizing equality or opportunity across racial, social, and economic lines. Schooling and education clearly has not delivered all that it has promised.

This chapter considers some individuals and forces responsible for the emergence of the common schools. After a consideration of the roles of those who taught in late eighteenth and early nineteenth century American culture, we examine changes in attitudes toward childrearing which took place during this period. The chapter concludes by looking at some of the forces and individuals responsible for promoting the Common School Movements in America.

THE TEACHER

Important redefinitions of attitudes and beliefs are frequently reflected in the language of a society. An example of this can be found in the increasing adoption and use of the word *teacher* during the early nineteenth century. This redefinition can provide us with important insight into changes that had been taking place in both education and American culture during this period. The use of the word *teacher* by about 1820, instead of the older one, *master*, to denote one who taught, was more than change in fashion of speech. The change of words went with a change in the nature of an occupation. It had consequences for those who taught, for the organizing of schools, and for the education of children.

(By one sociological definition, an *occupation* is a role or a set of roles. To fill an occupational role, specialized knowledge and skills, of varying kinds of degrees, are required. With occupational roles are status and prestige, also in varying degrees. There are norms and expectations of behavior that go beyond the job. Odd combinations of occupation and behavior seem—are—incongruous. Farmers do not generally play Mozart, and nuns do not smoke cigars.)

Those who taught before about 1820 were nearly always called *masters*, though of course there were *school dames, governesses, tutors*, and others. The term *teacher* was seldom used. *Masters* ideally knew the classics. The classics were the content of what was to be taught, and at the same time they determined the method of teaching. While *masters* taught beginning pupils, "abcedarians," that was not their only or primary task. The *teacher*, by contrast, was at the beginning concerned more than anything else with teaching the elementary subjects. The teacher's skill was to be in what we would call classroom management and was not expected to go beyond that. Masters were to have a commitment to teaching and for the moral and spiritual welfare of their students. Teachers were to be "consecrated," to be wholly devoted to the interests of their pupils, to be sort of lesser servants of the Lord. Lucy Larcom, later a professional writer, described in a cloying (but possibly autobiographical) verse what was wanted:

> In a dreary school-house
>   A girl, young and fair,
> Spent life, strength, and beauty.
>   "She scatters live seed:
> She works in wild thought-fields,
>   The starved soul to feed."

In 1838, a Pennsylvania superintendent of schools implied the difference of the out-of-school behavior of the teacher and the master:

> The profession of teaching is much elevated. Instances of bad moral character and intemperate habits, are hardly to be met with though formerly School

FIGURE 4-1
A district school teacher illustrated in the frontispiece to *The Child's Guide*, 1833. Reprinted in Clifton Johnson, *Old Time Schools and SchoolBooks* (New York: Macmillan, 1904), p. 255.

Masters, who above all others should be perfectly exemplary as a class, were not remarkable in this respect.

It is hard for us to think of a teacher who in the 1800s earned a substantial wage or who earned even fairly high status or prestige. We know of masters in the 1700s who enjoyed incomes that were substantial for the time. To repeat, Ronald Robertson in Virginia averaged £90 a year in earnings from his school, nearly twice the earnings of a skilled carpenter regularly employed. In 1775, three of Boston's public school masters were paid £100 and the other two, £120, and probably fees. One of them was also provided with a home.

As we see it, the change from *master* and what it implied, to *teacher* came from shifts in social values and from changes in the pupils who were the masters', and then the teachers', clientele. As to the change in social values, we must return to the "republican spirit" and one facet of Revolutionary thought. After the Revolution, in keeping with the republican spirit, it appeared that learning the classics or about the classics was not important. For some—we cannot say how many—the teaching of the classics was an affront, an insult to and the exploitation of the common man. As Massachusetts tavernkeeper William Manning wrote,

> Many are so rich that they can live without Labour. Also the merchant, phisition, lawyer & devine, the philosopher and school master, the Juditial and Executive Officers, & many others who could honestly git a living without bodily labours. . . . [T]hese professions naturally unite in their skems to make their callings as honourable & lucrative as possible. . . .

Specifically about school masters Manning wrote,

> [T]he few are always striving to oblige us to maintain grait men with grate salleryes & to maintain Grammer Schools in every town to teach our Children a b c all which is ondly to give imploy to gentlemens sons. . . . For there is no more need of a mans haveling all the languages to teach a Child to read and write & cifer than their is for a farmer to have the marinors art to hold plow.

Manning was an extremist, but classical learning, or any school learning very far beyond the rudiments, lost much of its value as a badge of social rank and position. By 1820, when the master had become nearly obsolete and had been largely replaced by the teacher, the educational qualifications for entering the traditional professions—medicine, divinity, and law—were very much reduced. Perhaps a parallel to the disappearance of the master was that of the peruke maker. Perukes, wigs for formal occasions, which for a hundred years had been badges of official and social position, also lost favor. Basil Hall, early-nineteenth-century traveler and commentator, was said to have seen the disappearance of perukes as evidence of the "universal ascendency of the democratic principle in the U.S." He was entirely right.

At the same time, as classical education was less valued, primary education for a larger proportion of children was, more than it had been formerly, felt to be of value. Jefferson saw general literacy as necessary for the democracy he envisioned. Noah Webster saw schooling as an aid to stronger nationalism. The appearance of Sunday schools and infant schools and the passing enthusiasm for monitorial schools were evidence of widespread conviction of the value of schooling. As more children attended school, more poor children attended. The lower the status of the clientele, the lower the prestige of the occupation that serves it.

Most masters were replaced by teachers. Others were replaced by those who taught in academies, who had a variety of titles. One source mentions *tutors, professors, professor-principals, principal tutors, tutor governesses, instructors*, and *perceptors*. Those who taught in academies seldom called themselves *teachers*. Until the public high schools became common, a *teacher* taught beginning pupils beginning subjects. A primary or district school teacher required less substantive knowledge. In part, the status of a profession depends upon the knowledge it employs.

The appearance of the *teacher* and the disappearance of the *master* had several effects. If less formal learning was needed by the teachers, it became seen as more appropriate, as well as cheaper, to employ women as teachers. For a hundred years or more, most teachers have been women. With required formal learning reduced and entry into teaching easy, teachers' salaries would be low during the 1800s. With pupils coming from poor families more often than from middle-class ones, the status of pupils tended to reduce the status of teachers, who themselves most often came from families of limited means.

Of course the title *master* lingered. Authors used it for nostalgia. Ichabod Crane in Washington Irving's "Legend of Sleepy Hollow" was a master. It was used in out-of-the-way rural places, as in Edward Eggleston's novel *The Hoosier School-master*. *Masters* survived in conservative Boston schools, where reformers would find their ways difficult to change. They appeared or reappeared in prestigious New England preparatory schools, presumably to add an air of age or Englishness. Generally, the *master* left the stage, to be most often replaced by the *teacher*.

THE AMERICAN CHILD

The early decades of the nineteenth century saw not only the emergence of the new role of teacher but also a redefinition of patterns of family life and childhood. It is clear that by the beginning of the 1820s family organization and childrearing practices in the United States were significantly different from those found in the early republic and also from those found in Western Europe. As least among white middle- and upper-class families, democratic ideals and principles were changing the aspirations parents had for their children and were also influencing their attitudes toward childrearing and education.

Eruopean visitors to the United States during this period had great interest in the differences between childrearing practices in their own countries and in America. For example, French penal reformer Alexis de Tocqueville devoted to the American family an entire chapter in his 1835 work *Democracy in America*. According to de Tocqueville, the American family was being radically altered as a result of the democratic experience. The autocratic rule of the father which characterized the European family had been abandoned:

> In America the family, in the Roman and aristocratic signification of the word, does not exist. All that remains of it are a few vestiges in the first years of childhood, when the father exercises, without opposition, that absolute domestic authority which the feebleness of his children renders necessary and which their interest, as well as his incontestable superiority, warrants.

De Tocqueville wrote that as the child approached adulthood, filial obedience became more and more relaxed, and the child was encouraged to become increasingly independent.

The independence of the American child was carefully observed and commented on by other visitors to the United States. Harriet Martineau (1802-1876), an English writer and reformer visiting during the mid-1830s, saw American children as being remarkably free and independent when compared with their European counterparts. Often European visitors saw this tendency toward independence on the part of the American child in a negative light. During the 1850s, Adam Gurowski complained about "the prodigality, the assumption, self-assertion and conceit" of the American child. In a similar case, a British naval officer, Captain Frederick Marrayat, described overhearing the following account between an American child and his parents in 1837:

'Johnny, my dear, come here,' says his mamma.
'I won't,' cries Johnny.
'You must, my love, you are all wet, and you'll catch cold.'
'I won't,' replied Johnny.
'Come, my sweet, and I've something for you.'
'I won't.'
'Oh! Mr. _____ , do, pray make Johnny come in.'
'Come in, Johnny,' says the father.
'I won't.'
'I tell you, come in directly, son—do you hear?'
'I won't,' replies the urchin, taking to his heels.
'A sturdy republican, sir,' says his father to me smiling at the boy's resolute disobedience.

It is important to note that many of these early visitors who were highly critical of the American child were also critical of their parents and American culture in general. It is clear that the assertiveness and individuality of many Americans offended the sensibilities of European observers of American culture. Materialism, restlessness, and self-centeredness were themes repeatedly raised by Europeans in discussing Americans during this period.

During the 1820s and 1830s there appeared for the first time a substantial body of literature written and published in America dealing with childrearing and child care. In 1826, for example, Dr. William Dewees, professor of mid-wifery at the University of Pennsylvania, published *A Treatise on the Physical and Medical Treatment of Children*. Among the earliest and most widely read works in America on pediatrics, Dewee's work reflected an increasing concern over the medical needs of children as distinguished from those of adults.

In a more popular vein were works on childrearing such as Lydia Maria Child's *The Mother's Book* (1813) and Jacob Abbott's *The Child at Home* (1833), which came into widespread use providing practical suggestions and ideas concerning the care and raising of children. Numerous themes emerge in these works and suggest that the observations and analyses of many European visitors concerning the nature of American childrearing and family organization were too simplistic. According to Robert Sunled, at least three different approaches to childrearing were evident in the child care books written during the first half of the nineteenth century. The first of these approaches could be found during the pre-Revolutionary eras and corresponded to what Philip Greven has described as an "authoritarian" approach to childrearing. The second corresponded roughly to Greven's "authoritative" approach and also clearly reflected the influence of the Enlightenment thinkers John Locke and Jean-Jacques Rousseau. The third and final approach taken toward childrearing in the early nineteenth century represented what was essentially a new point of view, emphasizing the child's natural development.

The first school of thought had its origins in the Calvinist tradition of the child being born in original sin. As Theodore Dwight explained in *The Father's Book* (1834), "No child has ever been known since the earliest period of the world, destitute of an evil disposition however sweet it appears." Parents had the duty of making sure that their children were prevented from following their naturally depraved tendencies. Obedience to the demands of adults alone could ensure the salvation of the child. When a child refused to follow the demands of a parent, it was felt to be critically important not to let children get their way. Sunled, for example, quotes a mother writing in *The Mother's Magazine* who explains how her sixteen-month-old daughter refused to say "dear mama" at the request of her father. Failing to get the child to change her mind, the parents then left the child alone in a room, where she screamed wildly for ten minutes. Ordered again to say "dear mama," the child refused and was whipped for her disobedience. This process was continued until finally after four hours the child submitted.

Such an example may seem extreme, but the fact that it was reported in an obviously positive light in a widely circulated magazine of the period indicates that such methods for dealing with children were probably acceptable among a significant number of parents. Physical punishment was not always necessary. Constant persuasion and the eventual breaking down of the child's will seems to have also been common.

A second widely prevalent approach to childhood seemed to be derived from the works of the English philosopher John Locke and resembled those of the French social theorist Jean-Jacques Rousseau. According to them, environment played a crucial role in shaping the child. Since children were highly vulnerable to the potential corruptions of adult society, an attempt was made to keep the child as free from corruption as possible. Although the perception of the child was different from the more traditional Calvinist approach, the emphasis upon strict parental guidance and control was much the same. Essentially in the Calvinist approach the child was seen as being corrupt, while the less rigid environmentalist approach saw the child as having the potential to be corrupted.

Corruption of the child was possible in many different ways. Many of the child care books of the period warned of ruinous consequences of masturbation. Disease, insanity, and even death were commonly cited as the consequences of such activities. Rather than discovering masturbation spontaneously, it was assumed by many of the authors of the period that "respectable" children were introduced to the evils of masturbation by servants, slaves, or depraved school children. Moral virtue was associated with cleanliness. Individuals such as Dr. Dewees set forth ideal goals of having children toilet trained by the age of one month. Lack of adequate early training encouraged the child's autoerotic tendencies. As Dewees warned,

> Children should not be permitted to indulge in bed long after daylight; as its warmth, the accumulation of urine and faeces, and the exercise of the imagination, but too often leads to the precocious development of the sexual instinct.

A third and final approach to the child emphasized the need to nurture and encourage the child's natural tendencies. Parents were seen as guides who encouraged the natural potential of their children. Lydia Maria Child in *The Mother's Book*, for example, maintained that

Children are not so much influenced by what we say and do in particular reference to them, as by the general effect of our characters and conversation. They are in a great degree creatures of imitation. If they see a mother fond of finery, they become fond of finery; if they see her selfish, it makes them selfish; if they see her extremely anxious for the attention of wealthy people, they learn to think wealth is the only good.

Clearly the foundations of many of our modern attitudes toward childrearing can be found in this third approach expressed by Child, which emphasizes the need for parents to nurture and guide the child.

Changes in attitudes toward childrearing were closely related to changes in schooling that took place during the early phases of the Common School Movement. The feminization of the teaching profession and the primacy of moral over intellectual instruction suggest models based upon principles of childrearing as much as upon traditional pedagogy.

ORIGINS OF THE COMMON SCHOOLS

As new attitudes toward children and childrearing emerged during the early decades of the nineteenth century, so too did new attitudes toward education. Free public elementary education for all citizens had been an ideal of intellectuals Thomas Jefferson, Benjamin Rush, and others since the time of the Revolution. Yet at the beginning of the nineteenth century, rather than being seen as the birthright of all citizens, free schooling was more often equated with charity or pauper schools such as those established by the Free School Society of New York, the Philadelphia Society for the Free Instruction of Indigent Boys, and the Benevolent Society of the City of Baltimore for the Education of the Female Poor.

As outlined in earlier chapters, programs supporting free public education date back to the early colonial period. Although laws such as those passed in Massachusetts in 1647—requiring towns to establish elementary schools for their children—could be found in a number of the colonies, their effectiveness was extremely limited. Property taxes levied to pay for the schools, were, as in our own era, extremely unpopular. Many towns lacked sufficiently large populations to be able to support a school adequately. Even if a town did have enough people living in it to support a school properly, they were often so scattered that it was difficult to establish the school in a convenient central location. Schoolmasters moving from one settlement to another, teaching children for a few months at a time, provided a limited solution to the problem.

As populations increased into the eighteenth century, most localities in New England established schools of their own, as they had in Dedham. Commonly referred to as *district schools*, these village or neighborhood schools were ungraded and served the needs of all the children within the community. Technically, the term *district* referred to the division of the town for purposes of schooling. They were restricted in size to distances that children could reasonably be expected to walk to school. Control of these schools was completely maintained by the local taxpayers.

As one might expect, the quality of education depended upon local taxpayers' commitment to the schools. When they worked well, the district schools not only provided children with good basic instruction, but they also tended to draw the community together by a common purpose or activity. Citizens of the district levied taxes, appointed instructors, determined the length of the school year, maintained the schoolhouse, and acted as final arbitrators in conflicts between students and teachers. More often than not, however, citizens' commitment to the school in their district was limited. Grossly inadequate funding characterized many of these schools, eventually leading to the use of rate-bills.

The rate-bill was a device that placed an additional tax on those families who had children attending school. In effect, the rate-bill was tuition charge intended to supplement local taxes. Unfortunately, the rate-bill imposed a burden on poorer families who were unable to pay this additonal tax. In rural areas, those who were so poor that they could not pay the rate for their children were also often too proud to be excused from it and to send their children to school as "charity cases." In cities, particularly during the early nineteenth century, the number of poor was often so large in many districts that there was no way that the schools could be properly supported with the payment of rate-bills.

The development of philanthropic educational programs, such as that of the Free School Society of New York, were attempts to overcome some of the problems inherent in the funding system of the district schools. Serving only the poor, the basis of their support was limited. Support for public schooling did not exist among the majority of the population. In general, given the choice of paying less in taxes or supporting the schools, most individuals seem to have chosen the easy way out.

The failure by taxpayers to support effectively the district schools reflects to a large extent the main needs and concerns of people during the period. In a primarily agricultural society, as in early nineteenth-century America, where land was cheap and opportunities were numerous, the need for schooling was probably not perceived as particularly important. Except for a limited number of professions, formal schooling did not in most instances contribute significantly to the average individual's success. On the frontier, where personal initiative, physical strength, and native shrewdness often counted for a great deal, schooling often counted for very little. In fact, formal education was frequently looked down upon as an aristocratic and unnecessary luxury.

In the South, public education received relatively little attention. Schooling continued well into the nineteenth century along much the same lines that it had followed during the provincial era. Schooling was basically perceived as a luxury whose pursuit was a matter of individual discretion. When free public schooling was supported, it was typically as philanthropy. The free school law adopted in South Carolina in 1811, for example, was intended only for orphans and poor children. Similar laws passed in Virginia at about the same time also provided only for the education of the poor.

Exceptions can be found to the South's tendency to ignore education as an important issue. At the meeting at Rockfish Gap, Virginia, in the summer of 1818, Thomas Jefferson not only outlined the plans that eventually lead to the establishment of the University of Virginia, but also reiterated the need for a state-supported system of primary education. Although figures such as Calvin Wiley effectively lobbied in states such as North Carolina during the late 1830s and 1840s for the support of public education, the tendency in the South prior to the Civil War was to disregard free universal education as an important matter.

Although admirable in many respects, philanthropic and charitable programs of education in both the North and South were inadequate to meet the demands of society. Support for the development of the common schools began to come from many different groups. Often the reason for these groups' interest in education were widely different. One of the earliest authors criticizing the charitable schools and urging the development of a broader-based system of public education was James G. Carter, whose *Essays upon Popular Education* were published in the mid-1820s. Carter called for a revival and improvement of public schools. He maintained that the poor and ignorant members of the population did not voluntarily seek education. Yet unless properly educated, they posed a serious revolutionary threat to the integrity of the republic. The government, through the enforcement of education, had the obligation to eradicate ignorance for the government's own political good.

Beginning with figures such as Carter, there is an interesting and subtle shift in the attitude taken toward schooling, when compared with the educational theorists of the late eighteenth century such as Webster, Rush, and Jefferson. Throughout the works of these earlier writers there was a consistent emphasis upon properly educating individuals so that they could assume the responsibilities of citizenship. With the growing waves of immigrants who entered the country in the 1830s and the 1840s, the schools were seen as having an increasingly important role in helping to bring about the process of assimilation and neutralizing the newcomers as a political threat. To be an American was to support and become part of Anglo-American institutions. As Calvin Stowe, a major figure in the Common School Movement, explained in 1836:

> It is altogether essential to our national strength and peace, if not even to our national existence, that the foreigners who settle on our soil, should cease to be Europeans and become Americans; and as our national language is English, and as our literature, our manners, and our institutions are of English origin, and the whole foundations of our society English, it is necessary that they become Anglo-American.

Biculturalism was seen as being un-American, and as being a potential threat to the political stability of the nation.

The primary impetus for the early support of the common schools has typically been seen as coming from a select group of liberal New England reformers. Yet interest in free public education was also an important issue for lower-middle- and working-class groups in the Northeast during the late 1820s and early 1830s.

Interest in education on the part of these groups was socially and economically motivated. Factory-produced items were beginning to threaten the traditional markets of skilled craftspersons and small businesspersons. Education would provide the means by which working-class and lower-middle-class children could achieve economic and social equality.

The workingmen's parties clearly associated education with privilege. Charity schools were inherently discriminatory. As Stephen Simpson argued in *The Working Man's Manual* . . . (1831),

> . . . the scanty pittance of education termed *charitable*, has never realized the *equal benefits of instruction*, to which the working people have been entitled as the producers of all the wealth of society. When it is solemnly inscribed upon our constitution, that education is an essential preliminary of government, its diffusive dispensation becomes a duty and a right of the first importance and magnitude: we are bound to consider it, not as an *accidental* but as an *integral* part of government.

The workingmen in their concern for education were reflecting views quite similar to those of the earlier republican educational theorists. Education was to act as an equalizer for the citizens of the republic. Ironically, in their criticism they often tended to repudiate many of the achievements of these same theorists. In Pennsylvania and Connecticut during the early 1830s, for example, the workingmen's groups mounted a major campaign against the granting of state funding to colleges and universities, since they tended to benefit the wealthy, rather than the general population.

The issues addressed by the workingmen's movement provide an interesting contrast to those issues addressed by leaders of the Common School Movement, such as Horace Mann and Henry Barnard. The workingmen's movement called for a new type of educational program: one that, as Rush Welter has explained, "would abridge—not enchance—the authority of the established leaders of the society."

Traditional pre-revisionist interpretations of the Common School Movement tend to present the programs of reformers such as Mann and Barnard as receiving widespread and immediate support from all members of the society. This was hardly the case. The movement itself was beset by fundamental contradictions. Following the older republican conception of education, the leaders of the Common School Movement saw education as serving Americans by helping them find their identities and realizing their full potential not only as individuals, but also as citizens. At the same time, the Common School Movement leaders felt it was their duty to sustain political stability by properly shaping the attitudes and values of the younger generation.

The goal of the Common School Movement—to provide for the personal development and education of the individual and at the same time to maintain political order and stability among the members of the society—often created serious contradictions and inconsistencies within the movement. Such inconsistencies were evident not only in the major programs that were put into effect by different state boards of education, but also in the personal philosophies of Horace Mann, Henry Barnard, and other members of the movement.

Undoubtedly, the leading figure in the Common School Movement was the Massachusetts educator Horace Mann (1796-1859). Originally trained as a lawyer, Mann supported major social and humanitarian causes such as the reform of debtor's laws, abolition, temperance, prison reform, and the improvement of the treatment and care of the mentally ill. By the middle of the 1830s Mann had a reputation throughout Massachusetts as a gifted politician, one whose ability might eventually lead him to the governorship of the state or to a seat in Congress.

It was therefore something of a surprise to Mann's friends when, in 1837, he accepted the post of secretary of the Massachusetts State Board of Education. In May of 1837, Mann had been approached by Edmund Dwight, a prominent industrialist from Springfield, about accepting the position as head of the recently established State Board of Education. Dwight had persuaded Governor Edward Everett (who eventually became the president of Harvard University) that the secretary's position was too important to the state's future to be held by "just an educator." Instead, Dwight maintained that the position required someone of broader experience. Mann, whose previous work indicated a strong interest in social and humanitarian reform, was considered an ideal choice for the position.

When Mann took over as Secretary of the Board of Education in 1837, the situation in the Massachusetts schools was extremely discouraging. Although innovations, for instance, the "English Classical School," which was the forerunner of the modern high school, had been introduced in Boston as early as 1821, few tangible improvements had been made in methods of school administration or instruction since the time of the Revolution. The schools that were successful were usually private and did not meet the needs of the general population. According to educational reformer James G. Carter, only one-third of Massachusetts school-age population attended school for some part of the year in 1837.

Part of the failure of the schools was a result of older methods and approaches to education and schooling, which were no longer able to fulfill the complex and changing needs of the industrial and urban society that was beginning to emerge in Massachusetts as well as in other parts of the country during this period. As Michael Katz has argued, when Horace Mann was born in 1796, no one could have predicted that within his lifetime the state's well-ordered Yankee farms would give way to burgeoning factories and mills. Old expectations and traditions were torn apart and new ideals and values were established in the radically changing society that was emerging during this period.

The new society that came into existence during Mann's lifetime forced schools to assume an increased importance. Between 1820 and 1850, the percentage of workers involved in agricultural occupations in Massachusetts fell from 58 percent to 15 percent. Traditional methods of learning no longer met the needs of many individuals—particularly those working in the newly industrialized sectors of the economy. The popular education proposed by the Common School Movement fulfilled the needs of many different individuals and interest groups within the culture. Utilitarian values were emphasized. It was widely assumed that education that promoted a disciplined working force would also bring about the growth of prosperity for both the individual and the society as a whole. As Mann explained in his *Fifth Report* (1842) as the secretary of the Board of Education,

> . . . Education is not only a moral renovator and a multiplier of intellectual power, but . . . also the most prolific parent of material riches. . . . It is not only the most honest and honorable, but the surest means of amassing property.

In his work with the Board of Education, Mann clearly saw the schools as an important vehicle for not only bringing about social reform, but also for maintaining the stability of the republic. Mann genuinely feared that the fabric of American society was in danger of being torn apart as a result of growing social pressures and conflicts. The burning of the Catholic Ursuline convent and school in Charlestown, across the river from Boston, by an antiforeign mob in 1834 was to Mann a "terrible outrage." Not only was it a violation of the rights of the Catholic nuns who lived in the convent and ran the school, but also a threat to the general welfare of the nation.

Mann saw industrialization, which increased personal prosperity and wealth, as having the potential to provide a fuller and more complete life for all citizens. But education was the key to Mann's reform of society. As he explained,

> Education, then beyond all other devices of human origin, is the great equalizer of the conditions of men—the balance wheel of the social machinery. . . . It gives each man the independence and the means by which he can resist the selfishness of other men. . . . The spread of education, by enlarging the cultivated class or caste, will open a wider area over which the social feelings will expand; and if this education should be universal and complete, it would do more than all things to obliterate factitious distinctions in society.

Mann was clearly espousing a conservative philosophy, one which suggests that public schooling would provide the talented and ambitious with the means to advance themselves socially and economically.

In certain respects Mann's educational philosophy reflected the ideas of Thomas Jefferson. Like Jefferson, he promoted a meritocracy, which was supported by a system of free universal public schools. Unlike Jefferson, however, Mann was more interested in promoting the education of the general population than in isolating and educating a special elite group. Leadership would come from talented individuals within the general populace who were recognized by their peers as being particularly capable. Significantly, however, these leaders would not be separated by education from the people who elected them.

In this respect, Mann placed a tremendous amount of faith in the educational system's ability to provide the general population with a strong sense of morality and with the ability to judge critically the political and social needs of the nation.

In this sense, the Common School Movement had as its purpose the training of an educated citizenry. For Mann, the Common Schools would create a uniform political consciousness—one in which the potential for political, religious, and social discord would be eliminated. Once the common schools were properly established, there would be no social issue or problem that could not eventually be solved by them through their educated citizenry.

Such an absolute faith in the schools as a tool of social reform was almost utopian in nature. As Mann argued,

> In universal education, every "follower of God and friend of humankind" will find the only sure means of carrying forward that particular form to which he is devoted. In whatever department of philanthropy he may be engaged, he will find that department to be only a segment of the great circle of benefi-cence, of which *Universal Education* is centre and circumference; and that it is only when these segments are fitly joined together, that the wheel of Progress can move harmoniously and resistlessly onward.

The development of Mann's educational philosophy is most thoroughly chronicled in the twelve annual reports (1837–1848) that he submitted while he was the secretary of the Massachusetts Board of Education. Remarkable for their insight and comprehensiveness, the *Reports* were widely circulated in both the United States and abroad. Taken as a collective whole, they represent perhaps the best source for understanding Mann's ideals and purpose as an educator.

Included in the twelve annual reports are discussions relating to almost every aspect of education and schooling. The development of better schoolhouses and responsible local boards of education is discussed at length in Mann's *First Report* (1837). Objecting to the tendency of private schools to encourage their students to adopt a limited political perspective, and to "wield the sword of polemics with fatal dexterity," Mann strongly emphasized the need to encourage and promote the development of common schools in their place.

Mann's insights into the instructional needs of the child are remarkable for their time. In his *Second Report* (1838), he addressed himself to the need for intellectual development on the part of the student. Discussing instruction in reading, spelling, and composition at length, Mann recognized that "Knowledge cannot be poured into a child's mind," but must be reached out and grasped by the children themselves. Rather than being a passive recipient in the process of learning, the child must be actively involved in the acquisition of knowledge. Mann placed a great deal of importance on the child's mastery of basic skills. Recognizing the importance of reading in his *Third Report* (1839). Mann advocated the establishment of a free circulating library in every school district throughout the state.

As Mann's work with the State Board of Education continued, his *Annual Reports* increasingly provided him the opportunity to address specific reform issues. The consolidation of small impractical school districts into larger ones was discussed in his *Fourth Report* (1840), with the basic qualifications for a teacher. In the 1840 *Report*, Mann emphasized the ability of teachers to teach subjects rather than the curriculums outlined in manuals. He criticized the memorization of facts and data that dominated most learning, rather than the understanding of principles. For Mann, the ability to communicate complex ideas, as well as to maintain order in the classroom was of critical importance in a teacher. As a skilled publicist, Mann used both the *Annual Reports* and *The Common School Journal*, which began publication in 1838, to promote the common schools. In his *Fifth Report* (1841), Mann included arguments, specifically directed toward the business community, which maintained that the schools would promote a suitable morality that would protect the rights of individuals with property.

Many different intellectual forces influenced Mann in his work. In 1837, when he was considering whether or not to accept the secretariat of the Board, Mann had read the work of the Scottish phrenologist George Combe. Combe's most important work, *The Constitution of Man* (1828), attempted to combine the utilitarian aspects of traditional Scottish philosophy with the phrenological theories of F. J. Gall (1809). Phrenology represented an attempt, crude by today's standards, to develop a psychology of human behavior. According to Gall, the human mind was divided into more than thirty faculties, or propensities, that included characteristics such as "benevolence," "self-esteem," "inhibition," and so on. By observing the measurements and configurations of the skull, it was felt that the mental capacity and character of an individual could be determined.

Significantly, it was believed that the negative propensities of an individual could be discouraged and positive tendencies encouraged by means of proper training. Some of phrenology's most extreme practitioners argued that by massaging certain parts of the skull, positive or negative propensities or tendencies in an individual could be stimulated. Thus by massaging the top of the skull where "veneration" was supposed to be housed, this characteristic could be encouraged in the individual.

Mann readily adopted phrenology into his philosophy of education. Basically, phrenology provided Mann with a means to predict and shape human behavior. Although now discredited, phrenology did provide a primitive theory of personality and psychology around which educators such as Mann could develop specific educational programs. By encouraging the total balanced development of the individual, phrenology encouraged the introduction of subjects such as music, art, and physical education into the common schools.

John D. Davies in *Phrenology: Fad and Science, a Nineteenth Century Crusade* (1955), points out that Mann's *Sixth Report* was heavily dependent upon Combe's *The Constitution of Man* for many of its ideas. Mann's interest in phrenology was to follow him through the rest of his life. Having met Combe and attended his lectures in Boston in 1838, Mann traveled extensively with him throughout the United States during the spring of 1840. In 1844, they again met and traveled together while Mann was on a six-month tour of European schools.

Mann's European tour provided the basis for his *Seventh Report* (1843). He was particularly impressed by the schools he observed in Prussia and discussed their programs at great length. To a large degree, Prussian schools were based on Pestalozzi's philosophy of gearing education to the developmental level of the chil-

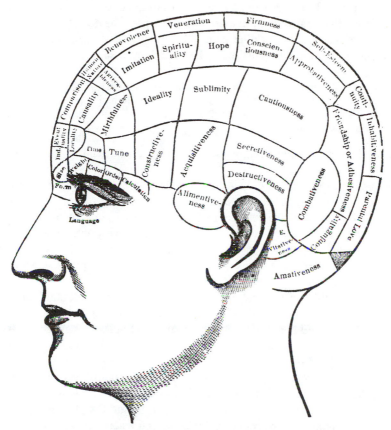

NUMBERING AND DEFINITION OF THE ORGANS.

1. AMATIVENESS, Love between the sexes.
A. CONJUGALITY, Matrimony—love of one. [etc.
2. PARENTAL LOVE, Regard for offspring, pets,
3. FRIENDSHIP, Adhesiveness—sociability.
4 INHABITIVENESS, Love of home
5. CONTINUITY, One thing at a time.
E. VITATIVENESS, Love of life.
6. COMBATIVENESS, Resistance—defense.
7. DESTRUCTIVENESS, Executiveness—force.
8. ALIMENTIVENESS, Appetite—hunger.
9. ACQUISITIVENE S, Accumulation.
10. SECRETIVENESS, Policy—management.
11. CAUTIOUSNESS, Prudence—provision.
12. APPROBATIVENESS, Ambition—display.
13. SELF-ESTEEM, Self-respect—dignity.
14. FIRMNESS, Decision—perseverance.
15. CONSCIENTIOUSNESS, Justice equity.
16. HOPE, Expectation—enterprise.
17. SPIRITUALITY, Intuition—faith—credulity.
18. VENERATION, Devotion—respect.
19 BENEVOLENCE, Kindness—goodness.

20. CONSTRUCTIVENESS, Mechanical ingenuity
21. IDEALITY, Refinement—taste—purity.
B. SUBLIMITY, Love of grandeur—infinitude.
22. IMITATION, Copying—patterning.
23. MIRTHFULNESS, Jocoseness—wit—fun.
24. INDIVIDUALITY, Observation.
25. FORM, Recollection of shape.
26. SIZE, Measuring by the eye.
27. WEIGHT, Balancing—climbing.
28. COLOR, Judgment of colors.
29. ORDER, Method system—arrangement
30. CALCULATION, Mental arithmetic.
31. LOCALITY, Recollection of places.
32. EVENTUALITY, Memory of facts.
33. TIME, Cognizance of duration.
34. TUNE, Sense of harmony and melody.
35. LANGUAGE, Expression of ideas.
36. CAUSALITY, Applying causes to effect. [tion.
37. COMPARISON, Inductive reasoning—illustra-
C. HUMAN NATURE, Perception of motives.
D. AGREEABLENESS, Pleasantness—suavity

FIGURE 4-2 Frontispiece to O.S. and L.N. Fowler, *New Illustrated Self-Instructor in Phrenology and Physiology* (New York: Fowler and Wells, 1859).

dren and their natural interests, and, according to Mann, many positive features of their curriculum recommended them to the American educators. Of the thousands of students Mann claimed to have observed while in Prussia, he explains that never once did he see a "child in tears from having been punished, or from fear of being punished." Rather than harsh discipline Mann saw teachers deal gently with their students as individuals, while providing them with basic instruction. According to Mann, the relationship the teachers had with their pupils seemed

> . . . to be one of duty first, and then affection, on the part of the teacher, . . . The teacher's manner was better than parental, for it had a parent's tenderness and vigilance, without the foolish doatings or indulgences to which parental affection is prone.

Pestalozzi's ideal of the teacher being a guide and respected friend of the student was clearly at work.

Mann was by no means the only American educator to visit and write about the Prussian schools. Calvin Stowe, for example, had been sent by the Ohio state legislature in 1836 to study the schools in Prussia. A year later he published a report on his trip that was circulated by the legislature in every school district in Ohio. Stating that he was impressed by the "excellent order and rigid economy with which all the Prussian institutions are conducted," Stowe's report had a widespread impact beyond Ohio.

Mann's visit to Europe further impressed upon him the importance of the schools as a vehicle for social reform. Mann observed the great gulf that separated the wealthy from the working class in countries such as England. By denying the working class access to free public schools, the English ruling class was threatening the country's political and social stability.

In his *Eighth Report* (1844), Mann discussed at some length the employment of women teachers and the need to develop effective teacher training institutes. With figures such as Charles Brooks, James G. Carter, Edmund Dwight, and Samuel R. Hall, Mann had advocated the establishment of special teacher training institutes as early as the late 1830s. In 1838, Dwight, a Boston businessman, contributed $10,000, to be matched, for the establishment of some sort of teacher training institute in Massachusetts. As head of the state board of education, Mann was left to develop the specific plans of the institution.

Attempts to establish teacher training programs date back to the beginning of the nineteenth century. Samuel R. Hall's private normal school, established in 1823, was unsuccessful. He later taught courses for would-be teachers at Phillips Academy at Andover, Massachusetts. A few academies, especially in New York State, offered teacher preparation courses, but this too was unsuccessful.

It was not until 1839 that the first state-supported teacher training institute, or *normal school*, was established by Mann and his colleagues in Lexington, Massachusetts. The normal school in Lexington was placed under the direction of Harvard graduate Cyrus Pierce. Only three students enrolled on the first day, although twelve eventually were enrolled for classes before the end of the first quarter. Several other normal schools were opened in rapid succession. In September 1839, a school was begun at Barre, Massachusetts; another in Bridgewater, Massachusetts, the following year. The importance that Mann placed upon the normal schools is indicated in an address he made for the dedication of the normal school in Bridge-water, Massachusetts, in August 1846. As he explained,

> I believe Normal Schools to be a new instrumentality in the advancement of the race. I believe that, without them, Free Schools themselves would be shorn of their strength and their healing power, and would at length become mere charity schools, and thus die out in fact and form.

Mann's desire that the normal schools would become strongly linked to the growth of the common schools was eventually borne out.

In the *Ninth Report* (1845), Mann emphasized the primacy of moral education over intellectual training. Basically Mann believed that the ideals of a republican democracy would never be fully realized until the common schools created "a more far-seeing intelligence and a purer morality than has ever yet existed among communities of men" (1849). Moral education for Mann provided a means of ensuring the promotion and development of the Republic:

Engraved by H.W. Smith.

Henry Barnard

FIGURE 4-3
Henry Barnard (1811-1900) at forty-five, editor of *American Journal of Education*. Barnard's *American Journal of Education*, 1 (1857).

> In order that men may be prepared for self-government, their apprenticeship must commence in childhood. The great moral attribute of self-government cannot be born and matured in a day: and if school children are not trained to it, we only prepare ourselves for disappointment, if we expect it from grown men.

Until his final annual report was submitted in 1848, Mann continued to use the reports to promote the idea of the common schools as providing the training necessary for the individual to become a useful citizen. While discussions of the state education code are included in the *Tenth Report* (1846), and the belief that education has the power to redeem the state is discussed in the *Eleventh Report* (1847), it is in the final *Twelfth Report* that Mann's ideas are best summarized.

Mann wrote the *Twelfth Report* after he had been elected to a seat in the U.S. House of Representatives in 1848 and had resigned as secretary of the School Board. In the report he drew together the basic principles and ideas he had been promoting for the past twelve years as an advocate of the common schools. Mann once again emphasized that the destiny of the school is the same as that of society:

> . . . the true business of the schoolroom connects itself, and becomes identical, with the great interests of society. The former is the infant, immature state of those interests; the latter, their developed, adult state. As "the child is father to the man," so may the training of the schoolroom expand into the institutions and fortunes of the state.

The crusade Mann led for the establishment of common schools represented part of a more general educational movement that developed in the second half of the nineteenth century through which schooling came to play an increasingly important role in American culture. As an idealist, Mann had little notion of the extent to which his ideas on free universal schooling would be used to maintain the existing political and social order. Michael Katz has argued that the purpose of the public schools over the course of at least the last hundred years has been the inculcation of attitudes into children that reflect the dominant social and industrial values of the culture. In his reform of the common schools, Mann had no way of knowing the extent to which bureaucratic structures would come to dominate the operation and organization of the public schools in the years following his death.

Mann obviously contributed to the development of the bureaucratic system that would eventually come to so totally dominate American schools. His opposition to democratic localism on the part of individual school boards and his development of an increasingly centralized system of schools throughout Massachusetts are perfect examples of how his work tended to encourage the subsequent development of a bureaucracy. Yet in assessing Mann's work, one is left with something of a paradox. Assuming that the development of free public schools was an important ideal to be realized for the culture, one must ask how these schools could be developed without a centralized administrative system and, with it, bureaucratic and often class-dominated structures.

Mann's work with the common schools was closely paralleled by that of Henry Barnard. Barnard was born in Hartford, Connecticut, in 1811. Like Mann, he was the product of a traditional Protestant upbringing. Educated in a local district school, Monson Academy in Massachusetts, and Hopkins Grammar School, Barnard entered Yale University when he was sixteen in 1826. Graduating in 1830, he taught for a single term at Wellsborough Academy in Pennsylvania. Teaching, however, did not agree with Barnard. In 1831 he returned to Hartford, where he became increasingly involved with Whig politics. Having spent a brief period observing the political scene in Washington, Barnard returned to Connecticut to study law at Yale. Passing the bar exam in 1834, he gravitated toward a political career.

Having traveled briefly in Europe, Barnard returned to the United States because of the death of his father. He was elected to the Connecticut legislature in 1837. Like Mann, Barnard was a Whig and supported a series of social and humanitarian causes similar to those supported by his Massachusetts counterpart. Included in the bills he sponsored in the legislature were programs to improve conditions for the blind, the deaf, and the mentally ill. Advocating the reorganization of the penal system in Connecticut, Barnard eventually became interested in the reform of the state's school system.

In 1838, Barnard introduced a bill in the legislature creating a Board of Commissioners to supervise the Common Schools. The board, under the supervision of a secretary, was to collect information on the schools and evaluate them with the purpose of improving their organization and the quality of education that they provided. Barnard's bill passed the legislature with little difficulty, and he accepted a position as one of the board's eight commissioners. Elected secretary of the board, Barnard intended to hold the position for a period of only six months. Persuaded to stay on for a four-year term, he became increasingly interested in using the schools to reform society. Barnard truly believed that with an educated populace most social problems would be eliminated. Vice and crime would be reduced, the quality of family life would be improved, justice and liberty would flourish.

Like Mann in Massachusetts, as secretary of the education board Barnard assumed the role of an agent for promoting the common school cause. During the late 1830s and early 1840s he traveled extensively throughout Connecticut, collecting school statistics, writing annual reports, and editing the *Connecticut Common School Journal*. It was as a publicist and editor that Barnard undoubtedly made his most important contribution to the development of education in the United States during the middle and late nineteenth century.

Beginning with his editorship of the *Connecticut Common School Journal* and continuing to the end of his life, Barnard systematically wrote about, edited, and assembled an extraordinary collection of documents and critical essays relating to education in Europe and the United States. In doing so, Barnard followed popular nineteenth-century tradition of disseminating educational ideas through the publication of popular journals and magazines. For example, as early as 1811, Albert Pickett published the first American educational magazine. Although Pickett's magazine ultimately proved to be a failure, the basic concept did not.

Between 1811 and 1830, according to Sheldon Davis, a total of nine journals pertaining to the subject of education were published in the United States.

In 1855, Barnard began the publication of what was to be the greatest of the nineteenth-century American educational journals, the *American Journal of Education*. Published in huge annual volumes until 1881, the journal was primarily underwritten by Barnard. The publication was the most comprehensive journal up until that time dealing with the subject of education. In addition to republishing important documents related to the history of schooling (a complete copy of the *New England Primer* was reprinted in one of the early issues, for example), the journal included biographies of important educators, descriptions of educational innovations, essays on school architecture, descriptions of the education of the deaf and blind, and as well discussions of juvenile reformatories and the education of the poor.

Although the journal's cost was far beyond the means and interest of the average teacher, it was widely available in major libraries, school systems, colleges, and teacher training institutions. In addition, the journal was circulated internationally to such places as Chile, Argentina, Scotland, Belgium, Canada, Germany, France, Switzerland, and Italy. Surviving documents from the period seem to indicate that the impact of the journal as a vehicle for disseminating and promoting new educational ideas was enormous, although its influence is hard to assess accurately.

Barnard's efforts were by no means limited to the *American Journal of Education*. In 1838, for example, he had presented an address on the unfortunate condition of most schoolhouses in the United States. In 1842, his ideas were further developed and published in a manual or architectural pattern book entitled *School Architecture, Or Contributions to the Improvement of School-Houses in the United States*.

Interest in the design of schoolhouses in the United States goes back to the beginning of the 1830s. In 1830, the American Institute of Instruction sponsored a competition on the construction of schoolhouses. Barnard credited his own interest in school architecture to Alonzo Potter and George B. Emerson's book *The School and the Schoolmaster*. Included in Barnard's *School Architecture* were not only designs discussed by Potter and Emerson in their work, but plans and elevations actually executed by Barnard himself for the Windsor and Washington district schoolhouses in Connecticut.

Barnard saw the well-designed school as not only a place where education could be properly conducted, but also as a model, worthy of imitation by the general population. As he explained in an article published in 1839 in Volume 2 of the *Connecticut Common School Journal*, every village, town and school in Connecticut

> . . . would have least one edifice in good taste,—in a conspicuous and agreeable situation,—a correct model of architecture,—pleasing to the eye of every spectator, and agreeable to those for whom the school house is designed. . . .
> How would such edifices adorn our streets, and arrest the eyes of the travellers

along our roads, rivers, and sea coast! What an influence, also, would models of this kind soon exercise on the taste of our people, and their views of domestic architecture, and the arrangement of their own grounds!

Barnard felt that most schoolhouses were badly sited, situated in noisy places too often close to highways, unattractive, and built at the least possible cost.

A careful examination of the designs in Barnard's *School Architecture* is revealing. As in almost any type of architecture, there is inherent in the designs for schools a clear philosophy and set of social values. The frequent selection and use of classic revival style the schoolhouses in Barnard's book reflects not only the then current interest in neoclassic style for both domestic and public architecture, but also recalls in a physical form the rationalism of the Greeks. The schoolhouse becomes a "sacred space" or literally a temple of wisdom. Similarly, the emphasis upon Gothic styles of architecture for schoolhouses, which was popular as a style in both England and the United States, recalled not only the tradition of the medieval universities, but also the tradition of ecclesiastical architecture. As a result, the school as a "sacred" architectural space was once again emphasized.

Barnard included in *School Architecture* much more than floor plans and elevations for schoolhouses. Toward the conclusion of the book, he went into detailed discussions of monitorial and other pedagogical systems. In addition, he discussed the use of pedagogical devices ranging from movable blackboards to globes of the earth, desk designs, and even ventilation and heating systems.

In 1842, the same year that *School Architecture* was published, Barnard lost the secretaryship of the Connecticut Board of Education as a result of the Democrats coming to power. He immediately set out on a fifteen-month tour of the United States, collecting materials for a history of American education. While collecting his data, Barnard also lectured on the need for the establishment of Common Schools to various state and local groups. On completing the trip, Barnard assumed the post of commissioner of Public Schools in Rhode Island, a position he held until 1849.

Barnard subsequently served as the principal of the Connecticut State Normal School and State Superintendent of Common Schools, Chancellor of the University of Wisconsin, and agent of the Wisconsin Normal School Regents. In 1867, Barnard was appointed as the first U.S. Commissioner of Education. With the change of political administrations in 1869, the Department of Education was made a bureau of the Department of the Interior. Barnard lost his job and returned to live in Connecticut, where he worked on his history of American education and the *American Journal of Education*, which he continued to publish until 1881.

Barnard's work as a proponent of the Common Schools was only exceeded by that of Horace Mann. His work as an educational administrator was largely a failure. As head of the University of Wisconsin, he never assumed a position of strong leadership, while his work as the U.S. Commissioner of Education was too short-lived to bear any fruit. Instead, Barnard's most lasting contribution seems to have been derived from his work as an editor and writer—one who provided critical direction and purpose to the relatively new enterprise of public education in the United States.

ACADEMIES

The development of the common schools during the 1830s and 1840s was accompanied by a continued growth and development of the academies. Until roughly the centennial year of 1876, the academies enrolled more students than the high schools. Thousands of academies had been established. There were military academies, monitorial academies, manual labor academies, and preparatory academies. There were academies for boys, for boys and girls, and for girls. An academy for Indians operated for nearly twenty years, and after the Civil War there were a few academies for blacks.

    The first military academy in the United States was, of course, the army academy at West Point, patterned after military schools in France. Before Sylvanius

FIGURE 4-4
Captian Alden Partridge, early superintendent of West Point, later founder of other military schools. Barnard's *American Journal of Education*, 13 (1863).

B. Thayer replaced Alden Partridge as superintendent in 1812, West Point seems to have had a course of study like that of many other academies. It was Thayer who laid the foundation of West Point's traditions of drill, polish, and discipline. Partridge established a private military school and later aided in the establishment of other military academies.

The United States Naval Academy at Annapolis, Maryland, was established forty years later by Secretary of the Navy George Bancroft, by administrative sleight of hand, without congressional approval. Until then, navy midshipmen had been expected to study at sea. For example, when the frigate *Potomac* sailed around the world (elapsed time 1,002 days), in its crew were nineteen midshipmen and Schoolmaster Francis Warriner, who was outranked by them. Bancroft was sure this was an unsatisfactory arrangement.

In the twenty years after the Revolution, Boston produced a generation of American intellectuals. Conservative, Federalist, self-styled "natural aristocrats," they were dissatisfied with what they saw as vestigal grammar schools, rudimentary academies, and tradition-bound Harvard. Several young intellectuals were sent to Europe by Harvard President John T. Kirtland to complete their preparation for Harvard professorships. One was Edward Everett, who became a famed orator, politician, and Harvard's president. A second, George Ticknor, was an unsuccessful reformer at Harvard. Two others, Joseph Green Cogswell and George Bancroft, later established the Round Hill School.

Cogswell visited von Fellenberg's school for young aristocrats twice in 1818. (That year Robert Owen of New Harmony sent his son, Robert Dale Owen, there.) At von Fellenberg's school for aristocrats the first concern also was for the development of the student's moral facilities. Students studied Latin, Greek, French, German, science, drawing, and music and exercised by doing calesthenics. The school for young aristocrats was a boarding school. About the same time Bancroft visited German secondary schools, *gymnasiums*, in which students studied and learned far more quickly and thoroughly what American students learned in the classical departments of academies and their first years of college.

Cogswell and Bancroft taught at Harvard upon their return, Cogswell as professor of science (and librarian) and Bancroft, after preaching a few months, as tutor (instructor) in Greek. The students saw Bancroft as a demanding tyrant in his classroom. After Harvard's "great rebellion" of 1822–23, forty-three of the seventy members of the senior class were expelled and President Kirtland was forced to retire. Cogswell and Bancroft resigned and founded Round Hill School, near Northampton, Massachusetts.

Like von Fellenberg's, Round Hill was a boarding school. Round Hill was concerned first with the development of "character." Cogswell and Bancroft undertook to provide a vigorous preparation for higher education, as the German gymnasiums did. Classes were small. Much of the teaching was tutorial, individual. Students began their studies there at the age of nine. When they had completed the Round Hill course of study, they were prepared to enter Harvard or Yale, sometimes even the junior or senior classes there. Round Hill was the prototype for

Eastern preparatory schools, the schools which, at least by legend, have prepared the sons of the elite for Ivy League colleges. Bancroft left Round Hill in 1831, and in 1834, Cogswell closed the school.

Compared with the preparatory school, the range and variety of academies is difficult to overstate. Before the Civil War, Colonel Dick Johnson's Choctaw Academy had an Indian student body. On the eve of the twentieth century, Orange Park Normal and Industrial School for Negroes was closed by Florida Superintendent of Schools William F. Sheats because it had admitted seventeen white students. Frederick William Coleman's academy in Virginia was a small log cabin copy of the University of Virginia, complete with quadrangle. Mr. Coleman heard recitations when he was ready, early or late. Many of his scholars entered college. Fairfield Academy in upstate New York offered medical school courses. Gardiner Lyceum in Maine was a school for "farmers, millwrights and other mechanics" from 1824 until 1831. Other smaller agricultural academies survived more briefly. To repeat, the academies were generally small. In New York State in 1850, even the best-

FIGURE 4-5
Emma Willard, founder of Troy Seminary, 1821, which became one of the first women's colleges. Barnard's *American Journal of Education*, 6 (1859).

Mary Lyon.

FIGURE 4-6
Mary Lyon, founder of Mt. Holyoke Seminary, an early women's college. Barnard's American Journal of Education, *10* *(1861)*.

funded academies averaged only 4.4 teachers and 108 students. In North Carolina then, 272 academies had 403 teachers and 8,000 pupils, an average of 1.5 teachers and 29 pupils each.

After their first beginnings, academies for females multiplied rapidly. From first to last their aim was to educate girls and women so that they would be better wives and mothers and for the good of society generally. They did not educate women for professions or occupations, except for teaching. By 1839, nearly 500 former students at Zilpah Grant's Ipswich Female Academy alone had become teachers, and twenty more taught in female seminaries.

In 1876, there were still questions concerning appropriate studies for women, where they would go to college, and whether they should go to professional school. Underlying these, of course, were questions concerning suitable occupations for women, and most fundamentally, women's roles in society. These issues and questions arose outside the academies, which had made their contributions.

The supporters of the public schools portrayed the academies as unfortunate and inadequate, and their criticisms have outlasted the academies. However, if one starts with the proposition that secondary education should be privately supported, as much of higher education still is, and if demand is so scattered that students must leave home, then perhaps academies had their virtues. They were responsive to community and student needs, as part of the cost for their survival. They were small enough to avoid impersonality. Students and their parents had wide choices in courses of study and academies' religious stances. Tuition costs surely prevented some from attending an academy, but the first high schools were not for the poor—wages not earned were an important consideration too for those planning to go beyond common school. Most young men and women in the 1800s had no such plan or wish.

The virtual extinction of types of schools has been rare in our past; only the academy and the Latin grammar school have suffered that fate. A brief post mortem is appropriate. As a first approximation, tuition-supported academies were replaced by tax-supported high schools. During Horace Mann's superintendency the enrollments in Massachusetts schools rose much faster than total enrollments in Massachusetts academies. In 1839, in the town of Cambridge, 69 percent of the pupils attended common schools. Seven years later, 90 percent did. It seems likely that teachers who were well thought of preferred to teach in public schools, instead of in private schools or academies. In Buffalo, New York, the new school system recruited half its teachers from local nonpublic schools in the later 1830s. Some sixty academies in New York State were transformed into high schools, and a very few became colleges. Others closed when buildings burned or respected principals left education, as Bruce Catton's father did during World War I. A few closed later when their endowments were exhausted. A scattering of academies survive, in rural New England, or as preparatory schools, or schools closely related to churches. In the last twenty years, hundreds of new academies have been established, as refuges from school desegregation or from what has been seen as the mediocrity of the public schools and their "immorality." But they are parts of more recent history of education.

CONCLUSION

The first half of the nineteenth century saw the emergence of a distinct American identity and the development of a school system consistent with it. New attitudes toward childrearing reflected a specific set of values and beliefs concerning the child and the family that were unique to American culture. Democratic ideals combined with the demands of a rapidly expanding industrial system encouraged the "Common School Revival.

New and important educational ideas were promoted by leaders of the Common School Movement such as Horace Mann, Henry Barnard, and Calvin Stowe. Older and more traditional approaches to schooling survived in the form of the academies. As had been the case with republican educational theorists after the Revolution, the leaders of the Common School Movement saw education as a means of reforming American culture. In doing so, they failed to realize that they

FIGURE 4-7
Rural school, Genesse Falls, New York, built about 1875 and said to have burned a half century later. Most schools were rural long after urbanization had begun. Barnard's *American Journal of Education*, 26 (1876), p. 301.

were promoting a philosophy that was specifically their own, rather than one that was universally held. Their faith in the effectiveness of the schools and their ability to reform American culture had at times almost religious overtones. This faith in the school's ability to reform American culture has continued into our own era, and only in recent decades has begun to be seriously questioned.

The significance of the Common School Movement ultimately lies in the patterns that it set for the subsequent development of education in the United States. The roles now defined for teachers and administrators within the school system, the relationship of the school to the family and to minority groups, systems of finance and administration clearly have their roots in the Common School Movement. As a result, the Common School Movement is of particular importance and interest to those concerned with understanding the history of American education.

Chapter Five
THE GROWTH OF THE COMMON SCHOOLS

The second half of the nineteenth century was the great period of expansion and growth for the common schools, and of the development of what David Tyack has called "the one best system." Common schools spread from New England and New York westward and southward after the Civil War. They served (though that was not always an appropriate word) older students in high schools and vocational schools and younger pupils in kindergartens. Partly because of compulsory attendance laws, a larger proportion of children attended schools.

As the common schools grew, there were strong arguments and seemingly good reasons for more centralized control, and also for more authority for state superintendents of schools, the establishment of the county superintendency, and the development of the city superintendency. With increasing enrollments, the division of the labor of teachers was more desirable. A need for coordination arose, and administrators, especially the city superintendents, acquired further duties and authority.

However, large segments of schooling remained outside the "one best system." Members of the Roman Catholic Church had preferred to build Catholic schools rather than send their children to Protestant-dominated public schools. Despite the efforts of radical Republicans and blacks after the Civil War, only a much-modified form of schooling was available to blacks. Girls and women were often consigned, at first, to different and inferior secondary schools, and were not admitted to colleges. American Indians also attended different segregated schools. The common school as it was extended was not for everyone at every level.

EXPANSION

The concept of the common school spread in part because it was an institution whose time had come. Horace Mann, and also Henry Barnard and others, expressed what many people, particularly influential people, felt. Mann's and Barnard's reports and papers were read nationally and approved and often acted upon. In other states there were also advocates of the common schools, who were respected and influential; Norman Angell of Michigan and John Swett of California were in their place and time ardent advocates. (A might-have-been of history opens an interesting speculation: if, for whatever reasons, Mann and Barnard had not been active in the Common School Movement, would it have been as strong and widespread? One of the authors thinks it might have been. That belief presupposes that public opinion or functional necessity, rather than inspired leadership, produced an institution. The question is illuminating because it shows alternative lines of historical explanation.) The common schools seem to have spread, too, because an extraordinarily large proportion of schoolmen and teachers had come from New England, presumably bringing with them devotion to the common schools. In large cities, particularly, some old residents felt threatened and were alarmed by the large numbers of people different from themselves. The common schools were established in some part to protect things as they had been, to protect against Irish and German immigrants in Buffalo, to protect against the Spanish-speaking residents of Los Angeles and newly freed slaves in Charleston, South Carolina. In some cities, the men Bayrd Still called "civic boosters" established common school systems. In any event, the common school revival spread fast and far. In California, common schools appeared within a year after the 1849 gold rush. By then common schools had been established or reestablished in the Old Northwest, bounded by the Ohio and Mississippi rivers, and in the states and territories west of there.

Organizationally, the "high school" was an extension of the common schools for older and more advanced pupils. If *high school* is understood as meaning a secondary school supported by taxes and controlled by public authorities, the line between academy and *high school* blurred because the later sharp distinction between "public" and "private" had not come into being. The source of the name *high school* was probably the Edinburgh High School, which had been founded in 1566 and was controlled and funded by the city. John Griscom, the monitorial school enthusiast and professor of chemistry, had visited it and had published descriptions. Bostonians may have borrowed the term. The *English Classical School*, an alternative to Latin grammar schools, was established in Boston in 1821 as a public secondary school. After 1824, it was called the *English High School*, It is thought of as the first high school in the United States.

The spread of high schools was slow at first, but by 1851 there were high schools in eighty American cities, and other high schools opened soon after. In some states new laws authorized the establishment of high schools. In other states courts held that common school laws had authorized the establishment of high schools. The most famous of these court cases was *Stuart et al* v. *School District No. 1 of Kalamazoo*, which was decided in 1874.

There was as much variation in the curricula of early high schools as there was in the academies. Some subjects were extensions of those of the common schools: the English High School of Boston offered the common school subjects of reading, arithmetic, and geography as well as more advanced courses. Others had curricula parallel to those of the academies. Some high schools offered the courses in Latin and Greek that had been taught in the Latin grammar schools and that were still needed for admission to colleges. Less often, high schools were seen as "people's colleges": a very few of them even awarded bachelor's degrees. Until nearly 1880, there were more academy than high school students. Enrollments in high schools increased after that, and academy enrollments declined.

The issue of the high school versus the academy was important in its consequences. However, most of the pupils, even at the end of the 1800s, had no plan or wish to continue their schooling. In 1880, only one adolescent in fifty was attending a high school, and fewer were attending an academy. Even in 1920, only one out of five adolescents would be attending high school. Only a tenth of those who went to high schools in the 1880s graduated. Students dropped out for all the reasons still heard, and many high schools offered only one or two years of instruction. The importance of completing high school—graduating—was a later convention. High school students in Dedham, Massachusetts, received a certificate for completing each year's work.

David Nassau has said that academies "were abandoned by parents unable to pay both tuition and taxes." It was more complicated than that, of course. Public high schools grew as cities grew, because in cities there were many potential pupils, and because real property—land and buildings—in the cities was valuable and profitable enough to bear taxes to support schools.

THE FORMING OF CITY SYSTEMS

From the first erratic beginnings of city school systems, in the 1830s, to their generally uniform organization by about 1900, is a history that has gotten considerable attention, although it has not been fully explored. The general tendency, clearly, was toward regularization and regulation, toward more elaborate formal organization and bureaucratization. But there were many cases of delayed modernization, and even some cases of regression when the city superintendent was weak or unfortunate. In a few cities, superintendencies were even abolished for a time.

The history of Chicago's schools is in many ways illustrative. The first school there to receive public funds, in 1833, was that of Miss Eliza Chapell, who had moved her charity school from a borrowed storeroom to the Presbyterian church. Miss Chappell's memoirs show that she was much more missionary than teacher, which should not be surprising.

After the time of Miss Chappell, who went on to better missionary fields, one first sees the enormous growth of enrollments in the Chicago schools. In 1837, the year of a particularly painful and costly panic, 325 children were enrolled. (The schools shut down because there were no tax revenues to support them.) Herrick, in her study of the Chicago schools, gives enrollment figures from time to time, which are shown in Table 5-1. The rate of increase in numbers of pupils was far greater in Chicago, and in the other big cities, than any seen in our century. In the eight years ending in 1845, enrollments tripled. In the thirteen years ending in 1850, they increased nearly ten times. In the next ten years, they again more than tripled, and in

TABLE 5-1   Chicago Pupils and Teachers, 1837-1970[a]

YEAR	ELEMENTARY ENROLLMENT[b]	HIGH SCHOOL ENROLLMENT[c]	TOTAL ENROLLMENT[d]	NUMBER OF TEACHERS[e]	TEACHER PUPIL RATIO
1837	325	—	325	4	1:81.2
1840	317	—	317	4	1:79.2
1850	1,919	—	1,919	21	1:91.4
1860	6,539	312	6,851	135	1:50.7
1870	27,342	602	38,939	537	1:72.5
1880	58,519	1,043	59,562	958	1:62.2
1890	131,341	2,825	135,541	2,711	1:50:0
1900	215,660	10,201	255,221	5,786	1:44.1
1910	257,620	17,781	300,472	6,357	1:47.3
1920	291,678	36,433	392,914	8,740	1:45.0
1930	326,000	103,851	440,161	13,479	1:32.7
1940	318,443	144,671	391,171	13,532	1:28.9
1950	293,142	96,786	389,928	13,423	1:29.6
1960	410,206	102,886	513,092	20,276	1:24.0
1970	433,319	142,843	576,153[f]	26,884	1:21.4

Notes:

[a]Data from Mary J. Herrick, *The Chicago Schools: A Social and Political History* (Beverly Hills: Sage, 1971), pp. 403, 406. Enrollment figures may be a third higher than average attendance in early years.

[b]Includes seventh and eighth graders in junior high school.

[c]Includes ninth graders in junior high school.

[d]Includes summer, evening, special students, 1890-1950. Normal school and college students not included.

[e]Includes special teachers, 1880, 1900, 1910, 1940, 1950, teachers not assigned to schools, 1970.

[f]Apparent discrepancy not explained.

the following ten years, nearly doubled again. By 1890, there were 135,431 pupils enrolled in Chicago schools. Because Chicago was one of the most prosperous and fastest-growing cities of the time, its school enrollments were among the fastest growing. The sheer weight of numbers was one of the most important shapers of city schools in the later 1800s.

Miss Chappell's school and the other schools of that time were not publicly controlled, although they were partly supported by taxes. A new city charter put Chicago schools under the city's control in 1839, only two years after Horace Mann had become de facto superintendent of Massachusetts schools. The first Chicago superintendent of schools, John Dore, from Boston, was appointed in 1854. It was not unusual that he was a New Englander; most of the early superintendents were. The first big-city superintendent, Oliver Steele, had been appointed in Buffalo seventeen years earlier. Dore was a *schoolman*, as they called themselves, who had previously taught, but he later became a Chicago businessman. Steele was a businessman, owner of a bookstore and bindery, before and after he was superintendent of schools, which seems to have been less common. But of Steele's seventeen successors in Buffalo before 1890, only four were schoolmen. Herrick gives no details as to why the Chicago schools were put under the control of the city government. The founders of the Buffalo school system were civic "boosters," who established the school system for the same reason they established police departments and fire departments, and built water systems: those were good for the city and for business.

It is convenient to talk about public schools as isolated institutions, but it must be remembered that in the 1800s, the schools were only part of a matrix of institutions intended to educate. In Chicago and elsewhere, many private schools continued after city public schools came into being. Herrick has not provided details about other educating institutions in Chicago. Those in Buffalo have been more thoroughly examined. In Buffalo, secondary studies could be undertaken at academies that thrived for a time even after a public high school was opened. There were private instructors in many subjects—one of the early Buffalo superintendents had been a private "writing," or penmanship, teacher. There were frequent lyceum sessions, and a privately supported school of art, and a large but privately supported library. There were, of course, newspapers. Parochial schools had appeared. The individual who wished to could, unless he was too poor, be educated in both practical and the finer things.

A Chicago Board of Education was appointed in 1857, replacing earlier "inspectors." In some places, including Buffalo, city governments continued to control the public schools directly. In others, such as Brooklyn and Pittsburgh, there was a school committee for each school. Their consolidation into one city-wide board of education, and its reduction in size, seemed at the time to be one of the greater advances of the late 1800s.

Dore was followed as superintendent by William Henry Wells of Connecticut. Wells had not attended college, but had been thought well enough of to be awarded an honorary master of arts degree by Dartmouth College. (Masters of arts were generally honorary then, but were normally awarded to a college's own graduates.) Before coming to Chicago, he had written an innovative grammar book.

The first Chicago high school opened in 1856, at least fifteen years after it was first proposed. In 1856, most big cities already had high schools. There were 169 pupils in the high school its first year, admitted by competitive examination. There were three programs. One was *Classical*, primarily the study of Latin and Greek, as preparation for college or, as some believed, to stregthen the mind. This was reminiscent of the Latin grammar schools. The second program was *English*. Greek and most of the Latin coursework was replaced by English literature and, by Herrick's count, sixteen other subjects. This was in the academy convention obviously.

NORMAL SCHOOLS AND TEACHER PREPARATION

The third program in the high school was a two-year program, open to students at least sixteen years old, a *normal* program for would-be teachers. They studied history, "mental philosophy" (a kind of prescientific psychology), and "theory of teaching." Teacher training was one of Wells's greatest interests. He had been Samuel A. Hall's student in the normal department in 1834 at Phillips Academy at

FIGURE 5-1   Chicago high school building in 1857. From *The American Journal of Education*, Vol. 3 (1858), p. 536.

Andover, Massachusetts. There were scattered efforts to prepare teachers in other academies, sometimes with state funding, but the first state normal school would not be established until 1839. A normal school in Albany, New York, was established five years later. David P. Page was the first principal there; his book, *Theory and Practice of Teaching . . .*, moralizing, advocating, giving practical suggestions for classroom management, would still be seen as a classic fifty years later. But there were only nine state-supported normal schools when the Chicago program opened in 1856, and there were no more than a few normal programs in cities. Even Boston had not established a normal school until 1852. It was part of a girl's high school when the Chicago program opened.

A few years later Edward A. Sheldon saw an "object lesson" display in Toronto, a formalized English version of the Pestalozzian teaching method. Sheldon returned to Oswego, New York, with the display; recruited Hermann Krüsi, Jr., son of one of Pestalozzi's assistants; and the Oswego normal school, state supported after 1866, became famous and successful. Thereafter, normal schools, supported by states, cities, or occasionally counties, rapidly increased in number.

In 1883, Colonel Francis W. Parker became a principal of the Cook County Normal School near Chicago. During the Civil War, Parker, who had enlisted as a private, won his promotions by bravery. He had studied in Europe and had been the successful superintendent in Quincy, Massachusetts. The "Quincy System," which he established, called for learning and teaching directed by the interests of the pupils and the creativity of the teacher. As a supervisor in Boston, Parker was not successful; the system there seemed too rigid to change. Parker was a latter-day romantic who believed first of all in the natural gifts of the individual, particularly the child, but also the teacher. With this he coupled, rather oddly, faith in science. In principle, judging by the curricula he suggested, the child would learn by inventiveness, and would learn about the world by learning science. But Parker's greatest strength was his faith, which cannot be recaptured in a few lines.

Wells "graded" the Chicago elementary pupils, placing each of 14,000 of them in one of ten grades. Although grading had often been discussed earlier, John Philbrick is given credit for having first "graded" a grammar school, in Quincy, Massachusetts, in 1847. Perhaps the idea had been a kind of translation from the old Latin grammar schools, which had had "forms" since their beginnings in America. Perhaps the idea was borrowed: Mann had been impressed by grades in German schools. "Grading" was quickly and widely adopted. Most often, there were eight grades in a grammar school, but in the South there were seven, and many of the city schools added kindergartens. Usually a "grade" covered a year's work (and a year in the school life of the pupil, or more if the pupil "failed"). Many city grade schools had promotions twice a year, and a few even more often. Buffalo's schools had only three grades, or "departments," although nine years of instruction after kindergarten was offered—perhaps this was not grading at all. Chicago and a few other cities numbered grades starting with the highest; the student in first grade was in the graduating class. (West Point and Annapolis still use this system.)

A graded school had immediately obvious advantages. A class could be taught as a whole, and the old endless routine of one-by-one recitation would have been abandoned. A teacher in a graded school could specialize in teaching one grade, and would be more productive: Adam Smith's principle of division of labor had been applied. A third advantage was that discipline, especially in the earlier grades, would be easier to maintain.

The difficulties were less obvious. One of them was, and is, that pupils could no longer advance at their own rate. Another probably more subtle disadvantage was, and is, that pupils met, studied, and played only with their agemates and tended to lose contact with the worlds of those who were older or younger. The advantages were more obvious than the difficulties, and one might judge that they were greater if classes were huge, as they were during Wells's superintendency. In his last year as superintendent, there were 121 enrolled pupils for each teacher. Even taking into account the high absence rate (perhaps in the general neighborhood of 30 percent), a class of 90 is hard to visualize, but classes were that large. Also, teachers were unprepared by today's standards. As late as 1870, fewer than half the Chicago grade school teachers had completed either high school or normal school. In those schools at that time perhaps the advantages of grading were greater than the disadvantages.

Grading the schools also added an organizational difficulty. If graded schools were to be effective and satisfactory, content overlaps or omissions had to be avoided. That made necessary courses of study, which took much of the time of early superintendents. Wells wrote *A Graded Course of Instruction with Instructions to Teachers*. Much of it was taken up with essays, most of which were surprisingly humane and progressive. The book was far better known for its detailed course of study, an elaborate catalogue of what was to be taught when. It was used in many school systems.

Wells resigned in 1865 because of poor eyesight and health. Chicago teachers loyal to him presented him with a $400 gold watch, a spectacular gift considering teachers' pay and the times. Wells stayed on in Chicago as a businessman and member of the Board of Education of Chicago and of the State of Illinois. He also helped establish the Chicago public libraries, the astronomical society, the Chicago Academy of Science, and the Chicago Historical Society. One infers that Chicago institutions for education also went much beyond the public schools.

AN ASIDE: *McGUFFEY'S* AND OTHERS

The knowledge and values that schools tried to teach in this era are preserved like fossils in the schoolbooks of the time. The most famous of them was *McGuffey's*, eventually a set of six readers, starting with a primer and ending with a reader for what would now be a capable high school student. (Webster's "Blue-Back Speller," survivor from early times, was probably next most famous.) *McGuffey's* is still well known because it was enormously popular. More than 100 million copies were sold.

FIGURE 5-2
William H. Wells, Chicago Super-
intendent of Schools, about 1860.
Barnard's *American Journal of
Education*, 8 (1860).

It is better known than competing readers, *Sanders* and *Appleton's,* for instance, not only because it outsold them, but because automobile manufacturer Henry Ford studied *McGuffey's*. He later purchased the log cabin in which the first compiler, William Holmes McGuffey, had been born and had it restored at Greenfield Village outside Detroit. Ford also encouraged McGuffey societies. Nevertheless, there were better reasons for remembering *McGuffey's*.

The first of the *McGuffey's Eclectic Readers* appeared in 1836 and was compiled by William H. McGuffey, a former teacher, and president of a new college in Cincinnati, Ohio. His wife and younger brother aided in the compilations. Later there were revisions by the publisher's editors. Compared with the readers published after 1920, the *McGuffey's Readers* were overmoralizing, although they lacked much of the grim Calvinism of the various editions of the *New England Primer*. They have been accused of upholding conventional Victorian morality, which, in general, they did. The *McGuffey's Readers* were not openly abolitionist, for which they have been sharply criticized. Perhaps selling books in the South was too important to the publishers. (Another publisher printed practically identical books in the South during the Civil War.) However, it should be recalled that most Northerners were not abolitionists before the Civil War, that Cincinnati was a border city, and that William Holmes McGuffey was a professor at the University of Virginia from 1845 until he retired in 1873. Conventional as *McGuffey's* was in other ways, it was first and last pacifistic, even in times of war.

Aside from values and issues, many of the *McGuffey's* selections were rememberable. Even Aesop's fable of the boy who cried "wolf" has remained in many minds. At worst, the *McGuffey's Readers* were stuffy. At best, they were much nearer to being literary than were the primers that appeared after 1920. The 1857 edition of the fifth reader had two selections from William Shakespeare (edited and simplified) and selections from Joseph Addison and George Gordon (Lord Byron). One *McGuffey's Reader* was criticized by some because English authors were favored. In it there were also selections by Washington Irving, Nathaniel Hawthorne, William Cullen Byrant, and John Greenleaf Whittier. The readers were criticized by some because they favored American writers.

CHICAGO, 1864

Josiah L. Pickard was Chicago superintendent of schools for twelve years from 1864 until 1877. Pickard, a native of Massachusetts, had been Wisconsin state superintendent of schools before he had come to Chicago. Pickard was Chicago superintendent during the last year of the Civil War, when whites' resentments of blacks, an early sort of "backlash," had resulted in the segregation of pupils from 1863 until 1865. He was superintendent of the Chicago schools at the time of the Chicago fire in the fall of 1871. A third of Chicago's school buildings were burned then, and after the fire the high school was closed so that the building could be used for the courts.

As they had in every other big city, Irish and German immigrants had poured into Chicago. In Pickard's time they had acquired political power. As in New York City, Catholic immigrants objected to the reading of the Bible in the schools, and Lutheran Germans joined with them in complaining. By forbidding the reading of the Bible, the Chicago Board of Education met that objection. Germans also succeeded in introducing German language in the schools, over the opposition of other ethnic groups. Discontinuing Bible readings was not common then, but many cities put German into the course of study. In a few places, such as Cincinnati, German became a language of instruction. The German version of *McGuffey's* primer is evidence of that.

In Chicago in the 1800s, the range of pupils attending the public schools increased enormously. At first the children of merchants and journeymen had attended private academies and schools, but they were increasingly drawn to the public schools—the establishment of the high school was probably related to that. Catholic parishes established schools, but many Catholic children attended public school. But many children, particularly the children of the poor, did not attend any school. In 1850, there were 13,500 school-aged children in Chicago, but only 1,919 enrolled in public schools. Herrick says enrollments in other schools were greater than in public schools, but perhaps half the children did not attend at all. Six years later Wells said that there were at least 3,000 children who had never been to school. A compulsory education law had been recommended as early as 1838, but it was 1883 before one was enacted in Illinois, thirty-one years after the first compulsory attendance law had been enacted in Massachusetts.

Like the earlier Massachusetts law, Illinois required all children between the ages of eight and fourteen to attend schools at least twelve weeks a year. The law was not fully enforced, and probably—in an age of child labor in sweatshops and before birth certificates—was not fully enforceable. There was not enough space in the schools for all the "truant" boys and girls. Nevertheless, in 1888 Chicago truant officers placed 9,799 children in public, parochial, or night schools. (In Chicago and in many other cities, night schools were at first for children who worked during the day.) The law was amended in 1889, to require eight consecutive and a total of sixteen weeks of school attendance each year.

In 1893, after several ineffective laws, the Illinois General Assembly passed an act forbidding the employment of children under the age of fourteen in workshops and factories. Compulsory education laws were generally ineffective unless there were also child labor laws. Although there were still children who worked in stores and still a diminishing number of truants, greater proportions of children attended school. As a result, the common schools in the cities, which most children would attend, required changed curricula, a subject we will return to.

Relatively little is known of Chicago teachers as individuals. Most of them were women. During the Civil War, women teachers outnumbered men teachers by sixteen to one and by twenty-three to one in 1885. There were several causes for the employment of women and girls rather than men as teachers. In 1860, men beginning teaching in the elementary schools were paid $500 a year; women $200. Twenty years later, when the starting pay for female high school teachers was $850 a year, men were paid $2,000. It is not difficult to cite a dozen or so speeches and papers arguing that women, because of their maternal—or perhaps submissive—nature, were best suited to be grade school teachers.

As Tyack has pointed out, the proportion of teachers who were women was greater where schools were graded; presumably it was easier for women to manage and teach a primary class, at least. However, there are still unexplained regional differences. Most teachers in Montana in 1880 were women, but most teachers in Indiana were men. It has been suggested that normal schools, because they cost time and therefore income, made teaching less attractive for men. The general matter should be explored further.

Most of the Chicago teachers were young. Some graduated from the normal program at eighteen, and those who graduated from high school were about that age. We would suppose that the other new teachers, appointed because of politicians' endorsements, were not much older. Not many of the woman teachers were married, although regulations against married teachers had not yet appeared. They

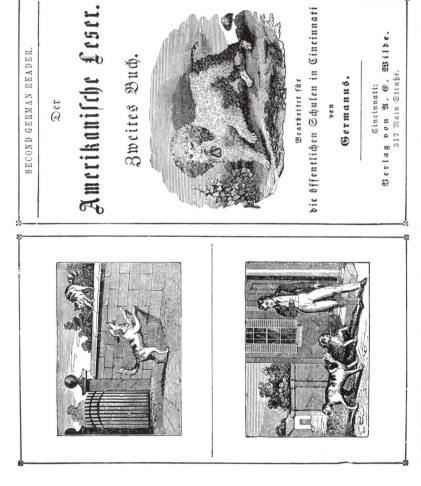

FIGURE 5-3 The extraordinary popularity of McGuffey's work is indicated by the fact that special German editions like the one illustrated above from 1854 were published for German Americans.

were not married because, by the middle-class conventions of the time, many were too young to marry. Herrick remarks that the average teacher then had only seven years of experience. Chicago teachers in the 1800s had more experience on the average than teachers in the 1960s, though less than now.

As far as we know, only three biographies of Chicago teachers have been printed. Eliza Chappell's biography suggests that she was a convert of the *New Reawakening*, passionately concerned with the redemption of souls, whether those of Indians or whites. She was the first public school teacher in Chicago, as some calculated it. In Chicago she married a missionary and accompanied him in his missionary tasks. She survived long enough to spend her last winters in the warmth of Southern California and Florida. At the time of her death, on New Year's Day, 1888, nearly 130,000 pupils were enrolled in the Chicago public schools.

The second printed biography of a Chicago teacher is that of Chester C. Dodge, who was largely inconsequential. The third Chicago teacher who escaped anonymity was Ella Flagg (later Ella Flagg Young). Her family moved to Chicago from Buffalo when she was thirteen. In Chicago she had been a monitorial instructor in arithmetic, then had completed the two-year normal course. At eighteen she was assistant principal of the elementary school from which she had graduated, then was in charge of what would now be called "observation, participation, and student teaching" in the normal program. When it was eliminated, she transferred to high school teaching. One has the impression of Ella Flagg as a whirlwind of energy, a woman of great determination. She would later be Chicago's first woman superintendent, and the first woman president of the NEA.

Pickard resigned in 1877 after a dispute with the board of education. By then the outlines of a city system had emerged. There were grade schools and high schools, and night schools for daytime workers. There was a normal school which, like those in most big cities, trained at least some new teachers in the system's ways. (Outside critics said city normal schools resulted in inbreeding, produced new teachers no different from the old by some kind of parthenogenesis or cloning.) Within a relatively few years the city would have a vocational school: Pickard had already introduced manual training on a trial basis. As in many other cities, the first manual training school and kindergartens were privately supported. Kindergarten classes became part of the Chicago system in 1892.

Chicago school organization and staffing when Pickard left had assumed the form that would last without basic changes for a hundred years or more. The schools were under the direction of a central board of education, instead of local school committees or city government directly. The board of education (usually) delegated authority and responsibility to the superintendent, who was becoming increasingly powerful. There were assistant superintendents who were the beginning of a central office staff. In every school there was a principal in authority, and sometimes even as assistant principal.

Pickard became a professor at the University of Iowa, and then president there. He established some of the first university courses in education in the United States, but only at the preparatory level. Later he wrote a book on the superintendency, one passage of which was a foretaste of what was to come. He saw the school as a factory, which was not new, but went on to describe the superintendent as a factory manager:

> In every branch of human labor the importance of supervision has grown with the specialization of labor. The more minute the division of labor, the greater the need of supervision. . . . [To each], what he has done is complete in itself. He has accepted his place in the plan about which he gives himself no anxiety. But his work is only a part, in the great plan. . . . He might acquire the knowledge, but at the expense of his efficiency in the special work he is to perform. Over him . . . stands one whose special work is to adjust the parts, make himself familiar with each, but freed from active work in any part. He is the overseer, the superintendent.

"MANUAL LABOR" SCHOOLS

In 1818, Joseph Green Cogswell, who would found Round Hill School, had visited a comples of schools at Hofwly, near Berne, Switzerland. The founder and principal of the schools was Phillip Emmanuel von Fellenberg, a Swiss aristocrat and one-time assistant to Pestalozzi. Von Fellenberg believed that, in the words of John Griscom, society was "divisible into three parts, the higher, the middling, and the poor." The higher were to be taught values; the lower, acceptance of their station in life. The Hofwyl schools were for the sons of the higher and the sons of the poor. They were boarding schools, intended, as we think of it now, both to educate and to socialize.

In von Fellenberg's school for the sons of the poor, pupils were taught piety and were to learn to be satisfied with their places in life. They were also taught elementary school subjects and, by working in shops and in the fields, vocational skills. That school was also an important model, a model for "manual labor" or "industrial" schools in the United States.

The apparent survival and application of von Fellenberg's model is informative. Its concepts were imported to the United States by several returning visitors, including John Griscom, who also visited Hofwyl in 1818. "Manual labor" academies were briefly popular in the United States for several reasons: exercise was good for students, costs were lower, and pupils would learn skills or trades. There was even a Society for Promoting Labor in Literary Institutions. But manual labor schools fell from popularity quickly, and the Society died before it held its first meeting. Perhaps it was inappropriate to teach trades and farming in academies that many attended so that they would not be mechanics or farmers.

It has been argued that the Morrill Act land grant universities showed the influence of the manual labor movement, and that may be. We will discuss land grant colleges in a later chapter. In the meantime, the manual labor academies were copied in Hawaii. New England missionaries had arrived there in 1821. Their first concern was to bring Christianity to the Hawaiians, the old fashioned hellfire-and-

FIGURE 5-4 Von Fellenberg's Institute at Hofwyl. From a nineteenth-century illustration republished in Paul Monroe, ed., *A Cyclopedia of Education*, Vol. 3 (New York: Macmillan, 1911).

brimstone Christianity which had regained favor in New England in the New Re-awakening. From this followed the familiar imperatives: to be saved one must know the Bible; for that it was necessary to know how to read, at first in one's own language and then in English. Common schools of a simple sort were established early. After that, it was important to teach Hawaiians everyday working skills. Girls and women were taught to spin and weave and sew, because cotton grew on Hawaii and the other islands, and inferentially so that the unclad naked shame of Hawaiian bodies would be hidden. Hawaiian students learned to farm, and they learned to be printers and bookbinders so that Bible translations and homilies could be given to prospective converts. The manual labor schools were not intended to be like academies in the United States.

In 1831, The Rev. Richard Armstrong came to Hawaii to do missionary work. Like several other missionaries, he became a government official, the "minister of education" of Hawaii. His son, Samuel Chapman Armstrong, who had "come home" to New England to attend college, became the commanding officer of a black regiment in the Civil War. He founded Hampton Institute in Virginia in 1868. Established for newly freed blacks, it operated on the lines of a manual labor school. That inspiration, he said in his autobiography, had come from the manual labor schools he had known in Hawaii. Manual labor schools, modeled directly after Hampton Institute and indirectly after the Hofwyl school, became one of the most popular, and, many thought, the most appropriate schools for free blacks. The influence of Hofwyl might have stopped there, but as it happened, it did not.

By the beginning of the 1880s, a few years after the Indian Victory at Little Big Horn, many concluded that it was cheaper (as well as more humane) to school Indians, or Native Americans, instead of shooting them. One possibility was to bring Indians, children or young adults, to school in the East. For a time Hampton Institute had an "Indian Department." Later, Indians attended Carlisle School in Pennsylvania, which followed Hampton Institute's—and von Fellenberg's—principles. We will return to the Carlisle School. Another obvious possibility was to build schools where the Indians were. In the Sioux reservation in what would become South Dakota, manual labor, or "work-and-study," schools were introduced. It was no accident, we are sure, that one of the first missionary teachers there in the 1880s, and the first superintendent of the reservation's schools, was Elaine Goodale, who had been a teacher at Hampton Institute. An "industrial room" was added to her schoolhouse immediately after she arrived. Manual labor schools were also established on the Navajo reservations in Southern Arizona and New Mexico. One of their promoters was a Navajo, J. C. Morgan, himself a graduate of Hampton Institute.

To trace the transit of the manual labor schools from Switzerland to the Navajo reservations, one starts by noting that the manual labor school, originated by von Fellenberg, became popular in the United States after John Griscom and others returned from visiting Hofwyl. We cannot show which missionaries, or missionary teachers, took the concept to Hawaii. Perhaps it was Richard Armstrong, who arrived in Hawaii the year the first manual labor school was opened there, was later an avid advirer of Horace Mann, and had a long-time interest in schools. We have General Armstrong's word that he brought the plan back from Hawaii. Richard Pratt, the founder of the Carlisle (Indian) School, was an admirer of Hampton Institute. Goodale, who set up manual labor schools for the Sioux, had taught enthusiastically at Hampton Institute, and Morgan had graduated from there. There are social reinventions, just as there are mechanical reinventions, but the record of the transmission of the manual labor school seems credible. Thriftiness aside, the manual labor school had benefits. Some benefits were to students. A sociologist might say that the manual labor schools were functional in that they contributed to the preservation of society. Perhaps, taking the long view, von Fellenberg's school for the poor did indeed do as he intended and teach them to accept their humble places in the world.

CATHOLICS AND SCHOOLING

The rapid growth and expansion of the common schools was accompanied by the development of an alternative educational system for the Catholic population in the United States. Opposition to Catholicism had been strong during the early Colonial period. Although greater toleration of Catholicism had developed during the late eighteenth and early nineteenth centuries, anti-Catholic feelings were never completely eliminated. A latent fear of Catholicism persisted among Protestants during the early nineteenth century and became intensified as increasing pressure resulted from the waves of large numbers of Catholic immigrants who came to the United States during the first half of the nineteenth century. In many respects a new phenomenon developed: *Catholic* became synonymous with foreigner.

Opposition to Catholic immigration to the United States became strong during the 1830s. Many native-born Americans feared that the massive Catholic immigration to the United States would transfer Papal, or "Romish," power to the North American continent. The Catholic Church in the United States was in fact going through a period of extraordinary growth. In Ohio, for example, there was not a single Catholic church in 1816. By 1830, there were twenty-four priests, twenty-one churches, a newspaper, college, and seminary.

Other factors during the late 1820s and early 1830s contributed to the "Catholic problem." In 1827, the Papal Jubilee of Leo XII was celebrated and led to an increased interest in Catholicism throughout the world. In the United States, Catholics attempted to win converts to their faith, which caused them to come increasingly to the attention of anti-Catholic groups within the country. Of even greater significance was the assembly by Bishop John England of Baltimore of the first Provincial Council of Catholicity, which met in Baltimore in October 1829. Ostensibly, England's purpose in calling the Council was to calm the fears of many native Americans about foreign churchmen taking control of the Catholic Church in the United States. It was intended to encourage the growth of a more American church with native, rather than foreign, leadership.

Rather than quieting nativistic fears, however, the Council had just the opposite effect. A total of thirty-eight decrees were issued by the Council. American Catholics were warned against corrupt translations of the Bible and were encouraged to build parochial schools for their children. The dangers inherent in a secular education were clearly outlined by the members of the Council. As they explained in their report,

> Listen not to those who would persuade you that religion can be separated from secular instruction. If your children, while they advance in human sciences, are not taught the science of the saints, their mind will be filled with every error, their hearts will be receptacles of every vice, and that very learning which they have acquired, in itself so good and so necessary, deprived of all that could shed on it the light of heaven, will be an additional means of destroying the happiness of the child, embittering still more the chalice of parental disappointment, and weakening the foundations of the social order.

Such statements tended to raise antagonism among non-Catholics.

During this early period, anti-Catholic sentiment was focused in New York, Philadelphia, Boston, and other urban centers. Organization of those opposed to the Catholics was relatively limited and ill defined. Beginning during the late 1820s, however, both in England and the United States an increasing number of tracts and articles critical of Catholicism were published. In New York on January 2, 1830, the first issue of the anti-Catholic newspaper *The Protestant* was published under the editorship of the Reverend George Bourne. Bourne saw himself as defending Protestantism against "Romish corruptions" and "monkish traditions." Although the newspaper initially met with opposition and underwent major editorial reorganization, its influence increased. Changing its name to *The Protestant Magazine* and becoming a monthly in 1833, it spawned other publications, such as *The Anti-Romanist*, which began publication as a weekly newspaper in 1834.

Anti-Catholic feelings were by no means limited to the press during the early 1830s. Under the leadership of Reverend W. C. Brownlee, the editor of *The Protestant*, and others, the New York Protestant Association was organized in 1832. The association was "to promote the principles of the Reformation by public discussions which shall illustrate the history and character of Popery." Meetings were open to the public, and Catholics were in regular attendance, although the Bishop of New York eventually prohibited priests from attending the meetings and answering the charges of the Protestants. Violence often interfered with the sessions. In May 1832, Catholics attending a meeting of the association became involved in a minor riot. At a meeting in 1835, where the subject "Is Popery Compatible with Civil Liberty?" was being discussed, a mob largely made up of Catholics broke into the hall where the meeting was being held, drove out the speakers, and destroyed the furniture.

Rioting and mob violence tended to create sympathy for the Protestant Association and focus attention on its cause. By the end of the decade published debates between the anti-Catholic and pro-Catholic groups were being regularly published in journals and newspapers. The outcome of these debates seems to have consistently been in the favor of the Catholics, and as a result a new type of strategy began to be employed by anti-Catholic groups. Beginning at this time a number of major anti-Catholic works were circulated and popularly received, including Anthony Gavin's *Master Key to Popery:* Scippio de Ricci's *Female Convents. Secrets of the Nunneries Disclosed*; Maria Monk's *Awful Disclosures of the Hotel Dieu Nunnery of Montreal*; and Richard Baxter's *Jesuit Juggling: Forty Popish Frauds Detected and Disclosed.* All these works depicted Catholicism as a highly immoral religion in which priests kept convents to avoid their vows of celibacy. They told of secret passageways connecting the homes of priests with convents and of the bodies of babies found abandoned under convents.

The establishment and running of schools by the Catholics was seen by many anti-Catholics as a deliberate attempt by the Catholic leadership to indoctrinate children, especially Protestant children, into their system of values and beliefs. Opposition was early directed against the organization of Catholic schools. In some instances, this opposition took the form of mob violence. In August 1834 the school run by a community of Ursuline teaching nuns was burned by an angry mob in Charlestown, Massachusetts.

The burning of the Ursuline convent in Charlestown brought national attention to the anti-Catholic movement. By 1836, the American Society to Promote the Principles of the Protestant Reformation had come into existence as an off-shoot of the New York Protestant Association. It was the first national group of its type. The group had two purposes: the first to distribute anti-Catholic materials that would make clear the threat of popery, and the second to convert Catholics to Protestantism. The group was extremely successful, sponsoring lecturers and organizing affiliate groups throughout the country.

If various Protestant groups feared the corruption of the Republic by the Catholics, the Catholics were likewise fearful of the corruption of their children's faith by Protestant educators and their schools. As the Common School Movement became an increasingly powerful force during the late 1830s and early 1840s, many Catholics saw it as posing a threat to the religious values that they held to be important. Religious materials were being consistently introduced into the curricula of the common schools. Above all, Catholics complained about the use of Protestant hymns, prayers, and, in particular, the King James version of the Bible as a regular part of the instruction. Even the reading of the Bible without interpretation was anti-Catholic.

The inclusion of "Christian" material in the curricula of the common schools had been suggested by nearly all the early leaders of the Common School Movement, including Horace Mann. Mann argued that a common core of Christianity could and should be taught in the common schools. Specific sectarian creeds and beliefs were to be transmitted through the home. Through appeals to the traditional Protestant doctrine that the Bible was the principal source of knowledge about Christianity, the Bible continued to be a major source of religious instruction in the common schools.

FIGURE 5-5 "The American River Ganges" by Thomas Nast, *Harper's Weekly*, Vol. 15, September 30, 1871, p. 916.

Mann's philosophy, while excluding the specific doctrines of any Protestant sect from the schools, did not exclude what may be termed a more general or universal Protestant outlook. It was this general Protestant philosophy, evident in the common schools, that many Catholics strongly opposed. They believed that their faith was the true faith. The recognition of other religious beliefs on an equal footing with Catholicism was a denial of the basic truths believed to be inherent in Catholicism.

It was in New York that the Catholic schools developed their strongest following. Although there were five Catholic schools in New York City when the first Plenary Council met in Baltimore in 1829, the schools were hardly able to meet the needs of the Catholic population of the city, which numbered approximately 35,000. Under the leadership of Catholic bishop John DuBois, attempts were made to cooperate with the Public School Society to provide Catholic children with schooling. Despite numerous attempts at compromise, the leaders of the Public School Society could not comprehend why Catholics, in particular the poor Irish, were unwilling to send their children to the Society's schools.

With the death of Bishop DuBois, John Hughes, DuBois's assistant, was ordained the bishop of New York. Hughes was forty-one when he became bishop and was highly energetic in defending the Catholic cause. Of poor Irish origins, Hughes established himself as a militant defender of Catholic interests.

When Hughes assumed the position of bishop in 1839, there were a total of about 60,000 Catholics living in New York City. Approximately 3,000 children attended the Catholic schools. Arguing that the entire population of Catholic children should be provided the opportunity to receive a Catholic education, Hughes sailed to Europe in the fall of 1839 to seek funds for a new college and seminary (later to become Fordham University) and to bring back priests and teachers who could work in the Catholic schools.

While Hughes was visiting Europe, the Governor of New York, William H. Seward, took a remarkable stand in his second annual report to the legislature. Seward had been informed that very few Irish Catholic children were attending the public schools. As a result, he called for a system of schools to be established at public expense that would be acceptable to the Catholics from a religious point of view. According to Seward, the Catholics had special educational needs. Calling for the establishment of schools in which teachers spoke the same language and were of the same religious faith as those whom they taught, Seward advocated a remarkably sensitive (for a Whig politician) and radical solution to the Catholic school problem.

The Catholic leadership, under the direction of Dr. John Power, who acted in Hughes's absence while he was in Europe, interpreted Seward's report as an invitation to apply for state funds to support their schools. Traveling to Albany and consulting with various legislators who were close to Seward, Power was encouraged to submit a request for a public subsidy for the Catholic schools in New York City.

The Catholics submitted a request to the New York Common Council legislature for financial support on the basis of need. The public opposition was overwhelming. Members of the Public School Society quickly objected to the petition.

Arguing that the Common School Fund was a civil fund intended to benefit all members of the community, the Public School Society asserted that the Catholics' schools served a limited and narrowly defined segment of the population. The Public School Society further argued, with some justification, that if public funds were given to the Catholics, then other sects would have an equal right to request support. Considering the limited resources available, the funds would be so seriously limited if the Catholic request received support that sectarian education would displace public or general education in New York City.

The Common Council rejected the Catholics' petition for funding after reviewing their request for a month. Hughes returned to the United States from Europe shortly afterward and launched into a major campaign to receive financial support for the Catholic schools. Compromises, including the revision of textbooks that were offensive to Catholics, with the Catholics were attempted by the Public School Society. What the Public School Society failed to understand was that Catholics were opposed not only to the schools and curricula of the Public School Society, but to the basic idea of common schooling as well. The Catholic outlook concerning the common schools and public education was clearly outlined in the Pastoral Letter of 1840 for the Provincial Council of Baltimore:

> . . . it is not through any reluctance on our part, to contribute whatever little we can to the prosperity of what are called the common institutions of the country, that we are always better pleased to have a separate system of education for the children of our communion, but because we have found by a painful experience, that in any common effort it was always expected our distinctive principles of religious belief and practice should be yielded to the demands of those who thought proper to charge us with error: . . .

Catholics' complaints were clearly justified. Readers, as the New York Common Council School Committee admitted, included passages offensive to the Catholics. The King James version of the Bible was used to the exclusion of any other translation. More important, the Catholics objected to non-Catholics interpreting scripture to their children.

In late September 1840, Hughes supervised the drafting of a new petition to the Common Council requesting funding for the Catholic schools. Significantly, the new request was not based on need, as the earlier request had been, but on a matter of conscience. It was argued that public school education was a threat to the morality of Catholic youth. Under the supervision of the Board of Aldermen, a debate was held, on October 29 and 30, to allow both the Catholics and the Protestants to present their respective points of view.

Hughes led the debate for the Catholics. Arguing that the Public School Society monopolized public education funds, he maintained that individuals who held different attitudes and beliefs concerning the education of their children were no less deserving of public support. Representing the position of the Public School Society was Theodore Sedwick. According to Sedwick, the Public School Society was not involved in any dogmatic Protestant instruction of the type that the Catholics were talking about, but instead a generalized moral education. He argued that sectarian views were not a part of the schools and should not be as long as they were supported by public funds.

Attempts were made by the committee of aldermen to reconcile the differences between the Public School Society and the Catholics. Compromises were proposed. Catholics offered to place their schools under the supervision of the Society. The Public School Society agreed to submit its textbooks to Catholics for review. Neither proposal was accepted by the other group.

After inspecting the schools of both groups and debating the issue for more than two months, the committee advised the Board of Aldermen, on January 11, 1841, to reject the Catholics' petition, which it did by a vote of fifteen to one. Having suffered defeat at the hands of the New York City aldermen, the Catholics took their case to the legislature in Albany.

Governor Seward, in his annual message in January 1841, again reconfirmed his support for the Catholics' receiving a share of the school fund. After prolonged discussion and debate, the legislature passed the MacLay Bill on April 9, 1842, which created a system of public common schools in New York City. Under the bill, no school teaching any religious doctrine was to receive financial support. This included the schools of the Public School Society. The bill also provided for Board of Education members to be elected by wards. The power of the Public School Society had been broken and, in its place, a more democratic ward system of representation established.

If the MacLay Bill represented a defeat for the Public School Society, it was by no means a victory for Catholics. The MacLay Bill had the effect of establishing a system of public schools in New York that were supposedly totally free of sectarian influences and that were ultimately under the control of a board of trustees drawn from the various wards of the city. The legislation also placed the schools under the supervision of the state superintendent of education. In July, following the passage of the bill, William J. Stone, a prominent nativist, was appointed to the superintendency. Despite the stipulation in the MacLay Bill that sectarian influences be excluded from the schools, Stone allowed the use of the King James version of the Bible in the schools during his term of office. Following various protests, Catholics received some relief by bringing pressure to bear through their elected trustees.

The Catholic school controversy had three major effects that are of particular importance for the subsequent history of American education and culture. The first was to exacerbate the feelings that were held by the nativists against the Catholics during the period. The second was to undermine the domination of the New York City schools by the Public School Society and to substitute in its place a system of public common schools administered by ward-elected commissioners or trustees. Finally, it encouraged Catholics to establish an extensive system of parochial schools.

THE DISPOSSESSED: BLACKS

Slavery in the South during the earlier 1800s had become a carefully regulated institution. Slave codes prohibited slaves from owning property, from leaving a master's land without specific permission, and from striking a white man even in self-defense. Throughout the South state laws prohibited slaves' being taught to read or write. In Mississippi, for example, an 1832 law made illegal the assembly of "slaves, free Negroes, or mulattoes" for the purpose of teaching them reading or writing. In Louisiana an 1830 law said that

> . . . all persons who shall teach, or permit or cause to be taught, any slave in this state, to read, or write, shall, upon conviction thereof, . . . be imprisoned not more [sic] than one month nor more than twelve months.

Legislation after 1820 would rest upon the conviction that education of slaves had the "tendency to excite dissatisfaction in their minds, and to produce insurrection and rebellion." In North Carolina a law provided for fines of from $100 to $200 upon any white selling a book to or teaching a slave to read. A free black teaching a slave to read could be lashed at least twenty times with a whip. A slave guilty of teaching another slave to read or write was to be sentenced to thirty-nine lashes. As the law implied, there were some free blacks and slaves who had learned to read.

The most important justification for not educating slaves was that educated slaves would be much more likely to rebel than would those who were kept in ignorance. Insurrections were a dread and a real problem. In 1800 "Colonel" Gabriel Prosser organized in revolt outside Richmond a thousand slaves. In 1822 free black Denmark Vesey attempted to organize a major revolt in Charleston, South Carolina. A rebellion in 1831 under the leadership of slave preacher Nat Turner in southeastern Virginia caused the death of sixty white men, women, and children.

Slave tradition, custom, and oral learning formed a subculture that could not be eradicated. The rhythms of African music would echo in spirituals and re-echo in jazz. On the isolated Sea Islands of Georgia, Gulla, an African language, has been preserved. Although some families were broken up when a member was "sold down the river" (to Louisiana sugar cane plantations), there were many stable and extended slave families.

Although slavery had been abolished in the northern states by 1825, blacks in the North were not welcomed, not treated as equals, and not encouraged to become educated. Even during the 1840s, during the Common School Revival, blacks were discriminated against in schooling. In New York City the "African School" had reopened, and in spite of the efforts of some blacks and their white supporters schools were segregated there. Chicago elementary schools were only briefly segregated. In Massachusetts segregated schools were banned in 1852. But these were exceptions. Because blacks could not become members of white literary societies and lyceums, they established black literary societies to provide libraries and reading rooms for blacks and to encourage the literary endeavors of their members.

As was to have been suspected, some abolitionists supported and encouraged the schooling of blacks, and so provided many with a ready excuse for not supporting it. Leon Litwak, in *North of Slavery: The Negro and Free States, 1790–1860*, provides one account of the interesting example of Prudence Crandall's school for black girls.

Crandall, a young Quaker, established in 1831 a successful academy for girls in Canterbury, Connecticut. In its second year she admitted a black. Parents of white girls immediately protested. Community support for the school ended. Crandall contacted leading abolitionists, including William Lloyd Garrison, about the possibility of opening the school for black girls and women only. With the support of major black leaders in the North, Crandall opened an academy for black women and girls in 1833.

Canterbury's citizens violently opposed the school. They argued that it would lower the value of town property, and that blacks living in the town would claim to be the equals of black students, and so equal to white citizens. They saw the school as an abolitionist plot to foist "upon the community a new species of gentility, in the shape of sable belles."

Canterbury townspeople offered to purchase Crandall's home and school, but she persisted. When the school opened in April 1833, Crandall and her students were repeatedly harassed. Manure was thrown down the school's well. A physician refused to treat ill students, and town officials threatened to enact vagrancy laws against them. The town appealed to the Connecticut state legislature to take action against the school.

It passed a law prohibiting the establishment of any school for the education of blacks who did not live in the state. Crandall refused to close the school and was arrested. When she was first tried, the jury could not reach a verdict. In a second trial she was convicted, but for technical reasons, the case was overturned in appellate court. Attacks against the school continued, and there was attempted arson. Finally, in 1834, Crandall closed her school and left Canterbury.

THE DISPOSSESSED: NATIVE AMERICANS, INDIANS

Between 1778 and 1871 the United States made a total of 389 treaties with tribal groups. Together they would put under federal control 1,000,000,000 acres of land, four-tenths of the area of the United States. "Reservations" would retain 155,000,000 acres for the Indians, one-seventh of the total, and that would later be halved. The federal government promised to provide medical, educational, and technical services.

In 1819, when the Office of Indian Affairs was established, government funds for Indian schools were available for the first time. As President James Monroe wished, Indians were to be introduced to "the habits and arts of civilization." Money for support of schools was turned over to Protestant missionary programs, which were to be responsible for establishing and operating the schools.

The Choctaw mission school was operated by missionaries of the Congregational Church. In 1822 The Reverend Cyrus Kingsbury, superintendent of the school, reported to Secretary of War John C. Calhoun that the school for Indian boys employed the monitorial method of instruction. In addition to employing the boys in various agriculture endeavors, some were being taught blacksmithing. Women attending the female school were being taught domestic skills. The school was as much as possible self-supporting.

By the middle of the 1820s, the Indian "civilization" policy was widely supported. In 1824 the Committee on Indian Affairs of the House of Representatives reported that since 1819 eighteen new Indian schools had been established under federal sponsorship. As the Committee reported,

> It requires but little research to convince every candid mind that the prospect of civilizing our Indians was never so promising as at this time. . . . The instruction and civilization of a few enterprising youths will have an immense influence on the tribes to which they belong.

According to the Committee the educational program it supported would grow in "geometrical proportion" as "civilized" Indians convinced others of the virtues of the white man's culture. That prediction was overly optimistic. Prior to the Civil War attempts to provide schooling for various Indian groups would largely be failures. Tribal resistance made the work of missionary educators extremely difficult. Few promoters of Indian schooling were aware that most Indians saw themselves as surrendering their own culture and tradition if they accepted the white man's civilization.

CONCLUSION

The mid-1800s saw massive growth of the common school movement. Blacks and Indians were neglected, but by the Civil War high schools were being added to common school system. Public high schools would replace nearly all the academies.

Accompanying the growth of the city schools was increasing regulation. Curriculum and textbooks were regularized and books such as *McGuffey's* were sold by the million. As enrollments increased, school administration became more important.

In the schools that developed in the nineteenth century are rooted many of the traditions responsible for shaping schools of our times. Their development encouraged that of Catholic schools, still important alternatives to public schooling. But the structure and intent of the schools was not unchangeable or unchanging and in the next decades alternative approaches would appear.

Chapter Six
SCHOOLING
AND INDUSTRIALISM

The year 1876 was an important psychological turning point for the American people. During its first century the United States had emerged as a major social, political, and economic power. Western expansion had opened new lands and provided new opportunities. Three foreign wars and a Civil War tested the strength and will of the American people. The population had grown tenfold, swollen by waves of European immigrants. The centennial provided an opportunity to pause and reflect on what had happened over the course of the preceding century and to consider the possibilities for the future.

Americans did not celebrate their centennial alone. Numerous foreigners came to the United States in 1876. Most came to participate in the Centennial Exhibition held in Fairmount Park in Philadelphia. If foreign visitors came to the United States to celebrate its accomplishments, they rarely left without commenting about the Americans and their culture. Among the most perceptive of these visitors, particularly concerning matters related to education, was the French educator M. Ferdinand Buisson.

Buisson came to the United States in 1876, as the French Commissioner of Education, to attend the Philadelphia Centennial Exhibition. Although mainly concerned with preparing exhibits for the fair, Buisson met numerous American educators and also visited schools throughout the country. His reactions to these experiences were recorded in the report that he and his staff submitted on their return to France.

Buisson explained that schooling in the United States had become an essential part of the system of state and local government. As he perceived it the Americans saw education as being far too important an issue to leave in private hands. They had united their national destiny with their system of public schools. As the early republican educational theorists had hoped, the schools served the function of educating the nation's children to be patriots.

Buisson also recognized that the public schools were to be the primary means by which immigrant children were drawn away from their traditional cultures and Americanized. In his comments, Buisson was clearly critical of the idea of biculturalism. His praise of the American school system focused on its ability to take its recently arrived immigrants and to assimilate them quickly into the mainstream of the culture.

Yet political and cultural socialization were not the only distinguishing features that Buisson recognized as part of the American public school system. Economic growth and development were also clearly linked to the American educational system:

> If the political future of the United States depends on the efficiency of her schools, her commercial future is no less directly interested. The conditions of labor in the New World are such that success depends, as it were, on a certain degree of education. . . . Education has a double value: it has besides its real value a kind of surplus value, resulting from its practical and commercial usefulness. . . . The wealth of the United States is incalculable precisely because intellectual wealth counts for an enormous proportion. We sometimes think that the eagerness of the Americans to support and improve schools is a kind of national pride, vanity or show. Not at all. It is a calculation, and a sound one; enormous advances are made, but it is known that they will be returned a hundredfold.

Buisson's comments are confirmed by the educational trends evident in American schools during the second half of the nineteenth century. Beginning approximately at the time of the Civil War, American education became increasingly focused on issues related to industrial and technical training. In the case of higher education, this interest can be seen in the passage of the Land Grant College Act on July 2, 1862.

INDUSTRY AND EDUCATION

The Land Grant College Act, or Morrill Act, granted federal funding for the support of colleges and universities whose primary purpose was to teach engineering and agriculture. Under the grant, payments for the sale of federally owned lands were turned over to the different states to set up agricultural and engineering colleges.

Each state received 30,000 acres of land for each of its senators and congressmen. Money from these sales was to be invested at a rate of no less than 5 percent a year, thus providing a perpetual endowment for the schools. A total of 17,430,000 acres of land was eventually turned over to the states. California, Ohio, Arkansas, and West Virginia used the money to establish state universities with agricultural and engineering programs. In Connecticut, the money received from the Land Grant College Act was used to support the Sheffield Scientific School at Yale. In New York, special funds were provided to Cornell for the establishment of its agricultural and engineering programs. The same type of program was set up in Indiana at Purdue University.

The establishment of the land grant colleges was clearly a major redirection in American higher education. But the program was not without controversy. Questions arose as to the relationship of these new technically oriented universities with the older and more traditional private colleges and universities. The land grant schools were also reflections of an increasing process of modernization and industrialization sweeping across American culture. Higher education was seen in a new light. In 1872, the dean of the college of agriculture at the University of Missouri was maintaining that the purpose of the college was to "teach the science of high production" and to make farming competitive in attracting the nation's most talented youth.

The establishment of the land grant colleges reflects an increasing tendency toward the "industrialization" of American education. This was also evident at the elementary and high school levels. For example, programs in art education were first established in American schools in Massachusetts during the late 1860s. These courses were not to improve the aesthetic sensibilities of the children attending the schools, but to train skilled draftsmen for industry.

Unitarian minister Edward Everett Hale maintained the need to establish art programs as part of the Massachusetts public school system was for their contribution to the development of the Massachusetts industrial system. As he explained,

> It will be impossible for Massachusetts to maintain any eminence in the higher manufactures if the great body of workmen of other countries are the superiors to our own in the arts of design, in the drafting of machinery, and in the habits of observation which spring from such accomplishments.

American interest in vocational training can be traced back to the early Colonial period. Besides traditional apprenticeship methods of instruction, proposals as early as the end of the seventeenth century can be found supporting the establishment of schools that would instruct children in basic trades.

Thomas Budd, for example, in his work *Good Order Established in Pennsylvania and New Jersey* (1685), had argued that schools should be established throughout the cities and towns of Pennsylvania and New Jersey that would not only teach Latin and English, but also provide instruction in trades such as the making of mathematical instruments, woodworking, clock making, weaving, and shoemaking. In his *Proposals Relating to the Education of Youth in Pennsylvania* (1749), Benjamin Franklin repeated many of Budd's arguments.

Yet the origins of what can accurately be called modern industrial education in the United States did not occur until the first decades of the nineteenth century. During the 1820s, vocational instruction was included as an important part of the educational programs of reform schools such as Boston's House of Reformation, and Philadelphia's and New York's Houses of Refuge. Training in these programs was simply to have the children attending the reform schools contribute to their own support and to teach morality and sound work habits.

The first major attempt to develop a systematic industrial education program in the United States was in conjunction with the school established during the 1820s by Robert Owen at New Harmony, Indiana. Owen, whose work at New Harmony was discussed in Chapter 3, placed particular emphasis upon manual and vocational training. Taxidermy, printing, engraving, drawing, carpentry, wheelwrighting, woodturning, blacksmithing, cabinet making, hatmaking, shoemaking, agriculture, washing, cooking, sewing, housekeeping, and dressmaking were among the subjects taught. Although Owen's utopian and educational experiment at New Harmony was ultimately a failure, it was an important early attempt to systematically introduce manual and industrial training into an educational program.

During the first half of the nineteenth century, a number of orphan asylums in the United States also included programs in vocational training. Among the best known was the program at Girard College in Philadelphia. Programs emphasizing several types of craft training were developed within a few years after the opening of the college in 1848. By 1864, provisions were made for the orphans at the college to learn trades as sophisticated as typesetting, printing, bookbinding, woodturning, photography, and even telegraphy.

Important programs in manual and industrial training were introduced by individuals such as General Samuel Chapman Armstrong at Hampton Institute in Virginia during the late 1860s, but it was not until the late 1870s that widespread interest in industrial education began to develop throughout the United States. Much of the foundation for this interest was the result of a modest exhibit of Russian drawings, tools, and models used for teaching manual and industrial arts that were on display at the 1876 Philadelphia Centennial Exposition.

The Russian materials were sent to the Exposition by the Moscow Imperial Technical School and were based on the work of its director, Victor Della Vos. Begun in 1830, the school was reorganized in 1868 under imperial sponsorship. Primarily for training draftsmen, industrial foremen, and chemists, as well as civil and mechanical engineers, the school provided not only theoretical training in various specialized fields, but also practical courses in subjects such as wood turning, carpentry, metal turning, fitting, and forging.

Under the supervision of Della Vos, the school's new system of manual and industrial training was developed during the late 1860s. It deemphasized apprenticeship training and focused instead on the principles of design inherent in the manual arts. Rather than following the traditional apprenticeship method in which a student learned a trade or craft by copying the work of a master craftsman, students under the Della Vos system learned the basic principles of design and fabrication that were the basis of the manual or merchanical arts. Della Vos's purpose was to teach students to become skilled in each craft area as quickly as possible and to learn the proper use of tools in each of the manual arts.

As part of his system of instruction, the following procedures were laid out: (1) each mechanical art or trade, such as metal forging, wood joinery, or carpentry, was assigned a separate instruction shop; (2) each shop had as many working places and separate sets of tools as students; (3) exercises done by the students were arranged in a hierarchy of difficulty; (4) all work was done from drawings rather than models; (5) drawings used by students in the beginning classes were prepared by students in the advanced classes; (6) students could not advance to a new project unless they had completed what they were working on and it had been approved by the instructor; (7) the grading of projects became stricter as the student advanced in the program; and (8) each instructor teaching a specialized trade, such as carpentry or forging, had to be an expert in his area. Training at the Imperial Technical School was at both the secondary level and the collegiate level and took three years to complete for each level.

When Della Vos's method was put on display at the Centennial Exposition in 1876, the possibilities of using it in an American context were immediately recognized. For example, John D. Runkle (1822-1902), the president of the Massachusetts Institute of Technology, recalled how

> At Philadelphia, in 1876, almost the first thing I saw was a small case containing three series of models, one of chipping and filing, one of forging, and one of machine tool work. I saw at once that they were not parts of machines, but simply graded models for teaching manipulations in those arts. In an instant, the problem I had been seeking to solve was clear to my mind; a plain distinction between a mechanic art and its application in some special trade became apparent.

Runkle's interest in the Russian exhibit was a result of his experience with the problem of providing shop training for engineering students. On his return from the Centennial Exposition, Runkle recommended the establishment of a program in shop training based upon the Della Vos Method.

On August 17, 1876, the trustees of M.I.T. approved not only a set of shops for the students in engineering, but also a School of Mechanic Arts at the secondary level for those interested in receiving general industrial training.

Runkle was soon promoting Della Vos's method in reports to the Massachusetts Board of Education and the National Education Association. According to Runkle, students from M.I.T. trained under the method were clearly superior in shop skills to students trained under the more traditional apprenticeship system. Claims were made that if the Della Vos method came into wide use in the schools, it would be possible to double national production and to increase the wages of laborers by 300 percent. Through the introduction of Della Vos's system, workers

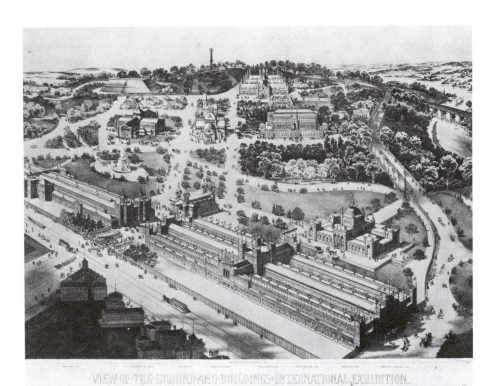

FIGURE 6-1 The Philadelphia Centennial Exposition, 1776, attracted millions of visitors. John D. Runkle saw there examples of the work in Victor Della Vos's Moscow school. The Corliss engine was in Machinery Hall, a glass-sided building a quarter mile long and covering almost thirteen acres. The Bettman Archive.

would be elevated not only in terms of their skills, but in their social status as well. Conflicts between labor and management would be eliminated. Unionism, which was just beginning to emerge as a force at this time, would cease as a result of not having a cause or reason to exist.

Runkle's suggestion of establishing mechanic arts schools as part of the public school system quickly came to the attention of Calvin Woodward. Woodward was a professor of mathematics and applied mechanics and dean of the Polytechnic (Engineering) faculty at Washington University, Saint Louis. An experienced secondary and university teacher, Woodward, like Runkle, faced the problem of providing engineering students with training in shop skills. Having established shop training as part of the university program as early as 1872, Woodward began to argue the need for industrial training, not only as part of the program of specialized polytechnical schools, but also in the public schools in general.

In 1877, Woodward acquired the use of an old dormitory known as the Philbert Mansion to set up a more extensive workshop for his students. Charles F.

White, who had attended the Worcester Free Institute and the Stevens Institute of Technology, became the shop superintendent. Under White's direction, graded exercises in the use of machine tools were introduced as part of the program. White had seen the Della Vos method at the Centennial Exposition and had developed his own exercises based on it. In the Philbert Mansion were a blacksmith shop, a machine shop equipped with vises and lathes, and a woodworking shop.

In May of 1878, in an address before the Saint Louis Social Science Association, Woodward called for the establishment of a secondary school emphasizing both intellectual and manual training. With the help of Samuel Cupples, a Saint Louis businessman and philanthropist, Woodward began to assemble the support necessary for a new secondary school. After lengthy discussion, it was agreed that the Manual Training School be established as a permanent part of Washington University's Polytechnic School. Instruction in the new school would include mathematics, drawing, the English branches of the high school curriculum, and training in the use of tools.

A new building was completed for the school in the summer of 1880. Opening for classes the following September, the school was to provide students with a liberal education that emphasized the development of mechanical arts and skills rather than a specific vocational training. The school's program took three years to complete. By electing to take a foreign language as part of their coursework, students were able to complete three years of college preparation at the school. Most students, however, were expected to enter the work force once they had completed their course of study at the school.

The Manual Training School was an immediate success. Enrollment increased from fifty students in September 1880 to 176 students when the first class graduated in June 1883. While interest quickly developed throughout the nation in the school and its programs, there emerged at the same time a strong antimanual-training sentiment among many educators. According to Lawrence Cremin, the debate that developed during the 1880s over the acceptance or rejection of manual training in the schools was the most vigorous pedagogical battle of the decade.

As one would expect, Woodward led the promanual-training forces. Support came from many sources. Graduates of the program vigorously promoted the establishment of new manual training schools throughout the country. On February 4, 1884, the second manual training school in the United States was opened in Chicago. Known as the Chicago Manual Training School, the school was privately supported. On March 3, 1884, the first publicly supported manual training high school was opened in Baltimore. The programs of these schools were closely modeled after those of Woodward's schools in Saint Louis. Before the end of the decade, manual training schools could also be found in cities such as Philadelphia, Toledo, Cincinnati, New Orleans, Brooklyn, and Cambridge, Massachusetts.

Woodward believed that manual training could provide students with a balanced general education. Writing in 1887, he argued that manual training programs would not only encourage students to stay in school longer, but also provide them with a superior intellectual background. Besides material success, the educa-

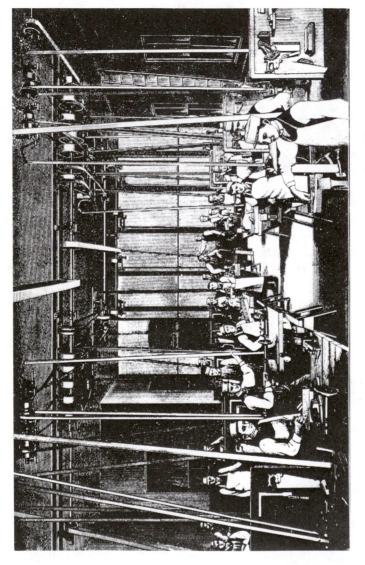

FIGURE 6-2 The woodworking shop of the Manual Training Institute, Washington University. From C.M. Woodward, *The Manual Training School* (Boston: D.C. Heath & Co., 1887), p. 26.

tion provided by the manual training schools would help the worker deal with the demands of an increasingly complex technological society:

> The new education will give more complete development, versatility, and adaptability to circumstance. No liberally trained workman can be a slave to method, or depend upon the demand for a particular article or kind of labor. It is only the uneducated, unintelligent mechanic who suffers from the invention of a new tool.

Significantly, opposition to Woodward's ideas came not only from traditional educators, but from an important part of the labor movement as well. A survey in New York in 1886 showed that the state's labor organizations favored trade schools and manual training by a margin of only two to one. Manual training further weakened traditional apprenticeship programs. Although cooperative efforts were gradually worked out between the various labor organizations and many of the early manual training programs, opposition came from powerful union leaders such as Samuel Gompers, who argued that the workmen produced by the manual training schools not only did botched work, but that they undercut the wages of skilled union workers as well.

Organized labor's opposition to manual training focused primarily on its introduction at the elementary level. Arguing that children were inadequately trained in various crafts, critics felt that emphasis on manual training denied the worker's children the opportunity to study more traditional subjects. D. J. O'Donoghue, writing in the *American Federationist* in 1895, for example, argued that

> . . . even now too many children are obliged to leave school and fight for a livelihood long before they are grounded in even a fair elementary education, and yet we are told, and many of us are gullible enough to believe, that the time which is now devoted to imparting such an education in our public schools could, with advantage, be reduced so that our children may receive a technical education—and their minds directed away from higher pursuit! . . . A little careful attention on the part of the careful workingman will readily demonstrate that the first aim of the average advocate of manual training in the public schools is that of *utility*, rather than physical or intellectual improvement.

Schoolmen presented similar arguments. Among the most important of these critics was William Torrey Harris. Harris was the superintendent of the Saint Louis public schools from 1868 to 1880. Among the most distinguished American educators of the second half of the nineteenth century, Harris later headed the Concord School of Philosophy and served as U.S. Commissioner of Education from 1889 until 1906. His work combined both the practical and the theoretical. Under his supervision, the Saint Louis schools became known throughout the nation as a center for innovation in education. As the leading Hegelian philosopher in the United States, Harris spearheaded what became known as the "Saint Louis Movement," or

"American Hegelian Movement," in philosophy. Harris was editor of the *Journal of Speculative Philosophy*, the first modern scholarly philosophy journal published in America. Besides providing a forum for the dissemination of German philosophical ideas, Harris's journal had the distinction of publishing the first articles of a young Vermont high school teacher named John Dewey.

Harris, like Horace Mann, believed that universal public elementary education would provide the children of the working class the tools by which to participate in the more general culture. He defined these tools as being grammar, literature and art, mathematics, geography, and history. Through their use, these "five windows of the soul" would allow the child the means by which to master both the mysteries of nature and of the human mind. Harris opposed the movement because it emphasized the physical development of individuals instead of their spiritual development. Harris felt that manual training did nothing to develop the higher faculties of the individual. Training in manual arts, such as woodworking or forging, provided children with only a limited knowledge of themselves and nature.

Described by the historian Merle Curti as a "conservator," Harris supported a capitalist economic system. He felt that socialism discouraged the initiative of the individual, an initiative that was critical to the creative growth and development of the culture. As a follower of the German philosopher Hegel, Harris saw the process of history as being an ever more powerful movement of the individual toward personal freedom and away from domination by the group. For Harris, manual training did not contribute to the development of the individual's spirit. Hence, Harris rejected the ideas outlined by Karl Marx in *Das Kapital (Capital)* and argued that in making his profits, the businessman or industrialist was in fact benefiting the entire society by developing more effective means of production and distribution, as well as by providing jobs for workers.

Despite arguments such as Harris's, support for the manual training movement increased during the last decades of the nineteenth century. Educators throughout the country argued that manual training would provide modern factory workers an effective means by which their children could receive the technical training necessary for them to be able to succeed in work.

Through the introduction of manual training in the schools, a partial solution was provided to the problems imposed by industrialization in the United States. The increasing use of mass production techniques meant that the worker did an increasingly narrow range of work. Under the older craftsman and artisan system, a clock, for instance, was made from beginning to end by a single highly trained individual. As an example, using mass production techniques factories employed dozens of workers doing different tasks to make a single clock. Although efficiency was gained, the new methods left the worker with little sense of accomplishment at having produced a complete item or gained an actual understanding of the work process.

The tradition of the craftsperson and skilled worker was giving way to a new ideal of efficiency. Unlike traditional craftsmen, the new industrial workers in most instances had neither the means nor the skills to provide their children with the training necessary to effectively enter the work force. As a result, it became necessary for the school to assume many of the functions of the more traditional education. According to many educators of the period, children would once again have reinforced in them the traditional values of industriousness, thrift, and pride in work through the virtues inherent in manual training.

Marvin Lazerson has maintained that the manual training movement was perceived as a means of reconstituting American society. It was also seen as a vehicle for social reform. By providing practical education and training that would be of value in the everyday world of work, manual training would help reduce truancy among the children of industrial workers.

Although compulsory education laws had been enacted in Massachusetts as early as 1852, such legislation had met with only limited success. Under the 1852 law, children under fifteen could only be employed if they had received three months of schooling in the year prior to their employment. Attempts to make the law apply to children working on farms and in stores, as well as to factory workers, failed. Similar legislation was passed prior to the Civil War in northern states such as Rhode Island, Connecticut, Vermont, New Hampshire, Maine, and Pennsylvania.

Factory owners and the parents of working children often found ways to get around the compulsory school attendance laws. Careful birth and school attendance records were deliberately not kept by many factory owners so that they could not be held responsible for violations of the compulsory schooling laws. Children were often moved from one factory to another every nine months to avoid the requirement of being in school at least three months each year. Parents often cooperated in having their children work in the factories rather than attend the schools.

Although greed, and possibly fear, often motivated the parents of child laborers to cooperate with factory owners in ignoring the laws, economic survival must also have been a factor for many parents in sending their children to work. A working child could contribute an additional quarter or third to the income of a family, which in a period of extremely low wages could provide the additional means necessary for a family to survive.

Lucy Larcom (1824–1893), a one-time child worker, recalled in her autobiography, *A New England Girlhood* (Boston, 1889), how important her working in a factory was for her family.

> When I took my next three months at the grammar school, everything there was changed, and I too was changed. . . . It was a great delight for me to study, and at the end of three months the master told me that I was prepared for high school.
> But alas! I could not go. The little money I could earn—one dollar a week, besides the price of my board—was needed in the family, and I must return to the mill. It was a severe disappointment to me, though I did not say so at home.

Stephen A. Knight, another former child worker, recalled working in a cotton mill during the mid-1830s for approximately fourteen hours per day, with a half hour out for breakfast and lunch. Knight was paid 42 cents per week, or 7 cents a day—an hourly rate of one-half cent!

The success of city and state reform schools by the late 1860s is indicated by their proliferation throughout the country. In their 1867 survey, *Report on the Prisons and Reformatories of the United States and Canada*, Enoch C. Wines and Theodore W. Dwight noted the existence of seven state reform schools outside of New York State, as well as municipally sponsored reform schools in cities such as Providence, Cincinnati, Louisville, Baltimore, Saint Louis, and Chicago.

As an attempt to prevent children from becoming delinquents, the New York Children's Aid society (1853), the Boston Children's Aid Society (1864), and other groups were organized. Their work was part of the earliest attempts in the United States to respond to the problems of children living in an urban environment. Earlier groups, such as the New York Association for Improving the Condition of the Poor (AICP) established in 1843, had attempted to address the miserable living conditions that had begun to develop in New York and other major cities by the end of the Jacksonian era. Arguing that individuals raised in the squalid moral and social conditions of the slums would be insensitive to Christian morality, the AICP attacked the overcrowded conditions of the slums, the lack of adequate sanitary facilities, poor ventilation in buildings, and the general conditions that they felt produced disease, intemperance, and a lack of morals among the urban poor.

The AICP assumed throughout its early years that an enlightened capitalist system could provide good housing for the working class and still make a substantial profit on its investment. Promoting the development of housing with superior structural and sanitary features, the AICP built its first model tenement in 1854. Located near Elizabeth and Mott Streets, near what today is Chinatown in New York City, the building had nearly 100 units renting from $5.50 to $8.50 per month. The project proved to be a financial failure and was sold by the AICP in 1867. Degenerating into one of the worst tenements in the city, the building was actually condemned by a committee of the AICP during the 1880s. Far too often investors sought the maximum profit possible from the buildings they owned. Tenements were built as cheaply as possible, while forcing together as many people as possible in the smallest amount of space.

If attempts to improve the physical conditions of the urban poor met with little success during this early period, greater success was achieved with the various child welfare agencies such as the New York Children's Aid Society. Founded by Charles Loring Brace in 1853, the society had as its purpose meeting the needs of the destitute children of New York. Brace, a minister, set up Sunday meetings, established industrial schools, opened lodging houses for newsboys, and established reading rooms for poor children. Acutely aware of the physical and personal needs of poor urban children. Brace and the Children's Aid Society were also intent on providing them with religious and moral training. In doing so, Brace felt that the integrity of the American political system would be maintained. Referring to the boys and girls served by the Children's Aid Society, Brace argued in his work. *The Dangerous Classes* of New York (1880) that they would

. . . soon form the great lower class of our city. They will influence elections; they may shape the policy of the city; they will, assuredly, if unreclaimed, poison society all around them. They will help to form the great multitude of robbers, thieves, vagrants, and prostitutes who are now such a burden upon the law-respecting community.

Other sources from the period confirm that the children of the poor were perceived as being potentially dangerous to the future political stability of the nation. Wines and Dwight in their 1867 report on prisons and reformatories strongly recommended that compulsory education laws be established in every state in order to insure that all children learn proper moral habits and industriousness.

Calling for the establishment of public nurseries and industrial schools, Wines and Dwight clearly saw such institutions as providing substitutes for the family. Arguing that the discipline of the industrial schools should be of the family character, they explained that the arrangements of the schools should be such that they would

. . . cultivate industrious habits, and prepare their inmates for the stations they are afterwards to fill.

Practical labor promoting moral development was advocated as fundamental to the purposes of industrial schools. Skills for the workshop or farm or home, suitable

FIGURE 6-3 The night school of the Children's Aid Society. From *Harper's New Monthly Magazine*, Vol. 47, August 1873, p. 327.

kinds of recreation, and particularly appropriate schooling would reform poor urban children and provide them with the kinds of character and skills necessary to become members of the larger American culture.

The initiators of child welfare reform programs, such as the Children's Aid Society, obviously did much to meet the immediate needs of poor children. They also consciously tried to impress upon their charges a specific set of moral values and limited economic expectations. We agree with Samuel Bowles and Herbert Gintis, who argue in *Schooling in Capitalist America* that most educational re- formers during the later nineteenth century did not question capitalists' ownership and control of production. The purpose of educators was to help "preserve and extend the capitalist order." Schools were intended to inculcate students with values supporting the existing social system. If they were successful—the point is moot without good evidence—the schools contributed to the strength of the existing order and also encouraged its further expansion and growth.

Nearly a century ago the French sociologist Emile Durkheim pointed out that almost all educational systems tend to perpetuate the existing values and traditions of the cultures of which they are parts. In fact, Durkheim argued that it would be foolish to imagine that an educational system could exist for very long if it did not serve to maintain the status quo. Conservatism, rather than change, is encouraged by most educational systems, a conservatism that preserves existing power struc- tures and sources of influence and privilege within the society. The extent to which this is true can be and has been debated at great length. Simple answers are not evi- dent. In any case, Durkheimian and anti-Durkheimian arguments both rest on the assumption that educational systems have been or are successful in transmitting to pupils values or traditions. There is no hard, clear demonstration, historical or sociological, that this is true.

If the present social order is accepted by the educator, he or she may still favor mobility of the individual within that system, and most educators have at least paid lip service to that. In carefully examining the past of American schools, it is clear that schooling has, even at the same time and place, held some back and given others the means to advance socially and economically. Nevertheless, school systems, like other organizations, usually function to preserve themselves and their existing practices. Even so, some have been able to use schools to meet their needs and approach their personal goals.

LYCEUMS AND LIBRARIES

During the first half of the nineteenth century, institutions other than schools played increasingly important roles in the education of many Americans. As early as 1826, Josiah Holbrook (1788-1854), a graduate of Yale, had organized the first lyceum in Massachusetts. Loosely organized, the purpose of the lyceum was to sponsor lecturers, to encourage the public discussion of ideas, and to provide read- ing material for the general public. According to Holbrook in his *Proposal for a*

Constitution for the American Lyceum (1828), the object of the lyceum was the promotion of "useful knowledge" among its members and the advancement of popular education by encouraging improvements in the common schools. Because the services of the leading speakers of the period were enlisted, interest in the lyceum movement spread rapidly. By 1830, approximately 3,000 communities in the United States had such organizations, providing a major source of adult education.

The lyceum movement, as shown by its widespread popularity, was an important vehicle of popular education. Closely paralleling the movement was the rapid proliferation and development of libraries. Although individuals including Benjamin Franklin had supported the development of free libraries in America as early as the middle of the eighteenth century, it was not until the beginning of the nineteenth century that libraries began to be available to the public on a widespread basis.

As early as 1820, the Boston Apprentice's Library was formed. In 1829 a similar library was set up in New York City. Mercantile libraries were organized in business districts in various East Coast and Midwestern cities. In 1849, New Hampshire passed the first law establishing libraries on a statewide basis. Yet, despite the steady growth of interest in libraries, it was not until the last quarter of the nineteenth century that successful attempts were undertaken to organize the library movement on a national basis.

Although a convention of leading American librarians was called as early as 1853 to set up a national library organization, it was not until 1876 that this goal was finally accomplished. Under the direction of Melvil Dewey, the librarian at Amherst College and the creator of the Dewey Decimal System, a meeting of librarians was held in October of 1876 as part of the Centennial Exposition in Philadelphia. Ninety men and thirteen women attended the meeting. By the meeting's end, the American Library Association had been organized with Justin Winsor, a Boston librarian, as its head.

At the American Library Association meeting, the U.S. Bureau of Education presented a massive two-volume report on the *Public Libraries of the United States.* The most detailed and comprehensive document produced until then addressing library organization and history, the report also included the first comprehensive explanation of Dewey's system of decimal classification for libraries. The report clearly reflected the new direction libraries were beginning to take. According to the report, the twenty-nine public libraries in the thirteen original colonies had approximately 45,000 volumes in 1776. A hundred years later, there were 3,682 libraries in the United States, with a total of 12,276,964 volumes and 1.5 million pamphlets. The sheer mass of material and information that had become available made it imperative that new systems of classifying and disseminating it become available.

The literature from this period clearly shows that the librarian was seen as being a special type of "public educator." Casting aside to some extent the traditional model of the scholar-librarian, librarians were recognized as being popular educators. As explained in the Education Bureau's report,

> . . . the librarian has silently, almost unconsciously, gained ascendency over the habits of thoughts and literary tastes of a multitude of readers, who find in the public library their only means of intellectual improvement. That educators should be able to know the direction and gauge the extent and results of this potential influence, and that librarians should not only understand their primary duties as purveyors of literary supplies to people, but also realize their high privileges and responsibilities as teachers, are matters of great import to the interest of public education.

Traditional interpretations have presented the growth and expansion of libraries after 1876 as being part of an idealistic, liberal humanitarian movement that functioned as a counterpart to the Common School Movement. Under what has been described by the historian Dee Garrison, in her work *Apostles of Culture*, as the "progressive interpretation," the public library has been looked upon as part of the general movement toward social reform and moral improvement coming out of the late nineteenth century.

Garrison has argued that the traditional interpretation of American library history has been too simplistic. According to her, the traditional approach places too much emphasis on the support for library development that came from the working classes. It does not take into sufficient consideration the extent to which the public libraries were seen by the middle and upper classes that sponsored them as a means of "arresting lower-class alienation from traditional culture." While altruism and humanistic ideals were undoubtedly key factors in the development of libraries in the United States during the second half of the nineteenth century, leaders in the development of their institutions tended to support moral and economic values that were consistent with their middle- and upper-class backgrounds.

Yet, despite the fact that most library leaders of the period were highly conservative, significant advances were made in the late nineteenth century to counter the paternalistic nature of most American librarians and their programs. Unlike the schools, which had much tighter control over their charges and the materials studied, librarians had relatively little control over what their patrons read. Although librarians made consistent attempts to discourage the reading of popular novels (in most cases, romances), little could be done effectively to shape the tastes and interests of most readers. Fiction collections were tolerated in many libraries only as a means of attracting readers into libraries. As the 1876 Bureau of Education report maintained,

> The old recipe for cooking hare, which begins with "first catch your hare" may well be applied to the process of elevating the tastes of the uncultivated masses. Let the library, then, contain just enough of the mere confectionary of literature to secure the interest in it of readers of the lowest—not depraved—tastes; but let this be so dealt out as may best make it serve its main purpose of a stepping stone to something better.

In the 1890s, innovations such as the "two-book" system, in which fiction readers

FIGURE 6-4
The New York Public Library by
E.J. Meeker. From *The Outlook*,
Vol. 83, May 19, 1906, p. 199.

were required to check out a nonfiction book for every volume of fiction that they took from the library, became popular among librarians.

These attempts by many librarians to impose what they considered suitable reading material were largely unsuccessful. A significant minority of librarians opposed placing restrictions on the selection and use of reading materials by their patrons; popular tastes could not be curbed. Strict censorship was impossible. The library by its nature encouraged the free flow of information, providing educational opportunties to a significant portion of the population. In doing so, the library movement, whether consciously or in spite of the intention and purpose of many of its founders, contributed significantly to the development of a free society.

THE DEVELOPMENT OF KINDERGARTENS

The contradictory tendencies of both formal and informal institutions of education to impose upper-middle-class values, as well as to provide limited opportunities for economic and social advancement, is particularly evident in the early kindergarten movement. The kindergarten movement was first transplanted from Germany to the United States just before the Civil War. Privately sponsored, and during its early years led by educators with strongly humanitarian concerns, the kindergartens were eventually absorbed into the public school system, where their original intent and purpose were radically redefined.

The kindergarten originated the 1830s and 1840s in Germany, but it achieved its greatest popularity in the United States. Conceived by German educator Friederich Froebel (1782–1852) as preschool instruction for children between the ages of three and seven, its curriculum emphasized not only the physical and intellectual development of children, but also their moral development.

Froebel began his first kindergarten in Blankenberg, Germany, in 1837. Its roots, however, went back to the earlier part of Froebel's life and also to the educational philosophies of Jean-Jacques Rousseau and Heinrich Pestalozzi. Froebel's own childhood seems to have been relatively unhappy and may explain part of his concern with early childhood education. Entering the University of Jena in 1799, for the next three years he concentrated his study mainly in mathematics, physics, and architecture. Evidently strongly influenced early in his life by the concepts of German philosophers Johann Fichte and Friederich von Schelling, Froebel developed his philosophy that all life was based on an eternal law of unity. According to Froebel's scheme, God was the ultimate or "Devine Unity." Since all things evolved from this devine unity, it was for Froebel the purpose of education to teach children to observe and understand the devine characteristics of all things in the world around them. Since the spirit of God infused all things, it followed that all things were interconnected. Although an individual, each was part of a larger whole. Following such a philosophy, it is not surprising that Froebel was an ardent German nationalist. He enlisted in the infantry to defend the German fatherland against Napoleon; Froebel's pursuit of unity realized itself not only as part of his educational philosophy, but of his political consciousness as well.

Froebel's philosophy was merged with much practical experience as a teacher. Having decided upon a career as an educator shortly after having completed his work at the university, he was involved in several educational enterprises. In 1808 he went to Yverdon, Switzerland, where he worked with Heinrich Pestalozzi. He left there in 1810 to continue his studies at the University of Göttingen. After four years in the army Froebel became principal of a school in Kielhau, Germany. There he wrote *The Spirit of Man* (1826), the most detailed exposition of his philosophy.

Froebel's political views eventually led him into difficulty with the Prussian government, which investigated his school for socialist influences and forced the school to close. Between 1831 and 1837 Froebel tried to set up schools in Switzerland, but met with strong opposition from local authorities because of his religious point of view and the fact that he was a foreigner.

Returning to Germany in 1837, Froebel set up the school in Blankenburg that was eventually to become known as the kindergarten (child's garden). Lacking adequate financial support, the school was finally forced to close in 1844. Attempting to promote the idea of the kindergarten, Froebel traveled throughout Germany during the next five years. In 1849, he set up a kindergarten in Libenstein, Germany, where he met the Baroness Bertha Von Marenholtz-Bülow. Quickly convinced of the value of Froebel's work, the baroness began to work intensively with him in the promotion of his ideas. Helping Froebel to establish a teacher training school, she attempted to enlist the support of leading educators for Froebel's work and in turn the support of the government. Despite the support of the baroness and prominent educators throughout Germany, the Prussian government not only did not lend its support to the establishment of kindergartens, but in August of 1851 also actually forbid them!

The rejection of the kindergarten in Germany was largely a result of its association in the minds of political leaders with a radical political ideology. Yet except in the broadest philosophical context, Froebel's ideas as an educator were apolitical. Froebel seriously considered emigrating to the United States. However, he died in June of 1852, and the promotion of the kindergarten was left to his followers.

Froebel's ideas concerning the education of young children were a radical departure from the traditional approaches. Abandoning the idea of John Locke that a child is a tabula rasa, or blank slate, upon whom ideas are impressed, Froebel argued that the child was a self-generating force. Education, rather than impressing ideas upon the child, had as its purpose helping children realize their natural potential. Through the process of education, children would have their inner potentials revealed to them.

Froebel included a wide range of activities in his curriculum for the kindergarten. Gardening, circle games, and group singing taught children how to work and play with one another and be part of a group. Of greatest importance to Froebel's pedagogical scheme was his set of "Gifts" and "Occupations." These involved a series of twenty teaching devices and tasks that would provide the child with an increasingly sophisticated understanding of the world in which they lived.

Froebel's system of Gifts and Occupations had as its purpose helping children to understand not only the spiritual relationship and unity supposedly inherent in all things, but also to provide them with the tools necessary to master and shape the world in which they lived. To what extent the Gifts succeeded in this purpose is, of course, impossible to know. It is interesting to note that the American architect Frank Lloyd Wright felt that the Froebelian materials had a major impact upon his growth and development as a designer. Recalling his using the kindergarten materials as a child during the 1870s, Wright commented that

> A small interior world of color and form now came within grasp of small fingers. Color and pattern, in the flat, in the round. Shapes that lay hidden behind the appearances all about. . . . Here was something for invention to seize, and use to create.

According to Wright, the virtue of the Froebelian materials

> . . . lay in the awakening of the child-mind to rhythmic structure in Nature—giving the child a sense of innate cause-and-effect otherwise far beyond child comprehension. I soon became susceptible to constructive pattern *evolving in everything* I saw. I learned to "see" this way and when I did, I did not care to draw casual incidentals of Nature. I wanted to design.

At least for Wright, the Froebelian materials had helped not only to master methods and materials, but also to understand the rhythmic unity that drew the world together.

In the United States limited discussions and experiments in kindergarten education were underway by the middle of the 1850s. Henry Barnard had published an article in the *American Journal of Education* describing the kindergarten display held in conjunction with the London educational exhibit of 1854. In 1856,

Margarethe Schurz, wife of a German political exile and former student of Froebel's, established a German-speaking kindergarten in Watertown, Wisconsin.

In 1859, Schurz visited Boston, where she met Elizabeth Peabody. Peabody was one of the famous Peabody sisters of Salem. Her sister Sophia was the wife of novelist Nathaniel Hawthorne and her other sister, Mary, the wife of Horance Mann. Among her several friends were leading figures of the New England intelligentsia, such as Ralph Waldo Emerson and Unitarian leader Dr. William Ellery Channing. Widely experienced as an educator, Peabody had been involved in several major educational and literary experiments associated with the Transcendentalist movement in philosophy. During the 1830s, Peabody had taught in Bronson Alcott's Temple School, which had attempted to help children develop the ability to express themselves with the ultimate purpose of leading them to a greater spiritual development. Peabody had also been involved in the founding of the utopian Brook Farm experiment and the great Transcendentalist literary magazine, the *Dial*.

Peabody's involvement with the Transcendentalist movement laid an important foundation for her acceptance of kindergarten ideals and practices. The Transcendentalists argued that the essence of human nature was spiritual and ideally in tune with God's universal spirit. Contradicting traditional religious views, the Transcendentalists believed that God was an "oversoul." Ideally, the human spirit would transcend the physical and material aspects of existence and become one with God's divine spirit.

Having been introduced by Schurz to the concept of the kindergarten, Peabody began to read and study Froebel's works. In 1860 she opened the first English-speaking kindergarten in the United States at 15 Pickney Street, Boston. Assisted by her widowed sister Mary Mann, Peabody actively promoted the ideals of kindergarten instruction. In 1863 with her sister Mary she published the *Kindergarten Guide*. Unsure of her knowledge and mastery of the kindergarten system, Peabody went to Europe in 1867-68 to study Frobelian theory more thoroughly. On her return to the United States she gave up teaching and focused her energies on the promotion of the kindergarten. Repudiating her earlier work, Peabody advanced her ideas by public lectures, private correspondence, and the publication of a new journal, the *Kindergarten Messenger.*

Peabody's efforts on behalf of the kindergarten met with remarkable success. An address by Peabody in Springfield, Massachusetts, engaged the interest of game manufacturer Milton Bradley in the idea of the kindergarten. In 1869 Bradley published Edward Weibe's *Paradise of Childhood*, the first American study of the Froebelian system. At the same time Bradley began to manufacture kindergarten materials. After several unsuccessful attempts, Peabody persuaded the Boston school system to open an experimental kindergarten. Unfortunately, the kindergarten proved to be a failure and was finally forced to close in 1869.

Successful introduction of the kindergarten into a public school system came about partly as a result of Peabody's efforts. Having met Saint Louis Superintendent of Schools William Torrey Harris on one of his frequent trips back to New England, Peabody sent him in 1870 and 1871 a long series of letters, urging him to set up kindergartens as part of the Saint Louis public school system. Initially, Harris had little interest in Peabody's proposal, although he did mention in his annual report of 1871 the possibility of adapting some kindergarten methods to instruction in the primary grades. The major impetus for the establishment of kindergartens in Saint Louis came from a young socialite, Susan Blow.

Susan Blow was the daughter of wealthy Saint Louis businessman Henry Blow. He had been an outspoken abolitionist and had a distinguished public career as a state senator, congressman, and minister to Venezuela and Brazil. In 1871 Blow had taken his family to Europe. While they visited Germay, his daughter Susan first saw a kindergarten class. Blow took extensive notes on what she had seen, and after she returned began to inquire into the possibilities of establishing a kindergarten in Saint Louis.

Initially, Blow's father offered to finance a private kindergarten to be directed by Susan. She apparently declined the offer and talked with Superintendent Harris about setting up a kindergarten as part of the school system. Harris agreed on a kindergarten on a trial basis and promised to assigned a teacher from a primary school to work with Blow and to provide classroom space.

Before Blow actually began the experiment, she went to New York City, where she studied for a year under the direction of Maria Boelte, a German who had studied kindergarten methods under the direction of Froebel's widow. Blow had tremendous hopes for the success of the kindergarten in Saint Louis. Writing to Harris from New York in the spring of 1873, she explained that

> . . . we shall see the day when this mustard seed will have grown into a mighty tree [sic], and I am more than ever anxious to see the system introduced into our Public Schools.

Blow's kindergarten began regular classes in August 1873, at the Des Peres School in Saint Louis. It is commonly recognized as the first successful public kindergarten program in the United States. Mary A. Timberlake was assigned to Blow as her assistant. Blow provided her own services on a voluntary basis. The kindergarten quickly proved to be an enormous success. By 1879, a total of 53 classes and 131 paid teachers were working in the kindergartens. Also working in the kindergartens were many unpaid assistants, most of whom were receiving training to become kindergarten teachers.

Numerous arguments were put forward opposing the establishment of the kindergartens. It was argued that setting up kindergartens would be extremely expensive, that they would spoil the children attending them, and that it would be almost impossible to find or train teachers who could effectively handle the demands imposed by the kindergarten curriculum.

Blow and others who shared her view argued for the establishment of the kindergartens primarily on the basis of the opportunities for happiness and personal growth that kindergartens would provide the child. Harris and the Saint Louis School Board had more pragmatic reasons for supporting the kindergarten. For

FIGURE 6-5 The interior of the Des Peres Kindergarten. Courtesy of the Audio-Visual Department of the St. Louis Public Schools.

example, Thomas Richeson, the president of the board, explained in the super-intendent's report for 1875 that

> It is in its industrial aspect chiefly that our recent experiments in Kinder-garten education promises the most satisfactory results. At a tender age, when the child is plastic in his nature, and easily moulded in any direction, he com-mences a training adapted to give him great skill in the use of his hands and eyes. . . . The influence of the Kindergarten will be felt on all subsequent education. The early impulse given to mechanical skill and to taste, in regard to form an design, in the Kindergarten, reinforced by a thorough course of instruction in industrial drawing in the primary and grammar schools, is suffi-cient to work a revolution in the manufactures of the country, and cause our goods to obtain the preference in foreign as well as domestic markets.

While Harris recognized that children would be better able to become useful workers in the industrial system as a result of the habits and skills they obtained through their kindergarten training, he was more concerned with the fact that the kinder-garten would provide children in the manufacturing districts of the city with an additional year of schooling. In his report for 1872-73, Harris argued that the kindergarten would remove children in poorer neighborhoods from the corruption of the streets. According to Harris,

> We do not look so much to gain in intellectual possessions as to the training of the will into correct habits, during the years previous to the seventh. . . . Such careful training in habits of regularity, punctuality, industry, cleanliness, self-control, and politeness, as are given in the ordinary primary school, and still more efficiently in the well-conducted kindergarten, are of priceless benefit to the community. They lessen the number of rough, ungovernable youths whose excesses are the menace of the peace of society.

Harris's comments reflect the increasingly important role the kindergartens were perceived as having in the reform of urban society during the later decades of the nineteenth century.

The kindergartens were seen as providing the poor child the opportunity to rise above the poverty and neglect that was supposedly so much a part of their lives. By providing the children with kindergarten instruction for three hours a day and having teachers work with the parents of these children, sweeping reforms and improvements were believed to be possible. Children, still flexible, could be shaped in ways that would allow them to overcome the debilitating environments in which they lived. The negative influence of the home and the neighborhood would give way to the supposedly superior influence of the schools and teachers. By culti-vating the spiritual and moral aspects of the child, as well as providing them with practical training, it was believed that the fragmentation and alienation caused by urbanization and industrialization could effectively be overcome. In doing so, the needs of the society as a whole would be met.

Paralleling the growth of the public kindergartens were charity kindergartens such as those sponsored by Mrs. Quincy Adams Shaw in Boston's North End, Jamaica Plain, and Brookline, beginning in the early 1870s. As part of the North End charity kindergarten, teachers spent half their days away from the classroom visiting parents and enrolling children in school. In this context, the teachers in many of the early charity kindergartens were fulfilling the roles of social workers.

As late as 1903, the kindergarten was seen as being an important vehicle for the Americanization of immigrant children. In an address included in the National Education Association Proceedings, Richard Gilder commented

> You cannot catch your citizen too early in order to make him a good citizen. The kindergarten age marks our opportunity to catch the little Russian, the little Italian, the little German, Pole, Syrian, and the rest and begin to make good American citizens of them.

As the kindergarten movement received greater support from the public schools, it moved away from working with parents and became more and more integrated into the general school system. By the end of the 1890s, the kindergarten had become a major part of American schooling. In 1873, according to the U.S. Bureau of Education, there were a total of twelve kindergartens in the United States, with 72 teachers and 1,252 students. By 1898, this number had increased to 4,363 kindergartens with 8,937 teachers and 189,604 students.

The rapid growth of kindergartens in the late nineteenth century was accompanied by important efforts to go beyond the work of Froebel. Anna E. Bryan, for example, argued in a major address to the National Education Association in the early 1890s that the use of Froebel's Gifts and Occupations discouraged spontaneity and creativity on the part of the child. A few years later, G. Stanley Hall rejected much of Froebel's work because it was not derived from systematically observing young children, while John Dewey argued against Froebel's concept that the child's mind contained certain specific universal principles.

Hall and Dewey, with kindergarten leaders such as Anna E. Bryan and Patty Smith Hill, laid the foundations for what would become the Progressive kindergarten movement. Rejecting what they saw as an overly romantic approach to culture by the traditional Froebelians, the progressives felt that the primary purpose of the kindergarten should be to help the individual child learn to cope with the demands of an increasingly complex culture and environment. Unlike the traditional Froebelians who saw morality as being fixed and defined within each individual, the progressive kindergarten supporters saw it as defined by the social environment in which the child lived. Essential to their philosophy was the realization that the children they were teaching were members of a larger and more complex society in which they would have to live and function as adults.

CONCLUSION

By the late 1860s, American culture was being reshaped by rapid industrialization and urbanization. Education, in turn, was affected. The demands of industry for workers with specific skills led the schools to develop programs in industrial arts. As the cities grew, and with them the problems resulting from rapid expansion and overcrowding, the school came to be looked at increasingly as a source of stability and direction for the culture.

The development of the land grant colleges, the manual training schools, free libraries and even the kindergarten were responses to the new social and political order. A new society was coming into being—one radically different from the agrarian society of America during the late eighteenth and early nineteenth centuries. With the creation of this new society there developed in turn a radically different educational system, shaped by the new industrial and urban culture.

Part Three
FARM TO CITY TO SUBURB

No man or woman now alive attended the Philadelphia Centennial Exposition. A very few old men and women remember having seen President Theodore Roosevelt, who best represented in politics the Progressive movement. The last surviving veterans of the World War I are now aged. The veterans of World War II, who remember from their childhood the privations and fears of the Depression, have grandchildren who have few firsthand recollections of the war in Vietnam.

During these times the United States was transformed, and transformed again. Ways of thinking had changed. Knowledge had increased, though some of the old was lost as the new was gained. In 1876 America was still more than anything else rural. Forty years later the big cities were thriving and attracting workers from farms as well as from abroad. By the 1950s many of us had moved again, from aging cities to recently built suburbs. Work had changed, often from farm to factory and sometimes from factory to office. Naturally, the schools changed between 1876 and the 1950s; their changes can be understood only by keeping in mind the changes in the society and culture of which they were a part.

Schools were also affected by shaping events in our history: the Progressive movement, in and out of politics; World War I; the Depression; another world war; and (relatively) peaceful and prosperous years.

WAYS OF THOUGHT, WAYS OF KNOWING

In 1876 faith in science was for most intellectuals unbounded. Science had or would shortly be the means of explaining, predicting, and controlling both the physical world and society. Engineering was already revolutionizing industry. The ills of society would be ended by a new "social science" which would provide remedies for all society's flaws. Within a half century, that faith had been in large part lost.

"Science," of course, survived, but took a different and in some ways more constraining form. Most simply, it then rested upon the conviction that, in spite of theories and in spite of rhetoric, things *are* what they seem, no more, no less. That puts crassly the positivistic view. In its purest and most readily explainable form, positivism is based on the proposition that all knowledge, all understanding comes from observation.

Scientific knowledge, then, was not knowledge of the laws and wisdom of God, but of accumulated sensory data. The classical laws of Newton's physics had not been "discovered," but had been invented, and new and better laws or theories could be invented. Some conventional scientific knowledge was no more than dogma and could be swept away, and at turn of century would be. Albert Einstein's first paper on relativity would appear in 1905.

In a quite similar way, conventional philosophy met the fate of classical physics. What was said was true, provably true, only if it could be logically deduced from a prior truth, but there were no logically demonstrable prior truths. Ludwig Wittgenstein (1889-1951) argued, and argued persuasively, that what had been said and written was not demonstrably true. The unmistakable inference was that most of it was meaningless, nonsense. To Marxist thinkers, the inference was that conventional thought was no more than ideology, a masking of reality.

At the same time the old vision of individuals as acting rationally and in their own interest was being replaced. Behavior came to be seen as the outcome of heredity and experience which in turn had been shaped by environment, a view drawn largely from Darwin's theory of evolution. To suppose that an individual would act on principle was unwarranted. Sigmund Freud saw experience as shaping not only the individual's knowledge, but also emotions and personality. The rational "mind" was replaced by id, ego, and superego.

In the fine arts too the old "realism" was refuted. Picasso in painting, Joyce in literature, and Schoenberg in music all abandoned the old rules, the old canons. Suggesting a date for the change of thought is a great hazard, but for most young intellectuals the old truths had been brought into question by, roughly, 1920. By the mid-1900s doubt had penetrated every thought. Possibly the three quarters of a century beginning in 1876 saw greater changes in ways of human thought than any time since Copernicus.

CITIES AND FACTORIES

Mass production required capital, management, materials, and labor. Capital came in large sums from investors, bank loans, and earnings. Material usually came from American farms and ranches, mines and forests. A new specialization, management, was appearing; since it was also applied to schools, it will be discussed in Chapter 8. Laborers, of whom little skill was required as industrialization progressed, were former journeymen, farm "hands," blacks and whites from the still poor South, and, by the millions, immigrants, most of them from Southern and Eastern Europe. The demands of the factory or mill determined hours of work and the exertion and repetitiveness of work. As factories grew, jobs were divided, subdivided, and divided again, in keeping with Adam Smith's principle of a hundred years before of division of labor. Then, craftsmen had made furniture and clocks—some now in museums— from inherited patterns, from boards and brass to finished pieces. By the 1920s, workers on the Ford Model "T" assembly line tightened only one nut on each car. With more power available, a thousand cumulative technological developments, and increases in efficiency, factory output increased year by year—in the 1920s faster than markets, contributing to the coming of the Depression. Larger investments in larger factories allowed the use of more expensive and more specialized machines. At best the factories were orderly collections of impressive machines; of punch presses and drop forges, turret lathes, shears and brakes, and a thousand others. At worst factories were dehumanizing and dangerous. Big factories had thousands, even tens of thousands, of workers. Most of them worked too-long hours in dangerous, disagreeable places: in the stench of meat packing houses, at moving conveyers where carcasses were methodically dismembered; in the sweatshops of New York City's garment district; and in the hot, humid, dusty cotton mills. Work was dangerous. About fifteen thousand workers were killed annually in factory accidents, and in the 1920s more than ten times as many were injured. Few factory workers belonged to unions before the 1930s and wages were low, usually less than $10 a week. Especially during the 1914-1918 wartime labor shortages, southern blacks were recruited to work in the North in war and other industries. Others heard of work for better pay and so came north. Southern and border cities already had large black populations. During World War I a half million blacks moved to northern cities, and the flow would resume during the Depression and World War II. Southern whites, especially poor mountain people from Appalachia, also come north for factory jobs.

Many, probably most, of the new factory workers were immigrants. Between 1890 and 1914 more than fifteen million immigrants came to the United States. More than half those living in big cities were immigrants or the daughters and sons of immigrants. By 1907 four-fifths of the new immigrants came from Southern or Eastern Europe; others came from Asia, the Caribbean, Mexico, and elsewhere. Most often they settled in cities near fellow countrymen.

Although there was too much variation for any ethnic community to be typical, "Buffalo Polonia," the Polish village of Buffalo, New York, can serve as an example. "Polonia" (the living place but also the spirit of the Poles) was near its zenith in 1914, before war cut off immigration. Polonia was then forty years old. It had grown east of the center of the city, because there was no nearer place and no housing cast off by others. The population of Polonia is difficult to estimate, but St. Stanislaus, the first Catholic parish, had once had more than thirty thousand communicants. By 1914 there were five Polish Catholic parishes.

Immigrants had come to Buffalo Polonia because Buffalo was prosperous, because they had friends and relatives there, because there were jobs, because *w ameryce kazdy ma dobrze* ("in America everyone has it good"). At least one non-Polish agent advertised for and recruited Polish workers. Many were from Prussian Poland, spoke German, and had friends or acquaintances who were German. ("Kaisertown," a German community, was adjacent to Polonia on the south.) Poles said they came to Buffalo *za chlebem* ("for the bread"), but that was a figure of speech. They came to Buffalo to earn money, but they did not come moneyless. Many had worked in factories in Germany, although others did come from the countryside in search of success. "Success" was owning "grunt," ground and house, and security. Poles of Buffalo worked, some remembered, to buy a cramped wood one-story house and then rented the best rooms to pay the mortgage and lived in small additions at the rear. As money was saved and families grew, there were additions to additions, until some houses stretched nearly to the back of deep lots. When money could be spent for it, houses were finished in bright, exuberant, rather old-fashioned ways. A paid-for one-story wood house and its furnishings, even on a lot only 20 feet wide, was proof of prosperity and success.

In Polonia's way of thinking, success came from hard physical work, from sweat, not from schooling. Polish boys did not hope to enter the professions, except perhaps the priesthood. Far more often, they hoped to become craftsmen, and many Polish boys and men attended vocational school at day or at night. But school was not to stand in the way of jobs or wages. Only one Polish child in five, we estimated, completed grammar school. (But only one Buffalo child in four completed grammar school then.)

Buffalo Polonia was, in the words of a man still living, expected "to last hundreds of years." (Although it seems unlikely that it will, there is still a Buffalo Polonia at the end of the 1980s.) It was above all a community, a place where people were linked both personally and institutionally. In the immigration many men had been joined by their wives and children. By 1914 there were third-generation Polonians and extended families: aunts, uncles, in-laws, and cousins sometimes living in the same house, more often in the same block and usually in the same parish. Beyond the families there was the Catholic Church. The "mother church," St. Stanislaus, was more imposing and impressive than the Catholic cathedral. St. Stanislaus's pastor was one of the most prominent men in Polonia, and in Buffalo. The church's teachings, celebrations, and feasts united Polonia, and the church was the symbol of hope for the Polish nation that had lived under

German, Austrian, and Russian rule for a hundred and more years. Children, especially before their first communion at about eleven years of age, attended parochial schools. There were many parish organizations: of choirs, altar boys, and ushers. There were women's circles, mothers' clubs, rosary societies, and others. Of course, there were Polish nuns who lived in parish convents and taught in parish schools. Beyond the church there were the Polish Falcons, a young men's gymnastic and patriotic society. *Dom Polski*, the Polish home, housed a score of organizations, a library, and meeting rooms. The Chopin Society sang traditional Polish songs. Polish men and women owned shops and stores, and there were others owned by Polish-speaking Jews (but to be Polish was to be Catholic). There was a Polish newspaper and sometimes two. At Christmas time the Polish market itself was a festival, with warmth and unnumbered greetings. There were sweet Polish holiday breads, Christmas sausage laced with oregano, and live ducks for czarina or duck blood soup. One could live and die in Polonia rarely hearing a word of English. Life and death occurred among relatives, friends, and acquaintances, supporting if binding. One could even be buried by a Polish undertaker.

There were incursions into Polonia, of course. Policemen were not Polish, and occasionally Poles were arrested for drunkenness or minor crimes, although Polinia was generally law abiding. Some Polish children attended public schools, especially after primary grades and religious instruction taught by the nuns in parish schools. There were no Polish teachers in the public schools. At least one Polish boy's first independent excursions out of Polonia were on an American-made bicycle, and at least one rich Pole owned an American-made Packard. The one-time bicyclist remembers a Polonia Christmas when he was given maple sugar candy, certainly an American candy. Most jobs were outside Polonia, in factories, machine shops, grain mills, at the blast furnaces. It was hard, dirty work. The first was not bad, the second a minor annoyance. Although German might do at first, a factory worker needed to learn English. Women worked in factories too, or outside Polonia as housemaids, and so also needed to know English. As strong as the community of Polonia was, it could not be insulated from the rest of America.

POLITICIANS AND OTHERS: PROGRESSIVE REFORMERS

Perhaps the Civil War had exhausted for a time American energy and enthusiasm for reforms. In any event, although there were some small reform parties and reform causes (for instance, free coinage of silver), after the Civil War a reform era did not come for thirty years or more. It was already slowing when it was brought to an end by the United States' entry into World War I.

President Theodore Roosevelt (a distant cousin of New Deal President Franklin D. Roosevelt) was inaugurated in Buffalo on September 14, 1901, after President McKinley died a lingering death from a gunshot wound by a perhaps deranged self-styled radical. Roosevelt, not yet forty-three when he became president, was as representative of the Progressive era as any man. Time for reform had come. There seemed to be dangers of an uprising of the lower class. It seemed to many that there was one law for the poor, another for the rich, and none at all for big business. Theodore Roosevelt became the most popular president since Andrew Jackson and the most powerful since Abraham Lincoln. Roosevelt was a whirlwind of energy. He had been a rancher, author, explorer, big-game hunter, and soldier and would be a Nobel Prize winner, as well as president. He was an enemy of corruption and of the "wealthy criminal class." He was an early conservationist, a foe of business monopolies, and a believer in just and popular rule.

There are several theories as to the origins of the Progressive movement. For each of them there are supporting arguments; for each of these arguments there are counterarguments. One driving force was increased faith in planning; political writer Walter Lippmann voiced that most persuasively. A second argument was that Progressive reformers were moved by fear, fear of loss of influence and middle-class status; this seems less persuasive than it was found to be at first. Third, it is argued by David J. Hogan that the Progressive movement was a response to the appearance of clearly defined social classes, and of the unrest and even violence of the lower class. His case study of Chicago is persuasive, though not conclusive. We find informative and useful his analysis of the aims of the Progressives. He sees them as threefold: justice, democracy, and efficiency. The second and third of these will receive most of our attention here. But, obviously, some reforms supported by the Progressives had precedents before the Progressive era.

But the time had come for changes, and the Progressives undertook them. Writers, intellectuals, journalists, politicians, engineers, and educators took part. The future was to be taken in hand so that a better future might be brought into being. There were to be changes in government; secret ballots; women's suffrage; an expanded civil service; responsible and honest city, state, and national government. Wretched, overcrowded, unhealthy slum housing was to be improved; the prisons reformed. Child labor in factories was to be ended; drinking prohibited. Outrageous freight rates would be corrected by government control. Trusts and monopolies harmful to the public were to be dismembered if necessary. Impulses for school reform were part of the same Progressive movement, and they too would be called "Progressive." The Progressive era in politics ended in 1917 when the United States entered the war against Germany and Austria.

WORLD WAR I AND OTHERS

U.S. participation in World War I disrupted and reshaped America's society and economy. For a variety of reasons, most debatable but many honorable, the United States entered the war, which was already two and a half years old, in April 1917. There was some resistance to going to war, most of it also honorable. The war required huge amounts of food, supplies, and weapons for the Allies, as well as for our own troops. Factories were converted, and a million women employed in war-related jobs.

On July 4, 1917 the first American soldiers were greeted in Paris, but even at the end of that year there were only 200,000 soldiers and marines in France, most of whom had not seen combat. But in the summer of 1918, when Russia had withdrawn from the war, 250,000 Americans opposed German attacks at Chateau-Thierry. In September more than 1,000,000 "doughboys" were in the Battle of the Meuse, and one-tenth of them were casualties. The Armistice took place on November 11, 1918. By then more than 5,000,000 men had served in the armed forces. It was the greatest military effort since the Civil War.

There were other more or less minor military actions before and after World War I. The Battle of Little Big Horn, Sitting Bull's triumph and General George A. Custer's defeat—and death—was fought the summer of the Philadelphia Centennial Exposition. Some of Custer's cavalrymen were killed by Sioux tomahawks. Only forty-two years later soldiers in France were killed by poison gas. (One of the least satisfying contributions of technology has been to make even ways of killing more efficient if less personal.) The Spanish-American War, 1898–1899, was fought in the Caribbean and in the Philippine Islands. "A splendid little war," Theodore Roosevelt had called it. In 1916 General John J. Pershing pursued Francisco "Pancho" Villa into the mountains of Mexico. In 1919, after World War I, U.S. and Japanese troops occupied the port of Vladivostok in Russia. Marines were stationed in Santo Domingo in the 1930s.

The decade after World War I was a time of rampant conservatism, a time when "the business of America was business." During those ten years there were three Republican presidents: Warren G. Harding (who would set standards for poor performance in the presidency that would last for a half century), Calvin Coolidge, and Herbert Hoover. In 1919 employers broke massive worker strikes and a "Red scare," an intense and senseless search for Bolsheviks. Partly because of a Progressive argument, the prohibition amendment became effective in 1919.

There was a brief postwar recession, but except for farmers the 1920s were times of prosperity. The phonograph became popular, and radio was making its appearance. Life had taken everyday forms which we might find quaint and inconvenient, but not entirely unfamiliar. True, refrigeration was by ice and the furnace burned coal, but most middle-class houses and apartments had bathtubs and central heating. There had been suburbs for most of a century, mainly for those who rode railroads and street cars, but in the 1920s commuting by automobile was no longer unusual.

DEPRESSION

The start of the Depression is remembered as "Black Thursday," October 24, 1929, the day of disaster in the stock market. Too many of the gullible or hopeful had purchased stock on margin, that is, on credit. Consumers buying on time had exhausted their credit. Prices of farm crops had fallen since the end of World War I. In spite of minor rallies and pauses, stocks would fall for two more years. By 1932 RCA stock had fallen from 100 to 2½, General Motors from 396¼ to 34. Since 1920 the price of a bushel of wheat had fallen from $1.98 a bushel to $.38, and the price of cotton from $.16 a pound to $.06.

Half the factory workers and a third of all workers were laid off, without jobs. In East Saint Louis, Illinois, the unemployment rate was 60 percent. But President Hoover insisted that relief and welfare payments were not the responsibility of the federal government. "The strength of our economy," Hoover maintained, was "unimpaired." The reputation of President Hoover did not recover. Businessmen and engineers had had their reputations so badly soiled that would not regain public confidence for fifteen years. In the seventy years before 1929, there had been two democratic presidents; Democratic presidents would be elected in seven of the next nine elections.

The lowest, hardest time of the Depression may have been in 1933. Banks suffering from the after-effects of the stock market crash had lost the confidence of their depositors, who in throngs tried to make withdrawals. Roosevelt was sworn into office on Saturday, March 4, 1933, and the next day declared a "bank holiday" to close banks officially and halt public panic. At his inauguration, Roosevelt said that "The great nation will endure as it had endured, will revive and prosper. . . . [T]he only thing we have to fear is fear itself—nameless, unreasoning, unjustified terror."

New legislation and new programs appeared at once. Nearly three dozen new agencies were created. Federal funds were appropriated for public welfare. The NRA, National Recovery Act, was intended to reduce competition and restore profits. For a year or two its symbol, a blue eagle, was everywhere. Several agencies provided jobs. The CWA, WPA, and PWA built the Holland Tunnel, Boulder Dan, and countless schools, courthouses, hospitals, and levees. Two and a half million men joined the Civilian Conservation Corps—the CCC—and reforested land, built fire trails, planted wind breaks, and dammed off gullies to stop erosion. The National Youth Administration—NYA—arranged and financed part-time work for high school and college students. The AAA supported farm prices. The FHA encouraged building and modernizing homes. (Critics complained of "alphabet soup.") One of the controversial sections of the NRA was Section 7a, which said that ". . . employees shall have the right to organize and bargain collectively . . . and shall be free from the interference, restraint, or coercion of employers." After hesitation Roosevelt gave further support to labor unions.

In 1936 Roosevelt was reelected by majorities in forty-six states, but Roosevelt was the most widely hated man in America. The "nine old men" of the Supreme Court declared the NRA and AAA to be unconstitutional. It was only after Roosevelt threatened to name six additional Supreme Court judges that the court relented. Distribution of welfare and work funds was never satisfactorily organized. Unemployment continued, and Roosevelt's attempt to balance the budget was followed by another stock market slump. In the summer of 1939, 9,500,000 workers were unemployed. The Great Depression came to an end only from an unwelcome event, the outbreak of World War II, when foreign orders for war-related supplies reorganized the U.S. economy. But whatever else, the New Deal established, lastingly, that the government of the United States was responsible for the well-being of its citizen, a principle that now seems so obvious that its source can be overlooked.

WORLD WAR II

The battle between the Japanese and the Chinese at the Marco Polo Bridge near Peking in 1937 was the first of what would become World War II. The German invasion of Poland on September 1, 1939 began the war in Europe; England and France went to war against Germany two days later. Although there were non-interventionists, most people, including President Roosevelt, had come to feel that the United States would, and even should, go to war. Nevertheless, the Japanese attack on Pearl Harbor on the morning of Sunday, December 7, 1941, was enormously shocking, as Roosevelt called it, "the day that shall live in infamy." The United States declared war against Japan, and three days later Germany and Italy declared war against the United States.

After Pearl Harbor there were floods of volunteers for the army, navy, and air corps. Even women were allowed to enlist as noncombatants. During the war nearly 15,000,000 men enlisted or were drafted into the armed forces. For the inductee, the "GI," there was most often a basic or boot camp, then more often than not a specialized training school, maybe on a college campus where there was available space because the college students too had gone to war. Then the serviceman went to sea or overseas to any of four or five continents.

The unsung heroes were the GIs, particularly the "dog faces," the infantrymen, suffering everything from malaria to frost bite, and enemy action. Nearly 400,000 Americans were killed in the war, three times as many as in World War I.

Life at home was almost immediately different. For three and a half years, until the final victories in 1945, the needs and demands of the war came first. Government control was wider than ever before. Industrial production was controlled by a priority system, and price ceilings were set by the OPA, Office of Price Management. Needs for equipment, supplies, and weapons, both for the United States and its allies, were vast: statistics on wartime production are more eloquent than words. As examples, airplanes, 300,000; tanks, 100,000; large guns, 400,000; cargo ships, 5,500, small arms ammunition, 44 billion rounds. There were hundreds of other war products.

War manufacturers demanded more workers. Nearly a million housewives took jobs. More than a million people moved from farm to factory, from country to city, from the South to the North and West. After mid-1943 the cost of living did not increase, but better times and more overtime increased incomes by 70 percent. There were strange and inconvenient shortages, from military needs or production dislocations. Matches were scarce, but there were fewer cigarettes to light. Because Japan had overrun the rubber plantations, there was a shortage of tires. To reduce their use, there was gasoline rationing. War and rumors of war seemed to overshadow all else.

Science and scientists, under the direction of Vannevar Busch and James B. Conant, also became part of the war effort. Physicists and chemists had been useful in some ways in the winning of World War I. But between the wars there were revolutionary theoretical developments, particularly in physics. As we have said, university faculties had grown in numbers and in expertise. World War II has been called the "War of the Physicists." The contributions of scientists were crucial and decisive. The successful defense of England against German bombing raids had depended upon early English radar. German submarine "wolf packs" were driven from the North Atlantic by U.S. navy airplanes and ships equipped with improved American radar that located submarines and automatically directed gunfire. Germans developed the V-1 "buzz bomb" (remote ancestor of the cruise missile) and V-2 "flying stovepipe" (direct ancestor of all ICBMs), too late to change the war's outcome, but inklings of what was to come.

The crowning and most terrifying of achievements was the atomic bomb. Albert Einstein had shown in 1915 that, at least in principle, matter could be converted into energy: $E = mc^2$. In the 1920s scientists produced far-reaching new theories about the structure of the atom. In 1939 German physicists demonstrated that some atoms of uranium could be split, releasing energy, and could produce an atomic bomb. An American atomic bomb was an imperative. Its development began in the summer of 1941. The first atomic reactor, under a grandstand at the University of Chicago, was built under the direction of Enrico Fermi. It first began operating—"went critical"—December 2, 1943. There were many technical problems. How could U-238—the isotope of uranium that was fissionable, or could be split—be separated from the U-235 that was 99.3 percent of the uranium produced? What were the physical properties of plutonium that did not occur at all in nature? They were determined from milligrams, specks, of plutonium made in the cyclotron at Washington University in Saint Louis. Oak Ridge, Tennessee, produced enriched uranium, and Handord, Washington, plutonium.

By early summer 1945, there were three atomic bombs. (No more could be produced in less than a year.) The first, "Trinity," was a test model to be fired statically atop a tower. The uranium bomb, "Little Boy," was long and slender, like a streamlined torpedo. A prototype of the plutonium bomb, "Fat Man," in the Sandia museum seems gross, obese, and of course deadly. "Trinity" was fired at sunrise on the morning of July 16, 1945 at Almagordo, New Mexico. The tower that supported it was vaporized; the desert sand beneath it melted into glass. The Atomic Age had begun.

President Roosevelt died of a brain hemorrhage on April 12, 1945, at Warm Springs, Georgia. That month Mussolini was killed by Italian partisans and Hitler committed suicide in a Berlin bomb shelter under attack. On September 2 the official Japanese surrender took place aboard the battleship *Missouri* in Tokyo Bay. Six years and a day after the invasion of Poland, World War II had ended.

PEACE, AND PLEASURE, IN THE SUBURBS

The war was over and won. The Depression was past and prosperity was back. The years after the war were years for enjoyment, for pleasure, for satisfaction. "Big spender" was a complimentary term, and there was money to be made. If there were to be other crusades, they would have to wait.

Nearly a million of the new veterans were discharged within a month. The GI Bill entitled them to mustering-out and unemployment pay, tuition, and an allowance while they attended school: more than a million veterans would go to college. Educational benefits were first seen by some as a kind of welfare, but in spite of overcrowded dormitories, rickety housing, and too-large classes, the veterans would be better students than most.

Although it would not be clear until later, the American economy had been transformed. Because wartime taxes had reduced the largest incomes, and wartime jobs and overtime had increased the smaller ones, of which there were many more, there had been a major redistribution of wealth, with a major increase in buying power. Demands for goods had accumulated from the war years and even from the Depression. Birth rates climbed, creating further demand. The veterans wanted, and many of them found, a life that was good in material things. Millions of new homes were built, most of them in the suburbs; for those best able to pay, "colonial" homes or spreading "ranch houses" built a room or two deep across a building lot and at least looking big and expensive. For others there were FHA- or GI Bill-financed boxes, built in many suburbs, the biggest of which were the Levittowns. The first of them would be built on Long Island, in the far suburbs of New York City. The 17,500 houses in it easily sold at $6,990 and up.

Part of the good life was early marriage, which became fashionable. In the 1950s women married on the average two years younger than before, and high school student marriages were not unusual. To sire or bear three, four, or more children was also fashionable. The best-selling childrearing manual, by Dr. Benjamin M. Spock, advocated "permissiveness." Mothers chauffeured children to Boy and Girl Scout meetings, to piano lessons, and so forth. The suburban "teenagers" (the term became popular then) had generous allowances or part-time jobs. They spent an average of $550 a year in the 1950s, on records, radios, cameras, movie tickets, and cosmetics. They made Elvis Presley one of the greatest stars of radio and movies, and eventually he was even allowed on television (from the waist up).

Before the war, most television had been experimental. After 1950 the manufacture of television sets became a major industry: two million sets a year were sold. Color television would appear, triumphantly, in 1955. Watching television became an absorbing and time-consuming pastime. Those who were children then remember Howdy Doody, Buffalo Bob, and Clarabelle and the Mouseketeers. Many still remember a theme song: "Mickey Mouse, Mickey Mouse! . . . M - I - C - K - E - Y   M - O - U - S - E!" Disney's "Davy Crockett" was an enormously popular television series. We remember explaining to a new immigrant high school student that Crocket was *langzeit gestorben*, long dead. The student was upset.

The suburbs, where affluent children, teenagers, and parents watched television, would not have been possible without the automobile. The great American love affair, it was often said, was between Americans and their automobiles. They increased, year by year, in size, power, speed, and ornateness. They made possible the new suburbs, stretching far beyond public transportation. They made downtown shopping districts obsolete, because of the lack of parking space. Shopping centers, surrounded by acres of macadamized parking lots, made their appearance. Korvettes, the first of the discount centers, appeared there. Drive-in theaters became common—in one sense or another.

In 1948 Democrat Harry S. Truman was elected to the presidency—pollsters and political experts had expected his opponent Thomas E. Dewey to win. Four years later Dwight D. Eisenhower, wartime commander in Europe, defeated Adlai E. Stevenson, witty idol of liberals. During Truman's presidency, South Korea was invaded; in behalf of the United Nations, the United States (and several other countries) sent troops commanded by General Douglas MacArthur, brilliant and headstrong, finally relieved for insubordination. Naturally, there were concerns at home—inflation, McCarthyism, strikes.

But in spite of all these, it was a time for pleasure, a time to relax after the privations of the Depression and the exertions of the war. Other crusades would wait.

Chapter Seven
PROGRESSIVE REFORM

The subject of this chapter is Progressive reform in cities. The free land was gone by 1890, and the need for farm labor was declining. Immigrants and rural Americans had gone to the cities. Chicago, as an example, had a population in 1900 of more than a million, ten times as many as in 1860. In the cities, social injustice was greatest, and the old small-town democracy had faded. America's social conscience was aroused, and fears arose. Two of the Progressive reformers' aims, the subjects of this chapter, were to remedy social injustice in the cities and preserve democracy there.

Although the geographical frontiers had gone, there were intellectual frontiers, far broader than before. As Cremin pointed out, nearly every discipline made important advances in the 1890s. Physics and chemistry were developing rapidly. Influenced by Darwinian theory, psychology, social theory, philosophy, and sociology were reconceptualized. So too were the theoretical foundations of education, William James's *Principles of Psychology* appeared in 1890. Other works, including Francis W. Parker's *Talks on Pedagogics* (1894), Edward L. Thorndike's *Animal Intelligence* (1898), James' *Talks to Teachers on Psychology* (1899), and John Dewey's *The School and Society* (1899), were to reformulate radically purposes and meanings of education during the first decades of the twentieth century.

BIG BUSINESS, DARWINISM, AND REFORMERS

The growth of business and industry during the later 1800s produced a new economic elite, the new rich, the big rich. By 1892 there were more than four thousand millionaires in the United States. Although some had acquired wealth by inheritance, others were "self-made" men. As one example, Rockefeller had begun his career as a clerk in a Cleveland commission house. As another, Andrew Carnegie had been a mill worker, a bobbin boy in a Pittsburgh cotton mill. The Rockefellers and the Carnegies got their wealth by disregarding the welfare of the public. Called "robber barons," like those of the Middle Ages, the business leaders of the United States claimed that their wealth was simply the result of hard work, thrift, and "good living" and that they deserved their wealth. Rockefeller maintained that his wealth had been given him by God. What was implied was that those who had less deserved less. Richard Hofstadter suggested that business leaders then adopted as their philosophy social Darwinism to justify social inequities, but it is doubtful that many of them were aware of Spencer's or Darwin's concepts. In *The Self-Made Man in America* (1954), Irwin G. Wyllie maintained that businessmen then based their belief in the "self-made man" upon deep-rooted Christian morality and from faith in reason that had its origins in the Enlightenment.

Although social Darwinism was largely unknown to business leaders, its application to social theory and reform was of increasing interest to American intellectuals. Two who had opposing views were Lester F. Ward and William Graham Sumner. Sumner, from 1872 until 1910 a professor at Yale, argued that progress could take place scientifically only if nature and the evolutionary process were allowed to take their natural course. Defending the status quo by social Darwinism, Sumner argued that those who held positions of power and influence did so because they were most suited to do so, as their survival in the system showed. Sumner opposed government reform because it upset the natural evolutionary process. He saw state-supported education as a way for improving society, to the extent to which it encouraged political order.

Lester Frank Ward's work was in contrast to that of Sumner. In *Dynamic Society* (1883) Ward drew upon Darwinian concepts to develop a theory of culture. In opposition to Sumner, he argued that when applied to a modern society, other forces altered the evolutionary process. The intellect could overcome natural man's desires, and methods to improve their evolutionary future could be developed by man. Ward emphasized the importance of "intellect" and "culture" in human evolution. If natural forces were left to themselves, they would tend to be destructive and counterproductive for the culture. Ward called for government reform and regulation. Ward's arguments, with those of other social scientists of the period, generated increased interest in reform.

Reform was pursued in many ways and received the support of many groups. Ministers, priests, and rabbis were among the leaders of the Progressives, as were journalists, politicians, and businesspeople. Intellectuals such as Jane Addams and John Dewey were among the reformers. By 1900 the Salvation Army claimed that in its ranks were twenty thousand privates and three thousand officers. The strength and zeal of the reformers was often impressive.

The reform movement had many origins, but probably the social settlement movement best typified its spirit, and was of great importance. It had begun in England in the early 1880s. Its origins were the beliefs of Christian Socialists Frederick Denison Maurice and Charles Kingsley. Strongly influenced by Hegel and Carlyle, the Christian Socialists believed in the unity of mankind and abhorred the artificial divisions created by social class and wealth. Kingsley promoted his beliefs in essays, articles, and books. Maurice brought them to the attention of the public by the establishment in London of the Working Man's College. Kingsley, Maurice, and art critic, writer, and social reformer John Ruskin were to inspire Samuel A. Barnett, the principal leader of the English settlement house movement.

Barnett was a Church of England priest who had worked in some of London's worst slums. To help the working people in his parish and take advantage of the energy and enthusiasm of university students with whom he had contact, Barnett organized in 1884 the first university settlement house. Named after a young English reformer who had died while trying to improve the lives of the poor, it was called Toynbee Hall. Rather than contributing to the poor as an act of charity, Barnett had young university educated men work and live in the worst neighborhoods in London and share their lives with the poor. In doing so, they would make their settlement house a center for culture and education and bring with it a new sense of community.

Toynbee Hall was an inspiration to Stanton Coit, who had graduated from Amherst and earned his Ph.D. at the University of Berlin. He spent three months at Toynbee Hall in 1886 and brought the settlement idea back to the United States. Strongly influenced by Felix Adler and the ideas of the Ethical Cultural Movement, Coit established a settlement house on Forsyth Street in New York's Lower East Side. But he returned to England in 1887, and his plan for the revitalization of American life collapsed.

Coit's place was quickly taken by several others. Four Smith College graduates led by Jane Robbins and Jean Fine were responsible setting up New York's College Settlement in late 1889. At the same time Jane Addams and Ellen Gates Starr began Hull House in Chicago. It was to become the most famous of the American settlement houses.

Addams's purpose was the regeneration of a democratic urban society. She saw herself and her coworkers as going into immigrant slums and taking over where city officials had failed. Through the settlement house a sense of order and community would be established. Programs based on the needs of the local community would be established. If filthy tenements were infested with lice, then Addams and her coworkers would show immigrant tenants how to exterminate them. If gangs of "street Arabs" and urchins were threats, the settlement house would organize the children into clubs, provide opportunities for them to take part in organized sports, and instruct them in arts and crafts. If immigrant mothers had to work, the settlement house would provide day care nurseries and kindergartens for their

FIGURE 7-1 A back-alley in the Hull House neighborhood of Chicago. From Jane Addams, *Twenty Years at Hull House* (New York: Macmillan, 1910), p. 95.

children. Immigrants were taught to read and speak English. Social clubs were organized. Music lessons were provided, and choral groups regularly gave concerts.

Addams's program was educational in the broadest sense. Hull House was to be a center for practical education and culture; John Dewey and Frank Lloyd Wright were among prominent speakers there. Reproductions of famous works of art covered the walls, and there were numerous exhibitions. But Hull House was probably most successful in practical matters with direct impact on the lives of the immigrants.

Addams accepted that industrialism and the factory had become permanent parts of America. She felt it was crucial that immigrant factory workers understand and appreciate the important parts they played in the industrial system. To help them become more aware of the importance of labor and of the role of the practical arts and crafts immigrants had brought with them, Addams, with the help of Ellen Gates Starr, set up the Hull House Labor Museum in 1900.

The programs developed at Hull House were important alternatives to the public schools' relatively restricted and narrow view of education. Increasingly, those in the settlement house movement set in motion reforms within the schools. As an example, Lillian Wald, of New York City's Henry Street Settlement, persuaded the New York City Health Department to hire school physicians and founded the Visiting Nurse Service of New York. Her colleague Elizabeth Farrell was responsible for the Board of Education's opening the first classes for handicapped children.

Among the individuals other than settlement house leaders who turned to questions of school and urban reform was Jacob Riis. He had come from Denmark in 1870. After a newcomer's difficulties in adjustments and settlement he became a reporter for the *New York Tribune*. His firsthand experiences as an immigrant suited him admirably to report on the lives and problems of the immigrants in New York City's Bowery. He was a police reporter for the *Tribune* for more than ten years. Riis's reputation as an urban reformer was permanently established in 1890 when his book *How the Other Half Lives* was published. Based on personal experience in the slums and tenements of New York City, it brought attention to the immigrant's poor wages, unhealthy working conditions, and the destruction of the integrity of the individual. He was particularly concerned for the children and felt that they did not deserve the tragic fates most of them would meet in the slums. Essentially an environmentalist, Riis argued that the city's corrupt environment threatened the institutions of democracy and that politics sprang from and was encouraged by unstable homes, poor schools, and an unhealthy physical environment. "A man cannot live like a pig and vote like a man," Riis wrote. Riis, like Addams, hoped that by proper education the importance of the home and the school would be reestablished in the lives of the immigrant poor. He felt that New York City schools, overcrowded, poorly designed, and extremely limited in curriculum, inadequately met the needs of poor children.

Riis strongly favored the establishment of industrial schools and wrote that "the industrial school plants itself squarely in the gap between the tenement and the public school." These schools would provide the transition from immigrant culture and the broader American culture. Like Horace Mann fifty years earlier, he felt that the schools should provide immigrant children with education adequate for voting and becoming good citizens.

Many of Riis's articles and books were illustrated, and he used a projector when he lectured. The illustrations were based on his research photographs. Consistently used to document educational conditions, Riis's pictures of childhood in New York are among the most valuable resources on urban life and education in the period. An excellent example of Riis's educational photographs is his "A Class in the Condemned Essex Street School". The inadequate facilities were clearly illustrated. On overcrowded, poorly lit, and badly heated classrooms such as this, Riis commented,

In New York we put boys in foul, dark class-rooms, where they grow crooked for want of proper desks; we bid them play in gloomy caverns which the sun never enters, forgetting that boys must have a chance to play properly, or

FIGURE 7-2 The Essex Street Market School; photograph by Jacob Riis. Courtesy of the Library of Congress.

they will play hooky; we turn them away by the thousands from even such delights as these, and in the same breath illogically threaten them with jail if they do not come.

Riis also focused attention on the need to establish playgrounds for children living in the poorer neighborhoods. Although legislation had been passed by 1887 in New York City calling for the establishment of small parks with playground equipment for children, none had been built by 1894, when Riis began to lobby for them. In *The Century* magazine, for example, he proposed that sufficient land be condemned around every school in the city to build a playground, a "people's park" in which children could play during their recesses and where mothers living in the neighborhood could take their babies during the day. The city government was unwilling to spend the money necessary to tear down the tenements surrounding schools.

Playgrounds would induce tenement and immigrant children to attend school more regularly. With the choice of staying at home in dark airless tenements, or coming to school where they could enjoy a playground full of air and light, Riis believed that the children would choose the latter. As he explained, "Instead of being repelled, children would be attracted to a school that was identified with their playground. Truancy would cease." Ideally, children would come to identify with the school. An identity and sense of self, rather than being shaped in the alleys and back streets of the tenement district, would be formed in the fresh air and wholesome environment of the playground.

Riis wished to make the schools community centers that would provide a wholesome alternative to the squalor and destructive environment of the tenements and streets.

> [T]he churches, clubs, schools, educational and helpful agencies . . . make a front of 756 running feet on the street, while the saloons, put side by side, stretch themselves over nearly a mile; so that ideals of citizenship are minting themselves on the minds of the people at the rate of seven saloon thoughts to one educational thought.

Riis's encouragement of the establishment of parks and improvement of physical conditions of the schools and tenements in New York City were his principal contributions as an urban reformer. He knew, however, that by itself physical reform of the urban environment would not be enough. While establishing better schools, recreation centers, and parks was critically important, the immigrant children and their parents must be properly educated if the conditions of the city and life within it were to be improved. Thus, Riis's reform attempts can best be understood as combining reform of the physical environment with the general moral and intellectual education of the individual.

Riis drew ideas from the Children's Aid Society, the Fresh Air Fund, and elsewhere. Sol Cohen has argued in *Progressives and Urban Reform* that Riis's ideas were not original and that Riis was "a great propagandist rather than a great innovator." Even if propagandistic in intent and purpose, Riis's photographs nonetheless tell clearly an invaluable story of the overcrowding, cramped, sordid conditions in the New York City schools—and reform, like all else, requires a variety of talents.

CRITICS OF THE SYSTEM

Although the reform movement of the 1890s focused initially on the physical conditions of the city, it expanded to address other social issues. In the case of the schools, increasing criticisms were made of their organization and curriculum. The most powerful of the school critics was Joseph Mayer Rice.

Rice was a young New York City pediatrician, who had studied education and psychology in Germany between 1888 and 1890. Back in the United States, Rice published a series of articles on education. The editor of *The Forum*, Walter Hines Page, was impressed, no doubt, by the prospect of the articles. And then, too, Rice's brother was *The Forum's* owner.

Under the sponsorship of *The Forum*, Rice toured the country examining every possible aspect of the public schools. He observed classrooms; talked to children, teachers, and parents; and interviewed school board members and administrators. His findings were published as a series of articles in *The Forum*.

Between January and June of 1892, Rice visited thirty-six cities and interviewed more than twelve hundred teachers. The first article in the series appeared the following October. They continued to be published until June 1893. They raised extraordinary controversy among educators and the general public. Rice reported that in city after city, political corruption, apathy, and incompetence were responsible for creating inadequate and badly run schools. In New York City, for example, a principal whom Rice had interviewed totally disregarded the idea that the children for whom she was responsible as a supervisor might have any knowledge or experience of their own. Rote memorization and parroted answer were the principal's ideal for a properly schooled child. As Rice explained,

> The principal's ideal lies in giving each child the ability to answer without hesitation, upon leaving her school, every one of the questions formulated by her. In order to reach the desired end, the school has been converted into the most dehumanizing institution that I have ever laid eyes upon, each child being treated as if he possessed a memory and the faculty of speech, but no individuality, no sensibilities, no soul.

Rice wrote that the principal and her program received high praise from the local superintendent. The school was based on the maxim of "save the minutes." Rather than thinking, children were commanded simply to absorb and memorize whatever was presented to them. When Rice asked the principal why the children were not allowed to move their heads or arms and legs when they were having their lessons, she responded saying, "Why should they look behind when the teacher is in front of them?" Rice's contempt for her approach was complete.

Rice's picture of the schools was in general a discouraging one. A teacher in Chicago was quoted as haranguing her students with the command: "Don't stop to think, tell me what you know." Bright spots did emerge at a few points. In La Porte, Indiana, Rice saw important progress in classes in art. (A Froebelian, W. N. Hailman, was superintendent there.) Francis W. Parker's Cook County Normal School was also providing outstanding models of teaching and instruction.

Rice called for basic and sweeping reforms. He maintained that if the schools were to improve, they must be totally divorced from local politics. School boards could have one and only one purpose in mind—providing the children under their charge the best education possible. In addition, proper supervision of teachers must be introduced into the schools. Incompetence would be checked and eliminated from the classroom as the result of proper examination and supervision on the part of the school's administration. Rice advocated in his proposals a system of accountability for the schools. His primary emphasis was on how the schools were administered and the quality of their curriculum.

Other critics and reformers addressed similar issues. At the meeting of the National Education Association in Saratoga Springs in 1892, a group that came to be known as the Committee of Ten on Secondary School Studies was organized by the NEA's National Council of Education. The committee, which was headed by Charles W. Eliot, the president of Harvard University, was established to try to determine a standard set of entrance requirements for those applying to college.

Until this time, most colleges required that applicants complete a Classical course of study at the secondary level. This normally included four years of Latin and two or three years of Greek. Students who had followed the English course of study were usually not admitted to universities or colleges. Under the leadership of the Committee of Ten, an attempt was made to broaden the criteria under which students would be admitted to college and university study.

Meeting over a period of a year and a half, the Committee of Ten completed its report in December 1893. A total of thirty thousand copies were sent throughout the country by the U.S. Bureau of Education. Against Eliot's desires, the report outlined four courses of study for the high school: Classical, Latin-Scientific, Modern Language, and English. In the Classical course, greater emphasis was placed on the inclusion of subjects such as English, history, and science. In general, the report argued that the primary purpose of the secondary schools was to prepare students for life, rather than just for college. At the same time, the report maintained that those individuals who had successfully completed the high school curriculum should be able to continue on to college without difficulty. From a practical point of view, the report of the Committee of Ten had the effect of making higher education more accessible to a larger number of people.

While the Committee of Ten was preparing its report, a second NEA committee was appointed in February 1893 to address the question of elementary education. Known as the Committee of Fifteen, this group was specifically charged to examine the training of teachers, the reorganization and combining of school subjects, and the organization of the schools. Under the direction of William H.

Maxwell, the superintendent of schools for Brooklyn, the Committee appointed three subcommittees including one on "correlation," reorganizing and combining school subjects.

The subcommittee on correlation was chaired by U.S. Commissioner of Education, William Torrey Harris, who write its report. At issue in the debates of the subcommittee on correlation was not only the course of study, but also the question of what the philosophical bases of education should be. By the end of the 1880s, a number of new educational theories had begun to emerge in the United States. Among these was Herbartianism. Based on the ideas of the German philosopher Johann Friederich Herbart and his followers, the Herbartian movement in the United States was led by Frank and Charles McMurry of the Illinois State Normal University and Charles DeGarmo of Swarthmore College.

Herbartianism is difficult to define precisely. There was much disagreement, even among those who considered themselves Herbartians. Basically, they rejected the traditional idea of mental "faculties." They saw little value in mental discipline, as reflected in exercises involving memorization and recitation. Instead they placed greater emphasis on the subject matter being taught.

Such an approach was in considerable conflict with views held by Harris. In February 1895, the Committee of Fifteen finally presented its report. In presenting the report of his subcommittee, Harris strongly opposed the Herbartians and their philosophy. While a number of issues were discussed, the most important was Harris's conviction that the Herbartian theory denied the concept of free will.

The arguments made for and against Herbartianism in the 1890s are tedious and obscure. What is perhaps most important is that an important choice was being made between philosophies. A new educational leadership was emerging. Whether or not they realized it, the curriculum reforms these new leaders were supporting implied more than a shift of philosophy. They were supporters of a new psychology. Harris's idealism was being replaced with materialism. New and different answers were being developed about how the human mind related to matter. But the subcommittee's report strongly upheld the traditional elementary curriculum.

PSYCHOLOGY AND THE NEW PEDAGOGY

Herbartianism was by no means the only new educational philosophy to emerge from the 1890s. Of far greater importance, for example, was the *child study movement*. Dating back to the 1880s, the child study movement was devoted to attempting the study and understanding of the child's behavior and development through systematic observation. The leader of the movement in the United States was the psychologist G. Stanley Hall.

Hall, the son of an old but impoverished Massachusetts farm family, was born in 1844 in rural hilly western Massachusetts. Exempted from the Civil War draft, he graduated from Williams College, studied theology for a year, and then studied in Germany for three years. After teaching at Antioch College in Ohio, he became William James's student at Harvard and completed his doctorate in psychology, the first in the United States. In 1882, at age thirty-eight, he was named a member of the faculty at newly established Johns Hopkins University in Baltimore, and his career had begun.

Hall was one of the founders of psychology in the United States; perhaps only William James was more important. He was *the* founder of child psychology. An admiring biographer called him the "playboy of Western scholarship." Hall's enthusiasms, "crazes" as he called them, led him into a variety of fields: theology and philosophy initially, then psychology, pedagogy (the science of teaching), child study, history, sex education, adolescence, and Freudian psychology all caught his interest. Unlike many researchers in education who would follow, Hall seems to have begun with an interest in "why," research to satisfy a need for knowledge. His interest in "how" was usually secondary. He was another of those individuals with inexhaustible energy. He was scholar, lecturer, journal founder, and editor, and after 1889, president of Clark University. He wrote hundreds of articles, supervised dozens of doctoral dissertations, and wrote half a dozen books. He was a founder and first president of the American Psychological Association. In the 1960s, he was described as having had values ". . . ominously parallel to twentieth century totalitarianism." It is true that he was nostalgic and felt that earlier times had been better times. With other prosperous citizens of his age he shared a longing for public order and was a staunch antifeminist. Staunch antifeminism was not rare then, but Hall gave it an aura, and so aided its perpetuation.

Hall's first paper on the contents of children's minds—what preschoolers did and did not know—was published in 1883 and marks the beginning of *child study* (or, in a Latin form, *paidology*). Hall returned to child study in the 1890s, when due to his influence several child study associations were established. The Department of Child Study of the NEA was established in 1893. There were thousands of published papers on child study, and tens of thousands of unpublished case studies. By 1896, aspects of childhood that had been studied included physical measurements, death rates, stammering, hearing losses, memory, games, children in primitive cultures, secret languages, imitation, home environment, and punishment. The child study movement had a common subject—the child. It had no common approach, no linking theory. For instance, a theoretical connection between children's heights and stammering is unimaginable. Child study was outlived by Hall, who lived and wrote until 1924. Child study was an idea whose day would never come.

In the late 1800s, psychology was emerging as a special discipline or branch of learning. It was founded upon a philosophical base and upon research by early German physiological neurologists. Psychological theories that now seem crude were developed. Hall's approach to psychology came from his long-time conviction, acquired at Williams, that human behavior should be interpreted in the light of Charles Darwin's evolutionary theory. That theory explained the improvement by adoption of each species, including mankind, Homo sapiens. It had been argued that the individual's growth followed the evolution of his species. "Phylogeny recapitulates ontogeny," in learned language. The growth of the body and intellect retraced that of the race. (A game of cowboys and Indians was the reliving of a barbaric "epoch.") This general theory, however dubious it seems nearly a century later, was the theoretical, or paradigmatic, basis for Hall's pscyhology of children and education. It would be disproved and discarded within a few years, but that is often the fate of theories.

From Hall's theory it followed that evolution, which was by nature right, should not be contradicted by education. Schooling should be adjusted to the age and "culture epoch" of the child. The Herbartians and the child study movement were eventually linked through the cultural epoch theory and the concept of recapitulation. Other theorists picked up these ideas, the most interesting and important of whom was John Dewey. Dewey, although a member of the Executive Committee of the National Herbart Society and a supporter and critic of the child study movement, cannot be accurately portrayed as a member of either group. Instead, he was an original thinker and force of his own—perhaps the most important in the history of American education.

Dewey had been born in 1859 in Burlington, Vermont. He attended traditional schools there. Evidently his early schooling had little impact upon him. Recalling his early childhood some years later, Dewey remembered that the most important part of his early education was outside the schoolroom, in the community of Burlington and the nearby countryside. Dewey went to high school in Burlington and when he was sixteen entered the University of Vermont.

While at the University of Vermont, Dewey developed what was to be a lifelong interest in philosophy. Upon completing his degree in 1879, he went to Oil City, Pennsylvania, where he taught high school for two years. Free to spend much of his time reading, Dewey began to pursue systematically the study of philosophy. Returning to Burlington, he taught briefly in a nearby village school. While in Burlington Dewey was tutored in philosophy by H. A. P. Torrey. It was then that he submitted, and William Torrey Harris accepted, several articles for the *Journal of Speculative Philosophy*.

While Dewey's interest in philosophy began to expand, an imaginative experiment in higher education was being undertaken in Baltimore, Maryland. A local businessman, Johns Hopkins, had endowed what became a research university based upon German models. Dewey read the university's inaugural address by evolutionist Julian Huxley. Highly impressed, Dewey decided to apply to study philosophy at the new university. Failing to receive a fellowship (the great sociologist Thorstein Veblin, a fellow student of Dewey's, was also refused support), Dewey borrowed $500 and entered the university in the fall of 1882, as a student of G. Stanley Hall. (Their relationship seems to have been a cool one.) Dewey received a fellowship the following year and completed his doctorate in 1884.

Johns Hopkins was a remarkable place to be in the early 1880s. It was expected that both advanced students and professors would be involved in original research. Dewey's early coursework was in history and political theory with Herbert B. Adams. During his second year he took courses in history and political science (Woodrow Wilson was a fellow student), animal physiology, elocution, and philosophy and logic. While at Hopkins, he studied under such major figures as G. Stanley Hall, Charles S. Pierce, and George Sylvester Morris.

Morris undoubtedly had the greatest impact on shaping Dewey's career. Under his supervision Dewey began to study the work of the German philosopher Hegel. More important, after Dewey finished his thesis, "The Psychology of Kant", in 1884, he went as an instructor with Morris to the University of Michigan where Morris had been made chairman of the Department of Philosophy. Dewey was to remain (except for a year teaching at the University of Minnesota) at Michigan for ten years. It was while teaching at Michigan that his interests in primary and secondary education began to develop. Beginning in 1871, the University began to admit graduates of any secondary school whose program had been approved by the university. Faculty committees were sent by the university to determine the quality of various schools' programs. Dewey often served on these committees. He also became active in the Michigan Schoolmasters Club, serving as its vice president in 1887 and 1888.

During this period, Dewey frequently spoke to teachers' groups and published a number of articles addressing general educational questions. While working with the schools in Michigan, Dewey became convinced that the quality of secondary schooling was ultimately dependent upon the type of instruction students had received in the earlier grades. While at Michigan, he became convinced that the schools were failing because of lack of coordination between programs, poorly conceived curricula, and limited understanding of methods of teaching.

In 1894, Dewey accepted an offer from the University of Chicago to head the combined departments of philosophy, psychology, and pedagogy. Included among his responsibilities at Chicago was the organization and administration of an experimental school for the university. Eventually known as the Laboratory School, Dewey saw the school as an ideal setting for experimental work in education. As he wrote in an early report,

> The conception underlying the school is that of a laboratory. It bears the same relation to work in pedagogy that a laboratory bears to biology, physics, or chemistry. Like any such laboratory, it has two main purposes: (1) to exhibit, test, verify and criticize theoretical statements and principles; (2) to add to the sum of facts and principles in its special line.

Dewey was not interested in creating a practice school for training teachers, but in creating a laboratory where pedagogical ideas could be practically tested.

Implicit in Dewey's work at the Laboratory School was the desire to establish a "science of education." Much of his work in education was based on the work of earlier educational theorists, including Johann Pestalozzi, Frederich Froebel, and Johann Herbart. Like them, he believed that children learned best by doing things for themselves and learning directly from the environment in which they lived.

Learning at the Laboratory School was seen as a synthetic process. In the textile room, for example, the children were able to learn about different textiles by processing and weaving them themselves. Looms, dying vats, and spinning wheels were included in the textile room. Samples of different types of fabrics were available for the students to study along with exhibits on their history and use. As Dewey explained: "You can concentrate the history of all mankind into the evolution of flax, cotton and wool fibers into clothing." Reading, writing, arithmetic, and spelling were related to the activities undertaken by the students in the textile room. Traditionally different subject matters were correlated and a unified curriculum was achieved.

The textile curriculum was one small example of the curriculum developed by Dewey and his colleagues at the Laboratory School. Essentially what Dewey attempted to do was to integrate the activities of the school with real-life experiences. "Learning by doing" became to motto for the school. Instead of being a place to learn lessons, the school became a process of directed learning.

Dewey argued in *The School and Society* (1899) that what the best and wisest parents wanted for their children, the community must want for its children as well. Only by helping each child to become all that he or she was capable of becoming could the community achieve its maximum potential. Dewey maintained that changes in the culture and society were necessitating the development of new curricula and methods that were responsive to the needs of the new society. He objected to traditional rote learning from textbooks and instead advocated a type of instruction that focused on the interests and activities of the child.

Dewey believed that children were active and inquiring beings with impulses, concerns, and desires of their own. Breaking with earlier traditions, he argued that the teacher's duty was not just to impart knowledge. Instead,

> His problem is that of inducing a vital, personal experiencing. Hence, what concerns him, as teacher, is the ways in which that subject may become part of experience; what there is in the child's present that is usable with reference to it; how such elements are to be used; how his own knowledge of the subject matter may assist in interpreting the child's needs and doings, and determine the medium in which the child should be placed in order that his growth may be properly directed. He is concerned, not with the subject-matter as such, but with the subject matter as a related factor in a total and growing experience.

For Dewey, the world of the child was a world of individuals with personal interests, rather than a realm of facts and laws. The ideal school and teacher respected these interests on the part of the student. At the same time the teacher attempted to shape the direction of the students' interests so that they conformed with social needs and requirements.

Dewey attempted to make the school into a cooperative community. He did this by making occupations such as cooking, weaving, carpentry, sewing, and metalwork the basis for much of the experience of the child. Dewey felt that by integrating traditional subjects, it would be possible to develop not only children's intellectual abilities, but their imaginative, emotional, creative, and social capacities

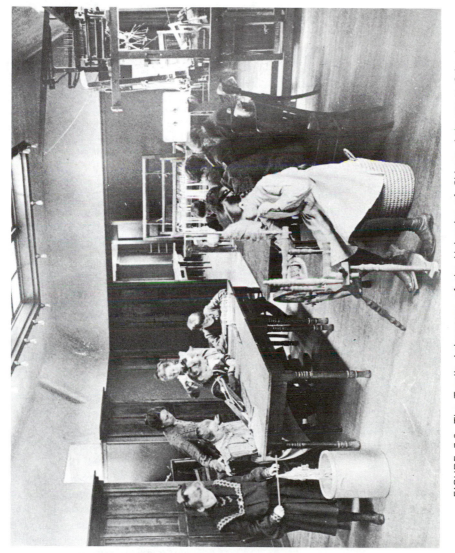

FIGURE 7-3 The Textile Laboratory of the University of Chicago Laboratory School, c. 1869. Courtesy of the Department of Education, University of Chicago.

as well. Textbooks were rarely used at the Laboratory School. Instead students were encouraged to search for information themselves, as well as to draw upon the skills and knowledge of highly trained and competent teachers.

Dewey's emphasis on learning by doing was adapted in many interesting ways by educators around the country. Increasingly, the community was seen as having the potential to educate the child. For example, in 1899, the Brooklyn Institute of Arts and Science began the first children's museum in the United States. Known as the Brooklyn Children's Museum, the purpose of the museum was explained in an early brochure:

> . . . to build up gradually for the children of Brooklyn and the surrounding neighborhood a collection that will delight and instruct the children who visit it; to bring together collections in every branch of natural history that is calculated to interest children, and to stimulate their powers of observation and reflection; and to illustrate by collections of pictures, cartoons, charts, models and maps, each of the important branches of knowledge which are taught in the elementary schools.

Children would visit the museum on a voluntary basis, attracted as a result of their natural interest and curiosity to its programs and activities. The museum would allow children living in the tenements and brownstones of Brooklyn to escape the urban environment in which they lived by taking advantage of a cheerful and exciting museum in a parklike setting.

As in the case of Dewey's curriculum, the Brooklyn Children's Museum hoped to bring children of all ages, whether or not they were attending school, into direct contact with the subjects and objects that

> . . . appeal to the interest of their daily life, in their school work, in their reading, in their games and rambles in the fields, and in the industries which are carried on about them.

Dewey had included an instructional museum as part of his plan for an ideal school described in *The School and Society*. While the Brooklyn Children's Museum represented one type of approach to hands-on education similar to that of Dewey's, a second interesting alternative was developed by the Saint Louis Board of Education in 1905.

As a result of the 1904 Louisiana Purchase Exposition in Saint Louis, interest had developed among teachers and school administrators in providing more hands-on learning experiences for children in the public schools. After the exposition was closed, the assistant superintendent of schools, Carl Rathmann, persuaded the school board to set aside funds for the establishment of an educational museum. A museum was started the following year, using exhibits left over from the World's Fair as well as specially purchased collections of lantern slides, botanical collections, and taxidermied animals.

The motto of the museum was "Bring the world to the child" and represented

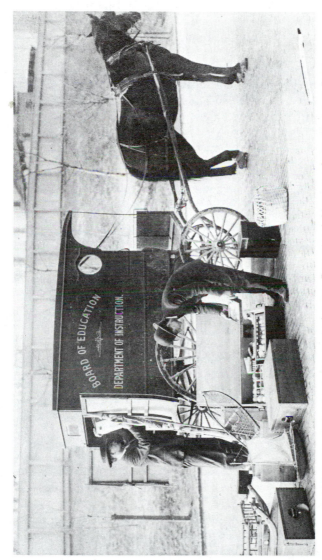

FIGURE 7-4 Deliveries being made for the Educational Museum of the St. Louis Public Schools, c. 1905. Courtesy of the Audio-Visual Department of the St. Louis Public Schools.

a continuation of the spirit of the Louisiana Purchase Exposition, which through its exhibits had brought the world to Saint Louis. Instead of having children visit the museum, collections of objects and slides were sent out to the public schools throughout the school system. Instead of just studying maps and materials in textbooks in geography class, students were given the opportunity actually to handle the raw materials and industrial products of a country. Under the guidance of their teacher, the students would be introduced to the climates, products, and occupations of different people from around the world. Stereoscope views, lantern slides, and photographs would provide students a clearer sense of the people they were studying, their ways of life, and the society in which they lived.

Parallels to the Dewey curriculum at the Laboratory School were to be found throughout the curriculum of the Educational Museum. Carl Rathmann, for example, explained in his first report concerning the Museum that

> By means of the cotton exhibit, we take the children to the cotton fields, where they study the plant, the method of preparing the soil, the harvesting; to the cotton gin, where the seed is separated from the lint; to the markets to see the bailing and the shipping; to the large cotton factories where the lint is spun and woven into fabrics; and to the refineries to learn how cotton seed oil, oil cake, cottonlene, and soap are made.

Lantern slides and photographs were used to develop comparisons between how cotton was processed in primitive cultures and how it was done in modern factories.

The development of "teaching" museums such as the Brooklyn Children's Museum and the Saint Louis Educational Museum are just a few examples of the influence of Dewey's work at the Laboratory School. By 1900, the school had come to the attention of educators throughout the country. Although Dewey left Chicago in 1904 to assume a position in the philosophy department of Columbia University, his influence in education continued to spread. The influence of Dewey on various schools and curricula and his role in the development of "progressive education" will be discussed in subsequent chapters.

YOUTH

Throughout his writings in the late 1890s, Dewey indicated that he saw American culture undergoing profound change. An urban industrial consciousness was increasingly dominating American culture. New values were emerging along with important changes in the social and economic system. Perhaps nowhere were these changes more evident than with the youth population.

During the late nineteenth century the role of youth in the economic and social system underwent a major alteration. Throughout the nineteenth century, youthful workers represented a critically important part of the labor force in the United States. By the turn of the century, however, younger workers were becoming less important in the economic system. Technological improvements in farming meant that fewer youths were needed to work in the agricultural sector of the economy. Increased industrial efficiency eliminated many jobs that had traditionally been assigned to younger workers. Older established workers opposed young workers since they undercut wages and threatened job security. Opportunities to enter the job market were more limited. Protective legislation in the field of child labor, while preventing children from being abused, also made it increasingly difficult for youths to enter the job market. Statistics cited by the contemporary educational historian, Joel Spring, indicate that the male labor force between the ages of fourteen and nineteen increased from 50 percent to 62 percent between 1890 and 1900.

As the need for youth labor decreased during the twentieth century, a corresponding growth in interest in the problems of youth developed. As early as 1904 the psychologist G. Stanley Hall published his pioneer two-volume study, *Adolescence*. Hall's definition of adolescence as a functional stage in human development was based as much on a social perception as on the recognition of a stage of physiological development. Unlike earlier times, when children with the onset of puberty were largely expected to enter into the responsibilities of adulthood, an intermediate period of transition, adolescence, was increasingly recognized as existing between the end of childhood and the acceptance of full adult responsibilities. The vicissitudes of this period of development for the youth were clearly defined by theorists such as Hall:

> The functions of every sense undergo reconstruction, . . . The voice changes, vascular instability, blushing, and flushing are increased. Sex asserts its mastery in field after field, and works its havoc in the form of secret vice, debauch, disease, and enfeebled heredity, cadences the soul to both its normal and abnormal rhythms, and sends many thousand youth a year to quacks, because neither parents, teachers, or physicians know how to deal with its problems.

The energy of youths during this period of their development was seen as having enormous potential. Hall, as well as individuals such as the pioneer social worker Jane Addams, argued that the energies of the youth population should be used for the betterment of the culture.

The development of an increasingly sophisticated technological culture beginning in the early decades of the twentieth century had the effect of making the services of the youth population more nearly superfluous. As the work of youth was needed less and less, enrollment in school began to increase dramatically. In 1900, according to Spring, 78.7 percent of the population between the ages of five and seventeen attended school.

With the decline of the need for youths in the labor force there was a corresponding increase in compulsory schooling. Although local compulsory education laws were passed during the early Colonial period, their implementation on a statewide basis did not begin until the middle of the nineteenth century when Massachusetts in 1852 passed the first statewide law requiring children to attend school. Yet, despite such laws, attendance in school throughout the nineteenth century was largely voluntary. Relatively little concern was given to teenagers who dropped out of school to find employment. Loopholes in the various attendance laws were easily found so long as there was a demand for the services of young workers.

The enforcement of compulsory education laws seems to have increased as adolescent workers were increasingly superfluous. Selwyn K. Troen has pointed out that in the 1870s, one-third of the employees in Macy's Department Store in New York City were cash girls, while the same proportion worked as cash boys in Marshall Field in Chicago during the 1880s. In 1902, Macy's and then Marshall Field, introduced a pneumatic tube system that eliminated the need for young messengers to carry money back and forth between the store's sales counters and the bookkeeping department. This relatively simple innovation, combined with the invention of devices such as the cash register in 1878, and their widespread adoption and use by the turn of the century almost completely eliminated the need for cash boys and cash girls. Technology was similarly affecting other areas of employment. Improvements in communications systems, such as the invention of the telephone, quickly eliminated the need for messenger boys to carry information between different offices in downtown business districts. As a result, another important source of youth employment was also eliminated.

Interestingly, as youth labor became less and less needed, greater efforts were made to regulate and limit it. Reformers increasingly saw child workers as exploited by the capitalist system. In addition, psychologists such as G. Stanley Hall began to warn that interference with the child's natural development would be destructive to it, and to the normal development of society as well.

The new psychology of Hall and the child study movement, as well as Dewey and his followers, stressed the physiological and psychological importance of play. "When children are robbed of playtime, they too often assert their right to it in manhood, as vagabonds, criminals, and prostitutes." These views not only supported the establishment of playgrounds, but led to increasing criticisms of child labor.

By 1904 the National Child Labor Committee had been organized. Headed by Felix Adler of the Ethical Culture School in New York, the committee board included Jane Addams and Lillian Wald. The purpose of the NCLC was the investigation of working conditions, the establishment of more stringent legislation, and the enforcement of existing laws. Promoting its cause by a wide range of activities, the NCLC made extensive use of photographs to document the working conditions of children.

Numerous books and articles were published then describing the conditions of child labor in America. The books included Ernest Poole's *The Street: Its Child Workers*, Robert Hunter's *Poverty*, and John Spargo's *The Bitter Cry of Children*. Articles condemning child labor appeared regularly in such periodicals as *The Survey, The Outlook, McClure's, The Independent*, and even the *Saturday Evening Post* and *Cosmopolitan*. Among the most interesting articles were the photo stories of Lewis Hine.

Hine, born in Oshkosh, Wisconsin, in 1874, went to New York City in 1901 to teach at the Ethical Culture School. In 1908 he resigned from teaching to be a full-time documentary photographer. As staff photographer for *The Survey*, Hine also undertook work for the NCLC. Traveling thousands of miles during the next several years, Hine photographed children working in canneries, coal mines, sweat-shops, and tenements and in cotton fields and cranberry bogs. In the reform tradition of Riis, Hine produced some of the era's great documentary and reform photographs.

   Although primarily a photographer, Hine often wrote about what he had photographed. In "Baltimore to Biloxi and Back," in *The Survey* in 1913, Hine described the conditions of children working in oyster and shrimp canneries. Seven- and eight-year-old children were forced out of bed at three o'clock in the morning to go to work shelling shrimps. Hine explained how

FIGURE 7-5 Cover photograph by Lewis Hine for the September 23, 1911 issue of *The Survey* magazine.

When they are picking shrimps, their fingers and even their shoes are attacked by a corrosive substance in the shrimp that is strong enough to eat the cans into which they are put. But the day's work on shrimp is much shorter than on oysters as fingers on the worker give out in spite of the fact that they are compelled to harden them in an alum solution at the end of the day. Moreover, the shrimp are packed in ice, and a few hours handling of these icy things is dangerous for any child.

Hine was also disturbed because children's work in the factories kept them from attending school. For pay of 25 or 50 cents a day they not only endangered their health, but were also deprived of any formal education. In those few instances where Hine did observe children going to school, he found that they attended only a few hours a day, often having worked since the early morning.

Hine fought to expose children working illegally in factories. His camera took him anywhere children were at work. Unlike Riis's, Hine's concern for reform went beyond the city. His photographs of "breaker boys" in coal mines in Pennsylvania, child cotton spinners working in rural factories in North Carolina, and child agricultural workers engaged in almost every task imaginable provide us with remarkable documentary sources for the history of child labor.

The work of Hine and groups such as the NCLC was eventually responsible for bringing about the passage of important state and federal legislation limiting child labor. When the NCLC was originally organized in 1904, there was little effective state legislation concerning child labor. By 1914, thirty-five states had a fourteen-year-age minimum, and an eight-hour-day maximum for workers under sixteen. Thirty-four states prohibited children from working at night, while thirty-six states had appointed factory inspectors to enforce child labor regulations.

By 1916, the federal Keating-Owen Act was passed. Providing for the protection of child laborers on a national level, the passage of the law was the triumph of the Progressive reformers, such as Hine, who were concerned with child labor reform. Failing to address the needs of domestic and agricultural workers, the law was eventually repealed in 1920. Its effects on reducing child labor and the child labor reform movement in general, however, are clearly evident in statistics from the period. In 1900, the census listed 790,623 children working who were between the ages of ten and thirteen and 959,555 working who were between fourteen and fifteen years of age. By 1920, these figures were reduced to 378,063 children working between the ages of ten and thirteen and 682,795 children working between fourteen and fifteen years of age.

CONCLUSION

This strain of the Progressive reform movement in education was an important attempt to deal with the problems created by an increasingly complex urban industrial society. Jane Addams, Jacob Riis, John Dewey, and other reformers had as their purpose the improvement of the environment in which people lived and were educated. Realizing that traditional models of education and reform were inadequate to meet the demands of the new society and culture emerging by the end of the nineteenth century, they provided important alternatives.

In retrospect, many of the innovations by these reformers seem naive and overly optimistic. Yet these reformers did help to create a better life for many people and laid the foundations for much of our modern education system.

Chapter Eight
EFFICIENCY
AND MANAGEMENT

It is worth noting again that the Progressive reformers had goals that could be characterized as social justice, democracy, and efficiency. This chapter is devoted to the pursuit of school efficiency, and to school managers who led that pursuit.

We see school efficiency as having often been a guise for authoritarian action. Many attempts to increase the efficiency of schools have been unsuccessful even by their own standards. But the general concept of efficiency in schools has a long history of its own and some distinguished ancestors.

The attempt to rationalize, or organize logically, is one that was attractive during the Enlightenment, in the 1700s. Benjamin Franklin, practical man of that time, had been a seeker for efficiency; that was the virtue of the Franklin stove. Arrangements sufficiently rational were like machines, which became admirable. We have noted that almost a hundred years before the Progressive era their supporters claimed that the monitorial schools were like machines. It was not coincidental, as John Griscom had written in 1823, that ". . . the establishment and progress of the Lancastrian or monitorial Schools, have been contemporaneous with the improvement of the Steam Engine, and with the wonderful applications of that new power to the wants of mankind." Nor do we think it coincidental that S. Chester Parker, dean of education at the University of Chicago when school efficiency came into fashion, was the first writer in three quarters of a century to praise the orderliness and systematic arrangements of the monitorial schools.

Reformers in the Progressive era pressed for efficiency, social justice, and democracy. A reformer might have pressed for any one of these goals, or two of them, or all of them. The difficulty, as is clear after a moment's reflection, is that the goals may be contradictory: the cost of efficiency in any conventional factory is the sacrifice of democracy, and the cost of social justice may be efficiency, as conventionally defined.

Toward the end of the 1800s the engineer's use of the word "efficiency" made its meaning somewhat more exact. An engineer calculated—and still calculates—efficiency by dividing the output of a machine by its input, when both were expressed in the same or interchangeable terms. Both the input and output of a machine can be measured as energy. Both the input and output of a factory can be measured in dollars. For lack of better standards, school inputs can be expressed in dollars also. The crowning, crippling handicap in the Progressive era was that outcomes could not be measured, and if measured could not be translated into dollars, except in the most simpleminded way.

SCHOOL CONTROL AND SCHOOL MANAGEMENT

The most influential men and women in the Progressive reform movement were members of the middle class and the well-off, members of the "elite." This was true of school reformers, and also of city reformers. The prominent and the successful, especially among the educators, often made statements supporting school reform. University presidents Eliot of Harvard, White of Cornell, and Harper of Chicago were staunch school reformers. They were joined, of course, by school superintendents, for instance, Ben Blewett of Saint Louis and William H. Maxwell of New York City. In New York City, supporters of school centralization were, as David Hammack has shown, business and professional men, advocates of efficiency in schools as well as in city government, and also old-fashioned Protestant moral reactionaries. The supporters of school reform in Philadelphia were prominent businessmen and lawyers.

One of the first aims of the reformers was to reduce the size of school boards, on the grounds that smaller boards and appropriate board members would enable school boards to function in ways similar to business boards of directors. School boards were reduced in size in many cities. The Saint Louis School Board was reduced from twenty-eight members to twenty-two, and then to twelve. The Philadelphia School Board was reduced from forty-two to twenty-one, and the New York City School Board from forty-six to seven, although that process took nearly twenty years.

As the size of school boards was reduced, the proportion of middle- and upper-class members in Saint Louis increased from 17 percent in 1896 to 86 percent in 1903. The Saint Louis School Board was made up then of three lawyers, four

FIGURE 8-1 The St. Louis School Board, c. 1875. Courtesy of the Audio-Visual Department of the St. Louis Public Schools.

businessmen, two engineers, a physician, a newspaper manager, and an educator. It is incontestable that most board members, at least since Scott Nearing's investigation of 1916, have been members of the middle class.

If it has generally been in the interest of the middle class to prevent school change to prevent social change, then the middle-class makeup of school boards has been a preventative of change. However, one might ask whether middle-class parents have indeed preferred the status quo in schooling. One might also ask if school board members have in general voted on the basis of their social class membership, a question which, as Charters pointed out some years ago, has not been answered. It could be argued that the decisions to be made by school boards were and are essentially moral decisions. If so, then a school board, like a jury, should represent as fully as possible the community from which it comes. However, if school board decisions contain technical elements, then knowledge as well as wisdom may be valuable. We are disinclined to offer personal judgment in the matter.

The school reformers, like the city reformers, felt that politics should be kept out of education. Lord Bryce, who had said that the quality of American life was pleasant, found little to admire in American political parties and party politicians: "We place at the head of the list of evils under which our municipal administration labors, the fact that so large a number of important offices have come to be filled by men possessing little, if any, fitness." Schisel notes that political scientists have found that nonpartisan elections favor, once again, members of the middle class. That aside, it is also argued that keeping politics out of school board elections and appointments has made the schools less responsive to local neighborhood influence. It must be granted that schools have been wonderously immune to such influences, but we have not seen persuasive evidence that party-affiliated board members have been effective in presenting local preferences in schooling.

Nearly all school superintendents avoided party politics. The party person who was a superintendent, as John Hancock of Ohio was, and who served as superintendent whenever a solid Republican was called for, was part of a small minority indeed. If *politics* is defined more broadly, then of course the control and financing of the schools is of necessity political—but that objection comes from a difference in definitions.

The reformers argued that more school decisions should be made by experts, as decisions in private businesses were made by experts. The most powerful of the school experts was, of course, the school superintendent, who in addition to being an executive was ideally an expert in all things educational. Decision making in and about schools was more and more the responsibility of the superintendent, as at least two surveys made at the time show.

The Progressive reformers of schools for efficiency argued that decision making should be centralized in the office of the superintendent, and then went on to advocate the development of city school district organizations very much like those of business organizations. Such school organizations were developed. However, the possible future disadvantages of such organizational patterns were not considered at the time. Large organizations may, or may not, function well when they are established. However, the same organizations become nearly impossible to change if they become obsolete or otherwise inappropriate. This, we have found in the last twenty-five years, is particularly true of public organizations, the staffs of which are protected by civil service regulations. To centralize and organize school decision making was to generate an organization that would be the greatest of bulwarks against subsequent change in schooling. The Progressive reformers did not foresee that difficulty, and perhaps could not have foreseen it, and that circumstance is partly extenuating.

Partly because they were outcomes of a kind of Progressive reform of schools, and partly because they accompanied it, "efficiency," the ready-made bromide, and scientific management and measurement in the schools should be discussed and considered in the wider context of Progressive reform.

EFFICIENCY IN THE SCHOOLS

Definite qualitative and quantitative standards must be determined for the product. . . . Where the material acted upon the labor processes passes through a number of progressive stages from the new material to the ultimate product, definite quantitative and qualitative standards must be determined for the product at each of these stages. . . . The worker must be kept up to standard qualifications for this kind of work during his entire service.

Pupils were the "material" and the "product."

Teaching was the "labor." Teachers were the "workers."

The author was Dr. Franklin P. Bobbitt, instructor in education at the University of Chicago. These passages were first published in 1913, when efficiency in the schools was a popular issue.

"Efficiency" in the schools had been borrowed from efficiency in factories. Although some school administrators had been concerned earlier about the efficiency of their schools, many more were converted to efficiency about 1910 when "efficiency" became a popular word and idea. It became then the most popular of remedies for all school evils, real or imagined.

Because of its origins, school efficiency and its popularity are more understandable with the history of industrial efficiency as background. For the same reason we have followed the history of industrial and business management. Even in factories, efficiency was useful, if it was useful, as a management tool. Efficiency required a different form of management, "scientific management." School administrators and others such as Bobbitt saw school efficiency as a tool, a tool for the scientific management of the school. If we are to tell the story of one, we must tell the history of both. In a sense, school efficiency rested upon educational measurement. After all, the meeting of "quantitative" standards could only be verified or demonstrated by measurement. There were unremitting efforts to pupils' abilities, school learning, and teacher effectiveness.

School efficiency was popular for several reasons. It was a defense against reformers. Attacked by Progressive reformers, particularly the "muckrakers" who were the advocacy journalists of their day, city school superintendents felt threatened and "vulnerable." For their own defense they needed to find ways of showing their usefulness and competence. For the school administrator there was another advantage of efficiency, because it served as an argument for greater centralization of control and power. Too, efficiency seemed to have the old fashioned virtues of practicality and frugality; that would have appealed to reform school board members. More benignly, perhaps some school administrators came to favor efficiency methods because businessmen and engineers had become the most admired and respected men in society and served as role models. Some professors of education also became ardent supporters of efficiency. Their zeal seems to have been excessive at times. It is difficult to believe that none of them was opportunistic.

It has been said that Benjamin Franklin was the first efficiency expert. That has a grain of truth in it. Franklin was surely interested in solutions to practical problems. Although practicality did not originate with Franklin, it was one of Americans' first interests, the interest which made Americans tinkerers and master mechanics, inventors, and engineers. In 1876 English visitors to the Philadelphia Centennial Exposition noted how well American machines worked. They also noted that hidden nonoperating parts of American machines were roughly made, although operating parts were made with great skill and precision. That was good enough. "Good enough" became an important consideration for American industry. (We most often complain because "good enough" is not good enough.)

It is not surprising that a like concept was applied to schooling at the time of the efficiency movement. In schooling, the near equivalent of "good enough" was "minimum essentials," the essentials (now often called "competencies") each student had to master to become a satisfactory worker and citizen. "Minimum essentials" received much consideration during the time of the school efficiency movement.

To repeat, school efficiency was largely an adaptation of industrial factory efficiency. The synthesis that produced industrial efficiency was primarily the contribution of Frederick W. Taylor. Taylor was the son of an old and well-to-do Philadelphia Quaker family. Born in 1856, Taylor is described by one of his biographers, Sudhir Kakar, as having a personality—formed by his first experiences—that was neurotically compulsive, as ritualistic and combative, profane but prudish. Kakar does not err on the side of generosity.

Probably not a likable man, Taylor had a streak of genius. He attended an academy in Germantown, by then a prosperous part of Philadelphia, and in Germany when his family made a prolonged visit there. Back in the United States, he was sent to Phillips Exeter to prepare to enter Harvard. Taylor was admitted to Harvard but did not attend because, he said, studies had weakened his eyes. One of Taylor's biographers has concluded that Taylor's eyestrain had psychological origins. But, on the other hand, young Philadelphia gentlemen had often started their careers with an apprenticeship, as Taylor did in 1874.

As an apprentice, incidentally, Taylor was an attendant at his firm's display at the Philadelphia Centennial Exposition. In 1878, at the age of twenty-two, he was employed by Midvale Steel Company, which produced heavy parts for railroads and for the navy. At Midvale he began the first of his tens of thousands of experiments on machining steel.

Taylor's objective was to cut away metal on a lathe, as quickly and inexpensively as possible. The problem was a complicated one, in which there were a dozen variables: depth of the cut, shape of the cutting edge, cooling, and so on. Taylor's work was a model of excellence in applied science. Among other things, he determined that a round cutting edge was quicker than a diamond-shaped one. Later he invented "high-speed" chromium-tungsten alloy steel, which is still in use for cutting edges.

Taylor was also interested in increasing the output of the worker. The first step was to replace traditional skills with technology, a process already many years old. Taylor's metal-cutting experts made part of machinists' traditional knowledge obsolete and useless, and made the lathe hand a worker semiskilled at best. Worker output could also be increased by division of work, or division of labor. That had served as one of the key concepts in Adam Smith's *Wealth of Nations* in 1776, although that idea was then already old, too. In 1835 Charles Babbage, an Englishman, had calculated that while one worker could make 20 pins in a day, ten workers could together make nearly 9,000 pins a day.

Like Adam Smith, Taylor saw the worker as being solely motivated by money or lack of it. This is demonstrably untrue. However, it was possible to think of a worker in terms of money. As another efficiency expert wrote in 1913,

> On a punch press costing $3,000, the yearly cost . . . would be $450. The operator of this machine would probably be paid $3 a day, a total of about $900 a year. The only apparent difference is that the machine is paid for in advance, while the labor is paid for in weekly, bimonthly, or monthly installments.

Taylor had not voiced that thought, but the thought did lead to the efficiency expert's conception of the worker, worker as machine, money driven rather than power belt driven. Like any other machine, the worker could be adjusted and readjusted. The other variables would be the worker's speed, strength, and endurance.

The most famous man-as-machine description was written by Taylor. The worker was called "Schmidt." The task, at Republic Steel, was loading ninety-pound iron pigs into railroad box cars. First there was a step-by-step analysis of activity and time required, from "(a) picking up the pig from the ground or pile" to "(e) walking back empty to get a load." Schmidt was selected from among the Republic Steel laborers. He was an "energetic little Pennsylvania Dutchman" who was known for "placing a very high value on a dollar." Like the other laborers, he had been loading into box cars twelve and a half tons of pig iron a day. For a 60-cent raise, to $1.85 a day, he was to move forty-seven tons of pig iron a day.

> ". . . you will do exactly as this man tells you tomorrow, from morning till night. . . . When he tells you to pick up a pig and walk, you pick it up and

you walk, and when he tells you to sit down and rest, you sit down. You do that right straight through the day. And what's more, no back talk. Do you understand that? When this man [Taylor's assistant] tells you to walk, you walk; when he tells you to sit down, you sit down, and you don't talk back at him. . . ."

Schmidt started to work, and all day long. . . . He worked when he was told to work, rested when he was told to rest, and at half past five that afternoon had his forty-seven and a half tons loaded on the car. . . .

Schmidt's work output increased by 280 percent, his pay by 60 percent. Taylor argued that increased overhead costs were part of the price of efficiency. Republic Steel had employed Taylor to increase profits, of course. There were many other applications of efficiency, and time-and-motion study, in factories whose products ranged from bicycles to field artillery.

In 1910, northeastern railroads applied to the Interstate Commerce Commission for a freight rate increase to cover the additional costs of wage increases. One of the attorneys arguing against the rate increase was Progressive liberal Louis Brandeis. Brandeis argued that the railroads' inefficiency cost $1 million a day. He called ten witnesses who testified on the application of efficiency and scientific management in industry.

The Interstate Commerce Commission hearings gained public attention, and "efficiency" was the hope of the hour. "Efficiency" was advocated for every part of life, even for churches and homes, and of course for schools. One author, Fletcher Durell, undertook building a formal philosophy with efficiency as its base. "Efficiency" was exported to France to aid in winning World War I. In Russia Lenin wrote a pamphlet in its praise.

"School efficiency" was the subject of many speeches and innumerable articles. Bobbitt's full-blown book-length presentation, from which the quotations at the beginning of this chapter are taken, appeared in 1913. The next year one of the few superintendents with public doubts said that "so many efficiency engineers [were] running handcarts through the schoolhouses in most large cities that grade teachers can hardly turn around without butting into two or three of them." In 1915, a National Society for the Study of Education yearbook on the measurement of teacher efficiency was published, and in 1916, efficiency and testing were important topics in the most important textbook on school administration.

Franklin Bobbit's 1913 book was a yearbook of the National Society for the Study of Education, the most prominent of scholarly education societies. The book was an exposition of Taylor's principles of efficiency and management, and of their application to schools. This would be valuable to teachers, Bobbitt said, because they would know exactly what was required of them. It would be valuable to supervisors, who could simply compare the achievements of a class with standards for its grade. The superintendent could "instantly locate the strong, the mediocre, and the weak teachers." He could assess differences in teaching methods and textbooks.

A simple calculation of efficiency in schools was in terms of dollar cost. (This was like the business input-output dollar efficiency, only by mistaken analogy. No

dollar measure of output was available or even sought.) The most prominent exposi-
tor of dollar efficiency was Frank Spaulding, who had earned a Ph.D. in Germany,
and having been superintendent of schools in Passaic, New Jersey, was superintendent of schools in Newton, Massachusetts. As early as 1909, he had said that
"The demand for efficiency . . . is urgent and universal."

Spaulding's definition of *efficiency* was nearest to that of the businessperson.
It was true, he said then, that school outputs were unmeasured and ultimately
unmeasurable. Measurements of instructional cost were to the informed eye measurements of inputs. Spaulding demonstrated his methods. First, he had discovered
that per pupil instructional costs in a small school in Newton were greater than in a
large school there. On the other hand, the large school had cost more, per pupil, to
build. These findings do not seem to be surprising or even particularly informative.

As a second example, he discussed the costs of high school instruction on a
per pupil per recitation basis. He found that

> . . . 5.9 pupil-recitations in Greek are of the same value as 23.8 recitations in
> French; that 12 pupil-recitations in science are equivalent in value to 19.2
> pupil-recitations in English; and that it takes 41.7 pupil-recitations in vocal
> music to equal the value of 13.9 pupil-recitations in art.

Presumably the audience found this at least somewhat impressive, even though hard
to follow and although "cost" and "value" were confused. The conclusion was
school efficiency reduced to dollar cost, pure and unmitigated.

> . . . I know nothing about the absolute value of a recitation in Greek as com-
> pared with a recitation in French or English. I am convinced, however, by
> very concrete and quite logical considerations, that when the obligations of
> the present year expire, we ought to purchase no more Greek instruction at
> the rate of 5.9 pupil-recitations per dollar. The price must go down, or we
> will invest in something else.

This was, of course, *efficiency* redefined as *economy*, and *economy* defined as
cheap. There seemed to be no other consideration.

SCIENTIFIC MANAGEMENT IN THE SCHOOLS

Management, as we will use the term here, means oversight of an enterprise and
organization, public or private. It means choosing goals and strategies and, on that
basis, distributing resources. Organizationally, management divides labor, logically
defines jobs, and distributes monetary and other rewards. Hastened by its inheritance from Taylor, management has been in part a systematic process of transfer-
ring skill from workers to management.

Patterns of school management have been derived largely from, and much
modified by, patterns of management of private enterprises. This took place more

than at any other time when schools adopted Taylor's "scientific management." "Scientific management" itself is more readily understandable against the background of the practice and theory of private enterprise management.

The simplest form of management is direct personal management by the owner. As an example of owner management, John W. Cannon was both captain—management—and owner of the record-making Mississippi River steamboat *Robert E. Lee* (New Orleans to Saint Louis, three days, three hours, forty-four minutes). In some industries there was little advantage in consolidation, or in elaborating management.

However, as industrial enterprises became ever larger and more complex, there was pressing need for coordination. At that point it was necessary to develop more detailed arrangements for management. The first of the elaborated management systems in the United States were the railroads' systems. Investments in railroads were huge for the time, far greater than in any other enterprise. By 1850, there were two railroads capitalized at over $10 million. In 1860, there were ten such railroads, and five capitalized at nearly twice that. Not only were they huge enterprises, but they were geographically dispersed—by 1855, there were at least thirteen railroads that each had more than 200 miles of track in use. It was necessary to coordinate operations. A locomotive derailed and damaged in Buffalo would affect the delivery of passengers and freight in New York City. The operation of a railroad increasingly called for technical expertise in operations, in maintenance of track and rolling stock, and also in accounting and other areas. Organized and centralized management was advantageous, and the appearance of the telegraph made it feasible.

In 1847, Benjamin H. Latrobe, chief engineer of the Baltimore and Ohio Railroad, put into operation a new management system. (Engineers would be important in these matters.) Financial accounting, receipts and disbursements, were to be the responsibility of a comptroller. There were separate departments for track maintenance, for rolling stock, and for transportation operations. The heads of the departments were to be responsible to the chief engineer or general superintendent, who with the comptroller reported to the Baltimore and Ohio's president and board of directors. Engineer David C. McCallum refined the management system for the Erie Railroad in 1855. He said then that the management of the Erie Railroad system called for, first an appropriate division of responsibilities, and with it, appropriate division of authority. It followed that there must be ways of verifying that responsibilities had been met and that therefore all "derelictions of duty" were to be reported at once (via telegraph most often) for quick correction. Concerning operations, daily or even hourly reports were required.

What McCallum formulated was the line of command portion of management organization. Additional staff positions for expert advisers would be added as the need and knowledge arose. (Although the language and spirit of this kind of organization and management have a military air, they did not arise in the military services, but in private enterprise. They were largely copied by the army and later by the navy. A later adaption to education is diagrammed in Figure 8-2).

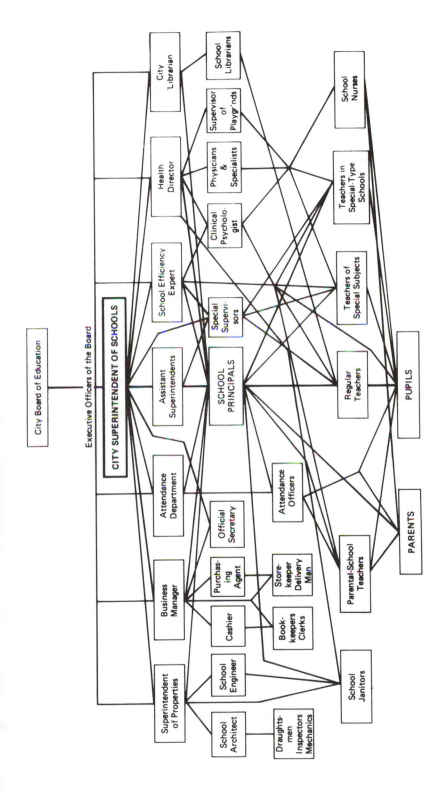

FIGURE 8-2 Plan of educational organization for a large-city school system. Adapted from Ellwood P. Cubberley, *Public School Administration* (Boston: Houghton Mifflin, 1916), pp. 172-73.

221

To management, Taylor made two important contributions. First, he offered a related set of ideas, a synthesis, and a refinement of the management techniques by then available. Second, perhaps without intent, he was instrumental in the popularization of a management plan, as well as his plan for worker efficiency. Taylor started with time-and-motion study, or the immediate development of efficiency. The next step, Taylor wrote, was the development of standards for tools and work. Then there was the task, to be worked out by a planning department, and with it bonus plans for payment for work. The "planning department" would develop the knowledge that would replace that of the journeyman, the skilled craftsman. A part of planning was to be the careful recording of production costs. Finally, Taylor's plan called for "functional foremen" whose primary responsibility was to teach workers how to perform tasks; this part of Taylor's scientific management was least often used.

As we have said, school administrators had appeared long before Taylor's scientific management and efficiency became popular. The drift of school administration toward business methods had started before the Interstate Commerce Commission hearings. W. E. Chancellor, who had written books on school administration in 1904 and 1908, had more often than not portrayed the city superintendent as a business manager. Early in 1910, Frank Spaulding was arguing not only that the school administration, as it then existed, was "grossly inefficient," but also that the training of the administrator should be based on "sound and simple business principles."

At the first meeting of the Department of Superintendence of the NEA after the Interstate Commerce Commission hearings, Spaulding was invited to deliver a major address. His topic was "Improving School Systems Through Scientific Management." Spaulding's version of "scientific management" bore little resemblance to Taylor's. Spaulding reported on the procedures that he had used with great success in Newton. He had eliminated small classes and reduced the number of classes offered, so that fewer teachers were needed. Spaulding used several graphs and charts that provided at least the pretext of science, although he had applied not much more than rudimentary cost accounting. His conception of what the school administrator should be was obvious.

An alternative form of efficiency would have been based on Bobbitt and at least indirectly upon Taylor. However, superintendents adopted Spaulding's formulas, and so could reduce schooling to dollars and meet the economy-minded critics on their own ground. Spaulding gave to the work of the administrator the appearance of scientific respectability. He contributed to the improvement of the status of administrators and also provided them with a professional reason for great emphasis upon the dollar aspects of education. If there were doubts of the effectiveness of Spaulding's approach, they might have been dispelled by witnessing Spaulding's career. For ten years he had kept his job at Newton, the "burial ground of superintendents," at one of the highest Massachusetts superintendents' salaries. In 1914, he would be appointed superintendent at Minneapolis at $8,000 a year, and three years later he would move to Cleveland at an annual salary of $12,000.

It was Spaulding's ideas, not Bobbitt's, that were accepted by most of those who wrote on educational administration after 1913. Spaulding's principles were easy to apply, economy was achieved, and the schools appeared to be run efficiently. Bobbitt's system would have required elaborate and expensive research and planning divisions, for which even the largest school systems had neither money nor talent. That aside, the public seemed to be primarily concerned with cost. Although he was praised, Bobbitt's description of children as "raw material" and of teachers as "workers" seems to have been too extreme.

The most widely used and most influential administration textbook of the time was Ellwood P. Cubberley's *Public School Administration* (1916). Cubberley incorporated into his text concepts from Chancellor, Spaulding, and Bobbit. The textbook pictured the superintendent as nearly superhuman. His was the office "up to which and down from which authority, direction, and inspiration flow." As Cubberley saw him, the superintendent was to be familiar with Bobbitt's efficiency and Spaulding's cost accounting, but was to be neither time-and-motion expert nor cost accountant. The superintendent was to be an executive in every way, much like the successful business executive, the captain of industry. Cubberley's definition of the role of the administrator left the teacher without authority outside the classroom. The teacher might advise, but was not to make important "administrative" decisions.

MEASUREMENT IN THE SCHOOLS

Returning to Taylor and Schmidt's efficiency, it is obvious that efficiency depended upon measurement. The necessary measurements were time (spent by Schmidt) and the weight of the pig iron he moved. Time and weight together, as tons per day, were the measure of Schmidt's productivity, which could also be described as cents per ton. If the efficiency and productivity of schools was to be calculated, it would be necessary to measure inputs (pupil and teacher attributes) and outputs (learning). Therefore, the popularity of school efficiency increased interest in productivity measures.

Factory mass production, pure science, and commerce also increased interest in measurement. At the beginning of the 1900s, Americans were increasingly impressed with the importance of pure science. Until then the sciences and scientists had been relatively unimportant in the development of new technology and new industries. However, the development of the electrical and chemical industries depended heavily upon pure sciences. Thomas Edison's electric business, which became General Electric, relied upon Charles Proteus Stienmitz for theoretical advice. Stienmitz was a German-trained physicist whose approach was mathematical and quantitative. It was clear that there were new areas of technology that required science and measurement.

Although pure science had gotten some attention in colleges since the 1820s, it was more important by 1900, when there were two hundred physicists in the

United States. One of the most prominent of them was Henry A. Rowland, professor at Johns Hopkins University whose vastly improved diffraction grating had made possible the much more accurate measurement of light spectra. Another prominent physicist was Albert A. Michelson, born in Poland, brought up in Murphy's Camp, California, and graduate of Annapolis Naval Academy. Michelson had studied in Germany and had begun there an investigation of "luminferous ether." This in turn required the most precise possible measurement of the velocity of light. For his measurement, Michelson was awarded a Nobel Prize in physics in 1907, the first to an American. Science in America was becoming more important, and measurement would be a necessary part of science.

The success of mass production was due, as we have said, to the standardization of products and their parts. This also required precise measurements of lengths and weights. To provide measurement standards, the Bureau of Weights and Standards was established in 1902. Fair standard weights for commerce and for the consumer were one of the goals of some Progressive reformers. *Cosmopolitan*, one of the popular magazines, carried a muckraker article on short weights. Measurement would not only aid in production. It would aid and protect the consumer, too.

Under the circumstances, interest in educational measurement increased. It had begun earlier, of course, with the work of Joseph Mayer Rice, who in the fall of 1894 turned from his exposés of the school to measurement. Rice's first question was whether and how much the length of spelling lessons affected pupils' ability. Spelling lessons' lengths were measured in minutes; ability to spell was to be measured by spelling tests. It was impractical for Rice himself to teach spelling, and he relied upon teachers for information on the length of spelling lessons. (Technically this was a *quasi-experimental research design*, which is still in use.) The spelling tests, fifty words long, were administered by Rice personally to, eventually, 14,000 pupils. Rice himself graded their papers. He concluded that there was no relationship between the length of spelling lessons and pupils' ability to spell. One might have inferred, therefore, that spelling lessons should be short. (It now seems that Rice's tests were too easy.) Rice's results, presented in 1896, did not please the superintendents. Perhaps they still resented his earlier muckraking, and the days of measuring educational products had not yet come.

In 1909, the year before the Interstate Commerce Commission rate hearings that publicized efficiency, Leonard P. Ayres, in *Laggards in Our Schools*, compared fifty-eight cities by the ages of pupils and the grades they were in. A city school system, he argued, was most efficient if none of its pupils were "retarded" or too old for the grade they were in. Since 75 percent of the pupils in Memphis black schools were "retarded," those were the least efficient of schools. There are obvious limits to the conclusions that might be reached this way. Ayres had mentioned none of them.

More direct measures, achievement tests, had already begun to appear. Several were developed by Robert L. Thorndike and his doctoral students at Teachers College, Columbia University. The first achievement tests, carefully validated, pretested, and standardized, were C. W. Stone's arithmetic tests, which appeared in

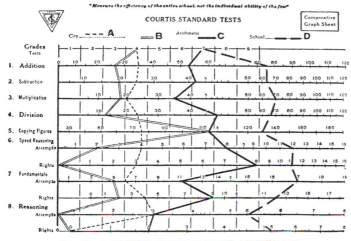

FIG. 30. A COURTIS SCORE CARD IN ARITHMETIC

(Reproduced by permission of Mr. S. A. Courtis)

In the figure above curves A and B are of two individuals in the same class. From an Indiana school. Note that A is practically normal except in the last test (shown by the fact that the curve is almost a straight line and lies almost wholly within the boundaries of the fourth grade), while B is below grade in every test but one and is particularly weak on reasoning.

Curves C and D are two measurements of the same child, one in September and the other in June. From a Michigan school. Note the correction of many defects and the balance of the final scores.

FIGURE 8-3   The development of the efficiency movement depended heavily on the results of quantitative research. Elaborate methods of recording the progress of students, such as this Courtis scorecard in arithmetic, came into widespread use as part of the movement. From Ellwood P. Cubberley, *Public School Administration* (Boston: Houghton Mifflin, 1916), p. 334.

1908. Thorndike's handwriting scale appeared the next year. Developing it was more complicated; there are objectively correct answers in arithmetic, but handwriting is good if it is judged to be good. S. A. Courtis's arithmetic tests, with grade-level norms, also appeared in 1909. In 1912, there was a measure of composition achievement; and in 1913, B. R. Buckingham's spelling test. In 1918, Walter S. Monroe listed 109 achievement tests. After that there were too many to list, or even to count. The interpretations of test scores rested on at least elementary statistics, which were made (relatively) accessible by Robert L. Thorndike in 1904 in *An Introduction to the Theory of Mental and Social Measurements.* The interrelations among measures were, as it developed, complex, and the interrelationship was never one to one. Thorndike provided information on correlations, calculations, that is, of the degree of interrelatedness. That was necessary, of course, because one set of scores by itself was uninformative.

Achievement tests, checklists, and other measurements were used in every imaginable way. Teacher outputs were measured. Two or more methods of teaching were compared. Schoolhouses were rated on long or short forms. The heights of boys and girls were measured annually and carefully tabulated.

A popular use of achievement measures was in school surveys. The *school surveys*—the term was borrowed from the municipal reformers' *social surveys*—

appeared about 1910. One bibliography lists six surveys in 1910 and 1911, seventeen in 1912 and 1913, twenty-one in 1914 and 1915, and twenty-three in 1915 and 1916. Surely there were many more. The most massive survey was that of the New York City schools, conducted by Paul H. Hanus of Harvard. That survey was in progress for three years and was reported in three volumes. It was the first survey to include achievement test results. Surveyers usually found that the schools were in most ways efficient, and provided evidence of the superintendent's competence and the system's merit. The schools of Boise, Idaho, were surveyed in 1910, 1913, and 1915 for reasons otherwise obscure, except that Boise School Superintendent Charles S. Meek was a survey enthusiast. School surveys would continue to be popular through the 1920s, and there are still occasional school surveys, though now for different purposes. In 1925, Jesse B. Sears in his book *The School Survey* explained the popularity of school surveys because of their resemblance to industrial efficiency studies: ". . . it was not strange that the public should take readily to the survey idea. People were already familiar with the work of the efficiency engineer and the accounting expert in business and industry."

Isolated, out of context, measurements are nearly meaningless, and our criticism of them in isolation would be as meaningless. Undeniably, the surveys

FIGURE 8-4 "What is a School Survey and Why" cartoon published in *The Richmond News-Leader,* reprinted in *The Survey*, Vol. XXXI, March 14, 1914, p. 747.

were misused in the name of efficiency, and their results were employed to gratify and defend superintents. Perhaps one of the shortcomings of the measurement movement was that some of its participants had concluded that a science of education, and from it basic truths, would come from the refinement of measurement without other consideration. That, as everyone should now know, is false.

CONCLUSION

Of course there were dissents to the centralization of school control, to efficiency in the schools, to scientific management, and to measurement. Although the dissents were generally inconspicuous and generally ineffectual, teachers did object. Teachers protested in the NEA Department of Classroom Teachers. In 1916, its president, Sara Helena Fahey, attacked school efficiency:

> Then there is the constant effort to standardize the human relations of child and teacher. The unobtrusive sterling qualities, which so often characterize the faithful overworked teacher, are not the first things in sight during a survey. There is often a startling contrast between paper efficiency and field efficiency.

Teachers also expressed themselves in other ways. First, they unionized. Second, as World War I created boom times and a labor shortage, teachers quit. They became clerks, telephone operators, and typists in the war industries. In part this was self-protection against inflation, but it was also in part protest.

Several university professors also dissented. In 1914, A. W. Rankin of the University of Minnesota told the NEA's Department of Classroom Teachers that "the superintendent learns to copy the manner of the factory head toward the operatives. He is an autocrat, an overlord, a taskmaster to the teachers. He reigns as a monarch." The next year W. A. Bagley of Teachers College, Columbia University, also addressed the Department of Classroom Teachers: ". . . Getting the next generation ready for its serious responsibilities is being accomplished more and more on the factory plan," he said, and he disapproved. His comments are eye-catching because Bagley had been a few years before an efficiency enthusiast. In 1913, John Dewey, in the American Federation of Teachers' *American Teacher*, was arguing that teaching should be, if it was to be anything, an intellectual activity. Teaching as an intellectual activity was clearly antithetical to factorylike efficiency. Even New York City Superintendent William H. Maxwell protested. The findings of the New York City survey were objectionable. Frank McMurray, one of the surveyers had, Maxwell said, concluded far too much from far too little. Maxwell's complaints, as the others' had, seemed to so almost unnoticed.

We have misgivings about the school reformers who have been the subjects of this chapter, and we have expressed most of them. Only two afterthoughts may be worth expressing here. First, although elaborated administrative organizations may have been promising, or even useful, when they were built, they were built more strongly than the builders could have known, and more lastingly than they could have intended. While the same organizations have sometimes instituted change, they have at other times been impervious to it. Second, if one is discomfited at the thought or experience of depersonalized education, one is discomfited at over-centralization, overregulation, and mechanization and routinization. However, we must add that there were other efforts and accomplishments of the Progressive administrators that we admire. We will discuss them in the next chapter.

Chapter Nine
SCIENTIFIC PEDAGOGY, TEACHERS, CURRICULUM, DEPRESSION, AND WAR

The 1910s had been the time of development and expansion of the one best system; the 1920s the time of its expansion; and the 1930s and 1940s the times of its maintenance. The system's principles of organization and administration were adopted by or forced upon city schools, small-town schools, and rural schools. As pupils stayed on longer, enrollments increased. As urbanization continued, city school enrollments increased more rapidly. Chicago, not the biggest of school systems, had 226,000 pupils by 1910. The growth of new suburbs transformed within a few years one-room schools into complete school systems.

As many have pointed out, the importance of schooling was greater than before. Growing up on a farm did not provide a knowledge of soil pH, especially if one's father was uninformed about it. There was no way of learning at home how to operate a punch press, the simplest (and maybe most vicious) factory machine. In 1918 Mississippi passed a compulsory school attendance law, and compulsory attendance became at least in principle universal. But increasing numbers of students stayed beyond fourteen or other minimum age set by law. The day of the high school came, and high school enrollments increased most of all. College and university enrollments also increased, although most of the students who did not complete high school did not enroll in colleges. Libraries multiplied, newspaper circulations increased, and motion pictures and radios appeared. Nevertheless, schools continued to become more important.

The ends of school business managers and those of democratic Progressives, supporters of John Dewey's theories, seemed completely incompatible. But there was one apparent exception, that of the Gary, Indiana, schools and the "Gary Plan."

There were fewer biographies of teachers, but sociological studies of teachers and teaching had begun to appear. The feminization of teaching reached its high point at the end of World War I when 86 percent of teachers were women. Accounts then of their lives in and out of school are often cheerless, although at least a few survivors remember it with nostalgia.

In at least some cities, for instance, in Chicago, schools were political battle-fields, with contests between political bosses, reformers, efficient school managers, and teachers. Being a teacher in Chicago could have been burdensome, sometimes oppressive: it need not have been boring.

Curriculum, at least as designed by some experts, was a painstaking compilation of skills for jobs, or sometimes skills for living. Others advocated curricula of a different sort, based upon the interests of pupils.

School systems varied, obviously, and the Depression's the effect upon them also varied. At worst, teachers as well as their pupils lived in poverty. Least badly, teachers were protected by their status as government workers from great financial hardship—but nearly always there was fear. If teachers escaped poverty during World War II, they suffered privation as costs of living increased and salaries stayed at their old levels. In some ways the schools could help the war effort. Of course the other priority was keeping the schools open in spite of shortages in money and work force.

After the war, schools were crowded by the "baby-boom" children, the generation now reaching their forties. Teacher's salaries remained small, and the cost of living soared. At least some issues educationists discussed might better have been considered ten years before.

THE GARY PLAN:
THE WHOLE CHILD AND EFFICIENCY

In 1906, the U.S. Steel Company built a huge complex of blast furnaces and steel mills on the empty, sandy, southern shore of Lake Michigan. It built a city there, Gary, Indiana, named after Elbert H. Gary, U.S. Steel founder. Willard A. Wirt was employed as school superintendent to build a new system of schools for the new city. It was a rare opportunity, and Wirt made the most of it. An admiring former student of Dewey, he installed workshops adjacent to classrooms to strengthen connections between school and work. The community became the school's laboratory. The schools were to become the hearts of the community.

Wirt was also a rockribbed Republican conservative capitalist and intended to make the Gary schools efficient, systematic, and economical. He developed the

Gary Plan, with classes exchanging places at appropriate times in gymnasiums, auditoriums, shops, and classrooms. Better utilization of school buildings and more careful organization was to keep costs low and promote efficiency.

The Gary Plan was admired by all progressives, by Dewey himself for its curriculum and ways of teaching and learning, and by administrators for its low cost and businesslike management. There were faulty details, but they would be remedied. Randolph Bourne, darling of politically progressive intellectuals, wrote a series of approving articles for *New Republic*. Those who objected to the Gary Plan did so for the same reasons that others supported it. Abraham Flexner, official of the Carnegie and Rockefeller foundations, growing more conservative as he grew older, objected to the curriculum because conventional subjects were not well taught, having been sacrificed for immediate and real experiences. Much later Callahan would criticize the Gary Plan because of Wirt's intent of efficiency. At least in appearance, the Gary schools were progressive in the two most important educationally progressive senses.

New York City rejected the Gary Plan when it was tangled in a political campaign there and because of the opposition of New York City school bureaucrats. Opponents even rioted before attempts to introduce it were abandoned in 1917. An evaluation of the Gary schools made with newly developed achievement tests raised doubts and opposition. Labor leaders in some cities objected to the Gary "platoon system" as cheapening schooling, and to anything connected with U.S. Steel or named for Elbert Gary. By the middle of the 1920s, the Gary Plan's unique popularity had passed.

No other plans or school systems got the support of Dewey's followers and also of efficiency enthusiasts. As an exception the Gary Plan may prove a rule. That Gary's popularity was isolated and unique seems to us to be evidence of the divergence of the views of educational progressives. Like political Progressivism, educational Progressivism had its origins in the reformers' beliefs in the 1890s. Progressive educators generally shared as a general aim the improvement of schooling and the improvement of society. In anything more specific than that, educational progressives did not agree among themselves, although the extent of their disagreement would not be clear until later. A new curriculum, businesslike management, and perhaps the science of education were Progressive, depending upon the view of the educator. That *Educational Progressivism* was a single unified movement was far more apparent than real.

Since the 1960s, historians of education have argued that progressives in education were more interested in preserving than in changing, that they oriented toward the conservative, that their hoped-for reforms would have resulted in a more conservative or more nearly static society, and that they intended to preserve capitalism. These arguments have been useful in dispelling the too-cheerful view that all that the progressives did was right and that schools and schooling in their time were in every way and at all times a blessing. They were not always a blessing nor were they ever a blessing for every pupil, nor did every progressive have a clear vision of a transformed society.

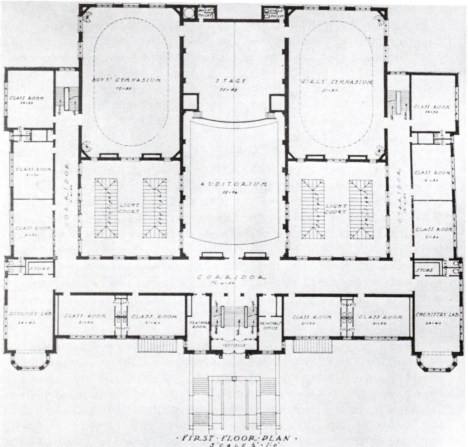

FIGURE 9-1 Exterior photograph and floor plan for the Froebel School, Gary, Indiana. From *Modern School Houses* (New York: The American Architect, 1915), plates 117 and 119.

Beyond that, the danger of overgeneralization seems to us great. It comes, as Kaestle has pointed out, from failing to distinguish the intent and effect of progressives. More than that it comes from not specifying which progressive, and with what intent and with what effect. The distinctions should be kept in mind.

THE SCIENCE OF EDUCATION, CONTINUED

Some deny that there is a science of education or that there can be one. However, argument as to the existence or possibility of a science of education in general is nearly meaningless, since there is no generally acceptable meaning of *science*. At one extreme, *science* is anything systematically arranged; by that definition it could be said that there is a science of philately, that is, stamp collecting. In one sense philosophy, as the careful ordering and examining of human experience is a "science." At the other extreme, a "science" is made up of a set of "laws" or theories that allow precise prediction and control. Physics comes closest to being such a science. The "science of education" has been thought of in all these terms, and probably others. Among its supporters, it has probably most often been thought of as becoming a science in somewhat the same sense that engineering is a science. One of those who believed most strongly in such a science of education was Charles H. Judd of the University of Chicago. Education, he said in 1918, was becoming a science because, in the first place, it was studied by the scientific method (although he did not define "*scientific method*"). The sources of the science would be history of theory and practice, psychology and educational psychology, statistics, experiment, and the study of "retardation" and of administrative problems. It is a far more comprehensive formulation than that of the science of education as no more than a science of administration and management. Judd's visualization strikes us now as oddly composed, but his was a science in which influential men strongly believed. Whether "scientific" or not, or in what way scientific, the *science of education* and research in education have had important effects upon schooling. Even those who feel that a science of education has been premature, or empty pretense, or a false hope, and that educational research has been a misguided failure and a pure liability, cannot deny its importance. Our strongest conviction is that it has been important, is important, and will be important.

Educational researchers have not, with rare and odd exceptions, worked in isolation. They have most often been university professors, less often college professors, or occasionally public school or foundation officials. The origin or employment of many educational researchers and scholars in the early 1900s was Teachers College, Columbia University. Therefore, the history of Teachers College is an important part of the history of the science of education.

Like any other branch of inquiry, the science of education had its founders who set precedents and established patterns or paradigms. The most important of these founders in the order in which they appeared were G. Stanley Hall, Joseph Mayer Rice, and Edward L. Thorndike.

Teachers College, Columbia University

Research of most kinds is shaped, naturally, by the interests and talents of researchers. It is also shaped and supported by the institutions where they have been trained and where they carry on their work. This has been true of the scientists of education. In the earlier years of the science of education, the most important of these institutions was Teachers College, Columbia University.

Before 1900, increasing numbers of colleges and universities were offering graduate or undergraduate courses in education, or *pedagogy* (the science of teaching). The beginnings are difficult to specify, because of the existence of honorary faculty appointments and precollege-level and not-for-credit courses. However, Josiah L. Pickard, who left the superintendency of the Chicago schools in 1877 to become president of the University of Iowa, started education courses there. William H. Payne, appointed to the University of Michigan in 1979, had been the first identifiable full-time university professor of education. G. Stanley Hall had been named professor of psychology and pedagogy at Johns Hopkins University in 1884.

Institutions and professorships suggest the underlying development. Education—teaching and administration—was at least potentially professional, based upon science and knowledge. That conviction led to the establishment of schools or departments of education intended primarily to offer graduate study and to support research. Clark University did so after G. Stanley Hall became its first president in 1888. There were other attempts, some short-lived and others only indifferently successful. A few developed substantial strengths. The outstanding success was that of Teachers College.

Teachers College was the creation of Nicholas Murray Butler, member of the department of philosophy of Columbia University, who had been encouraged by Columbia President F. A. P. Barnard, and of Grace Hoadley Dodge, progressive-minded heiress. Teachers College was established in 1889, and became a part of Columbia University in 1893. In 1897, James Earl Russell, who had earned a Ph.D. at Leipzig in Germany (and had become acquainted with Joseph Mayer Rice), became its president. Russell had a miraculous ability to identify the most promising young scholars and lead them to prominence. He recruited Edward L. Thorndike, who would become the most prominent educational psychologist and researcher of his time; Paul Monroe, an industrious and methodical man, who would establish the field of history of education; Frank McMurray, who developed a new curriculum based on the new psychology, and who would be joined by his brother Charles A. McMurray, survivor of an unsuccessful attempt to establish a "School of Pedagogy" at the University of Buffalo; and Susan Blow and Patty Hill Smith, kindergarten reformers. George S. Counts, a new kind of sociologist of education and educational comparativist, and William H. Kilpatrick, inventor of the "project method" and disciple of John Dewey, would join the Teachers College faculty later. Dewey himself, who had had unpleasant misunderstandings with President William Rainey Harper of the University of Chicago, became a member of the philosophy depart-

FIGURE 9-2 Teachers College, Columbia University, c. 1900. Courtesy of Special Collections, Teachers College, Columbia University.

ment of Columbia University in 1905. Although he was not a member of the Teachers College faculty, he would serve as guide and inspirer. Russell recruited a number of subject matter specialists whose names are now less familiar, but who were outstanding in their time. Such outstanding graduates, as George D. Strayer in educational administration, were kept on as faculty members.

Russell had, Cremin has said, four goals for Teachers College: it would provide liberal arts education, academic scholarship, professional knowledge, and technical skill. Russell's success in recruiting and his broad formulation of purpose and aim were sources of Teachers College's marvelous growth and success. By 1917 it had twenty-five hundred students. There were other successful schools and departments of education at Stanford University, University of Chicago, and other universities, but Teachers College, Columbia University was by far the most prominent and successful of them all.

The rise of Teachers College is important not because of its fame or its material success. As measured by endowment, Teachers College has not been wealthy, and it is neither financially supported nor controlled by Columbia University. It is important because it was a "visible," formal college, the home of communities of scholars who continued and extended thought about schooling, and so modified practice. It was important also for the researchers and scholars it trained. It has by now awarded thousands of doctorates in education. In the ten years ending in 1927, Teachers College awarded a third of all doctoral degrees awarded in education in the United States. Teachers College is no longer more important than all other schools of education combined, but in the 1980s, Teachers College is still a prominent school of education, perhaps the most prominent.

Founders

Three men were especially important in the development of the science of education. The first of these was G. Stanley Hall. The second was Joseph Mayer Rice, who has also appeared previously. The third was Edward L. Thorndike, psychologist and statistician.

Hall had unlimited, unending curiosity. His research as to the "why" of child behavior and child learning was in part a result of that curiosity. By intent, his research was "empirical," based upon observation. At least in the beginning it was anchored in Darwinism and the theories of genetic psychology, to which Hall was then committed. Hall's greatest legacy to educational research may have been an interest in learning "why," or as it would now be put, to discovering underlying variables.

Cremin dated the beginning of Educational Progressivism as 1892, when Joseph Mayer Rice's scathing critiques of schools appeared in *Forum*. Rice then turned to empirical research. His first results, in "Futility of the Spelling Grind," also appeared in *Forum*, five years later, in 1897. Rice asked if spending more time on spelling lessons made pupils better spellers and concluded that it did not. His other, similar studies followed.

Nontheoretical and utterly practical, presenting his results as columns of numbers, Rice's research was intended only to answer "how," how, in the first instance, to teach spelling. We can only guess why his approach had changed since the first *Forum* series. Rice, a near recluse, never wrote about himself, and his papers were burned immediately after his death. Rice set precedents for educational research, precedents more often followed than those of Hall. Rice proceeded without theory to find immediate practical solutions for practical problems. What was to be decided was how long to make spelling lessons. "How" was at the core of the question and the research. Unlike Hall, Rice was a quantifier. He used, relied upon, and published numbers. He used an experimental design, or to be more exact, a quasi-experimental design. He did not attempt to control the length of spelling lessons, but instead tested pupils in classes that had had spelling lessons of varying lengths and tested them afterward. In educational research, this "after-only" design has been a standard one since. It has serious shortcomings, but is the simplest research design and sometimes the only feasible one. We would guess that Rice borrowed the design from medical research. He had been trained as a physician, and the after-only design had been used by French physician Claude Bernard fifty years earlier. To repeat, Rice set precedents by addressing the question "how," by quantification (the use of numbers), and in research design.

Rice's precedents were followed in 1909 in Leonard Ayres's *Laggards in Our Schools*. To measure school "efficiency," Ayres tabulated the proportion of pupils who were "retarded," older than expected for their grade level. This too addressed a question of "how," how "efficient" the school systems were. The experimental design was after-only, and the results were quantified, that is, expressed in numbers. Ayres's work was the link to efficiency studies and to the administrative progressives. "How" questions have predominated in educational research since.

Hall's child study research had begun some years before the founding of Teachers College, and Rice's was not conducted there. Edward L. Thorndike, the third of the founders, spent nearly all his career there.

Thorndike's key contribution to psychology was the "law of effect." It had its origins in Thorndike's study of animal psychology; some of his early research had been with chickens, cats, and dogs. Thorndike assumed that human and animal learning were alike in kind if different in degree and that, therefore, the principles of animal psychology could be applied to humans. In 1898 Thorndike published *Animal Intelligence*, which led to the Law of Effect. Often modified by Thorndike, it said that behavior rewarded was "stamped in" and that behavior punished was "stamped out." The relationship between stimulus and reward was strengthened if there was a reward, weakened if there was a punishment. All behavior was explained as a resulting from a linking of stimulus and response. This view of learning and behavior made the concept of "mind" unnecessary and thought nonexistent. Behavior was only the result of reinforced "original tendencies." Mankind was not innately evil, as Calvin had long ago maintained. It was not innately good, as Jean-Jacques Rosseau had maintained. It simply *was*.

Thorndike developed a psychology of learning at least apparently especially suitable for education. By contrast, German Gestalt psychology, which appeared a few years later, was a psychology of experience, and Freud's was a personality psychology. Each had its supporters, but Thorndike's was by far the more popular. More concretely, Thorndike indirectly influenced B. F. Skinner, whose "operant conditioning" would become important in educational psychology in the 1960s, 1970s, and 1980s.

To repeat, Thorndike had introduced descriptive and inferential statistics into educational research. His *Introduction to the Theory of Mental and Social Measurement* (1904) had made available to researchers ways of computing correlations and some understanding of sampling and of significance tests.

Although he has been the subject of a thorough biographical study, Thorndike's personality remains enigmatic. A one-time colleague remembers him as utterly matter-of-fact, cold, and distant. Thorndike was once asked to account for his success and said it was because he had strong eyes and good health. A less informative or more matter-of-fact answer is unimaginable. He believed that intelligence was in large part inherited and was accused of being politically and socially conservative. But he demanded—and got—retractions of those accusations. His last studies, in some ways stiff and mechanical, were of the "quality of life," concerned with the satisfactions and enjoyments of society at large, surely progressive and liberal interests. Thorndike was indeed a "seminal figure," as Cremin said, a kind of father figure for later researchers, his apparently humdrum personal life notwithstanding.

MEASUREMENT OF INTELLIGENCE, ACHIEVEMENT, ETC.

Much of research in the science of education was at first in the development or adaptation of tests. This seemed the best way of developing the science, and the pursuit of efficiency demanded that "inputs" and "outputs" be measured. Ever since Henry Barnard educators had gathered columns and pages of numbers, compulsively counting nearly everything. To some, it seemed that numbers attracted educators almost as a candle attracts moths.

There were scholarly precedents for counting, for quantification. In Belgium, A. Quitelet, astronomer and public health official, had by 1850 gathered physical, anthropometric data on the dimensions of men. His statistical approach had been borrowed by Florence Nightingale to show the terrible shortcomings of Crimean War hospitals. In England, Francis Galton, who was interested in all things but most interested in heritability and eugenics, tentatively undertook measurements of mental ability. Psychologist J. McKeen Cattell had administered "mental tests" to University of Pennsylvania undergraduates in 1900.

One of the most important developments for educational measurement came from psychology and from France. It was the "intelligence test," developed in Paris by psychologists Alfred Binet and Theodore Simon. In 1900 Binet had begun the development of a means for identifying pupils in need of special education. The first version of the Simon and Binet test was published in 1905. It was not based upon a theory of intelligence; Binet had set these aside. The test had a long series of short subtests or tasks, beginning with the simplest and ending with the most complicated. Binet is quoted as having said that "it matters very little what the tests are, as long as they are numerous. Administered to one child at a time, with child and test administrator sitting across a table, it allowed the computation of a child's "mental age." German psychologist William Stern suggested dividing mental age by chronological or calendar age (and multiplying by a hundred) and the "intelligence quotient" or "IQ" had been coined.

The 1908 version of the test was translated and first used in the United States by Henry H. Goddard, a man of unbounded enthusiasms, at the Vineland (New Jersey) Training School for retarded children. In 1908 there were fifty-six subtests, for measuring mental ages from three upward to thirteen. As an example, one subtest was "catch" sentences for eleven-year-olds:

> There was found in the park today the body of an unfortunate young girl, frightfully mutilated, and chopped into 18 pieces. It is thought that she committed suicide.

About half the eleven-year-olds tested could see the absurdity of this and other similar sentences. (This sentence was quickly replaced with a less bloodcurdling one.)

In *The Mismeasure of Man* by Stephen Jay Gould is a scathing criticism of Goddard, who surely was a man of unbounded criticisms. Gould says that Goddard's first error was "reification," the error of supposing that if something has a name, it exists. Intelligence, Goddard thought, did exist, as a measurable and unitary thing. Thorndike's dictum is useful as a starting point for explaining reification. With minor variations, Thorndike said again and again that if a thing exists, it exists in some amount and is therefore measurable. That is plausible and, incidentally, cannot be shown to be false. But the inverse is not true: that a "thing" can be measured does not show that it exists. That one can measure an IQ demonstrates only that one can measure an IQ.

Second, Goddard was categorically convinced that intelligence, that is, IQ, was inherited. He demonstrated this by writing the supposed history of the Kallikak family, in which mental deficiency was said to be passed down from generation to generation. But even Goddard finally came to see this as at best an oversimplification. (Eugenics, "the study of agencies . . . which may improve or impair . . . future generations either physically or mentally," has an interesting history of its own, which we cannot follow here.)

The measurement of intelligence was a matter of fascination, as it still is. But, granting the fascination and the importance of IQ testing, and agreeing that in many cases IQ scores predict pupils' success in school, there were and are doubts about what is measured, and as to how much it is an outcome of heritability and learning, or of the two in some interaction. We would suspect that other kinds of training may influence outcomes. As one example, subtest 18 of the 1908 version of the Simon-Binet test was "execution of a triple order" for the six-year-old:

> "Here is a key; please put it on that chair. Then please close the door. Then . . . please bring me that box. Do you understand? First put the key on the chair, then close the door, then bring the box. Now, go ahead."

Of course some amount of thought—to use that soon-to-be outdated word—by the child was called for. But one would have suspected that obedience was called for too. That might have been reasonable, since the Simon-Binet test had been intended to identify the children who would not be successful in classrooms. As another example, subtest 23, for seven-year-olds, required that the child copy, legibly in ink, "See little Paul." Later research showed that there was no important correlation, or relationship, generally between handwriting and "intelligence." At best, the item was influenced by the training of the child.

Soon after the Simon-Binet test was published, it was shown that children from wealthier, higher socioeconomic status homes performed better on it. This immediately raised doubts. IQ tests were not intended to measure socioeconomic status, after all. Another question that was perplexing then to the thoughtful—and which is perplexing still—is whether IQ tests measured some general ability called "intelligence" or some combination of abilities. That discussion was for a long time hot and has not yet ended. These perplexities puzzle the writers and, we hope, will puzzle the reader. However, they did not for a moment stand in the way of IQ enthusiasts.

One of the most prominent of these was Louis B. Terman at Stanford University, who devoted his life, or at least most of his professional career, to the measurement of intelligence and to determining the consequences of high IQs. In 1916, he published the Stanford-Binet Intelligence Test, which was the most widely used American version of the individually administered intelligence tests and which in revision is still commonly used.

In 1917, 1918, and 1919, 1,726,966 soldiers, sailors, and marines underwent 1,793,313 mental tests. (There were retests and cross-validations. The precise numbers are in the 880-page official history.) It was testified that mental, or psychological, tests, identifying misfits at one extreme and potential officers at the other, made military personnel assignments more efficient and effective, and so helped win the war. Certainly they popularized mental, or psychological, testing.

Whatever else, the psychologists were prompt. On the day the United States declared war, April 7, 1917, American Psychological Association President Robert M. Yerkes wrote that

> In the present perilous situation it is obviously desirable that the psychologists of this country act unitedly in the interests of defense. [But psychologist Hugo Münsterberg, driven to a frenzy by American hostility to Germany, had committed suicide.] Our knowledge and our methods are of importance to the military service, and it is our duty to cooperate . . . toward the increased efficiency of our Army and Navy. . . .

Seven weeks later a committee of psychologists met at Vineland, New Jersey, and in ten days designed what would be known as "Army Alpha," a personnel classification test. It was followed later by "Beta," for men who did not read English. The tests were the first widely used group tests and were administered to up to five hundred men at a time.

Alpha and Beta were quickly—hastily?—assembled from available tests, among them A. S. Otis's intelligence test. There were strong correlates, and Army Alpha and Beta did measure something. However, weighing, scoring, and subtests were changed until it is difficult to say what they did measure. They yielded results that would be debated for twenty years; whites scored higher than blacks, Northerners higher than Southerners, sailors higher than soldiers, and so on. Army Alpha and Army Beta convinced the public that useful group, paper-and-pencil tests could be constructed, even in spite of mare's-nests of army red tape and bureaucratic confusion. (There was a delay because army officers had mistaken *psychologists*, experts in mental measurements, for *psychiatrists*, treating the mentally ill.) The official history shows great industry and considerable ingenuity by the army psychologists. The popular acceptance of mental testing had been attained.

Thorndike and some of his students, and other researchers as well, had developed scaled achievement tests even before Army Alpha and Beta. The first normed and scaled achievement test was C. W. Stone's, published in 1908. Many tests were constructed, and many applications found for them. Walter Monroe said that in 1922 there were seventeen arithmetic tests and nearly a hundred more for other academic subjects. The number of psychological tests increased in roughly the same proportion.

The study and development of measurements did not end in 1920, of course, and there are still numerous educational measurement experts gainfully employed.

The purposes for which measurements and educational psychology were used were as one might have predicted. Titles of two National Society for the Study of Education yearbooks indicate them well enough. In 1916, a yearbook was titled *Standards and Tests for the Measurement of the Efficiency of Schools and School Systems*, and a 1922 yearbook, *The Measurement of Educational Products*. To utilize measurement for efficiency, at least seventeen city system bureaus of research had been established as early as 1916. There were a number of state bureaus of research, and university bureaus: the University of Illinois Bureau of Educational Research listed with pride seventy-nine of its publications between 1918 and 1927. (At least a few had residual value fifty years later. Educational research was not always uninformative.) A few private philanthropical foundations also conducted research and supported financially some further research. Achievement measures, in particular, were used in dozens and hundreds of school surveys.

In 1928, Walter S. Monroe listed what he saw as the most important areas of research then: reading, by Judd and his colleagues; school finance, under the direction of George D. Strayer of Teachers College; a recently completed study by Thorndike on the measurement of intelligence; a "genetic study of genius" at Stanford University, directed by Lewis B. Terman, in which the lives and fortunes of 650 extremely high-IQ students would be followed for thirty years; and a study of nature versus nurture, sponsored by the National Society for the Study of Education, also directed by Terman. There were also school surveys and research in the teaching of school subjects. These undertakings do not strike us as having had substantial positive long-range effects.

Researchers encountered serious difficulties. Experiments when repeated gave differing results. Findings sometimes seemed trivial: that George Washington had an estimated IQ of 135, or that it was more efficient to teach children the use of the period first, then the use of the comma. (But even a fragment of good research may seem ridiculous when out of context, standing alone.) Some research must have been utterly frustrating.

The psychologists and other scientists of education had enormously underestimated the difficulties, the complications, the number of possible and plausible dead ends, the variety and vagary of human behavior. Few of them considered the possibility that measurements and psychology might be misused. It was not realized that putting the science of education at the service of efficiency might be costly if efficiency lost its lure—as it did. But there would be another day.

TEACHERS

Generally, teachers did not leave records of themselves; they seldom wrote at all of their teaching. Rarely, teachers' letters and papers are preserved in some collection, as are those of Oliver Cromwell Applegate of Ashland, Oregon. Even more rarely a teacher, such as Beatrice Stephens Nathan, has left behind memoirs or reminiscences. Careful interviewing of now elderly survivors would be illuminating, but the results of such interviews have not yet been published. Far more often than not, we must rely upon surveys and sociological studies, sometimes written with much precision, but usually with limited intent.

The first of the plentiful statistical studies of teachers was Lotus D. Coffman's dissertation, *The Social Composition of the Teaching Population*. Coffman, who was in 1910 beginning a distinguished career, gathered data on 5,215 teachers. It pictures with more or less accuracy the country, village, and small-city teacher of the time. Her median—approximately typical—age was about 25; almost 10 percent of the teachers were still in their teens. Only 1 percent of Coffman's teachers had been born outside the United States, and only 12 percent had foreign-born parents. (Even this proportion of teachers of foreign extraction troubled Coffman.) None of the teachers had been born in Greece or Italy, the origins of masses of new immigrants. Most teachers had been raised on farms in relatively large families with relatively low incomes. Women teachers outnumbered men by three to one in Coffman's sample, four to one in another sample that year.

The median teacher had only four years of schooling beyond elementary school, but substantially more than the average woman then. Only one teacher in ten claimed four years of college or the equivalent. The median teacher was in her fourth year of teaching and her annual salary was just under $500. Apparently one teacher in ten quit each year, and one teacher in ten was a beginner.

Coffman's data do not clearly show it, but many teachers began and ended their teaching in the same school in the same classroom. For others there were two patterns of occupational mobility. One was geographic, from country one room school to village school to small-city school. The other was from lower grades to higher grades, and perhaps to high school, where salaries and prestige were higher. A few teachers followed both pathways.

City teachers were still in the minority, although there were tens of thousands of them. We know less about them, but their origins and career patterns seem to have been at least somewhat different. In Buffalo, the new elementary school teacher in 1910 had attended normal school or its equivalent for two years beyond high school. Almost none of them had Italian surnames; perhaps one in five surnames was Irish (and presumably Catholic). Many seem to have been of German ancestry. Only a very few of the teachers beginning in the system, perhaps one in twenty, claimed teaching experience elsewhere, and nearly all seem to have been Buffalo residents. Most of them were in their early twenties, none younger than that. Prospective high school teachers—a minority within a minority—were, except for prospective vocational teachers, more cosmopolitan, with degrees from many colleges.

In September 1915, Beatrice Stevens, a twenty-year-old normal school graduate, began her teaching career in a one-room school in the mountains of California. She boarded with a rancher's family and from there rode horseback or walked to the school. There were nine pupils: the youngest, age six; the oldest, seventeen years old. Progressive administration had already begun to impose uniformity. Pupils were assigned to grades, and there was a standard course of study and a countywide examination for graduation. Stevens's yearly salary was $600.

After two years in her one-room school, she taught in a two-room school in a small town in the San Joaquin Valley. There were thirty-five pupils in her class, in grades 5 through 8. She remembered a Model-T truck that was used as a school bus, and living in a ramshackle, noisy hotel, and taking her class to swim in an irrigation ditch. The next year she taught in a larger school near her family's home, and then was one of the first teachers in one of the new junior high schools that were coming into fashion. There she saw children classified by IQ testing.

Frances R. Donovan's *The Schoolma'am* appeared forty years after Coffman. Their descriptions were in many ways alike. Donovan found that fewer than 4 percent of the teachers in 1930 had been foreign born and that only one teacher in five was married then. Most married teachers were teaching in country schools, where monthly salaries averaged $22. There were forty-six thousand black women teaching then, the invisible women of their time. Except for a very few, black teachers taught only black pupils. Only one teacher in five was forty years old or older, only one in fourteen over fifty.

The era of the normal schools was already passing. Among new high school teachers, four out of five were college graduates, and 12 percent of the city school systems required that new high school teachers have a master's degree. In Chicago a high school teacher could earn as much as $4,800 a year, when a new eight-cylinder Buick cost perhaps $800. But the average teacher salary was only $1,325 a year, and the average teacher earned less than the average carpenter, less in fact than almost anyone except farmhands, clerks, and factory workers. Teachers' salaries were no longer so low, but they certainly were not high.

In smaller towns, especially, there was religious bigotry. "There are communities today," Donovan wrote, "that prefer Methodist chemistry and Spanish taught with a Baptist accent." But in one Buffalo school in the 1930s there were lessons about Hanukkah as well as about Christmas. The diversity of city dwellers resulted in diversity of teachers from and in the cities. In Chicago, ". . . teachers vary almost as widely as the population itself in their cultural origins, their religious affiliations, their political beliefs, their economic prejudices, their social philosophies." Teachers were daughters (occasionally sons) of professionals or businesspeople or, increasingly often, of blue-collar workers. Washington D.C.'s black high school teachers were leading black intellectuals. Black teachers in border and southern cities taught in black schools. In most northern cities there were few black teachers. In Buffalo, into the 1930s they could have been counted on the fingers of one hand.

Another description of teachers at about the same time was in Willard Waller's *Sociology of Teaching*. Still important as sociology, it is also a picture, a grim one, of the life of a teacher in a small town. What a teacher was and did, Waller wrote, was governed by the public image, the stereotype, of teacher. Long ago the teacher stereotype had contributed to the forming of the common schools: by the early twentieth century the school perpetuated the stereotype of teacher, whose role was narrowly defined by others' expectations. In the school the important "others," Waller wrote, were pupils, with whom the teacher was always "at war." If the school was to function, the teacher was necessarily a despot, perhaps polite and kind and cheerful, but a despot nevertheless. The successful teacher maintained a distance from students, was isolated from them.

Outside the schools, Waller wrote, the teacher was a "stranger" in both usual and sociological senses. She came from elsewhere. The stereotyped role that separated her from her pupils also separated her from the rest of the community. Innocent amusement for others was forbidden to her. Custom determined where she should room. She was required to attend church, even to teach Sunday school. The stereotype discouraged suitors, Waller wrote. But perhaps Waller overstated: there are still a few small-town teachers from those times alive, and a substantial number of them married men from the places where they taught. Still, narrow rules and binding expectations did limit the lives of teachers.

THE CASE OF CHICAGO: POLITICS AND THE SCHOOLS

George S. Counts described a battlefield in *School and Society in Chicago* (1928). It was a battlefield of political bosses; ethnic voting blocks; progressive, efficiency-seeking school administrators; and even democratic Progressives. And some battles were fought over schools. That was true of many cities, perhaps of all cities. But in Chicago the battles were rowdier, and Chicago was different in another important way. In Chicago teachers—organized teachers—were important and powerful combatants.

"Machine politics" was not new in the 1920s. Municipal graft and municipal corruption had been one of the first targets of the political progressives more than twenty years before. It was not confined to Chiacago. Other cities had famous or infamous bosses: Tweed in New York, Pendergast in Kansas City, Crump in Memphis, and the list could go on. The generally reigning boss in Chicago was William Hale "Big Al" Thompson, who once promised that when he was mayor he would "punch the snoot" of the King of England. (That helped bring out the Irish vote.) Thompson was elected mayor in 1915, and left office in 1923, after a grand jury indicted his friends. He was elected again in 1927, with the support of Hearst newspapers and the alleged support of bootlegging gangster Al Capone.

Chicago, the fastest-growing American city—3 million inhabitants in its first hundred years—had large ethnic communities: German, Polish, Czech, Italian, Greek, and others. Ethnic voting blocs could control the outcomes of elections. (As a side effect, this resulted in the appointment of black teachers in Chicago's schools.)

Earlier there had been democratic Progressives in Chicago. John Dewey had been professor of pedagogy and psychology at the University of Chicago. Before him, Colonel Francis W. Parker had been a normal school principal. Dewey's student Ella Flagg Young had been Chicago superintendent of schools from 1909 until 1915. Administrative progressivism for efficiency was already being advocated in Chicago before 1900. University of Chicago President William Rainey Harper recommended centralization of authority, a "professional" superintendent, and reducing the size of the school board (which would make it more than ever middle class). Progressive administrator William McAndrew was appointed superintendent in 1924, by a reform, politically progressive-minded, mayor. McAndrew had written that

> [T]he fixing of responsibility, groups of workers responsible to the designated heads, an orderly graduation of duties and appropriate powers, must be maintained, or chaos, confusion, and waste ensue. These books [standard works on school management] chart the school system to show the regulation of authority.

Apparently on another occasion, he wrote

> Every organization which is planned to secure results devotes its energies not only to plans for maintaining and increasing efficiency, but to continuous follow-up of such plans to see that the efficiency comes to pass.

This naturally displeased teachers, but McAndrew also displeased school board members named by Thompson, who had again been elected mayor. McAndrew was suspended, charged with "insubordination" and being a "stool pigeon of the King of England."

Three women played important parts in the governance of the Chicago schools: Ella Flagg Young, Catherine Goggin, and Margaret Haley. Catherine Goggin and Margaret Haley were the leaders of the Chicago Teachers Federation (CTF), which had been founded in 1897. Its members were women elementary teachers in the Chicago schools, and within a year or two after its founding it had more members than the NEA. The CFT was active on behalf of teachers and schools more generally, and in other public issues. Goggin (who was killed in a traffic accident in 1916) and Haley believed that teachers' natural interests were the same as those of workers, that teachers were white-bloused blue-collar workers. The CTF at Goggin's and Haley's urging became an American Federation of Labor (AFT) affiliate. The affiliation was later discontinued to comply with a school board resolution, but the CTF's interests continued to be those of the unions. The CTF, for instance, strongly supported child labor laws, as did the unions.

Haley and the CTF were, naturally, interested in the financial support of the Chicago schools. The CTF discovered that Chicago's public utility companies—electric, gas, telephone, and public transportation—were not paying taxes on the value of their franchises, although Illinois law made them taxable. CTF's attorneys argued a series of suits and appeals until taxes were paid. CTF also discovered that several of Chicago's largest industrial firms, among them Pullman and Swift, were not paying tax based upon their assets, although Illinois laws made them subject to it. Again, suits followed. The Chicago Board of Education still owned scraps of the land set aside for schools by the Ordinance of 1785. It was leased by contracts that called for rental payments equal to 6 percent of its value. The *Chicago Tribune* building, on one of the most valuable sites in the city, did not pay increased rents, under the terms of a contract change in 1895. Again suits were filed, but the CTF was unsuccessful. Its hope, in suits against utilities, corporations, and leasers of school land, was to increase the revenues of the board of education, which it did.

Haley and the CTF had expected the board's increased revenues to be used to increase salaries, which were low in the 1900s, and sometimes paid belatedly. Instead, the board used its new revenue for building and repairing schools. There were finally raises, but not until 1920. Another of CTF's concerns was pensions for teachers. A teacher pension law was passed in 1895, five years after Chicago had started a pension system for its policemen. But contributions, as little as $6 a year, were too small to pay the scheduled pensions of $600 a year. A dozen years after the pension system was adopted, the CTF succeeded in having it changed; payments by teachers were larger and were accompanied by payments by the board of education, and pensions were reduced. Later the CTF became the trustee of the pension fund. Haley and the CTF urged and finally secured a teacher tenure law, and arbitrary and political firings of teachers were prevented.

The CTF also resisted the establishment of junior high schools, as did labor unions. It appeared to them, as it did to other unions in other cities, that junior high schools might be used to divert working-class pupils from high schools and into vocational schools; the term *industrial education*, long out of use, reappeared. Perhaps it was natural to doubt what sounded like and looked like von Fellenberg's school for peasants. The CTF also opposed the classification of pupils on the basis of IQ scores and the discontinuance of the teachers' councils, which had provided upward communication to accompany McAndrew's downward orders.

Counts's most important point in *School and Society in Chicago* was that the schools were enmeshed in society, politics, and the economy. They were not pristine, isolated institutions above politics and worldly concerns. With that there could be no disagreeing. From Counts's book it is entirely clear that teachers' lives were not always bucolic, that they were not always even mildly pleased with their pay and the wisdom of their superiors, and that they were sometimes little more than captives of the schools.

CURRICULUM BUILDING:
KNOWLEDGE AND THE CHILD

Before the end of the 1920s, curriculum research, design, and construction had become a recognized enterprise. In many ways it was the central and crucial issue in education. There was nothing more important in schools, after all, than what was to be learned. The implications were great, if not immediately clear.

Knowledge—what was to be learned—was most conventionally and simply subject matter, the substance and content of conventional school courses. In another view it was the accumulated knowledge within the culture. That knowledge was, in the wider view, artificially and harmfully compartmentalized by academic disciplines and conventional school subjects. From still another perspective, valuable knowledge was know-how, the knowledge needed for jobs and for lives. Valuable knowledge was practical knowledge. Knowledge that could not be used was not knowledge worth having. We will return to one assumption about the structure of knowledge.

Curriculum construction also depended upon assumptions, far more often than not implicit, about the nature of the child. Some aspects of the child's nature and learning were essentially psychological. Clearly, the child was not a bundle of "faculties," as phrenologists had believed a century before. Thorndike and the other experimental psychologists had disposed of that. Dewey had argued that one crucial consideration was the "interests" of the child, since what interested a child would be rewarding and therefore would hasten learning. That point could be argued, or ignored.

The child was seen as a learner, but also as a future member of society. A member of society might not be much other than a faithful and productive worker and law abiding, or be a fully participating and creative citizen. This was linked to further assumptions as to whether society was essentially fixed and static, evolving if at all only by natural law, or whether, as many progressives saw it, society was to be reformed, "restructured," by its members so that it would be more democratic and less oppressive. The acceptance or rejection of assumptions was implicit far more often than explicit. Dewey had an admirable but largely abstract position.

Even if it was accepted, its applications were difficult. Understandably, there were several approaches to the construction of curriculum.

Activity Analysis

Activity analysis for curriculum building implied the precedence of social needs over individual needs, of a society largely unchanging, and of the pupil as future worker and perhaps as a future "good citizen." Activity analysis was from all appearances a descendant of Taylor's job analysis in the shop. In this vein it was a part of the science of education and the curriculum builder was the "great engineer." Not surprisingly, one of its chief advocates and practitioners was Franklin Bobbitt. His *How to Make a Curriculum* (1924) and W. W. Charters's *Curriculum Construction*, published a year before, were standard expositions.

Activity analysis started by exhaustively describing a task. If performance of a task was to be learned, its components were to be learned. To design a spelling curriculum, Leonard P. Ayres tabulated 23,629 words in business and personal letters and identified the 542 most commonly used ones. Bobbitt and his associates tabulated 11,000 topics in *Readers Guide*. In a study he directed, 1,243 traits of good citizenship were compiled. Activity analysis as a basis for curriculum design was applied to nearly every field. We were particularly interested in the *Commonwealth Teacher-Training Study* because studies in the 1970s were remarkably similar to it. We see them as resting on an assumption that is categorically wrong.

The *Commonwealth* investigators, W. W. Charters, Douglas Waples, and their assistants, tabulated traits, or abilities, of good teachers, employing another minor variation. There were eighty-three major traits, alphabetically arranged from "accuracy" to "wittiness." This seems to us no more than a compilation of platitudes. The larger and more serious part of the study was activity analysis. To list what teachers did, Charters and Waples sent 22,000 questionnaires to teachers in summer schools, who returned 6,000 of them. Previous studies were combed, then more teachers were queried. There were in all 235,340 "activity statements." Duplicates were discarded, the near completeness of the list verified, and the items were classified. Precisely 1,001 activities were compiled in a 168-page list. This was to serve to evaluate education courses and textbooks and courses in student teaching, methods, and theory or teacher training programs as a whole.

The minute division of activity and learning was primarily from shop efficiency studies, but in curriculum design the concept was not, even in the early 1900s, new. As we have said, the approach had been anticipated by Joseph Lancaster and other monitorial school enthusiasts, who used the analogy of school as factory. Almost no one mentioned the parallels and possible precedents, but the underlying concepts had survived.

There was later interest in "competence based education," and especially in "competence based teacher education." The similarity of the *Commonwealth* list and the *Florida Catalog of Teacher Competencies*, computer generated in 1976, is remarkable. By the late 1970s there was a rather extensive literature on competence based teacher education. As far as we know, the *Commonwealth Study* was never cited in it. The general approach had again been reinvented. In this case, history does seem to demonstrate that nothing is learned from history.

Activity analysis as a basis for curriculum design was largely abandoned in the 1930s, for several reasons. First, it was as Cremin said enormously laborious, tedious, and time consuming to compile lengthy near-complete lists. Second, activity analysis seemed to lead to unimportant conclusions. In his *Universities, American, British, German*, Abraham Flexner singled out the *Commonwealth Study* to illustrate that research in education was more and more "Technical, trivial, and sometimes absurd" and wrote that it was ". . . based, apparently, upon the assumption that American teachers have neither native sense nor ordinary good breeding." We would certainly agree that activity and competence analysis have often been elaborations of the obvious. A third serious shortcoming was that in the name objectivity, activity analysis was concerned with what *is* to the exclusion of what *should* be.

Boyd H. Bode criticized it in those terms in the later 1920s. Bobbitt seemed to feel that the sole concern with what *was* was a strength. Of his compilations from *Readers Guide* he said, "They do not show, nor do they attempt to show, what educators . . . think the world should be concerned with. They show that it is concerned with." Bode's criticism deserves thought: Bobbitt seems condemned by his own words. If present practice is unsatisfactory, it should not be perpetuated by schooling. Ayers's notion that the spelling of the most common words should be learned first is reasonable enough, but professional education and spelling lessons are, or should be, different.

We add one further objection: We believe that fruitful knowledge, and therefore fruitful learning—professional or otherwise—is most often a knowledge of interrelationships. There is indeed more to playing a sonata than depressing piano keys three thousand times, and a cathedral is more than a high pile of rocks. Knowledge is by nature molecular, with bits of information in combination, rather than atomic with bits of information isolated. Activity analysis was as near to atomic as its practitioners could make it.

Project Method

The *project method* was one of many other approaches to curriculum. Its originator was William Heard Kilpatrick. Progressive by nature, Kilpatrick was one-time student of Dewey, later Dewey's colleague at Columbia University, and Dewey's popularizer. If anyone was, Kilpatrick was a democratic Progressive by nature and had had progressive leanings even before he had become familiar with Dewey and his work. He began his career as a public school teacher and administrator. He was also a careful critical scholar; it was Kilpatrick who clarified the life and career of Adam Roelansen and the beginnings of schooling in New Amsterdam, and the principles of Froebel. Kilpatrick was scholar, progressive, and, above all, Dewey's evangelist. His skill as a lecturer deserves to be legendary. It is said that

FIGURE 9-3 Outline of the Project Method in use for a curriculum on boats at the Lincoln School, Teachers College, Columbia University. Reprinted in Harold A. Rugg and Ann Shumaker, *The Child-Centered School* (New York: World Book, 1928), pp. 100–101.

each member of his classes, some of which had enrollments of hundreds, felt personally involved. He popularized, and therefore necessarily simplified.

In his most important simplification, the *project method*, which he formally introduced in a 1917 journal article, Kilpatrick posited that what the child did and found rewarding would determine what was learned. What the child found rewarding was a "wholehearted purposeful act." Citing Thorndike (although the connection is not entirely clear to us), he said that without wholehearted purposefulness an act would not produce learning that was substantial and unified. With this there was another premise: learning should be ethical and moral. Since ethics and morals had their origins in society, the child was to learn in society. The "rugged individualist" was not, from Kilpatrick's point of view, an admirable individual.

The spirit of the object lesson could permeate school programs, at least in a few cases. In the 1930s Julia Weber Gordon spent four years teaching in a one-room school in rural New Jersey. Her account, *Country School Diary*, described teaching in the spirit of the project method. There were projects as such, a presentation of "Pinocchio," a train ride, gardens, or a school newspaper. Learning came from each of them: how to make a puppet, how a steam engine worked, the value of fertilizer, writing, and calculating how long it had taken to produce the school newspaper. Gordon's concern for the interests and needs of the pupils appeared again and again. Her school must have been a pleasant place, at least compared with the school one of us was attending then.

Cremin pointed out the difference between Dewey's intent and Kilpatrick's project method. Dewey had said that the interest of the child should be engaged, but had insisted that society's accumulated knowledge was of equal importance. Kilpatrick's project method pushed helter-skelter toward child centeredness. For romantics with limitless faith in the innate virtue and goodness of the child, this was an entrancing formulation, even though only a distant approximation of Dewey's intent. For many of the tens of thousands who heard Kilpatrick speak of it, the project method had enormous merit. One of them may have been Julia Weber Gordon.

THE GREAT DEPRESSION

Although the Great Depression would cause stress and change as well as privation, some innovations from the 1910s and 1920s would survive. One survivor was the Gary Plan, part of which, as should have occurred to the reader, is still standard and conventional practice in high schools and junior high schools. Renewed interest in it and its wide adoption was due more to the efforts of Alice Barrows than to those of Gary Superintendent Willard A. Wirt. Barrows, a Vassar graduate and member of the Eastern Establishment, wrote that the first day she visited the Gary schools was "one of the most astonishing and exhilarating experiences of my life." Barrows was a convert and would become an evangelist. When Wirt became educational consultant for the introduction of the Gary Plan in New York City, Barrows became his secretary and the Gary Plan's publicist. After the plan to introduce the Gary Plan in New York City failed, Barrows became a staff member of the U.S. Bureau of Education. She would remain there until her retirement in 1942, and her efforts in behalf of the *platoon school* would be unceasing. (*Gary Plan* had become a controversial term, so the name was changed.) Barrows conducted more than a dozen surveys of city school systems, and every report advocated platoon schools. She organized conferences on the platoon school and frequently spoke in its behalf—in one twenty-four-day period, fifty times. She wrote articles supporting it for *School Life*, the Bureau's magazine. She taught summer school courses on the platoon schools

Before 1930 there were platoon schools in two hundred cities, and the platoon school thrived during the Depression in the 1930s. Barrows's campaign has been most successful and should be a classic case in the study of innovation.

And yet there is doubt. After visiting platoon schools Barrows had written that "I liked the spirit of the children and teachers. . . . It was free and natural. . . . I felt those children were learning how to think, that the school was a community in which they were engaged in worthwhile activities that had meaning to them." That might have been difficult to observe in high schools at the end of the 1980s, although students and classes were still exchanging places on carefully planned schedules. Perhaps Barrows's humaneness and idealism had in the end served Wirt's efficiency.

During the Depression the spirit of the project method, its concentration on the interests and needs of the child, would continue to gain support. Not until the 1950s would there be dark days for child-centered schooling. But in the late 1960s child-centered schools would again be prominent. Educators would then discuss *Summerhill* and free schools.

The Depression would lead to the eclipse of the business management of the schools; far from being a cure-all, it could be catastrophic, and school administrators would portray themselves in a different light. After a forty-year lapse, some school administrators in the 1980s would be proudly businesslike, but that of course was much later. Thorndike and other established educational researchers would continue their work, but nevertheless research would lag. Research seemed to democratic Progressives to deal with what *was*, when what *should* be was far more important.

The economic effects of the Depression struck some school systems far more severely than others. Poor schools, rural, Southern, black schools—the ones already impoverished—were most greatly affected. Some schools simply closed. Others shortened the school year, Alabama rural schools by 36 percent, for instance. While enrollments, especially high school enrollments, rose, the number of teachers fell somewhat. The salaries of those who continued to teach fell more slowly than did the cost of living, but that was not repayment for feelings of insecurity. Night school, summer school, and other "marginal" instruction was ended. In Chicago, junior high schools were closed, and the junior college discontinued. Child psychologists, truant officers, and some teachers were laid off. Teachers were paid in "tax warrants," school board IOUs, which some stores would not accept and others discounted by 20 percent. When she wrote about it thirty-five years later, one Oklahoma teacher remembered that many of her pupils had had only one meal a day, or none. In the Great Plains states, droughts and dust storms came with the Depression. Pupils at one school brought their own drinking water from home in fruit jars. Schools were dismissed because of the dust storms; midafternoon was as dark as night. One teacher remembered crying when there was a payday without pay. Beatrice Stevens Nathan, by then married and teaching near San Francisco Bay, remembered teacher contributions and PTA card parties and rummage sales to help pupils. Her school distributed used clothing to its neediest pupils. The fund provided free milk and paid for the repair of shoes and glasses and for emergency dental and medical care. Things were better, teachers remembered, after public relief was established, along with the WPA. In the mid-1930s, two Oklahoma teachers, man and wife, arranged a field trip for their students to Carlsbad Caverns in New Mexico. The cost was $5 per pupil.

FIGURE 9-4 "Victim of Drought." Photograph by Lewis Hine.
From *Coronet*, Vol. 5, February 1939, p. 155.

In the early 1930s, the despair of the public was shared by writers, journalists, educators, and intellectuals. Many expected a revolution momentarily and felt that a new form of society and the redistribution of wealth were urgently needed. For Progressive followers of Dewey, the crisis was especially significant. Progressive school reform had begun in the Progressive era when social reform had been the most important goal. Dewey's intent in reforming schools had been, implicitly or explicitly, to reform society, and Dewey, as well as many other reformers of the Progressive era, had been inclined toward socialism. For many Progressive educators it was time for a change.

Counts put the argument more strongly, "like a rousing sermon," and introduced the concept of social class, and, implicitly, the concept of social class struggle:

> If Progressive Education is to be genuinely progressive it must emancipate itself from the influences of this [middle] class, face squarely and courageously every social issue, come to grips with life in all its stark reality, establish an organic relation with the community, develop a realistic and comprehensive theory of welfare, and become somewhat less frightened than it is today at the bogeys of *imposition* and *indoctrination*.

Counts's proposal, put in the form of a rhetorical question, was "Dare the Schools Build a New Social Order?" The question was rhetorical and the expected answer was "yes." A few did answer "no." Journalist Agnew de Lima wrote that teachers were too "docile," too well protected by tenure, "unlikely to challenge the status quo." Teachers were too timid and too disinterested to effect a new social order. They could not.

Another *New Republic* writer said that

> [T]he word *progressive* in progressive education never carried political or sociological implications; that it is descriptive only of educational techniques which *progress* in keeping with psychological and other findings.

Schools, then, should not affect the social order. Counts replied within disdain. There were objections, too, to use of the schools for "indoctrination." "Indoctrination" seemed on its face to be inappropriate if schools were dedicated to the development and perfection of democracy. For another reason, then, schools should not undertake the building of a new social order—the means were inappropriate for the end.

Looking back, one sees that the schools, that is, the teachers, could not build a new social order because the means were inappropriate and insufficient. It now seems remarkable that Counts raised the question. Why "dare" what apparently could not, perhaps should not, almost certainly would not, be done? But, of course, we now have an additional half century of experience, some of it quite unpleasant.

The beginning of the road to recovery from the Depression seemed to come at Franklin D. Roosevelt's inauguration in 1933. However, Roosevelt, especially in his first term, was uninterested in social reform as such. When in his second term he did secure the passage of the Social Security Act and the establishment of the National Labor Relations Board, the Progressive reconstructionists, who had by then moved to radical liberalism and socialism, were unappeased. But the antipathy was mutual. Roosevelt and his New Dealers did not enlist schools or teachers to secure reforms.

WORLD WAR II . . . AND AFTER

As at the time of World War I, a teacher shortage developed. Teachers, this time 350,000 of them, left classrooms to enter the armed forces or defense industries, or simply for better pay. High school students dropped out because jobs were plentiful. College students were drafted, or enlisted. (There were no general draft deferments for college students, as there would be in the Vietnam war.) The number of women in college also declined, partly because of the jobs available. Armed forces service schools—preflight and intensive programs for translators, as examples—appeared on many campuses.

Wartime needs magnified the importance of scientific research, particularly research in physics and in engineering. American physics researchers had become highly competent, both as experimenters and as theorists. The number of Ph.D.'s awarded in physics had quadrupled in the 1920s, and the "intellectual migration" of German Jewish scientists had further strengthened university physics departments. Even in the later 1930s, the United States's research capability had been the greatest in the world. Research during the war, the development of radar and atom bombs, of shaped explosive charges and of other devices, made it plausible to claim that World War II was the "physicists' war." Postwar changes in industry and the economy would clearly make research even more valuable. Defense research would continue because Russia, with atomic bombs and intercontinental ballistic missiles, seemed threatening.

The war had great economic and social consequences. The war and the Depression also changed ways of thinking and talking about schools. The justification of school administration as business management had been one of the lesser victims of the Depression. Jesse H. Newlon, superintendent of schools in Denver and later professor at Teachers College, Columbia University, had written the first influential argument against school administration based on business management justifications:

> Education should, of course, be efficiently and economically administered, but it should be kept in mind always that efficiency and economy must be defined in terms of purposes and responsibilities and that economy and parsimony are not synonyms in the parlance of public affairs. The fundamental desideratum is that the schools be kept free if they are to serve the primary purpose of social education.

If the purpose of the schools was to serve democracy, the logical first essential was that the schools be democratically organized and controlled. Decisions were to be made by all involved. The basis for school administration was expertise rather than authority. After the war one spokesman for administrators wrote that

> Actual leadership, as judged by the contribution made or the solution arrived at, may come from a classroom teacher, a parent, or the administrator. The role of the administrator may or may not involve the introduction of the idea finally accepted. In many situations, the administrator's leadership role will be that of encouraging others to participate effectively.

"Group dynamics" became an important part of educational thought and research about the time of World War II, as support for "democratic leadership" (and of course as a condemnation of "authoritarian" leadership and governments). The best-known research was an experiment by Kurt Lewin, one of the academic refugees from Nazi Germany. At Iowa State University in the last of the 1930s he and his assistants conducted experiments to determine the effects of "democratic," "laissez-faire," and "autocratic" leadership. The boys who were his experimental subjects showed greater satisfaction and less aggressiveness when the leader was "democratic," and activities continued even when the democratic leader was absent. This experiment was widely cited for its implications both for teaching and for supervision, even though most attempts to replicate it were unsuccessful. It was still mentioned in some sociology of education textbooks forty years later.

By the end of World War II in 1945 the larger universities had developed into the institutions we know. Their pattern of organization followed that of William Rainey Harper's University of Chicago, with an undergraduate college, several professional schools, and a graduate school. Some college professors and most university professors had earned Ph.D.s. They had been trained as specialists, as scholars who were to make contributions to a narrow corner of an established field, perhaps to detailed knowledge to the works of Denis Diderot, or of the learning of planaria (water worms). Scholarly knowledge has become far too vast for even the gifted mind to grasp. Professors had been organized into departments, which multiplied as new disciplines emerged. One department of sociology became a department of sociology and anthropology, and a department of anthropology then spawned the department of linguistics. Research often took precedence over teaching.

By 1945 colleges were far removed from those of the 1880s. Denominational ties were less strong, and their presidents were no longer invariably ministers. Some early colleges had closed, but others had proved to be astonishingly hardy. Transylvania University (in Lexington, Kentucky), one-time forerunner of the comprehensive university, then reduced to a college and even to an academy, had survived war; cholera, typhoid, and influenza epidemics; financial crises; and internal strife. Its faculty members had been at one time or another charged with teaching Darwinism and other heresy and of being wartime Nazi collaborators. It had been a men's college and then it admitted women. At the end of the war its enrollment would quadruple.

Because colleges still saw themselves as *in loco parentis*—in place of parents—and because faculty members were less interested, "deans of men" and "deans of women" had been named to satisfy the colleges' obligations. (One of us recalls a dean of women berating his fiancée for holding hands in a dormitory lounge.) College women were required to "check in" at dormitories before a given hour, as if "sinfulness" never occurred in daylight. The grades of even twenty-seven-year-old ex–air force majors were sent automatically to their fathers.

Passed before the end of war, partly to prevent unemployment, the "G.I. Bill of Rights" allowed a million veterans to attend college. They were generally intent students, not interested in being "College Joes" or BMOCs (big men on campus). In the later 1940s, colleges and universities were crowded with GI Bill students. Nearby apartments were rented for students, while others lived in temporary, sometimes corrugated iron, buildings. Classes started early and ended late, and were as big as classrooms would allow.

Some returning veterans enrolled in junior colleges, the first of which William Rainer Harper of the University of Chicago had been instrumental in establishing in the early 1900s. The thirteenth and fourteenth years of schooling, he had argued, were part of a general preuniversity education. A few of the junior colleges had once been four-year colleges. Most of the junior colleges were publicly controlled and publicly supported. Many would offer vocational and technical courses as well as liberal arts curricula. They would come to be known as "community colleges."

High schools' enrollments had grown substantially during the Depression and then declined during the war. But few returning veterans enrolled in high schools, and birth rates had been low during the Depression. Although there were proposals for reform which we will describe later, most high school curricula were still based on the recommendations of the Committee of Ten in 1893 and the "Seven Cardinal Principles" of 1918.

The end of the war was followed by the "baby boom," an enormous increase in the number of births. By 1950 the baby-boom children were appearing in elementary schools. In wartime other employment had drawn teachers from the schools, and teacher pay had not risen as the cost of living had. The elementary schools were badly overcrowded and administrators searched earnestly for teachers. The teacher shortage would last into the 1960s and would extend to the high schools as pupils born during the baby boom progressed through the schools.

Part Four
YEARS OF TURMOIL

GOOD TIMES AND BAD

When Dwight D. Eisenhower became president at the beginning of 1953, the triumphs, failures, and changes of the thirty-five years to follow were unanticipated, nearly unimagined. The social and political issues that would dominate most of those years had not arisen, and even at most seemed unimportant. The cultural changes that would accompany and sometimes lead to them were also unanticipated. The most important of the new technological developments had not gotten beyond research and development laboratories or descriptions in science fiction. There would be real and genuine triumphs: in medicine, a vaccine for polio; for engineers, a man walking on the moon; for blacks, civil rights so long denied. War in Korea was ending and even the name of Vietnam was unfamiliar. Mass violence seemd a thing of the past. Assassinations were almost unthought of. No impeachment proceeding had ever resulted in a president's leaving office. The Depression was remembered, but a financial crisis in which prices increased had not yet been experienced in America.

There were, as always, exceptions, but Americans were pleased and hopeful. Perhaps the least anticipated change was the loss of hope and confidence. What follows is a short preliminary draft of the political, technological, economic, cultural history of thirty-five years, and the changes in values and mood that accompanied it. Difficult to write and inaccurate as that history may prove to be, it cannot be ignored.

In times of turmoil and doubt, schools were attacked and buffeted. When tempers of the times changed, the schools changed more slowly and were especially vulnerable to criticism and attack. Schools are a salient of society subject to attack and difficult to defend: a criticism of the schools is often a thinly veiled criticism of society in general. Schools have been criticized justly, and unjustly; opinions on that will differ.

FIVE FAILED PRESIDENCIES

Harry S. Truman had not been nominated or elected to the vice presidency on the assumption that he would, or even might, become president, and became president unexpectedly on the death of Franklin D. Roosevelt on April 12, 1945, in the last days of World War II. He inherited—almost literally—war issues and peace issues, and the domestic issues that followed the war. If he became president almost unintentionally, he was elected in 1948 almost accidently. Thomas E. Dewey, former governor of New York state, had led in presidential polls from the beginning. Only a last-minute shift by voters defeated him. It was in 1950, during Truman's presidency, that North Korean and Chinese troops invaded South Korea. At first, the invaders overran U.S. and Korean defending troops, but in behalf of the United Nations and with some help from other nations, the Chinese and Korean troops were forced to retreat northward. A truce was signed at the beginning of President Eisenhower's administration.

President Dwight D. Eisenhower, native of Kansas, West Point graduate, and commander of Allied Forces in Europe in World War II, seemed as candidate and as president to be a kind and almost fatherly figure. Elected as a Republican, he believed that the president should act only when necessary. At the time it seemed to some to be lassitude, but in times of neoconservatism, it is often seen as admirable restraint. It is said that he was elected to limit change. But during his administration the Soviet Union's first space satellite, *Sputnik*, orbited the earth, leading to the space race. In 1954 the Supreme Court, headed by Chief Justice Earl Warren, an Eisenhower appointee, unanimously ruled that "separate but equal" schools were not equal, and were therefore unconstitutional. The decision would obviously have far-reaching consequences, and as a precedent would lead to other Supreme Court decisions ending segregation generally. Eisenhower seemed unenthusiastic about the decision, but enforced it. He survived severe illnesses to serve two terms as president.

John F. Kennedy, Harvard graduate and New Englander of Irish ancestry, defeated by a razor's edge Richard M. Nixon, Eisenhower's vice president and Republican nominee ("razor's edge" in two senses: narrowly, by 0.17 percent of the votes, and because in television debates Nixon seemed not to be clean shaven—the new medium of television was crucial.)

Kennedy was youthful, the youngest president ever elected, and youthfulness was admirable. He was brave, witty, and compassionate. He recruited for government the ablest of minds. In his first three months in the presidency he asked Congress thirty-nine times for new legislation and appropriations, most of them to improve the quality of American life. There was a new successful agricultural policy. To aid schools—one of Kennedy's first concerns—there were appropriations for colleges and universities, public schools, and vocational education. There were programs for the jobless and to improve housing. The Russians were persuaded or forced to remove their ICBM missiles from Cuba. Massive aid was provided for declining American "inner cities." It was a promising beginning, even though marred by a bungled CIA-directed attempt to land an invasion force at the Bay of Pigs in Cuba. Some conservatives and reactionaries, members of the John Birch Society, hated Kennedy for, they said, being "soft on communism" and for a dozen other cardinal sins.

At 12:30 P.M., Friday, November 22, 1963, in Dallas, Texas, President Kennedy was killed by Lee Harvey Oswald. Those who remember say that Kennedy's death was nearly as great a shock as Pearl Harbor, a greater shock than Franklin Roosevelt's death by natural causes. Until after the president's funeral, Monday afternoon, television coverage was continuous. There was no time, attention, or spirit for any other matter. But in a suburb of Dallas, pupils in a fourth grade class had clapped when they had been told of Kennedy's death.

Harry S. Truman had not been a great president, but he had exceeded expectations for him. President Eisenhower had detractors, but seemed to most people to be an appropriate president for his time. Kennedy had great promise. The presidents that followed them would leave the White House with their reputations damaged or ruined.

Lyndon B. Johnson, Kennedy's vice president, was sworn in a few hours after Kennedy's assassination. Johnson was from the hill country of Texas north of San Antonio, the first president from the South in a hundred years. He was elected president less than a year after Kennedy's assassination, in 1964. The martydom of Kennedy helped. The Republican nomination of Barry Goldwater, honorable senator from Arizona and archconservative, also helped. Johnson was a masterful politician.

Johnson secured the passage of Kennedy's New Frontier bills and then declared the "War on Poverty." The War on Poverty was intended to set free the one American in five or six caught in poverty, in which poverty resulted in poor health, poor schooling, hopelessness, and continued poverty. That Johnson had country manners and enormous conceit was probably unimportant, although journalists emphasized them. Johnson was magnificently successful in dealing with Congress.

Whites, blacks, and Hispanics were the underculture. The War on Poverty was to provide help for those who were trapped by poverty. Whites in the Appalachians were stranded by shifts in technology, or caught in city slums. Blacks, many of whom had moved to the North during the Depression, during the war boom years, and after, were isolated, more than ever before, in city "ghettoes," where there were too few jobs and too much crime. Ghetto schools were much too unsuccessful in teaching rudiments, in preventing dropping out, and in inducting these members of the underculture into the common culture.

Those who did not speak English—most of whom spoke Spanish as a first language—were also at a disadvantage. Some Spanish-speaking communities were made up of Mexicans who had come to the United States legally or illegally—"wetbacks" was the scornful term for the latter—and their descendants. Puerto Ricans, who had been U.S. citizens since 1917, had come to the mainland to cultivate and harvest vegetables and fruits. Many others had come directly to cities in the northeast, especially New York, after World War II. Airline fares had been low, jobs more plentiful and better paying on the mainland, and welfare payments more generous. The most recent wave of Spanish-speaking immigrants had been refugees from Castro's communist Cuba.

Members of ethnic minorities, blacks, and the poor were to be aided by the War on Poverty. It was to provide jobs, better schooling, medical care, and community development. Johnson wanted to be remembered as another Franklin D. Roosevelt.

Kennedy had proposed the reforms that would lead to his "Great Society" and later to the "War on Poverty." Johnson quickly persuaded Congress to pass the needed legislation and began to put them into effect. But Johnson also sent aid and 550,000 soldiers, sailors, marines, and airmen to Vietnam. More than 56,000 of them would be killed. The war was also costly in terms of money.

The war in Vietnam was brought into American living rooms by television, which was important in arousing public opposition to the war. On campuses there were antiwar teach-ins. College students led by Students for Democratic Action (SDS) demonstrated at a hundred colleges and universities. Students burned draft registration cards and draftees refused to be inducted into the armed forces. Many fled to Canada, some even to Sweden. The war ended Johnson's popularity. Johnson's was the first of the presidencies marred or ruined. He did not seek reelection and probably prevented the election of the Democratic nominee, Hubert H. Humphrey, which led to the election of Republican Richard M. Nixon.

While Nixon and Secretary of State Henry Kissinger did bring hostilities to an end, although not until after the bombing of Cambodia, which produced a final round of heated demonstrations. As everyone knows, Nixon's presidency was ended by the scandal of Watergate. During the next presidential campaign, Republican henchmen broke into Democratic headquarters in the Watergate complex in Washington. On the surface it was tawdry political espionage, but no more than that. The break-in did not much affect the election's outcome; Nixon's reelection was by a landslide. The unraveling of the Watergate conspiracy cannot be told here, but when Nixon resigned from the presidency on August 8, 1974 it was clear that he had encouraged perjury and conspired to obstruct justice. Above all, he had demeaned the presidency.

In 1973 Gerald R. Ford had become vice president after Spiro Agnew, who had been elected to that office, had been forced to resign to avoid prosecution for bribes he had accepted as governor of Maryland. Ford became president upon Nixon's resignation. "Our long national nightmare is over," Ford said. A month later he pardoned ex-president Nixon. Ford immediately became the target of every liberal satirist and editor. The pardon may have cost Ford the election, although inflation and a business slump also put him at a disadvantage.

Democrat Jimmy Carter (a distant descendant of the Carter family that had employed Philip Fithian so long ago) defeated Ford. A determined and astute politician, although a Washington "outsider," he inspired the confidence of the voters. Carter's presidency was damaged by misfortune and hurt by ineptness. That his administration failed to gain the release of American hostages held by Iran damaged its reputation and, Carter thought later, led to his defeat.

Ronald Reagan, one-time sports announcer, actor, union president, radio commentator, and ex-governor of California was an enormously popular and benign seeming presidential candidate. He defeated Carter because of his likeableness and popularity, because of Carter's misfortunes, and because of the public's concern at the increasing cost of gas and oil and other forms of energy, the rate of inflation (in some years more than 10 percent), and the high rate of employment. The invasion of Afghanistan by the Soviet Union had chilled foreign relations. Inflation was reduced, although the actions of the Federal Reserve System had greater effects than the president's. The price was the unemployment of one worker in ten and mortgage interest rates that were as high as 20 percent and monthly payments that made it impossible for many to buy a home. Because the Soviet Union, the "evil kingdom," as President Reagan referred to it, seemed increasingly threatening, appropriations for the armed forces were greatly increased, partly at the cost of social programs and schools and partly at the cost of a national debt snowballing to almost inconceivable amounts.

The Reagan administration seemed likely to end disgraced by "Irangate," an inept, unsuccessful, ill-considered, and probably illegal attempt by Lieutenant Colonel Oliver North and other National Security staff members to arrange the sale of arms to Iran in exchange for hostages and to use the profit from those transactions to bolster the "contras," the armed opponents of the government of Nicaragua. Early in 1988 there were accusations aimed at Reagan cabinet members and other high ranking government officials.

Five successive presidencies had ended in disgrace or near disgrace, unpopular and discredited. Johnson's administration had been a victim—one of the less important ones—of the war in Vietnam. Nixon's presidency ended with the president's resigning to avoid impeachment because of conspiracy after the fact of the Watergate break-in. Ford's two years in office had been marred by his pardon of Nixon. Carter had been largely discredited because of unsuccessful attempts to rescue or have released hostages held by Iran, and Reagan by another unsuccessful attempt to gain their release, as inept as Carter's and lacking in honesty and honor. There were surely several causes for Americans' mood of uncertainty, pessimism, distrust, and withdrawal. The failed presidencies were influential ones.

TECHNOLOGY: GAINS AND LOSSES

The development of technology is especially relevant to the recent history of education for several reasons. Obviously, it has and will affect the occupations for which students are to be prepared. The shape of the economy of the United States, and of the world as a whole, has been, is being, and will be drastically altered by technological developments. Technology and the economic changes it has produced have greatly altered American society and will inevitably produce further changes. Technology's failures, some real, some prospective, and some entirely too real, have undermined public confidence.

Until nearly 1900 most inventions and discoveries had come from craftsmen, engineers, and others of native ingenuity. There were important discoveries and inventions, naturally, but in general they were not based on the findings or theories of "pure" science. Frederick Taylor has been more important in this account for other contributions, but his development of methods to machine metal parts was by cut-and-try rather than theory.

By cut-and-try, rule of thumb, and good luck, the production of power developed. Primitive waterwheels had by the late 1800s developed into hydraulic turbines which were efficient even by present standards. The steam engine, at first slow and unwieldy, developed step by step, gaining power and losing weight. At the Philadelphia Centennial Exposition the Corliss steam engine had been a marvel that had supplied power to all the exhibition's displays of working machines. For a time an automobile powered by a steam engine held national speed records. Within twenty years the Corliss engine and the automobile steamer had been made obsolete, the former by the dynamo and the latter by the gasolene engine. For a decade or more atomic energy seemed an admirable solution for the need for more power and reduced supplies of oil, gas, and coal.

Communications had also been revolutionized. Rotary presses that could print tens of thousands of newspapers an hour replaced flatbed presses that had printed at perhaps a fiftieth of that speed. In 1860 the pony express carried mail as fast as a mustang could gallop from St. Joseph, Missouri, to Sacramento, California, in ten days and nights. But the pony express was replaced in less than a year by a telegraph line, which could carry messages as fast as a telegrapher could tap out Morse code. In 1866 a telegraph line was laid under the Atlantic to Europe. There was a first, crude telephone at the Philadelphia Exposition; tradition has a visiting dignitary exclaiming that "By God, it talks!" The sinking of the *Titanic* in 1912 was reported to the world by "wireless telegraph," Morse code transmitted by radio. The first regular broadcasting service began by broadcasting election returns on the night of November 2, 1920, and a year and a half later the first radio commercial was heard. The first FM signals were broadcast in 1941, and commercial television broadcasting began at the end of World War II.

Personal transportation had developed from horseback to airplane in one long lifetime. The '49ers who went overland to California in search of gold had spent a summer crossing the continent. The first Japanese mission to the United States had reached Washington after forty-four days of travel from San Francisco. After completion of the transcontinental railroad, a week had been time enough to go from the Atlantic to the Pacific. By the 1940s there had been one-day transcontinental airline service. For commuters, the horse car had been replaced by the electric street car, which was being replaced by the personal automobile, which would soon travel on the new interstate superhighways. As personal transportation had improved, the transportation of freight had improved in speed and in economy.

Manufacturing methods had also improved, step by step, with the development of machine tools, interchangeable parts, assembly lines, and a hundred minor improvements and new materials. Thousands of new and comparatively inexpensive products, from pocket watches to automobiles, had appeared.

All these inventions had appeared before the 1950s. They had given the world the shape with which we are still familiar, but they did not prepare us for the discoveries and inventions of the next thirty years. The briefest of lists of these innovations would include electronic devices, including color television, radar and microwave cooking, and computers. It would also include factory automation and the use of robots; new medical diagnostic devices; new insecticides and herbicides; atomic reactors for the generation of electricity; and the development of space probes, crew-carrying space vehicles, and shuttles.

These were or at least seemed to be the gains of technology. But there were failures, and fears of failures, some well founded, some anticipatory, at least a few imaginary, and all undermining confidence. Even television, in most ways an innocuous source of entertainment, had its costs in making children and adults spectators rather than participants. Although computers and automation created new jobs, that they eliminated more jobs than they created seems incontestable. There are numberless stories of "computer errors," of subscriptions, prescriptions, travel reservations, and other services gone wrong. Even medical technology had its failures; as the most glaring example, the appearance of birth defects resulting from the use of thalidomide to prevent morning sickness. Many of the new petrochemicals were useful, even valuable, but DDT killed birds as well as insect pests, and PCB was said to be the most deadly of human poisons, and the thousands of deaths resulting from the release of a chemical in Bhopal, India, were not imaginary. Whether the hazards were exaggerated or not, the accidental near meltdown of the atomic reactor at Three Mile Island near Harrisburg, Pennsylvania, was real enough, as was the destruction of the reactor in Chernobel in Russia. The limits of the technology of space travel appeared in color on millions television screens when the shuttle *Challenger* exploded in the sky. To recall one early unfounded alarm, it was not true that cranberries carried lethal doses of DDT. It was not true that the

Concorde, the supersonic transport airplane, dangerously depleted ozone and so would cause skin cancer. Technological failures, predictions of technological failures, and even irresponsibly fabricated accounts of technological failures had dampened public confidence and added to its apprehension.

THE AMERICAN ECONOMY: PROFITS AND LOSSES

The economy of the United States generally flourished in the years after World War II. There were pauses and minor recessions, but more often there were at least as many jobs as workers, and after a postwar burst of inflation, wages increased more rapidly than did inflation and the cost of living. But in a number of ways the economy was weaker in the 1980s. Unemployment rates increased, worker productivity increased more slowly, salaries and wages increased too little to compensate for inflation, and new jobs on average paid less well. The weaknesses in the U.S. economy were summarized by Lester C. Thurow.

New jobs, better jobs, and higher income in the 1960s came from economic growth, the increase in gross national product. It was increasing at an average of 3.8 percent a year then, but in the years from 1979 until 1985 the annual rate of growth of the gross national product was only 2.0 percent, not much more than half as great. In the same periods the average yearly increase in worker productivity fell from 2.7 percent to 0.9 percent, that is, by two-thirds. (It was not that workers were less qualified; there were other causes of slowing increases in productivity.) The average hourly pay of workers actually decreased by 0.4 percent a year between 1979 and 1985, after correcting for the effects of inflation.

In the 1960s the average rate of unemployment, the proportion of workers looking for jobs, was 4.8 percent. In the earlier 1980s, it was 8.1 percent, more than half again as high. There were more than 10,000,000 new jobs between 1979 and 1985, but new jobs then paid less well than new jobs had before. In the years from 1963 to 1973, nearly half the new jobs created paid $29,600 a year or more. In the years from 1979 to 1985, the proportion of new jobs paying as well after inflation was only a fifth as great, and the percentage of new jobs paying less than $7,400 a year more than doubled: more men and women were employed, but more of them were employed at lower pay. The increasing number of households headed by women led to increasing numbers of families with low incomes, since women's wages and salaries were much lower than men's. To maintain a relatively comfortable middle-class standard of living, many families depended upon two incomes.

While the U.S. economy faltered, those of most other industrial nations thrived. The American economy grew too slowly. There were too few jobs, and many fewer well paid new jobs. To earn wages seemed not too difficult in the late 1980s, but to earn a good wage or salary was much more difficult than it had been. Worker productivity was increasing only a little, and only slowly. The incomes of the rich were increasing more rapidly than were those of others. According to

Thurow, too little was saved, too little was spent for research and development. And, of course, pupils learned too slowly and too little; the schools were not efficient and not effective. As this is written, the American economy shows some signs of improvement. Be that as it may, the economy, like technology, was disappointing. There was less confidence in the economy, as there was in government and in technology.

RETREAT TO INDIVIDUALISM

J. Anthony Lukas's *Common Ground: A Turbulent Decade in the Lives of Three American Families* is an absorbing and finely detailed account of events in Boston in the late 1960s and 1970s. One of its most important characters is Colin Diver, a Harvard Law School graduate who spent most of that decade as a member of the staff of Boston's mayor and Massachusetts' governor, attempting to implement school desegregation and end other forms of racial inequity. His wife, Joan Diver, a foundation official, also devoted much of her professional and personal time and attention to those issues. But near the end of the 1970s they sold their house in a "gentrified" part of Boston and moved to a hundred-and-fifty-year-old house in the suburb of Newton Corner.

The final paragraphs of *Common Ground* describe Colin Diver's careful, painstaking restoration of the carefully made white picket fence around the Newton Corner house that seems symbolic of his partial withdrawal from public affairs, although he continued his interest and concern. Many had had no interest in public affairs, and others abandoned those interests completely. America seemed to have entered a time when individualism was more prominent, more respected.

The trait of individualism was an old and often-admired one in America; de Tocqueville had written about it in 1835, and others had commented on the upbringing of "republican," individualistic, children (pp. 98–101). Ralph Waldo Emerson had written and delivered a famous address entitled "Self-reliance," in praise of personal independence, especially in thought.

Individualism had freed entrepreneurs from the conventions that limited them. The "rugged individualism" of "self-made" Andrew Carnegie, John D. Rockefeller, and other successful businessmen had been honored in the late 1800s, when they had acquired immense new fortunes. Respected and admired before the Depression, "rugged individualism" had seemed to William Heard Kilpatrick and his sympathizers an unfortunate personal characteristic. To overcome it, if there was to be a new or even an improved social order, it would be desirable to teach far more valuable "cooperation."

One of the main theses of *Habits of the Heart*, a sociological commentary by Robert H. Bellah and four coauthors, is that in the most recent decades Americans have retired into individualism and that older loyalties, to community, to church, to values and tradition, have lost much of their importance. *Habits of the Heart* describes individualism as "utilitarian" or "expressive."

Utilitarian individualism, they write, comes from the credo, the guiding belief, of the business manager. Utilitarian individualists have separated their occupational or professional lives from their personal lives. The principles of management have provided orientation for them. They work energetically and wholeheartedly for the benefits they can gain from their positions, knowledge, and skill. For each the first concern is gain, an improved "bottom line," greater profits, and for themselves greater earnings and greater prestige. Concern for the public good, civic values, and "citizenship" are irrelevant; the utilitarian individualist works and lives for his—or her—personal benefit.

Expressive individualism has its base, its origin, in psychology, which was first an academic discipline and then a way of treatment, therapy. The principles of psychology and of psychotherapy, Bellah and his coauthors argue, have spread from specialist researchers to well-educated intellectuals to the public at large. Therapists, it occurs to us, write columns for popular magazines and for newspapers, as well as for the research journals in their fields. The ways of thinking about the "self" and about "needs" that psychotherapists have developed and employ in therapy justify expressive individualism. But the authors ". . . wonder if psychological sophistication has not been bought at the cost of moral impoverishment." The utilitarian individualist seeks gain: the expressive individualist seeks the development and fulfillment of the "self," "authenticity," and "actualization." It puts the matter more crudely than Bellah and his coauthors, but a motto from the beginning of the 1970s comes to mind: "If it feels good, do it!"

In this brief summary we cannot include the reservations of the authors of *Habits of the Heart*, or their finer distinctions. But by its nature individualism without limits, without concern for community, for the general welfare, bleeds confidence from public institutions and costs them much of their strength.

One of those public institutions is the school.

SOCIAL CHANGES: SCHOOL CHANGES

In the most recent history of the schools there have been three major issues; these have served as the topics of the three final chapters of this book. One of these issues has been racial injustices and inequities and the ways in which they could be overcome. The second issue has been the enhancement or at least the preservation of rights, especially those of students. The third, with roots reaching farther into the past, has been the generally conservative efforts to ensure the teaching in the old ways of conventional information (if not knowledge), and to limit the dollar cost of schooling. Naturally, there have been times when supporters of some positions on more than one of these issues have shared efforts and goals. We will if possible point out when these occurred.

Chapter Ten
EQUALITY
IN SCHOOLS

The Constitution as well as morality demand that the schools treat equally, without regard to race, all who attend them.

This proposition and questions coming out of it have been since the 1950s the basis of one of the most important issues about schooling. The proposition is difficult to deny, but complying with it has been arduous. Nor have its meanings been entirely clear. Did schools discriminate against blacks even if the schools provided for them were in every way equal to those provided for whites? The 1954 case of *Brown* v. *Topeka* answered that question and is the most important of landmarks, the most important of victories, for the men and women dedicated to equality in the schools.

But other questions followed. One of those was how to define "equality." Did that mean simply that all pupils would attend the same schools? Even after desegregation, was the treatment of black and white pupils equal, and if not how could there be equality? Or should "equality" mean outcome, of learning? Was "equality" equity? For fairness, should there have been compensatory education to make up for past injustices by the schools?

Efforts to satisfy the general proposition (and efforts to avoid it), and the answering of the questions it raised, are the subjects of this chapter.

There were arguments and efforts to improve the schooling of blacks and the children of other minority groups long before *Brown*. They are part of the history of these efforts at school reform. Court decisions intended to end school segregation are a central and important part of their history and of this chapter, and opposition to them was also important in its time. By many standards, equality in schooling has not been reached, and these failures must be acknowledged.

BEFORE DESEGREGATION

In what would become the United States the inception of efforts to secure equality in schooling without regard to race had begun far back. In Philadelphia, Anthony Benezet had proposed in 1770 that there be "African schools" and a few years later had been the master of an African school for girls. Prudence Crandall's academy had been another attempt to better schooling for blacks.

For blacks the great turning point was the Civil War. The Emancipation Proclamation freed all slaves in the southern Confederacy and the Thirteenth Amendment, ratified in December 1865, freed all slaves.

As Union troops marched southward during the Civil War, it became necessary to resettle blacks who had fled from their masters and had been displaced by the war. General Thomas W. Sherman and other Northerners also called for schooling for blacks, and there were quick responses from Northern philanthropic associations for freedmen. Money, food, clothing, ministers, and teachers were sent to the South to refugee former slaves. Schooling was not the first concern of the freedman programs, but it soon became an important one.

The first well-known effort to provide schooling for former slaves was the Port Royal experiment in schooling, which began in 1862. Union sailors and soldiers had driven Confederate forces from the Sea Islands off the coast of Georgia near Port Royal. The planters had fled, and the plight of their slaves left behind was desperate. With other aid, seventy-six teachers arrived there that year. Some left in disgust; one stayed on for decades.

Hundreds of other teachers supported by the philanthropic societies were sent to the South to teach freed slaves. The federal Freedman's Bureau, established in 1865, supported schools and also hospitals. Perhaps three thousand northern teachers went to the South to teach in the Freedman's Bureau's schools. Freed slaves, blacks from the North, and Southern whites also taught blacks, by 1869 600,000 of them.

Booker T. Washington's boyhood schooling about that time demonstrates the variety of, and slender support for, schooling for blacks. He attended a school in Malden, West Virginia, that had begun in the home of a black preacher. It was supported by the Freedman's Bureau ($200 for a new schoolhouse), by local taxes ($40 a month for four months a year), and by tuition paid by black parents. His teacher there was a black veteran from Ohio. Three years later, after graduating from Hampton Institute, Washington taught in the same one-room, one-teacher

THE FREEDMAN'S
SPELLING-BOOK.

PUBLISHED BY THE

AMERICAN TRACT SOCIETY,

NO. 28 CORNHILL, BOSTON.

SECOND READER. 35

LESSON XV.

cock	wash	pig	too
crows	dawn	dig	two
food	bound	hoo	scrub
wake	clean	plow	bake
home	know	noise	eyes
cheer	knives	kneel	school

What letter is silent in hoe? in clean? Say just, not *jist*; catch, not *cotch*; sit, not *set*; father, not *fader*.

THE FREEDMAN'S HOME.

SEE this home! How neat, how warm, how full of cheer, it looks! It seems as if the sun shone in there all the day long. But it takes more than the light of the sun to make a home bright all the time. Do you know what it is? It is love.

FIGURE 10-1 Title page and illustration from spelling and reading books printed for the Freedman's Bureau schools. Repr. Robert C. Morris, *Reading, 'Riting, and Reconstruction: The Education of Freedmen in the South, 1961-1878* (Chicago: University of Chicago, 1981), plates 7,8.

school, where there were as many as ninety daytime pupils and a nighttime class equally as large. He somehow found time to establish a library and a debating society.

By 1865 black colleges had been established; Fisk University in Nashville, Tennessee; Tallegeda College in Tallegeda, Alabama; and what would become Atlanta University. At first they offered secondary school instruction. Only Howard University in Washington, D.C., founded in 1866, offered college-level courses.

The best-known and most influential of schools for blacks was Hampton Normal and Agricultural School of Virginia, established in 1868 with the support of the American Missionary Association. The driving force at Hampton was General Samuel Chapman Armstrong. The son of a missionary to Hawaii, Armstrong had been commander of a black regiment during the Civil War and then an agent of the Freedman's Bureau. He established the school for blacks patterned on the Hilo, Hawaii, Boarding and Manual Labor School. Its emphasis was on teaching basic occupational skills combined with a work-study program. Armstrong felt it was well suited for recently liberated blacks (as it may have been for von Fellenberg's peasant pupils forty years before).

A 159-acre plantation at the mouth of the James River was purchased as the site for the school. Hampton was to train students to be of service, to themselves and to white communities. It opened with two teachers and fifteen students. With strong support from prominent men, including former teacher and brigadier general and future president James A. Garfield, and Mark Hopkins, president of Williams College, the school was rapidly expanded. Armstrong's purpose was clear:

> [T]o train selected Negro youth who should go out and teach and lead their people, first by getting land and homes; to give them not a dollar that they could earn for themselves; to teach them respect for labor; to replace drudgery with skilled hands; and to these ends, to build up an industrial system, for the sake not only of self-support and intelligent labor, but also for the sake of character. And it seemed equally clear that the people of the country would support a wise work of the freedmen.

An 1873-74 Hampton Institute catalogue outlined a three-year teacher training course with emphasis on English grammar and composition, mathematics, history, and natural science. In agriculture, subjects such as crop and livestock management and crop rotation were studied. The commercial course emphasized bookkeeping. The mechanical course provided instruction on household industries, sewing, printing, mechanical drawing, and penmanship.

Perhaps the Hampton student nearest to Armstrong's ideals was Booker T. Washington, who would become famous. In his autobiography Washington described walking part of the 500 miles from his home in Malden, West Virginia, to attend Hampton. He arrived after a three-week journey with only fifty cents in his pocket. After applying for admission to Mary F. Mackie, the head teacher, she directed him to clean a classroom. Washington wrote that "the sweeping of that room was my college examination." He swept the floor three times and dusted four times. Mackie

FIGURE 10-2 Hampton Normal and Agricultural Institute shortly after its founding. From Mary F. Armstrong and Helen W. Ludlow, *Hampton and Its Students* (New York: G.P. Putnam, 1875), frontispiece.

accepted him, and he quickly became a model student. After graduating, three years teaching, and a year of study of theology, he returned to Hampton as its first black instructor.

Washington's papers show that he was a politic and sometimes dissimulating man. Publicly, if not privately, Washington said the black man's place was in the agrarian south. Schooling of blacks had as one of its primary aims "the fitting of him to live friendly and peaceably with his white neighbors both socially and politically." Washington accommodated and conformed. He was shaped by the attitudes and beliefs of his time rather than shaping them. (Or perhaps he had learned too well at Hampton.) In 1881, recommended by Armstrong, Washington was appointed head of Tuskegee Institute, an industrial school for blacks in the heart of Alabama. Washington modeled Tuskegee after Hampton Institute. It was in constant need of money in its early years, but Washington was an inspired fund raiser. By the beginning of the 1890s Washington had fully formulated the philosophy of Tuskegee and the means by which racial equality could be achieved:

> The Tuskegee idea is that correct education begins at the bottom, and expands naturally as the necessities of the people expand. As the race grows in knowledge, experience, culture, taste, and wealth, its wants are bound to become more diverse; and to satisfy these wants there will be a constantly increasing variety of professional businessmen and women.

Washington said that blacks in America would be accepted in time by whites as a result of their having demonstrated merit and worth.

In that scheme of things, equality and respect had to be learned. Washington said that agitation by the black population for social equality was "the extremist folly." Speaking at the Cotton States Exposition in Atlanta in 1895, he renounced demanding social equality for blacks. The futures of blacks and whites were inevitably linked, but "in all things that are purely social we can be as separate as the fingers, yet one as the hand in all things essential to human progress." The segregationist governor of Georgia congratulated Washington after his speech. It was extraordinarily well received by the white public; black protests about its denial of racial equality were largely ignored. The consequences of Washington's position would be felt well into the twentieth century. It also established him as the principal spokesman for America's black community.

There had been earlier government supported schools for Indians, but their counterpart of Hampton Institute was Carlisle Indian Barracks. It was established by Captain Richard Henry Pratt in 1879. He had been in charge of seventy-two Kiowas, Cheyennes, and Comaches captured in the Red River War and sent to Florida. Pratt was convinced that they would profit from instruction, that they should abandon tribal ways and adopt the white civilization and culture. When the government ordered them returned to the West, most of them requested permission to stay in the East and continue their education. Private contributions made it possible to send seventeen of them to Hampton Institute. With the help of Pratt, Armstrong began the training of his Indian charges. With the permission of Carl

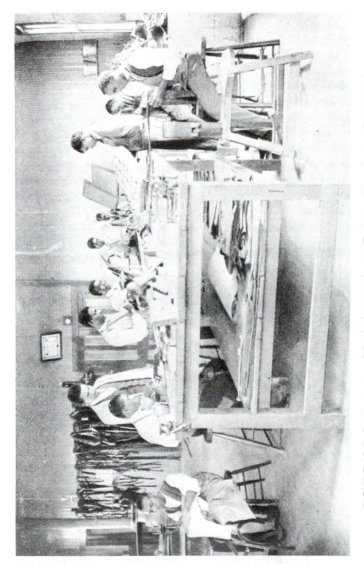

FIGURE 10-3 Students at work in the harness shop at Tuskegee. From Booker T. Washington, ed., *Tuskegee and Its People: Their Ideals and Achievements* (New York: D. Appleton and Company, 1906), pp. 270-71.

Schurz, Secretary of the Interior, the next year Pratt recruited forty Sioux boys and six Sioux girls to attend Hampton Institute at government expense. A year later he had permission and support to open the Indian school in a deserted barracks at Carlisle, Pennsylvania. Not surprisingly, the Carlisle school emphasized industrial and manual training, following the approach to the education of blacks at Hampton Institute.

The Carlisle school seemed at first to be successful, but probably was not in the long term. When students there completed their training, they returned to the reservations, where they could not use their new skills. Many shed the veneer of culture that had been imposed upon them and reassumed their Indian identities. In a well-known and illustrative case, Plenty Horses, a young Sioux, killed Lt. Edward W. Casey during the troubles at Pine Ridge in 1891. Plenty Horses explained at his trial that he had killed to wipe away the stain put upon him and to win a place of respect among his people.

By 1900 it was clear that federal school programs for Indians were of little benefit. As an example, there were four or five thousand Navajo school-aged children in 1901, but only three hundred of them were attending schools. There were attempts of minor reforms later, but only a few Indians had the educational opportunities of whites, and they had only limited success.

Although Washington seemed to ignore it, racism was pervasive in the South, and in all America, in the later 1800s. The demonstrations of members of the Ku Klux Klan, the Knights of the White Camellia, and White Empires were evidence: if more was needed, there were hundreds of lynchings of blacks. Blacks became the scapegoats of white Southern politics.

In *The Strange Career of Jim Crow*, C. Van Woodward described the "Jim Crow" laws. Black men were disfranchised by laws requiring that voters be property owners and that they be able to read. Housing was segregated by city ordinances and restrictive clauses in deeds. Theaters, parks, even taxis and telephone booths were segregated. In two states schoolbooks used by one race could not be used by the other. A visitor from the Union of South Africa said he could see little difference in the treatment of blacks in the United States and in the Union of South Africa.

In most of the South there was public schooling for black children, but of a terribly, unjustly inferior kind. Buildings were old, often rickety, unpainted, far too small, far too overcrowded. Black teachers' salaries were smaller than white teachers' salaries, which were much smaller than salaries outside the South. Compared with schools for southern whites, schools for southern blacks were no better supported in 1930 than they had been in 1875, and their relative level of support declined until 1930. Although there were exceptions, such as the "M" Street School in Washington and Dunbar High School in Norfolk, Virginia, high schools for blacks were slow to develop, and slower still to meet accreditation requirements. For each accredited black high school in the South in 1928-29, there were twenty-five accredited high schools for whites. In Mississippi there were two hundred thirty-five accredited high schools for whites, none for blacks.

FIGURE 10-4 A group of young Indians before and after their education at Carlisle. From "Indian Education at Hampton and Carlisle," *Harper's New Monthly Magazine*, Vol. 62, April 1881, pp. 660-61.

A thin scattering of blacks attended college. Of that scattering, a small fraction attended otherwise white colleges, such as Antioch in Yellow Springs, Ohio. Most attended black colleges. Private church-related black colleges had been established at the close of the Civil War and, although very poor, they provided scholarships and schooling for some who were in need. Other blacks attended black land grant "A&M" schools or black normal schools. Only Howard University in Washington, D.C., was thought of by whites as academically respectable.

THE COURTS AND THE SCHOOLS

The first lawsuit to desegregate public schools had been *Roberts* v. *Boston*, decided in 1849. Although Charles Sumner, a famous and eloquent abolitionist, had argued for desegregation of the schools, the court found that separate schools for blacks were legal.

The Fourteenth Amendment, ratified in 1868, seemed to protect blacks from discrimination by the states, and therefore from discrimination in schooling. It said

> No state shall make or enforce any law which shall abridge the privileges or immunities of citizens of the United States; nor shall any State deprive any person of life, liberty, or property, without the due process of law; nor deny to any person within its jurisdiction equal protection of the laws.

Nevertheless, in 1896 the Supreme Court said in *Plessy* v. *Ferguson*, a case concerning the segregation of railroad passengers, that

> We consider the underlying fallacy of the railroad's argument [in opposition to segregation] to consist in the assumption that the enforced separation of the two races stamps the colored race with a badge of inferiority. If this be so, it is not by reason of anything found in the act, but solely because the colored race chooses to put that construction upon it.

Only Justice John Marshall Harlan disagreed, saying that the Constitution was "colorblind." The Supreme Court ruled that "separate but equal" railroad coaches, and by implication schools, were not in violation of the Fourteenth Amendment. The 1899 Supreme Court decision in *Cumming* v. *Richmond County* explicitly approved segregated schools.

In the 1930s the political power and influence of blacks was slight, and in the Depression social injustices seemed less important. The leaders of the NAACP (National Association for the Advancement of Colored People, usually spoken of as the "N-double-A-C-P") decided that lawsuits were the best route for aiding blacks and ending segregation. There were suits and appeals in criminal cases where juries had been all white, about housing restrictions, and about other issues, as well as those about schooling. The NAACP's legal strategy was planned by Charles H.

Houston, dean of the Howard University Law School, and later by Thurgood Marshall, who would become a Supreme Court justice.

The first line of attack was to argue that "separate but equal" schools were in fact not equal. The NAACP was not successful in its first court actions. But when Donald Murray was denied admission to the University of Maryland law school in 1935, Houston argued that the University of Maryland branch for blacks, the Princess Anne Academy, offered not much more than secondary school instruction, and of course had no law school. "Separate" was not equal, clearly. A Maryland court ordered that Murray be admitted to the University of Maryland law school.

The State of Missouri promised to open a law school for blacks, but a promise was not enough. In *Gaines* v. *Canada* the Supreme Court directed that Lloyd Gaines be admitted to the University of Missouri Law School.

The University of Oklahoma admitted George W. McLaurin to its doctoral program in education but isolated him from other students. The court said that McLaurin was at a disadvantage and that the university's action was unconstitutional. Again, an implication: separate cannot be equal.

In 1950, Oliver Brown of Topeka, Kansas, a black welder and part-time minister, had attempted to register his daughter in the all-white elementary school that was closest to her home. She was not admitted. The NAACP protested, and then a suit was filed even though the black teachers and P.T.A. of Topeka supported segregation of the schools.

The suit was appealed to the Supreme Court. The NAACP's case, directed by Marshall though argued by Robert Carter, was supported by a thirty-two-page brief from the U.S. solicitor general. The Supreme Court's decision was difficult to predict. Chief Justice Earl Warren had been appointed only six months before. He was thought of as a states' rights man and had supported the internment of Japanese-Americans in World War II. The significance of the decision was clear, however. One justice came from his hospital bed for the occasion. Reporters had not been given the usual printed copies of the decision. Chief Justice Warren had written the decision and read it in the courtroom.

> To separate . . . [black children] from others of similar age and qualifications solely because of their race generates a feeling of inferiority as to their status in the community that may affect their hearts and minds in a way never to be undone. . . . We conclude that in the field of public education the doctrine of "separate but equal" has no place. Separate educational facilities are inherently unequal. We hold that the plaintiffs . . . are, by reason of the segregation complained of, deprived of equal protection of the laws guaranteed by the Fourteenth Amendment.

There were bitter protests at once, many of them. Kluger compiled some: the Constitution had been reduced to " 'a mere scrap of paper.' " The decision " 'flagrantly ignored all law and precedent . . .'." It was " 'the most serious blow that had yet been struck against the rights of the states.' " Governor Byrnes of South Carolina was ' "shocked.' "

In 1955 the Supreme Court, in a decision referred to as *Brown II*, began to specify how the schools named in the *Brown* suits were to make plans for desegregation with "all deliberate speed." The phrase "all deliberate speed" is an ambiguous one, with uncertain meaning. The next year the court extended its reasoning in *Brown* to public transportation. That decision freed Martin Luther King, who had been leading the Montgomery, Alabama, boycott of segregated buses.

If the Constitution and the *Brown* decisions required that the schools be "colorblind," then pupils were to be assigned to schools or classes regardless of their race. But in 1967 ability grouping, "tracking," was found to be unconstitutional if it resulted in classes predominately black or white. In the *Green* v. *New Kent County* case, the Supreme Court ruled that schools must be desegregated, that "colorblindness" was not in itself in keeping with the Court's previous decisions.

School systems and local and state governments developed many legal arguments, and subterfuges, to avoid or delay desegregation. There were also attempts to block school desegregation by other means. Some of the earlier efforts were in the south, but there were also attempts in the north.

Some politicians shared resentment against desegregation and some tried to use it for political gain. One of them was Arkansas Governor Orval Faubus, who was running for reelection in 1957. The Little Rock, Arkansas, Board of Education announced that it would begin desegregation that fall by enrolling nine black students at Central High School there, which two thousand white students attended. Faubus claimed that there would be violence and, to prevent black students from

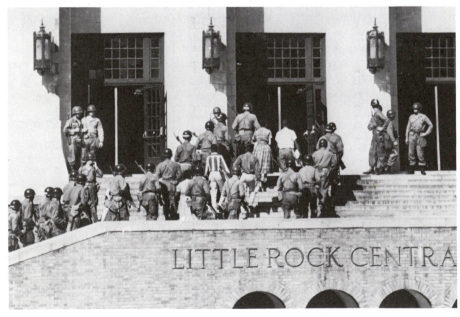

FIGURE 10-5 On September 25, 1957, federal troops escorted nine black students into the previously all-white Little Rock Central High School. Courtesy of United Press International.

entering Central High School, called out the National Guard. In spite of personal pleas by President Eisenhower and federal officials, Faubus refused to have the black students admitted. When they were, a white mob pushed through police barricades, and it was necessary to send the black students home. Seeing no alternative, President Eisenhower sent combat soldiers from the 101st Airborne Division to Central High School. The soldiers, with bayonets fixed, broke up the mobs and the nine black students returned to Central High. Faubus was reelected; the cost to the federal government was $4,051,000. Resistance to school desegregation became a notorious cause. The "Bonnie Blue Flag" of the Confederacy and even the song "Dixie" became symbols of militant and sometimes violent white supremacy rather than those of a romanticized lost cause.

There were also attempts to prevent the desegregation of colleges and universities. In 1961, James A. Meredith, a black applicant, was denied admission to the University of Mississippi. With the help of the NAACP, Meredith won suits in federal courts, and again applied for admission. Governor Ross Barnett denied the application on the ground that states' rights took precedence over federal court orders. Attorney General Robert F. Kennedy tried unsuccessfully to arrange Meredith's admission. Barnett physically blocked Meredith's way. When Meredith returned to the campus he was accompanied by one hundred federal marshals. There were tear gas and Molotov cocktails—homemade fire bombs—and rifle fire. National Guardsmen came to the aid of the marshalls. A reporter and an onlooker were killed, but the marshalls and the National Guardsmen did not return the rifle and shotgun fire, although nearly two hundred of them were wounded or injured. When the regular army arrived, forty soldiers were also injured too. There were two hundred arrests. The next morning Meredith was admitted to the University of Mississippi.

The efforts over ten years to desegregate the New York City schools was watched nationally. They show some of the difficulties in school desegregation in the largest cities. Our account follows in general that of Diane Ravitch, *The Troubled Crusade*.

In 1955, in 8 percent of New York's schools more than 90 percent of the pupils were black or Puerto Rican. Segregation was de facto, in fact but not by law. The New York City school board condemned segregation and had named a "commission" to plan desegregation.

There were interrelated obstacles to desegregation. Many white parents opposed school desegregation, especially if it required "cross busing," busing white pupils into schools in black neighborhoods. Either as a rationalization for opposing desegregation or sincerely, many favored the "neighborhood school." It was convenient, aware of local needs, and ideally the focus of the community. Sheer numbers had already made desegregation nearly impossible. In the 1950s the white population of New York City fell by 800,000, and 700,000 blacks and Puerto Ricans arrived. As early as 1959 whites had boycotted two neighborhood schools. The difficulties became greater in 1961. Citywide achievement scores had fallen below national averages. There were charges of payoffs and irregularity with school construction funds. That year the United Federation of Teachers (UFT) became the teachers' official bargaining agent; it would greatly affect educational policy in New York City. An organization opposed to pupil transfers, Parents and Taxpayers (PAT), appeared.

In 1963, New York Commissioner (Superintendent) of Schools James Allen, Jr., intending to speed desegregation, ordered New York State school systems to report their progress toward desegregation, a *segregated school* being defined as more than 50 percent "minority"—black and Puerto Rican. By then more than 40 percent of the pupils in New York City schools were members of minority groups, and 400,000 white children attended parochial and private schools. Integration by Allen's standard was becoming almost impossible. Nevertheless, minority action groups continued to demand school integration.

The board and Superintendent Calvin Gross proposed desegregation without forced busing of pupils. Angering both integrationists and neighborhood supporters. Milton A. Galamison, then the most important integrationist leader, demanded a schedule for desegregation and planned a school boycott. White liberals were becoming doubtful, but on February 4, 1963, schools were picketed. There were thirty-five hundred demonstrators at the board of education building, and a third of a million children stayed home. The board asked Commissioner Allen to prepare an integration plan. The PAT also picketed and planned a mass rally. Galamison planned a second boycott. The next spring his supporters attempted to block the opening of the New York World's Fair.

The Allen report pleased the integrationists, even though it admitted that the complete desegregation of New York City schools was no longer possible. The report called for neighborhood elementary (K-4) schools, new "middle" (5-8) schools that would be desegregated, and comprehensive high schools to replace vocational high schools and increase integration. Even at the time the plan seemed to some too simpleminded and as inadequate as treating a broken leg with aspirin.

In 1964 New York City had elected a Republican reform mayor, John V. Lindsay. He would not support the school board, which had been named by a Democratic mayor. President Johnson's War on Poverty funded community action organizations intended to give the poor greater power. Preston Wilcox, a community organizer and Columbia University faculty member, organized parents who were more concerned with quality of schooling for blacks than with desegregation.

In 1966, a new middle school, IS 201, was completed in East Harlem. Although school board officials had said it was to be integrated, it could not be. The leader of the IS 201 activists said before television cameras that "either they bring white children in to integrate 201 or they let the community run the school—let us pick the principal and the teachers, let us set the educational standards and make sure they are met." Local control was replacing desegregation as the issue. Perhaps the obvious had been demonstrated: New York City schools could not be desegregated.

In Boston, Federal District Court Judge Wendell Arthur Garrity, Jr., ordered and directed the desegregation of the schools. The issue there had been complicated by political maneuvring and a large and defensive Irish-American community. It seemed to some that some court-designed plans for busing students were ill considered and inept. In Charlestown High School, where tension was greatest, there were boycotts, sit-ins, marches, picketing, and riots. Lukas's account of school desegregation in Boston is to us dismaying. The desegregation of schools had its costs, which were not small.

REMEDIES AND DIAGNOSES

As school work has usually been judged, "minority group members" (blacks, hispanic Americans, native American Indians) have as groups done less well, impoverished pupils have done less well, and impoverished minority members have done least well. There have been many efforts to improve the school achievement of minority group members and the children of the poor. Court orders, laws, financial aid, curriculum revisions, organizational changes, and other remedies have been applied. These remedies have implied diagnoses, the nature of which make the remedies more readily understandable. It has been argued that

> Conventional achievement tests are biased, and the differences in academic performance are not real.
>
> The basic cause has been racial segregation in schools.
>
> Curricula and materials of instruction have been inappropriate for the poor and the black, and obviously unsuited for pupils who have not spoken English as their native language.
>
> Teachers have discriminated against minority group members and poor children and have been poorly prepared to teach them.
>
> The organization of schools in ways recommended by business management-oriented administrators has resulted in poor pupil performance.

Test Bias

That minority group members and other low-socioeconomic-status children have in general scored lower on IQ, achievement, and aptitude tests is indisputable. Evidence on that point has been accumulating since World War I, when the army tested draftees. Those lower scores, it has been argued, come from flaws in tests. It has been charged that, most fundamentally, there have been no clear, theoretical definitions of intelligence, of what IQ tests measured. The measurement of "aptitude" as distinguished from achievement was for most purposes impractical. The standard tests were culturally biased, designed on the assumption that the pupil had a conventional middle-class background—that was the most frequent criticism. Aside from that, it was said that some pupils scored low because they were not used to multiple-choice items and did not understand that test scores might be important.

We agree that there is no adequate definition of what an IQ test measures and that it cannot be assumed that what an IQ measures is "intelligence." We also agree that both IQ and achievement tests have often been used for administrative convenience or other inappropriate reasons. We are inclined to agree that there have been no successful ways of distinguishing between achievement and ability by test. But making "culture-free" tests still seems extraordinarily difficult. A careful, systematic effort by Alison Davis and Kenneth Eels in the early 1940s failed to produce any item, much less a test, that was culture free, on which blacks did not score lower. Test scores were and still are predictable at far better than a chance level from pupils' socioeconomic status. (All agree that on standard tests some minority pupils score higher than some whites and that many minority group members score higher than most whites.)

School Segregation

There were high hopes that differences in the academic performances of blacks would increase to the level of the performance of whites when schools were desegregated. Evaluations have not yielded uniform results, but the general conclusion is that blacks' achievement scores have risen somewhat, perhaps 15 percent, when they have been in desegregated schools. The differences in Scholastic Aptitude Test scores of whites and blacks has become somewhat smaller, though primarily because whites' scores have fallen. But other factors seem far more closely related than school desegregation to pupil achievement scores: parents' socioeconomic status, parents' values, and the pupils' sense of controlling their own destiny are all much more important.

Books and Lessons

Black academic performance, it was argued, suffered because conventional schoolbooks and courses of study ignored or even belittled blacks. Blacks, it was argued, had been robbed of their place in history. The typical preprimer, first reading book, neither pictured nor mentioned blacks. "Dick and Jane" and their counterparts in other preprimers lived in suburbs. They played on smooth, neatly cut lawns, and their houses had white picket fences around them. It was as if there had been no blacks at all, no slums, not even any cities. Upper-grade readers and literature books were scarcely better. The first and easiest steps were to change preprimer and primer illustrations. New stories were written, the first for use in the Detroit schools.

History texts had had casts that were nearly all white, except for an occasional Indian. Partly, this had reflected America's view of its past: Who had heard of the assault on Confederate Battery Wagner by the black soldiers of the Union's 54th Massachusetts Infantry in 1863? Who had ever heard of black cowboys, although there had been many of them? Perhaps it had also been the result of publishers' interest in selling books of the South. New edition and new texts carefully mentioned black historical figures: Benjamin Bannecker, Nat Turner, Frederick

FIGURE 10-6 The "Dick and Jane" readers of the 1950s and 1960s reflected life in a comfortable middle-class suburban setting. Courtesy of the New York Public Library Picture Collection.

Douglass, George Washington Carver, Martin Luther King, and others. Later it was pointed out that schoolbooks typecast, stereotyped, women and showed them only as homemakers or in women's traditional occupations. There were more changes and history books noted women: Dolley Madison, Harriet Tubman, Harriet Beecher Stowe, Frances Perkins, Eleanor Roosevelt, and others.

The appearance in reading books of blacks and of the cities in which they lived probably increased black pupils' interest, and presumably improved their achievement. The inclusion of blacks in school history books righted a wrong and corrected an omission. For black activists and their sympathizers, minor revisions of whites' lessons and whites' books was not enough. It seemed even to moderates among them that there could not be true equality for blacks until they came to have self-respect as blacks. As a motto, shorthand, "Black is beautiful!" Extremists, far more often outside than in schools, talked about "Negritude," about "black power," and, threateningly, "the fire next time."

Teacher Bias

Some social psychologists were, and are, convinced that important determinants of pupils' behaviors are self-expectations and that self-expectations are shaped by the expectations of others.

There were all too many indications that most white teachers, like most other whites, had racist prejudices. One study even showed that most white teachers reacted negatively even to blacks' patterns of speech and evaluated compositions as less good in every way if they heard a composition, even if written by a white, when it was tape recorded by a black pupil. Even teachers who did not identify the reader as black evaluated unfavorably the compositions they read. The racial bias of white teachers is lamentable: we hope it is declining.

That pupil performance was influenced by teacher expectations seemed to be demonstrated in a widely read and cited book, *Pygmalion in the Classroom*, by Rosenthal and Jacobson. They led teachers to believe that scores on a new test had identified certain of their pupils as potential "late bloomers." The test was irrelevant, but the pupils identified as "late bloomers" did improve in performance. The improvement was said to be the result of heightened teacher expectations. Later researchers could not duplicate the results in *Pygmalion in the Classroom*, and there were flaws in the experimental design. But our intuition says that expectations do influence pupil performance.

Teacher attitudes, expectations, and behavior may be shaped by pupil socio-economic status, as Ray C. Rist demonstrated in a study in which all those observed were black. He noted that a black kindergarten teacher seated pupils who were on welfare at the back of the room, and then systematically slighted them, gave them far less attention than she gave other pupils, and spent far less time in their individual instruction. There is no overemphasizing racial prejudice and its effects. But there is also prejudice against the children of the poor.

The proportion of teachers who were and are black was and is smaller than the proportion of blacks in the population of the United States. It was and is much smaller than the proportion of pupils who are black. The least dishonorable explanation for the relative rarity of black teachers in northern cities is that first-generation immigrants to the cities have not become teachers. One of the conventions of segregated schools was that it was permissible for whites to teach blacks but not for blacks to teach whites. The routine procedures of school personnel administrators sometimes institutionalized racism. In one system, to save travel expenses, they recruited teachers, even when the teacher shortage was severe, only at nearby colleges. However, nearby colleges admitted few blacks. Therefore there were few blacks among new teachers.

There are now many other occupational opportunities for black college graduates. Consequently, recruiting black teachers is more difficult than before. Many black teacher candidates have not performed satisfactorily on required standard or competency tests. These may be additional occurrences of racial bias in testing, about which we have written. Perhaps some of the difficulties prospective black teachers have encountered have been lingering after-effects of the inferiority of schools for blacks. It would be beneficial and equitable if there were more black teachers. Righting this imbalance will be difficult.

The System

We cannot view the "system" with anything like an open mind. It did not deserve it. In every big city there was a shorthand expression for the rules and regulations of the school system's central offices: "110 Livingston Street says" (New York City); "City Hall says" (Buffalo); "911 Locust says" (Saint Louis); "Lindsey-Hopkins says" (Miami). A more general term was "downtown." All these meant systemwide regulations and the office of the superintendent of schools and his or her assistants and staff. On days when "downtown" prevented the obviously appropriate, the teacher, or for that matter the building principal, mentioned "downtown" only when the word was accompanied with expletives.

In some downtown central offices of the city systems, the "sup'inten't" was mentioned only with a tone of awe and fear. Some, of course not all, the city superintendents were egocentric, autocratic, and punitive. The feelings of power and prestige were important rewards for some of them. Even the superintendent, however, would join in the condemnation state departments of education, of "Albany" (New York) or "Jeff City" (Missouri) or "Tallahasee" (Florida) or wherever. Again, there were more general terms: "state department" (not the Department of State, but the much more immediate state department of education) or "state ed." In "state ed" there were references to "Washington" and the "Feds."

This was in part a late example of what David B. Tyack called in his book of the same name "the one best system," the pattern of school administration evolved from business management methods, stressing uniformity and accountability. We are convinced that part of it was to avoid responsibility and so avoid blame. Risk-free if counterproductive control by "downtown" had attracted into school administration many men and a few women who by disposition avoided risks, "kept their noses clean," and obeyed.

The "one best system" reduced dishonesty and favoritism. It set careful procedures for purchasing and for hiring and firing, and nearly eliminated personal favoritism. In the development of city school systems, efficiency had been the first goal. As a prerequisite of efficiency, there was uniformity in school systems, of curriculum, of instructional supplies, of personnel practices, of accounting, of record keeping. Elaborate organizational pyramids had been erected. Even in moderately large systems, a teacher might have been four levels away from the superintendent, via (1) the departmental chair, (2) the building principal, (3) an assistant superintendent, (4) an associate superintendent, finally to the superintendent. The path to the superintendent might also have been by way of supervisors and coordinators. Although it was to be said that, as an asset, the one best system did establish orderly procedures, it was not certain advantages of the one best system were outweighed by their costs.

The ranks and tiers of administrators in the city systems seemed to reach as high and as far as the eye could see. Above and beyond the administrators there were the city school boards. As they had been for fifty years and more, the city school boards were made up of professionals and other members of the middle class, almost without representation by members of the lower class, and with only an occasional black member. Reformers asked whether it was reasonable to expect such school boards to be sympathetic to the needs and wishes of the blue-collar workers' families, or to the families of the unemployed.

The authority of state departments of education had been extended. A part of that had come from state legislatures. They had by law set responsibilities for teacher certification, for curriculum (for instance in New York State, lessons on the evil of tobacco and alcohol). State legislatures had composed formulas for state aid. State aid had been intended to give additional state funds to the proper districts. (That aid may have outweighed the drawbacks, but the drawbacks were real.) In New York State, "state ed" insisted on a numeration, a carefully tabulated sum of school head counts, for every pupil present each day in every school. While knowing where the individual pupil was had value, knowing where all the pupils were had its costs—in teacher time, in school clerk time, in administrator time. It is not at all difficult to find ridiculous examples of the outcomes of state aid formulas. In the early 1960s, in one North Carolina fishermen's community, an agriculture teacher was hired because the state would pay his salary, and in spite of the fact that the nearest farm was 35 miles away, by boat. He fertilized the sand with fish heads and entrails—the Pilgrims had known how—and indeed harvested the first home-grown tomatoes the fishermen had ever seen.

There was increasing pressure and influence, too, from Washington. It came from newly enacted laws about desegregation and other matters. For instance, Congress, as the law was interpreted, required that teaching staffs be desegregated, and sometimes that they be rotated. That there were advantages to having black teachers teach black pupils seemed not to matter. That teachers in all-white schools near the city limits had never taught a black pupil and wanted very much not to, also seemed not to matter. There could be other examples. What is entirely clear is that the federal government also played a more important part in the day-to-day management of the schools.

There were two remedies for the overcentralization of school administration, as critics saw it. One, which might have been called the insider approach, was to decentralize school administrative patterns, to have decisions made as near as was feasible to the pupil. It was generally agreed that there were some parts of administration—accounting, purchasing, and maybe personnel—that could best be managed by "downtown," the central office. Nevertheless, there would be advantages in local control of teacher assignment, choosing instructional materials, and supervision of teachers.

The more extreme solution was local control. This required that the neighborhood school boards, which the superintendents had been to so much trouble to extinguish, be established. The neighborhood boards were to have the power to set policy, to appoint principals and perhaps local superintendents, and even teachers. At least the local boards would express local preferences and have the power to put them into practice.

In New York City, the IS 201 activists saw local control as appropriate, since IS 201 could not be integrated. The idea of local control had wide appeal, not only to black activists, but also to white liberals. IS 201 activists called the city school board the "Board of Genocide" and, with supporters, took control of the board of education meeting in December 1966. They held it for three days and elected their own board. The legal, appointed board seemed ridiculous and powerless.

The decentralization of New York City schools gained Mayor Lindsay's support. He appointed a panel chaired by McGeorge Bundy, then president of the Ford Foundation. Mario Fantini and Marilyn Gittell, avid supporters of local control, were the panel's staff chief and chief consultant. It recommended that at least thirty local semiautonomous districts be established.

One of the "demonstration districts" was Ocean Hill-Brownsville. Rhody McCoy, "a militant Black with pent-up rage," was named as its administrator. He nominated as a building principal Herman Ferguson, under indictment for conspiracy to commit murder. On the advice of the Ocean Hill-Brownsville personnel committee, he "ended the employment" of nineteen tenured teachers and administrators. The board of education and the UFT, their union, came to their support. McCoy was directed to reinstate ten of them, but did not. The UFT struck New York City schools. Black and white racism and anti-Semitism

FIGURE 10-7 Students wait outside as non-striking teachers hold a press conference at the entrance of Junior High School 271 in the Ocean Hill-Brownsville district of Brooklyn, September 15, 1968. Courtesy of United Press International.

added to tensions. A thousand police officers were assigned to protect teachers returning to Ocean Hill-Brownsville after the strike, but there were disturbances and schools were closed. Another UFT strike lasted for five weeks. The Ocean Hill-Brownsville governing board, which had claimed independence, was told by a judge that it was "no more than an unofficial body of citizen advisors without power to transfer or suspend . . . [or] to countermand any orders of the Board of Education." After much more negotiation, the New York State Legislature did approve the decentralization of the city's school system, following in broad outline the recommendations of the Bundy panel.

But the decentralization of the New York City school system did not result in genuine local control. Perhaps there was decentralization in form, but not of power. In local board elections, only a few citizens voted, and their votes were often divided among several candidates, who lost to candidates sponsored by the UFT. The academic achievement of New York City pupils did not improve substantially. The results of New York City's decentralization were evidence that decentralization would not be, at least by itself, an adequate remedy for the poor academic performance of minority group pupils.

UNENDED QUEST

Lyndon Johnson's War on Poverty had broader aims than did the desegregation and improvement of schools. Although it did not produce changes as rapidly as had been hoped, it did produce changes outside and inside the school. Outside the school, the gaps between the incomes of blacks and whites with equal educations decreased, and there was less segregation in housing. Many schools were successfully desegregated, although how many was not clear because of differences in definitions of "desegregation." The gaps between the achievement scores of whites and blacks lessened. (But the doubter would note that declines in whites' scores contributed more to that than did increases in blacks' scores.)

Still, there was evidence that the education of whites and blacks was not equal, even if "equality" was defined as equality of access. Relatively few blacks entered teacher education programs, as we have said. While this is of special concern to us, we note that not many blacks are entering the other professions and that the percentage of law and medicine students actually declined in the mid-1980s. For some, the consequences of *Brown* have been a disappointment because the academic achievement of blacks is still on the average lower than that of whites.

Some of us who for thirty years and more have devoted effort to desegregating the schools have done so because separate schools seemed immoral, even if equal. For us, the appearance of all-black city school systems and all-white suburban systems is almost disheartening. If separate schools were immoral, separate school systems also seem so, no matter if equal.

Chapter Eleven
IN PURSUIT
OF FREEDOM

The school must protect and enhance the freedom and dignity of its students and must not impede their natural development. They must not be exploited or constrained by the society in which they live.

These propositions are, in simplified form, one basis for criticism of the schools, and of society. Arguments for them and changes in schooling to comply with them are the subject of this chapter.

The propositions are not new, and probably do not too much misrepresent the main points of Jean-Jacques Rousseau in his novel *Émile*, published in 1762. Rousseau's ideal man was the "noble savage," the man unspoiled by society. The ideal had great appeal to Lord Byron and other romantics of the earlier 1800s. It was linked to the thought of Pestalozzi, and so to that of the utopians of New Harmony. Others who preceded Dewey, including Bronson Alcott and Francis W. Parker, would probably have sympathized with them. Joseph Meyer Rice's first series in *Forum* concentrated on the "lockstep" schools imposed upon their pupils.

The status of "youth," as distinct from that of "child" and mature adult, had become more distinct during the later 1800s, as industrialization and urbanization limited youth's employment and association with relatives and other workers. It became more obvious as the youth population increased, almost doubling in the 1890s, from 14,200,000 to 26,700,000. In *School and Society* (1899) and through his work at the Laboratory School of the University of Chicago, John Dewey argued clearly for the need to develop schools that compensated youth for the loss of opportunities to learn that came from the growth of large-scale industry. Dewey believed that the school must take the places of the farms and homes that had formerly been educators.

Other organizations were increasingly important in providing youth with compensating experience. The Boy Scouts were organized in England by Sir Robert Baden-Powell in 1907. The Boy Scouts quickly appeared in the United States, and soon became popular. During the same time the Young Men's Christian Association and Boys' Clubs spread rapidly, and the Girl Scouts and Campfire Girls appeared. All these organizations provided alternative kinds of learning, nature lore, and crafts. They also kept youths and older boys and girls occupied.

At the end of World War I youth was increasingly marginal in the work force, and the importance of youth as consumer rather than as producer was apparent. A distinctive youth culture or subculture emerged then, identifying itself by its music, its fashions in dress, and its social behavior. The values of the culture of the "flapper" and "Jazz Age" was seen by some critics then as reflecting the decadence of youth and of America in general. Youth, they said, was increasingly immoral. Drinking, petting, and the lack of meaning and purpose in the lives of youth were often discussed. Comments made starting in the 1960s, but about drugs other than alcohol and about premarital intercourse instead of petting, would be similar. The universal problems of the Depression and nationwide efforts of World War II muted or obscured for a time the youth culture. The "Beat Generation" in the 1950s rejected American "ideals." Its most prominent spokesman was Jack Kerouac. His book, *On the Road*, would strongly influence Tom Hayden, who in the 1960s would be the most important leader of campus activists.

Historically, the interest of college students in public issues has been a some-time thing. College students had been enthusiastic supporters of the American Revolution. Generally, they had limited interest in abolition, although college men north and south eagerly enlisted to fight in the Civil War and the world wars. In the 1930s some college students became Marxists, but Stalin's brutality and his agreement with Nazi Germany in 1939 were disenchanting. In the 1950s political activity by the "silent generation" of college students was unusual.

For youth in the late 1950s, several symbols might be chosen. They fought with their parents about "D.A." or "duck's ass" haircuts for men and toreador pants for women. Perhaps nothing reflected the spirit of youth in the late 1950s better than *MAD Magazine*'s character Alfred E. Newman. His philosophy was summarized by his motto, "What, me worry?" He personified the detachment that much of youth clearly felt. *MAD*'s wide popularity among them and its open criticism of the idealized suburban life-style sought by most Americans was a telling indicator that all was not well. Tom Hayden would say youth didn't " 'even give a damn about the apathy.' "

By the end of the 1950s some educators had become more sensitive to the alienation of youth. Sociologist of education Edgar Z. Friedenberg's *The Vanishing*

Adolescent was published in 1959. He argued that emphasis upon conformity and group adjustment directly interfered with the adolescent's sense of self. Rather than being given the opportunity to differentiate one's self from the culture and to establish an identity, the adolescent was homogenized and depersonalized by schools and other institutions. Friedenberg called for a redirection of the schools, and the recognition of a far wider range of competence in the students they taught:

> Schools ought to be a place where you cannot only go to be a scholar, a fighter, a lover, a repairman, a writer, or a scientist, but learn that you are good at it, and in which your awareness and pride in being good at it becomes a part of your sense of being you. More emphasis on the sciences, higher standards, stricter discipline; these of themselves will not help at all. They may hinder. A school that while raising standards in certain academic areas, treats the students more than ever as an object or an instrument, simply becomes a more potent source of alienation.

Friedenberg was among the first to recognize that schools not only failed to help youths realize a sense of self and purpose in their lives, but, even worse, that they were keeping from many adolescents and youths the autonomy and self-direction that would lead them to meaningful adult roles. Later, in the 1960s, there was more criticism of the schools for failing to meet individuals' needs. Paul Goodman in *Growing Up Absurd* reiterated many of Friedenberg's points. In *Compulsory Miseducation* he described the educational system as a "compulsory trap."

Later, the Panel on Youth of the President's Science Advisory Committee was established to address the problem of youth. Its chairman was James Coleman, the principal author of the 1964 report *Equality of Educational Opportunity*. The Panel on Youth report, *Youth: Transition to Adulthood*, commonly known as "Coleman II," was published in 1974.

The extent to which the schools had been relied upon to introduce youth and adolescents to adult life was seriously questioned by the report. As the labor of the young had become less necessary for the society and the economy, more schooling had been required. Schooling had come to be seen as the only means of preparing for and helping make the transition to adulthood. The report went on to challenge the schools' effectiveness in doing this.

> Schooling, as we know it, is not a complete environment giving all the necessary opportunities for becoming an adult. School is a certain kind of environment: individualistic, oriented toward cognitive achievement, imposing dependency on and withholding authority and responsibility from the role of students.

The report said that school had expanded to fill the time formerly given other activities. Rather than emphasizing the development of cognitive skills, schools had emphasized the development of responsible action and leadership—skills crucial for becoming an adult. The schools provided no experience corresponding to these other out-of-school activities.

Youth: Transition to Adulthood began by arguing that youth (aged 14 to 24), which in earlier periods had been in regular contact with many older individuals, knew among older individuals only parents and teachers. Age segregation had once served to protect youth from the harsh work of the adult world, and from adults who were unsuitable as associates. In addition, segregation of youths and children had served a custodial function, so that adults might get on with their own work. However, age segregation also separated youth from the world of adults, and from roles and activities they would soon have to become engaged in. The report strongly argued that benefits of integrating youth with the adult population clearly outweighed advantages of segregating the two groups. Age integration would benefit adults, lessening conflicts between youth and the adult population, as well as enlivening the environment of adults by the presence of youth.

Second, the report pointed out the costs of age segregation among the young. Because of the organization of schools, the way they had been "graded," in-school segregation by age had become almost universal. For instance, high school students had little contact with college students. Segregating by age made it easier for the schools to teach groups of students, since the members of each group were approximately the same age, level of development, and maturity. It also prevented older children from taking advantage of younger children. But by integrating age groups of pupils, pupils would have a wider range of experience and perceptions, from which they could grow and develop.

Third, students segregated by age were at different stages of physiological development. There was a two-year difference in girls and boys at puberty, for example.

Fourth, schooling and work were not integrated. Most youths first went to school and then went to work. Having left school, they received little further formal education. The report suggested several approaches to continuing education for individuals in the work force: recurrent education, in which the individual would work for a time and then return to school for further training; career education that focused on schooling for the individual, dealing with future occupations he or she might have; and work-study programs that combine youths with adults working in real occupations while also receiving formal schooling.

Fifth, the report questioned the extent to which youth's time should be segmented. For example, should students be allowed to attend schools only two or three days a week and engage in other activities, for instance, job training or instruction in an art or craft, the rest of their time? Logically extending the question, should a youth capable of learning the required content of the curriculum in half the usual time be required to attend school full time?

Sixth, the report considered the proper scope of formal schooling. Should nonacademic activities, such as drivers' education, be part of the curricula of schools? The report argued that such activities were often distorted by the schools and were better dealt with outside the schools.

Seventh, the report discussed the legal rights and status of youths. It was argued that they were frequently constrained by laws that supposedly benefited them. While protecting many youths, compulsory attendance laws and restrictive child labor laws restrained others and barred them from activities and experience from which they might later benefit.

The report advocated radical shifts in approaches to youth. Smaller, less impersonal schools might be established. Many students might alternate work and school. Young people could be parts of work organizations where they could also learn. Youth organizations should be established or expanded. Employment possibilities should be increased, and a lower minimum wage for youthful workers would encourage employers to hire them. There were other suggestions.

Youth: The Transition to Adulthood recognized clearly the extraordinary problems faced by youth of the 1960s. At the same time it recognized the extraordinary ambiguity of youth's status:

> People below the age of majority are simultaneously the most indulged and oppressed part of the population. Both civil and criminal law accord minors special consideration and shield them from the full legal consequences of their acts. On the other hand, until reaching ages prescribed by law, children and young people are compelled to attend school, excluded from gainful employments, denied the right to drive automobiles, prohibited from buying alcoholic beverages, firearms and cigarettes, barred from the most interesting movies, and deprived of countless pleasures and liberties available to adults.

As the report said, ". . . the increase in the magnitude of the socialization task in the United States . . . was completely outside the bounds of previous and prospective experience."

COUNTERCULTURE ON CAMPUS

On May 13, 1960, the House Un-American Activities Committee held hearings in the San Francisco courthouse. Students, who had come to attend the hearings, were thrown down the courthouse steps. On May 14, 1970, National Guard rifle fire at Kent State University in Ohio wounded nine students and killed four: these dates and events mark as well as any the beginning and end of the times of student activism.

Part of the inspiration for student demonstrations would come from the blacks' civil rights movement in the South. On February 1, 1960 four black college students had ordered coffee at the lunch counter in a Woolworth store in Greensboro, North Carolina. They had been ignored and a sit-in protest against segregation had begun. In two weeks the Woolworth sit-in had spread to fifteen cities, and Woolworths in the north were picketed by white students until blacks were served at Woolworth lunch counters. The sit-ins had led to establishing the Student Nonviolent Coordinating Committee. Its style, politics, and success made it an example for the SDS.

The SDS (Students for Democratic Action) would become the most important student organization during those years. Its history and that of demonstrations then is difficult to reconstruct; records are scanty and memories differ. Some remember an event as fearful, others as laughable. Some chapters of the SDS were opposed in principle to keeping records, and not unrealistically felt that surveillance by the FBI and police made records a danger. The sensations of the time, of fear, of anger, of the smell of tear gas and sometimes the sound of gunfire, were not much written about at the time. There is an informative history of the thought of SDS's most important leaders, James Miller's book *"Democracy in the Streets"*.

SDS had evolved from the Student League for Industrial Democracy. It had been founded far back, in 1905; Upton Sinclair had helped organize it, and Jack London had been its first president. The SDS's most important leaders at the beginning were Alan Haber and Tom Hayden, both at the University of Michigan at Ann Arbor.

Tom Hayden would write most of the "Port Huron Statement," defining the principles and purposes of the SDS. Hayden was well read; he was most influenced by C. Wright Mills, whose book *The Power Elite* forecast totalitarian control by a few who held near-monopolies of wealth and power. The "Statement's" name came from the location of a United Auto Workers camp at Port Huron, Michigan; photos show clapboarded cottages and a rustic hall, something like those at an old-time Bible camp. The statement was adopted there on June 15, 1962, after review and revisions by "participatory democracy," a first principle of SDS.

The Port Huron Statement is a massive document, twenty-five thousand words, forty-five pages of tightly packed print. It has sixteen sections, dealing with values, students, society, politics, defense policy, and other matters. It began by saying that "We are the people of this generation, bred in at least modest comfort, housed now in universities, looking uncomfortably at the world we inherit." Parts of it have eloquence; a few phrases are eye catching: ". . . The dreams of the past were perverted by Stalinism." "Men have unrealized potential for self-cultivation, self-direction, self-understanding, and creativity." "The cumbersome academic bureaucracy. . . ." ". . . Automation . . . is imparting the opportunity for men around the world to rise in dignity from their knees. . . ."

Students' encounter at the San Francisco courthouse with HUAC and the police had been unplanned, unintended, but their treatment was an incitement to political action. The most notable demonstrations at the beginning of the student protest movement were at the University of California. The Berkeley "Free Speech Movement" started with a minor incident. In the summer of 1964 the Republican National Convention had met in San Francisco. The supporters of Barry Goldwater complained that the university was being used unfairly to organize support for the nomination of Governor William Scranton. In September the Berkeley administration began to enforce old regulations prohibiting soliciting funds and organizing political drives there.

On September 29, members of the Student Nonviolent Coordinating Committee, the Congress of Racial Equality, SLATE (a campus political party with Marxist leanings), and the Trotskyist Young Socialist Alliance set up tables to solicit funds and political support. (Tom Hayden was in Berkeley, but did not play an important part.) A university administrator identified five students, but allowed the booths to remain open. The students identified by the administrator were ordered to appear the following afternoon before the dean of men. By 3:30 at least four hundred students had gathered outside the dean's office. A petition circulated and signed by the students said they had also manned political booths in conscious violation of the university rules and that they should be subject to the same disciplinary measures as the students who had been called before the dean. They also demanded that all disciplinary charges be dropped.

University Chancellor Edward Strong refused to meet the student's demands. He asked that the students who had been called to the dean's office and the three demonstration leaders meet with him and discuss disciplinary actions for violating the university's regulation against solicitation of funds. None of them appeared in his office, and a strike was quickly organized. Mario Savio, a sophomore, quickly emerged as the leader. A sit-in was begun in Sproul Hall, the administration building. Money was collected for food and bedding. The Berkeley "Free Speech Movement" was underway.

Jack Weinberg, a Berkeley graduate student in mathematics, was an activist CORE member, a vocal advocate of the use of drugs, and at the time on parole from jail. He had solicited funds. At the start of a rally, Deans George S. Murphy and Peter Van Houten and a university police lieutenant asked Weinberg to leave

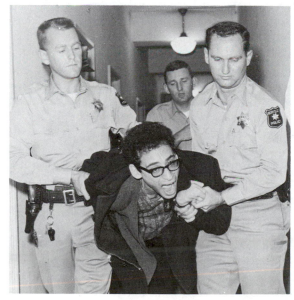

FIGURE 11-1
A University of California at Berkeley student chanting "Freedom Now" is carried to jail, December 3, 1964. Courtesy of United Press International.

the campus. He refused and was arrested for trespassing. He went limp when the police car arrived and he was carried to it. Two hundred students lay down in front of and in back of the police car. Savio climbed into the car with Weinberg, who remained in it for thirty-two hours while Savio, the other student leaders, and university administrators negotiated. The Berkeley conflict was concerned with freedom of speech, but was also a conflict clearly arising from the aspirations of youth and its opposition to established authority. It was a classic generational conflict.

Three days later it was announced that the university would request that the police stop the demonstration; 643 policemen prepared to come on campus, but negotiators reached a compromise. The students and police dispersed. Weeks of negotiation followed, and the campus was relatively peaceful. But in November four student leaders were summoned before the Faculty Committee on Student Affairs, and the conflict heightened. The university regents directed that the student leaders answer charges that they had committed violent acts against the university police. Specifically, Mario Savio was accused of having bitten a policeman. Savio and the three other leaders were threatened with expulsion. On December 1, activists presented an ultimatum. If charges were not dropped within twenty-four hours, there would be a general strike. The next day Sproul Hall was again occupied by students. Joan Baez, who had taken part in earlier demonstrations, led nearly a thousand students singing the "Lord's Prayer" and "We Shall Overcome" to the administration building. Chancellor Strong pleaded with the students to leave the building. They refused. At the order of Governor Ronald Reagan, the police entered and arrested 814 protesters, of whom 590 were students.

On Thursday, December 3, 1964, students struck and set up picket lines to close down the university. Only half the scheduled classes met. The following Monday, December 7, the president of the university, Clark Kerr, addressed eighteen thousand students and professors in the university's Greek theater. Kerr agreed that the university would not press the prosecution of those involved in the demonstrations and that censorship was not to be imposed upon the student protesters.

These concessions were remarkably liberal, even radical, responses to the demonstrations. Some would argue that university officials had capitulated, surrendered, but their approach was consistent with the university's liberal policies. It is worth noting that, protests and protesters notwithstanding, the University of California at Berkeley had a national reputation for being the most liberal in the United States. That year the American Association of University Professors had awarded the university administration there the Alexander Meiklejohn Prize for its consistent support of academic freedom.

On December 8, the Berkeley faculty senate supported a resolution that would have forbid the university to place any restrictions on speech or political activity. Critic Lewis Feuer argued that the actions of the Berkeley faculty "in effect created a moral and political vacuum in the heart of the university." Allan Bloom, writing about Cornell administrators twenty-five years later, took the extreme view and wrote about "the decomposition of the university."

Elsewhere, and certainly at Berkeley, student demonstrations divided the faculty and put some in a nearly impossible quandary. Conservative or nonpolitical faculty members—most often found in engineering and other professional schools—"simply went home and closed the shutters," as Bloom put it. ". . . They just did not want trouble and did not feel it was their fight." Some younger faculty members—especially in the arts and sciences—were in complete sympathy with the SDS and other demonstrators. Social and economic injustices were so great, the threat of governmental oppression so great, the war in Vietnam so immoral, that the welfare of a university or college seemed unimportant. (For many of them, it was never of great importance, since they identified themselves with their discipline rather than with the college or university where they happened to be employed.) Many others agreed with all or most of the aims of demonstrators, but were doubtful about or opposed the demonstrators' means. Obviously, the best of purposes did not justify the worst of means. But under the circumstances the choices to be made were between evils; perhaps supporting somewhat objectionable means was less objectionable if it helped end the slaughter in Vietnam or monstrous injustices. For faculty members with conflicting convictions such choices were excruciating.

In the 1960s there were demonstrations at hundreds of colleges and universities. There were even demonstrations overseas—those in Paris were televised in the United States. In the most violent of demonstrations there was arson, vandalism, and violence. But in one small university, smashing a picture of President Nixon was the most violent act (and was viewed with great concern). Any cause might serve: drugs on campus, recruiters for Dow Chemical (manufacturer of napalm) or the CIA, a history course on imperialism, suppression of black basketball players. There were endless varieties in demands and negotiations, in police tactics and counter-tactics, marches, building occupations, police assaults and sometimes counter-assaults, barricades, Molotov cocktails, and police clubbings. Former students remember stolid "peace officers" wearing battle visors, carrying "crowd-control" clubs, sometimes shields, and occasionally shotguns. Aging policemen and sheriff's deputies remember running, shouting "crazies."

The assassination of Martin Luther King in the spring of 1968 produced flame-filled nights in one of the worst "long hot summers" and added to indignation that swelled to rage. Robert Kennedy was assassinated two months later, adding further to the rage. After the second Kennedy death, the nomination of Eugene McCarthy by the Democrats at their convention in Chicago offered the greatest promise for the end of war in Vietnam. His defeat by Hubert H. Humphrey ended that hope. Members of at least a half dozen youth organizations and McCarthy supporters noisily, lustily demonstrated. The Chicago police charged: "Those are our children in the streets, and the policemen are attacking them," a journalist said. The anger mounted again and fueled more campus demonstrations.

The issue at Columbia University in the spring of 1968 was building a gymnasium on a steep slope that had no other practical use. Adjacent black communities had been consulted and had approved—a part of the gymnasium was to be set aside for their use. But the Students' Afro-American Society complained, and a

FIGURE 11-2 Columbia University students and others climb out of windows of the office of Columbia president Grayson Kirk, April 24, 1968. Courtesy of United Press International.

cause had been found. Students also demanded that the university end research for defense, and there were other issues.

On April 23, 1968, three hundred students led by SDS members occupied Hamilton Hall and held the dean of students hostage. Several other buildings were also occupied, and students formed "communes." Hayden rushed to the campus and went to Mathematics Hall. He remembered four years later that "I was in Columbia, living with people who felt such international solidarity with people around the world and such solidarity with students across the US and such revolutionary pride in their ability to live together for a week under such danger." Incidentally, his language was a good example of SDS speakers'.

Another account by a demonstrator was *The Strawberry Statement* (1968) by James Simon Kunen. Kunen had graduated from a prep school and was one of the privileged students attending Columbia. He wrote

> We think how lucky we are to be able to go to school, to have nice clothes and fine things and to eat well and have money and be healthy. How lucky we are really. But we remain unhappy. . . . We're unhappy because of the war, and because of poverty and the hopelessness of politics, but also because we sometimes get put down by girls or boys, as the case may be, or feel lonely and alone and lost.

Kunen described his and his friends' preoccupation with the notion that there college years were the best of their lives. Yet something was very wrong. College was in reality "exhausting, confusing, boring, troubled, frustrating and meaningless," and life could only become more difficult. Since that was unacceptable,

Kunen and his friends ". . . took adaptive measures, which consisted chiefly of constructing an alternative world in which we felt a bit more comfortable." The day after the demonstration began he was one of about two hundred students who began the occupation of President Grayson Kirk's office in Lowe Library building. Only twenty-seven of the students left when police arrived. Kunen and the others who stayed were not arrested and the occupation went on.

Kunen described some comic moments. The first day of the occupation he had slipped out to get the baseball scores and had returned. A professor in his academic robes was described as climbing through a window "like Batman" to warn the protesters that their action would set off a massive right-wing reaction among the faculty. Kunen spent the night in President Kirk's office and took great pleasure in using Kirk's after-shave lotion and toothpaste. At four o'clock in the afternoon Kunen slipped out again to attend crew practice. When the practice was over he rejoined the sit-in.

Students discussed piling in front of the windows paintings and sculptures on display in the building so that the police would have to destroy them if they entered the building. One student suggested using poles to push the police off the ledges of the building if they tried to recapture it. When criticized for the violence of his suggested action, he tried to explain that he would push the police off the ledges "in a nonviolent way." After spending another night in the occupied offices Kunen left in the morning to bus to Boston, where he rowed for the university in a crew race. Two days later he returned to the occupied campus and was once again actively involved in the student demonstrations.

Kunen described the occupation of Mathematics Hall and writing home to his parents. He explained how he tried in his letter to justify to his father spending his father's money while he was rebelling. He argued that the danger of going to college was learning things and that his actions had been strongly influenced by the reading that he had done for Contemporary Civilization (C 1001 y). But in the end he admitted that "after sealing the letter, I realize my conception of the philosophy of law comes not so much from Rousseau as from Fess Parker as Davy Crockett. I remember him saying you should decide what is right and then go ahead and do it." Kunen went on to describe being arrested and booked for trespassing and getting the names and addresses of various woman students involved in the sit-ins.

The last demonstration, the demonstration that ended demonstrations, was at Kent State University in Ohio. There was no tradition of radicalism among the twenty thousand students there. The events leading to tragedy started with a beer blast that spilled out of taverns into a street. A car's windows were broken and storefronts smashed, and police using tear gas chased the students back to campus. Eight hundred students attended a meeting the next evening. The ROTC building was set afire, and students cut firemen's hoses.

The National Guard was called out, and five hundred armed Guardsmen appeared on the campus. James Rhodes, governor of Ohio and candidate for the Republican nomination to the Senate also appeared. At a press conference he said that "We're going to drive them out. . . . They're the worst type of people that we harbor in America." Perhaps he thought his stand would win the election. (It did not.) The mayor of Kent, the president, and vice president, and others also came close to incitement.

There were classes that Monday, May 4, 1970. At noontime, student demonstrators and spectators, perhaps three thousand of them in all, gathered. The National Guard fired tear gas canisters into the crowd to disburse it. Some students threw rocks at the National Guard soldiers, and a major-general threw them back at the students. Infuriated, or possibly threatened, a few National Guard soldiers knelt to improve accuracy and opened rifle fire on students on a distant rise. Four students were killed, nine others wounded. (One became a paraplegic.) As Miller said, "the days of the revolutionary fantasy were over." The alternate worlds created by Kunen and his friends were not bulletproof. In Jackson, Mississippi, machine guns, shotguns, and rifles killed two black students and wounded nine and punctured other alternate worlds.

Innumerable sociologists and psychologists had explanations for the student demonstrations of the 1960s. The one most often heard was that of youth's alienation, of which we have written. But a general theory is not a sufficient historical explanation of a set of unique events.

Some said that the insurgence of youth was intergenerational conflict, the perennial revolt of child against parents. Permissive childrearing, recommended in best-selling books by Dr. Benjamin M. Spock, had been fashionable in the 1950s and was said to have produced rebellious youth. A general explanation was that the strengthening of the youth culture was simply because of the increase in the number of youths. Each of these views is plausible.

But events had also led to the rebellion by youth. General prosperity made the need for personal financial security less important. The War on Poverty and plans for "The New Society" had raised hopes and expectations that were unfulfilled. Assassinations had threatened time-honored faith. The civil rights movement had provided precedents and examples that might be followed. The SDS and its organizers were dedicated, ingenious, and resourceful.

Above all, there was the war in Vietnam. Participation by the United States had increased gradually, without clear foresight as to the outcome or possible costs. It was to many youths and many others a morally abhorrent war, imperialism and colonialism at their worst, genocide, an effort to obliterate a nation. It was a brutalizing war, a war in which cities were "bombed to be saved," in which mothers and children were massacred. Not incidentally, for many students it was potentially personally dangerous; fear was a powerful motivator. Many men attending college had draft deferments that would end at graduation.

Demonstrations ended suddenly, for several reasons. Rifle bullets punctured illusions. The SDS and other radicals had failed to gain the support of workers; "hard hats," construction workers, had tried to break up a New York City peace demonstration. Efforts to aid those in poverty had been abandoned. The SDS had collapsed in 1969, leaving only the "Weathermen," violence prone, wildly eccentric. Wanton violence, drugs, even hard rock, had caused great alarm. Military action in

Vietnam seemed to be coming to an end. There was no reason to suppose that the alienation of youth had lessened. Perhaps it contributed to the privatism of the late 1980s.

ALTERNATIVE SCHOOLS

By the mid-1960s and into the 1970s there were many critics and criticisms of elementary and high schools. Alternative programs at both levels were proposed and implemented. Known as "free schools" or "alternative schools," these school experiments were diverse in philosophies and purposes. In general, they shared a belief that traditional schools were not meeting the needs of children and that new types of schools should be established to provide alternatives to the traditional public school system.

Alternative schools were set up both privately and as part of existing public school systems. Philosophically they drew on many different sources. By the mid-1960s, a great deal of interest had developed in the programs and curricula developed by many of the English primary schools. In these programs, an emphasis was placed on the need of children to learn from their environment, to learn to live with other people including both children and adults, to assume responsibility, and to enjoy learning. A strong emphasis was also placed upon children being carefully guided in their learning by their teachers. As the 1967 Plowden Committee, which reported on the schools to the English Parliament, explained: "From the start, there must be teaching as well as learning: children are not 'free' to develop interests or skills of which they have no knowledge; they must have guidance from their teachers."

The philosophy of the English primary schools was by no means new, and reflected many basic themes found in Dewey's Laboratory School at the University of Chicago, as well as in the programs of the Progressive Education movement. Popular interest in the English primary schools was stimulated by a series of articles by Joseph Featherston published in *The New Republic* in August and September 1967. At the same time, increasing interest developed in the work of the radical British educator A. S. Neill, whose book *Summerhill: A Radical Approach to Child Rearing*, described his nontraditional approach to schooling. Neill argued that students would learn only if they had the need or desire to learn. Rote memorization, discipline, exams, and all of the traditional paraphernalia of most school systems destroyed the spirit of many students, according to Neill, as well as the desire to learn. Neill ultimately argued for an approach to education that encouraged "freedom without license."

Neill's *Summerhill*, Jonathan Kozol's National Book Award-winning *Death at an Early Age* (1967), together with various works by John Holt such as *Why Children Fail* (1965), Nat Hentoff's *Our Children Are Dying* (1966), and Herbert Kohl's *36 Children* (1967), generated widespread interest in what was believed to be the failure of the educational system to meet the needs of many children.

Basing their ideas loosely upon the ideas of these and other authors, teachers, concerned private citizens, and parents promoted alternative types of educational programs.

Criticisms of the schools were made not only by these popular authors. For example, among historians of education, a significant revisionist movement began to merge. The schools were no longer described as vehicles of personal freedom and economic advancement, but instead their potential for perpetuating existing social, political, and economic systems was emphasized. The "Great School Myth" was thrown into doubt by Raymond Callahan, Michael Katz, and others.

Tremendous confusion gathered around the definition of "free" or "alternative" schools. Many of the founders of these schools believed that the public schools had become too large and impersonal and that children were not allowed to develop naturally in such settings. The idea of "freeing" children from the traditional schools became a theme underlying the development of many of the alternative schools.

The first alternative schools were private ventures. Gradually others appeared as parts of public school systems. A variety of free schools or alternative schools, begun as early as 1966, addressed the needs of specific groups within the culture. For blacks and ethnic minorities, freedom schools, street corner and storefront schools, and academies were started. Middle-class whites promoted various "free" schools: open classroom experiments, Montessori-type schools, and community-oriented schools. In a loose sense, all these approaches were alternative types of education.

Many of the alternative schools reflected the wider unrest and disaffection in American society. Educators and parents frequently felt inadequate to handle the problems that were so common among many of their students. The Philadelphia Parkway School, which was one of the first public alternative schools started in the United States, was consciously begun in

> . . . a background of violence, increasing use of narcotics, under-achievement, dropouts, vandalism, and arson in the Philadelphia school system—these despite every effort at improvement by a blue-ribbon school board, its president, former mayor Richard Cilworth and his new school superintendent.

Terence Deal and Robert Nolan, in their article "Alternative Schools: A Conceptual Map," argued that while the alternative school movement drew much of its energy from the social critiques of the 1960s, the alternative school movement also drew upon themes from the Progressive Education movement. Among these were (1) the needs and experiences of the student as a starting point for schooling; (2) the teacher in the role of adviser; (3) the recognition of the school as a social community; (4) active instead of passive learning; (5) an emphasis upon drawing on a variety of learning resources, especially those found within the community; (6) recognizing skills as means of achieving something, rather than ends in themselves; (7) student participation in at least some of the important decision making for the school; and (8) an emphasis upon the individuality of students and teachers.

In 1975, there were approximately five thousand public alternative schools operating in the United States. The number of private alternative schools then was much more difficult to determine, since many of the older private schools in the United States included elements consistent with the aims and ideals of the newer free schools or alternative schools. Too, records of these schools are often much more difficult to obtain.

In interviews conducted with alternative school teachers and administrators during the mid-1970s, an attempt was made to determine some reasons why people became involved in establishing alternative programs. An administrator responsible for establishing an alternative high school in suburban Saint Louis explained that

> We had in this district the two types of students. The affluent white students who were dissatisfied with the Vietnamese war, and the militant black students who were tired of being put down. These two forces coverged onto our high school about the spring of 1970. It was pretty obvious we needed to rethink what we were doing at the high school.

The Vietnam war, the Kent State killings, and the general turmoil evident in the society were cited again and again by teachers and administrators when asked why they had become involved in setting up or teaching in an alternative school. One teacher, for example, explained how

> Students would not accept things because you told them to do it. If they couldn't see how it would apply to their practical life they wouldn't bother with it. . . . These kids were going off to the war after they graduated. With my first year in the alternative school there were the Kent State killings and the kids were questioning not only the school, but the government and the president. I was questioning them too. I saw the ridiculousness of my teaching sociology units when the kids were going to be shipped off to Vietnam in the next month.

War and social crisis had affected young Americans also.

CONCLUSION

After the Kent State disaster most college and university campuses were calm, almost funereal. Students seemed stoic and to withdraw into privatism. Faculties and administrators did agree to increasing student roles in policymaking and personnel decisions, but students were less interested. What had once been unacceptable student behavior was more widely tolerated, but seemed less likely to occur openly. At one school where students had once smoked pot openly, the serving and sale of beer was banned. The number of required courses was already being reduced before the 1960s and would in the early 1970s be further reduced. But by the later 1980s the number of specific courses required for graduation was on the increase.

Independent alternative schools, often governed by participatory democratic discussions and relying upon dedicated but badly paid teachers or volunteers, generally had short lives. The "open classroom," which had been imported from England, and in which pupils spent much of their time in independent study and work, had mixed results in the United States. Some pupils, most often from middle-class homes, thrived in them, but, especially when pupils were from lower-class backgrounds, the achievement score gains of children in open classes seemed less than of those in "structured," teacher-directed, carefully controlled classrooms.

Alternative schools would provide a conceptual basis for the "magnet schools" popular in the 1980s. Their supporters felt that for the benefit of society schools should be public, tax supported, and attended by children of all races and social backgrounds. Nevertheless, children, or rather their parents, should have choices as to kind of schooling—traditional, in the progressive tradition, Montessori, centering upon science, the performing arts, the humanities, whatever. It was something like a bus line: even if it was owned by the public and every member of the public was entitled to ride it, the passenger had a choice of where to go and which route to follow to get there.

But an era of reform, when zeal was at least as great as it had been in the Progressive era at turn of century, was passing. Perhaps in time to come there would be another such era.

Chapter Twelve
SCHOOL CRISIS, SCHOOL RESPONSE

The schools must preserve and perpetuate knowledge.

The schools must prepare students to meet the needs of the economy and national defense.

The schools must prepare all its pupils for what is required by the everyday world.

Conservative dissatisfaction with the schools has been perennial, but seldom as strong, or as widely accepted, as in the late 1970s and the 1980s. Partly, this came from developments in society generally, outside the schools. Schools, and other institutions, seemed to have lost public confidence and public support. Partly, dissatisfaction was because of shortcomings, real or alleged, in the schools themselves. Naturally, there were efforts by educators to remedy the shortcomings of the schools, and state legislators imposed upon the schools what seemed to them to be appropriate solutions.

The most general, most widespread, source of dissatisfaction came from what may have been long-term changes in cultural values or relatively transient shifts in public mood. The long-haired often activist youth of the 1960s had been in a way symbolic of the times. In the same way, the "Yuppies" (young upperwardly mobile persons) were symbolic of the later 1980s. Neither "Hippies" nor "Yuppies" were in the majority in their time, but the symbols were often taken to be real, and did show the feelings then.

Yuppies, sometimes real enough, often magnified in number, had as their first goals increasing their incomes and improving their life-styles. They had little interest in their communities or in public affairs and little interest in matters that would not add to their profit or pleasure. They, and it seemed society at large, had retreated to privatism, the pursuit of personal rather than public goals. As Tyack, Lowe, and Hansott put it, "the traditional aims of public schools—the creation of citizens who shared a sense of common purpose—became eclipsed."

The national economy, which had prospered and grown steadily since World War II, slowed. Inflation lowered standards of living. The level of unemployment increased until it was greater than at any time since the Depression. In the 1960s there had seemed to be a good job for anyone who wanted one. Ten years later, jobs, all jobs, were scarce, and were scarcer for youth. (Most scarce for black youth, but that was seeming less important.)

The economy and the level of jobs available were already being affected by the uses of computers. Computer-controlled machines replaced factory workers, especially in work requiring some skill. (Fetch-and-carry and floor-sweeping work was still done by workers.) Special-purpose computers controlled microwave ovens and stoves and were standard factory equipment in new cars. Often the filling station mechanic, who if competent had been able to make almost any automobile repair, could only shrug and direct the owner to a dealer service department that had, it was to be hoped, sophisticated diagnostic equipment and technological expertise. Court briefs, memoranda, term papers, and articles for publication could be prepared without the services of a secretary-typist. He or she need only operate the photocopy machine, and that too was being computerized. Even computer operations were deskilled; for instance, punching computer cards, which in the 1960s had required dexterity and some technical skill, was almost a thing of the past. The process of de-skilling work, which had begun with the Industrial Revolution, was being continued and speeded.

Birth rates during the Depression of the 1930s had fallen. In the prosperous and hopeful years after World War II, children seemed part of the good life, and in the time of the "baby boom," birth rates had soared, increasing substantially for the first time since records had been kept. Birth rates declined in the 1960s and the decline has continued, although there has been an "echo," an increase in the number of births as the "baby-boom" generation reached the age of parenthood. Obviously the number of school pupils would decline. For the schools, especially since they had become accustomed to growing enrollments, adjustments would be difficult.

The schools themselves, and educators, were other sources of dissatisfaction. In the years of the Great Society, there had been high hopes and strong expectations that the schools would end the inequalities in society. Socioeconomic inequalities in school achievement persisted, as did racial ones, though the latter did grow smaller. Nationally, pupils' achievement test scores declined. Possibly the decline in achievement was not real, and the seeming decline was the result of faulty test design or statistical procedures, but that point was hard to prove, and to the public the decline was a disappointment and concern. That illiterate youths, at least a few of them, had graduated from high school showed a gross failure by the schools and the too-great costs of social promotion seemed scandalous and outrageous. The schools could no longer teach religion (although they could still teach *about* religion). Some school texts and school curricula reflected the "relativism" of social scientists, the hypothesis that there was no basis for believing that one culture, or set of beliefs and morality, was better than others. Therefore, the schools at least seemed to have ceased teaching "values," "citizenship," or "character."

Much had been heard of marvelous new technological developments in education: teaching machines, programmed learning, teaching by television, computerized instruction, and others. These later looked more like fads than the great improvements they had been publicized as. Perhaps this was a case of another perennial shortcoming, of educators promising that schooling would be the "universal panacea" (to recall Horace Mann's phrase), promising more than they could deliver. Great expectations had led too often to great disillusion rather than great accomplishment.

SPOKESMEN FOR CONSERVATISM

Conservative criticism of the schools had not begun in 1945, of course, but after 1945 it was frequent, pointed, and often persuasive. It appeared in newspapers, in *Life* and other big-circulation magazines, congressional hearings, books, and motion pictures. In itself, it could be the subject of a book; only the most important ideas and representative spokesmen appear here. Critics argued, to put it in the most general terms, that changes in schooling after 1920 had not been improvements, that the school did not aid in the growth of the intellect, that they did not meet society's needs, that public schools had escaped the control of the public, and that they did not train the technologists needed for defense.

Some objections that had been raised before the war were repeated more strongly. One critic, the most important of the educational "perennialists," was Robert M. Hutchins. Hutchins was a prodigy who had been dean of Yale's Law School at age twenty-three, even though he was not a lawyer, and at thirty president of the University of Chicago. He argued that the schools should deal primarily with ideas and matters of the intellect and should teach from sources that demonstrated intellectual processes. The intent of this schooling was to prepare for citizenship. This approach to schooling was, if not reactionary, surely very old, traceable to Aristotle and classical Greek thought. It was the basis of the University of Chicago's four-year undergraduate program in general education, beginning after two years of high school. It was also the basis of the great books course of study at St. John's College in Annapolis, Maryland.

Another criticism that was made again after the war was that schools did not teach what the nature of society required. This was put in general terms by William C. Bagley, a dissident professor at Teachers College, who called himself an "essentialist." A specific case was argued by Rudolph Flesch in the widely read *Why Johnny Can't Read* in 1955. Girls and boys in the primary grades, he said, were taught only to memorize the shapes and patterns of words, beginning with the most common ones as determined by research on frequency of use. Primers and readers written on that basis had stories that were "meaningless, stupid, totally uninteresting to a six-year-old or anyone else." Many children who were taught that way with those primers learned to read well, but at the end of the 1970s, it was generally agreed that pupils in the primary grades read better in 1955 than primary grade pupils had read earlier. Ailment or not, Flesch had a universal remedy—phonics, the sounding out of words. He ended his book with illustrated letters and seventy pages of phonics exercises that would have pleased Noah Webster. Flesch's book was republished in the 1980s.

There were also attacks upon "educationists," what would now be called the "establishment," against their claims of superior knowledge, against "quackery in the public schools," as Albert Lynd titled his book. Lynd searched for and found the most trivial educational research and its greatest elaborations:

$$(\text{Teaching load} = \text{SP } [\text{CP} - 2 \text{ Dup}/10 + (\text{NP} - 20 \text{ CP})/100] \\ \times [\text{PL} + 55/100] \text{ PC}/2 [\text{PL} + 55/100]).$$

He quoted the most overblown course descriptions. The grounding assumptions of Dewey's philosophy of pragmatism or instrumentalism, with which he disagreed, were carefully put, and the gaps between Dewey's philosophy and Kilpatrick's applications were carefully noted. The control of the schools, Lynd wrote, had been taken from parents and communities. Instruction and curriculum were based upon a philosophy that was not generally accepted.

(Nathan wrote that she had retired partly because of her dissatisfaction with Progressive Education. Instruction in basics, in penmanship, spelling, reading by phonics, grammar, even arithmetic, had been deemphasized or abandoned. Homemaking, manual arts, and music lessons had taken time from basic instruction. Principals in the schools had become autocrats. Democracy in the schools had been destroyed. Exit Beatrice Stevens Nathan, gray haired, in great anger.)

Another criticism, much more intense than it had been before the war, was that the schools were not teaching patriotism. That criticism is comprehensible, if not excusable. An American Legion committee, the Sons and Daughters of the American Revolution, and other archpatriotic organizations instigated charges against the public school. They claimed that the "social studies" and history that were taught in the public schools were damaging because they were not patriotic, and were often socialistic—sometimes even communistic. Harold Rugg's social study textbooks in particular were condemned, but it was claimed that many other textbooks were tainted with "Red," communist, propaganda.

On October 4, 1957, the Soviet Union launched *Sputnik I*, the first man-

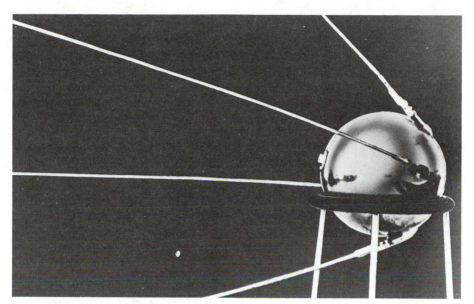

FIGURE 12-1 The Russian's Sputnik launched in late 1957 was the first man-made object to orbit the earth and marked the beginning of the space race and a new thrust in American education. Courtesy of United Press International.

made satellite. No bigger than a bushel basket and broadcasting only intermittent beeps, it became the symbol of Russian scientific and military superiority. If a satellite could be put into orbit, an atomic warhead could be fired at any target anywhere in the United States. The "missile gap" threatened the future of America, or at least it was felt that it did. When, a little later, Russia launched *Sputnik II*, which weighed half a ton and carried a dog as passenger, President Eisenhower appointed an adviser on science, the first ever. Every resource, technical, financial, and educational, was to be employed to overtake the Russian lead in space.

In his widely read *Inside Russia*, John Gunther wrote that Russian tenth graders were better educated in science than were average American college graduates. Ex-President Hoover emerged from oblivion long enough to say that Russia was turning out two or three times as many scientists as the United States. But the most important spokesman was Admiral Hyman G. Rickover, naval engineer and atomic energy specialist. He had directed the design and construction of the first atomic-powered submarine, *U.S.S. Nautilus*, and the first nuclear power plant. He was legendary as a hard-driving, demanding commander, satisfied only by perfection.

Rickover said again and again that the schools' first concern should be intellectual training. That training should be speeded and intensified. American students should learn more and learn it more quickly. It was particularly important that the most capable students be the best trained ones. For them there should be special classes, or special schools as there were in England. Their university training should be assured, as it was in Europe, by scholarships and living allowances. Scientists should have greater prestige. For slower students he suggested "minimum competency tests" to guarantee the value of high school diplomas. Teachers' salaries should be increased, and teachers should be more carefully selected on the basis of their academic qualifications.

Congressman Clarence Cannon, chairman of the House of Representatives Committee on Appropriations, endorsed these views in the preface to one of Rickover's books. "[T]oday a nation's position is largely determined by the respect accorded its science and technology."

There were perennialist critics, essentialist critics, antipragmatists, and those concerned for the future of science and technology. There were also all-purpose critics. One of these was Augustin G. Rudd, apparently a spokesman for the Sons of the American Revolution. His *Bending the Twig*, subtitled "The Revolution in Education and Its Effects on our Children," was a three-hundred page tirade against Progressive Education. It was atheistic, socialistic, communistic, indoctrinating, and Marxist, he said. Rudd quoted every imaginable authority, including Cecil B. De Mille. Students from progressive schools were said to be ignorant of or incapable in history, geography, mathematics, spelling, grammar, English, and punctuation. Rudd was one of those who were, to borrow a phrase, "mad as hell." There were many other critics, some of them capable and prominent, others scurrilous and as outrageous as outraged. The educator's natural impulse is to come to the defense of educators under attack. Having controlled that impulse, we conclude that some of the critics, including Hutchins, Lynd, and Rickover, capably presented arguments that were legitimate, sound, and logical, even if one did not accept the premises that were their starting point and did not accept their conclusions. But there were also unacceptable arguments, condemnations by innuendo, guilt by association, arguments ad hominem (against the arguer, rather than against the argument).

Beginning before 1950, but especially after the launching of *Sputnik* in 1957, there were new concerns for the quality of education, for the need for intellectual competence and excellence. These were required for the defense and progress of society. *Sputnik* was the symbol of the need, which gained significance from several sources. World War II had speeded technological and social change. The Cold War and fear of Russian intentions added urgency to the need. In 1961, President Kennedy approved the Apollo space program and moon explorations. In a way a response to the symbol of *Sputnik*, it created additional needs for technology and science, and additional opportunities for technologists and scientists. There were also nondefense opportunities for highly trained experts. As scientific research increased, knowledge increased exponentially, "exploded" as some said. There was much more to be learned. It has been suggested that, as post-war babies neared college age and colleges again became crowded, parents grew more anxious about their children being admitted to college. To an extent, all these factors changed schooling and the schools.

The National Citizens Commission for the Public Schools, chaired by Roy B. Larson of Time-Life, expressed business people's concern. In 1951, the Ford

Foundation established the Fund for the Advancement of Education, which would be a prestigious force for change. The National Science Foundation, a government agency, funded the first summer institute for science teachers in 1954, and by 1960, there would be sixty-seven NIE-sponsored summer institutes. In 1956, NSF underwrote the production of teaching films for science. That year the Course Content Improvement Program had a budget of $18,000. In 1957, NSF granted it $450,000. Its intent was to write an entirely new physics course of study. It was headed by Professor Jerold Zacharias of the physics department of Massachusetts Institute of Technology. There would be many more grants for the preparation of new courses of study, new curricula.

In the early 1960s conservative criticisms waned. Excellence, rigor, and economy had seemed less important than did equality. But Nathan Glazer wrote

> I see very little that the federal government can do today to advance racial equality. . . . The legislation of the 1960s and 1970s was directed by problems of access, opportunity, and equality of treatment. I do not think these are issues now—today, in effect, they have been reduced to nonissues.

But by the early 1980s conservative criticisms were numerous and widely publicized. The report of the National Commission on Excellence in Education, *A Nation at Risk*, published in 1983, was the most important of these. It began with stridence:

> Our nation is at risk. Our once unchallenged preeminence in commerce, industry, science, and technological innovation is being overtaken by competitors throughout the world. . . . The educational foundations of our society are presently being eroded by a rising tide of mediocrity that threatens our very future as a Nation and as a people. . . .
> If an unfriendly foreign power had attempted to impose on America the mediocre educational performance that exists today, we might well have viewed it as an act of war. As it stands, we have allowed this to happen to ourselves. We have even squandered the gains in student achievement made in the wake of the *Sputnik* challenge. . . . We have, in effect, been committing an act of unthinkable unilateral educational disarmament.

The risk, the report went on to say, was that foreign producers, for instance, of automobiles and of steel, were more efficient than were American ones. The "intellectual, moral, and spiritual strengths of our people" were also at risk. A page summarizing falling test scores followed.

High school curricula, the report said, had been "homogenized, diluted, and diffused." Expectations were too low; there was too little homework, too little of the student's time was spent in studying mathematics and science. There were too many high school electives, textbooks had been "written down," oversimplified. Students spent too little time at schools, and too little of that time was used for academic instruction. Teachers were badly prepared and had weak academic backgrounds. Too much of their undergraduate coursework had been in education. There was already a shortage of qualified mathematics and science teachers.

The Commission recommended that high schools require for graduation four years of English, three years of mathematics, three years of science, three years of social studies, and a semester course in computer science. For college-bound students, two years of a foreign language were to be required.

Grades were to indicate achievement. Colleges were to raise admission requirements. Students were to be tested for achievement. Texts were to be upgraded. More homework was to be assigned. The length of the school year and the school day were to be increased. Teachers were to be better prepared, better paid, and there were to be career ladders.

The report closed with "A Word to Parents and Students" and final exhortations. It was signed by four university presidents, four school administrators, two professors, one teacher, and five others. It was the most prominent of the proposals for conservative reforms. The curriculum it proposed was in many ways like those that had been recommended by the Committee of Ten in 1896.

Mortimer J. Adler's book, *The Paideia Proposal*, had appeared in 1982. Adler had been an associate of Robert M. Hutchins and zealous advocate of the Great Books program for out-of-school liberal education. Adler restated the recommendations he had been making for forty years or more. In *The Paideia Proposal*, he said that

> There should be a required course of study for all. . . . This means that the course of study should be a single track along which all move—at different speeds, perhaps, and under different conditions. There may be regional modifications of the required course of study to differences among students or regions. But these differences . . . must not result in a differentiation of tracks along which different groups of students move. The only result should be a differentiation of the ways differing students move along the same track. [We are not sure that "regions" was not a euphemism, a code word, referring to the childred of the poor or of blacks.]

Limiting the curriculum had been one of the recommendations of the Committee of Ten in 1896, but even the Committee of Ten had not recommended a single curriculum. Differences among the abilities of students was to be compensated for by "pre-school tutoring of children according to their needs" and grouping them by "ability grouping" instead of age. *The Paideia Proposal* had, whatever, an admirably clear aim and proposed method. It was of considerable interest for a year or two.

In 1982 James Coleman et al., in *High School Achievement: Public, Catholic, and Private Schools Compared*, had published a comparison of the performance of students in common schools with those in private schools. They found that, all things taken into account, the students in the private schools had higher achievement scores: expectations were higher, there was more homework, tighter control. Coleman's findings pained public school people, naturally. John Goodlad, in *A Place Called School*, described the curriculum as sterile, students as passive, and teachers as dominating. Theodore R. Sizer, in *Horace's Compromise: The Dilemma of the American High School*, ruefully and sadly described the compromises

"Horace Smith," a fictitious capable teacher, was forced to make because of school bureaucracies and the schools' contradictory aims. In an address in Washington, the Secretary of Education spoke of "input," "output," and "accountability," all key words in factory and business management applied to schools. There were numerous other critics and criticisms. In 1987 a savage diatribe on the failure of higher education appeared. Allan Bloom's 1987 *Closing of the American Mind*, about universities—in fact, Cornell University—was subtitled "How Higher Education Has Failed Democracy and Impoverished the Souls of Today's Students."

In the field of education at least, criticisms are far more likely to seem credible than are criticisms of criticisms. Nevertheless, there were responses to conservative criticisms and the change in emphasis from equality to excellence. If schools' emphases and resources were to be shifted to the cultivation of excellence, efforts to remedy inequality must be reduced. Otherwise, school budgets must be increased, a prospect that seemed out of tune with the times. As an obvious example, if school days or school years were to be longer, it would be necessary to increase teacher pay; the biggest teacher union, the American Federation of Teachers, emphasized that. If those of greater promise were to be attracted to teaching, it would be necessary to increase teacher salaries. The political uses of *A Nation at Risk*, especially by President Reagan, were obvious and objectionable.

But criticisms continued. "Excellence," which had in the 1960s given way to "equality" and "freedom," was again becoming the first priority, at least in discussions of schools. The immediate effects seemed not to be great. Achievement scores did not show any great increases. School budgets were not greatly increased. It was far less difficult to gain popular support for the new priority than to apply it.

COMPETENCY AND COMPETENCY TESTING

Competency testing appeared in the 1970s, partly as a result of a new—or renewed—way of thinking about what was to be learned and how it was to be measured. It seems to have become popular because an influential part of the public had lost confidence in the schools. Pupils were tested and teachers were tested for "competencies." ("Competencies" would come to mean discrete required behaviors. It did not have the same meaning as "competence.")

Describing learning in terms of the specific, concrete bits of behavior that were its outcomes had an appealing simplicity about it. It ended the need or opportunity to consider attitudes, motivation, appreciation, level of cognitive skill, and other kinds of learning and the conditions, the psychologists' "intervening variables," leading to learning. The objectives—purposes—of instruction would be concrete. It would end discussion of kinds of learning that were not clearly defined or readily measured.

In a general way, this approach was "positivism," although that word is defined in so many ways that it has no great value. To put it most simply, perhaps too simply, specifying what was learned as "competencies" rested upon the proposition that what you saw was what you got and that there was nothing else.

The psychological base for the proposition had its beginnings at least as far back as Thorndike (pp. 237-38, 241). His stimulus and response learning theory and research had seemed it invalidate earlier views of mental "faculties" and seemed to make unnecessary the concept of "mind," or even the use of the word. The general approach was followed by B. F. Skinner, who described learning as "operant conditioning." Skinner saw that approach as being all inclusive. He wrote that no theory, or at least no other theory, of learning was needed. Skinner was in a general way an intellectual, but he argued for nonintellectualism, even antiintellectualism.

The psychological view seemed to imply that behavior was to be seen as a series of acts, each independent. That view was the one upon which the *Commonwealth Study* had been based, and the base for curriculum developed by Bobbitt and others in the 1920s by activity analysis (pp. 248-49). These, as has been said, rested upon a view of the nature of knowledge we do not share. Perhaps activity analysis was the precedent for seeing learning as resulting in specific, discrete acts, or perhaps describing learning in that way was a reinvention. As far as we know, the matter has not been investigated.

The next step was to list or catalogue the discrete acts, the discrete behaviors, that were desired or required. A list of all imaginable, or, rather, all imagined, acts was encyclopedic, running into the thousands. *The Florida Catalogue of Teaching Competencies*, published in 1976, was a thick volume. From listing to testing was a short, simple step, except of course the test could only measure a few behaviors.

Critics pointed out in horror that some high school graduates had not learned the competencies necessary for everyday life and jobs. *A Nation at Risk* would say that "Some 23 million American adults are functionally illiterate by the simplest tests of everyday reading, writing, and composition" and that "about 13 percent of all 17-year-olds in the United States can be considered functionally illiterate." It would also be pointed out that many adults could not fill out a job application or read a simple road map. *A Nation at Risk* went on to say that "business and military leaders complain that they are required to spend millions of dollars on costly remedial education and training programs in such skills as reading, spelling, and computation."

Therefore, the schools were not accomplishing what they had been intended to, and "accountability" was necessary: "accountability" would be a motto in the later 1970s and the 1980s. There must be verification that students, before they graduated from high school and perhaps at several places along the way, had indeed learned the least that they could be expected to learn. Legislatures demanded demonstrations of competencies. By one recent count, thirty-seven states required that students pass a competency test before graduating from high school.

It was also discovered that some teachers were lacking in competencies. Their grammar was faulty, their general knowledge was deficient. Many were teaching "out of certificate," teaching subjects for which they were not certified and which they had not been prepared to teach. In most states and cities the American teacher organizations successfully opposed the testing of teachers who had already been employed. In Texas, where events have been described by Lorrie A. Shepard and Amelia E. Kreitzer, a bill requiring teacher testing was passed. The recommendations of a Select Committee chaired by H. Ross Perot had included teacher testing and legislators had declined to pass a bill increasing taxes unless teachers were tested: "No test, no tax."

Subject matter tests were planned, but there was not the necessary time and money to develop them. The teachers were required to take a literacy test. Four thousand educators selected skills, and a thousand reviewed the test items. Teachers were required to pass a multiple-choice fifty-five-item reading test and a thirty-item grammar test, and write a hundred-and-fifty-word composition.

Teachers prepared with videotapes, in all-day and inservice workshops, by using a three-hundred-page "study book," and with the help of a hundred and thirty "presenters" trained by the University of Texas. On their first attempt, 96.7 percent of the teachers passed the test. The Commissioner of Education was reported as saying that the "teachers did fantastic" (a slip of the tongue, we hope). Another 2.3 percent of the Texas teachers passed the test on their second attempt.

Competency tests, not surprisingly, had both costs and benefits. Both the high school competency tests and the Texas teacher competency tests seemed to discriminate against blacks. Almost 90 percent of white teachers in Texas passed the test on the first attempt, but fewer than 82 percent of black teachers passed then. In Florida, ten times as many blacks as whites failed the high school competency test. A suit in behalf of a black student who had failed the test was found in his favor, since most of the time he had spent in school had been in a separate but not equal segregated school. He was protected by the Fourteenth Amendment, the judge ruled, and ordered a four-year postponement in the requirement that the test be passed before a student graduated from high school. When the test was administered a year or two before graduation, remedial instruction often improved the performance of the substandard student. If the student did not, even in spite of remedial work, pass the competency test, he or she did not receive a high school diploma. Of course, he still did not know how to read.

As a more tangible matter, the dollar cost of competency testing could be high. Test items had to be carefully selected for face validity. If it could not be demonstrated that high school test items measured something included in the schools' curriculum, the test's validity could be and often was challenged in the courts. A teacher test had necessarily to measure competencies necessary for teaching. Shepard and Kreitzer said that the cost of preparing the Texas teacher test was $5,065,000. Inservice and workshop costs for preparing the teachers were $3,000,000, and the cost of a day's pay for the 202,000 teachers who took the test was $26,260,000. With other costs to the schools, the total was $35,614,000. Therefore, the cost of identifying each nonliterate teacher was more than $18,000.

There were also other considerations. Teaching to the test could distort curriculum. A test intended to set minimum standards might also tend to set maximums. For teachers in general, the test could be demeaning and costly in morale.

Shepard and Kreitzer felt that other statewide teacher tests would be unlikely. Possibly the crest of enthusiasm for teacher testing at least had passed.

TEACHER SHORTAGE, TEACHER SURPLUS

In the 1950s there was a painful shortage of teachers. There were more positions than candidates, more classes than teachers. By 1970 there were more would-be teachers than positions for teachers. In the late 1980s there were again teacher shortages in some subjects and in some places, and it seemed likely that the need for teachers would increase. Both the teacher shortage and the teacher surplus were the result of demographics, the uneven growth of the population of the United States. They were also affected by the economy, and by salaries.

In the 1930s, the annual number of births in the United States was low. Marriages were postponed, and perhaps in bad times it seemed hard to afford a child. Elementary school enrollments fell, but were partly offset by increased high school enrollments, as students there stayed in school for lack of jobs.

Teaching was a desirable occupation then, because as a general thing, teacher salaries fell less than did salaries in other occupations and the cost of living. Teachers' job security was relatively good. The cost of living considered, teacher salaries were high, higher than before or since, and there were more eager applicants than available teaching positions.

Enrollments during World War II were stable or even declined. The children of the Depression, comparatively few in number, were in the primary grades. Students dropped out of high school to accept wartime jobs. To repeat, the growth of defense industries before and during World War II drew many teachers from their classrooms, and others served in the armed forces. Salaries of teachers remained low, because of a wartime regulation forbidding pay increases. Aside from that, teacher salaries, like those of other government employees, tend to "lag," to increase or decrease more slowly than other salaries. One of us knew a Virginia elementary school teacher-principal who, with eleven years of experience, had an annual salary then of just over $1,100.

Immediately after the end of the war, veterans studying under the GI Bill flooded into colleges, where enrollments increased so much that there was a shortage of college faculty. The "baby boom" began, and the number of babies born each year roughly doubled. The first of the babies born then were entering kindergarten at the beginning of the 1950s.

Unfortunately, teacher salaries had increased much more slowly than had the cost of living, there were other better-paying and more attractive occupations, and teaching attracted too few newcomers. As the children born during the baby boom progressed through the grades and high school in the 1950s and early 1960s, the teacher shortage worsened. New teachers who were recent college graduates had to be recruited from among the relatively small number of those who had been born during the Depression.

The big-city schools, which had once been the most desirable places to teach, felt the shortage more than the suburban schools. Prosperous communities there could offer higher salaries and had more well-mannered middle-class pupils, whose families had moved from the cities. The administrator in charge of teacher personnel in one of the largest city systems said in mid-October of one of those years that he had hired all the teacher applicants, qualified or not, "living or dead, preferably but not necessarily the former." He exaggerated only a little. There were still eighty-odd classes in the system without teachers, even substitute teachers.

When the demand for teachers was greater than the supply of teachers, qualifications were lowered. One expedient was to issue to teachers who did not have the usual qualifications "temporary" certificates. A second was to have teachers of a specialty in which teachers were less scarce teach another subject. For instance, in Buffalo in the early 1960s there were more than a hundred and fifty industrial arts teachers teaching other subjects. Some who could not meet even the standards for "temporary" teachers were appointed as substitutes, and taught for years, with the schedules and responsibilities of other teachers. Some teacher education institutions developed special programs for "retreading" older college graduates who were interested in becoming teachers. There is no reason to suppose that they did not become competent teachers, but their careers would be relatively short.

Beginning roughly in 1965, those born during the baby boom were entering college. Many of them entered teacher education programs. But elementary school enrollments had declined and high school enrollments were declining. As Tyack has pointed out, dropout rates of high schools had already fallen, and increasing high school enrollments could not compensate for falling elementary school enrollments, as they had in the Depression.

The need for teachers was declining as the number of prospective teachers increased. Experienced teachers delayed their departure from the schools. As the economy slackened, other jobs in other occupations were hard to find. Yearly teacher turnover in the schools had usually been somewhere between 10 and 15 percent, but in some school systems it fell to 1 percent. The market for teachers was flooded. In Buffalo in those years, four thousand certified prospective teachers went without public school employment. Experienced teachers were "retrenched," laid off; one school system retrenched teachers with more than ten years of seniority: teacher union contracts generally required that the most recently employed teachers be retrenched first—"last in, first out." That was a time-honored union rule. One of its costs was the retrenchment of many of the black teachers who had recently been hired.

American Federation of Teachers: Teacher Bargaining

The first recorded teachers' strike had been in San Antonio, Texas, in 1902, where teacher salaries were low and where Franklin Bobbitt would conduct one of the first school surveys. That year the CTF (Chicago Teachers Federation) affiliation with the AFL (American Federation of Labor) was far more important because of the CTF's large membership and strong leadership. In 1916 Chicago teacher organizations and those from four other cities formed the AFT (American Federation of Teachers), a national component of the AFL. A court order had forced the Chicago local to withdraw, but the AFT had continued.

The membership of the AFT had increased rapidly at first, but then lagged in the 1920s. Unions were not well thought of in the conservative times after World War I, and union membership generally was declining. In New York City the AFT local was active in leftist and communist causes—politics and "bread-and-butter" union goals seemed to be in conflict. AFT policy prevented strikes, and teachers generally opposed them. George Counts, who was opposed to communism in the AFT, was elected its president in 1939. In 1941 the AFT locals in New York City and Philadelphia were expelled because of their communist links. A third of the AFT's members belonged to the expelled locals. Nevertheless, the AFT's membership had grown to forty-seven thousand by 1947.

That year members of an independent teacher organization in Buffalo, New York, struck for a week. The strike was not supported by Buffalo AFL unions and was opposed by the city government and the state superintendent of schools. Nevertheless, the strike closed all the Buffalo schools, and the striking teachers won substantial pay raises. The Buffalo strike was an important precedent. AFT locals would strike in the future, and the NEA (National Education Association) found it necessary to abandon its anti-strike policy.

For the AFT the crucial victory was in New York City. It had been preceded there by years of effort. The union had been handicapped by conflict among factions within it, and there had been competing organizations locally. The union had a national opponent, the NEA, a "company union," dominated from its beginning by school administrators. The NEA position was that it was "unprofessional" to strike, that at most teachers should negotiate rather than bargain. The Buffalo strike had led to the New York State Taylor Law, designed to prevent government employee strikes by setting severe penalties against those who did.

The competing teacher organizations in New York City were finally combined and became the UFT (United Federation of Teachers). There was support from the United Auto Workers and from the garment workers' union, which was powerful in New York City, and from the AFL. A one-day strike in November 1960 persuaded the Board of Education to allow teachers to select a bargaining organization, and at Christmastime in 1961 the UFT was designated. David Selden, UFT organizer, said later that

> In reality, standard collective bargaining suits the educational enterprise very well—even better than it does many private enterprises. Though school systems do not operate for profit, their organizational structures are much like those of private manufacturing firms.

Teacher strikes would be numerous in the 1960s and 1970s. For some teachers caught between commitments to students and union, they could be wrenching. In the 1980s it was difficult or impossible to find a large school system in which there was not an AFT or NEA affiliated bargaining agent.

FIGURE 12-2   New York City teachers hold a strike rally outside of City Hall on April 11, 1964. Courtesy of United Press International.

One result, expected and obvious, was higher salaries for teachers. There were improvements in working conditions, periods for planning and time for lunch, and in some places smaller class sizes. Perhaps there was a cost in public esteem, and teachers were less often seen as dedicated, tireless, having a "calling."

Predictions

At the end of the 1980s the teacher surplus had eased, and there were "spot" shortages of teachers. There were more vacant positions than new teachers in the sciences and in mathematics, and in teaching English as a second language. Some cities, New York most prominent among them, had teacher shortages.

There are grave risks in forecasting the numbers of pupils and of new teachers, and some past predictions have been embarassingly wrong. However, predictions for the next few years seem worth making: for the next few years the number of pupils will be roughly constant; the baby boomers are becoming parents, there will be some increase in enrollments in pre-kindergarten programs, and high school dropout rates may decrease somewhat. The number of teachers will not increase much. But because many teachers would be leaving teaching within a few years, the demand for teachers is likely to increase. Those who were earlier unable to find positions as teachers are not likely to enter teaching tardily. It seems likely that the number of those completing college and certification programs will increase slowly.

In past decades, the classroom careers of teachers have generally followed a general pattern, and it seems more likely than not that the pattern will continue, at least for a few years. To simplify, most teaching careers have been brief or long; fewer have left teaching in their middle years. New teachers have often left teaching within a very few years of their first appointment. Perhaps some have left teaching because of "reality shock": teaching was not what they had expected it to be. The investment in time and money to prepare for teaching has not been great, and there have been other opportunities. Women had left teaching when they married, although as two-income families became usual, that happened less often than it once had. Other women left teaching to rear their own children, although as there were more childless families and more provisions for child care, this too became less common. For these reasons and others, half of those who have become teachers have left teaching after not much more than five years. But when the teaching surplus developed, the newest teachers were "retrenched," and also because there was less likelihood that older, more experienced teachers would quit, the average age of teachers increased.

Those who had not left teaching after only a few years were likely to continue, to stay for a career. A relatively few left their classrooms to become guidance counselors or administrators, but many teachers would stay on until retirement. Their ages then would depend upon state retirement systems and might be as low as the late fifties. Some stayed on until they were eligible for Social Security benefits, but very few, literally one in a thousand in a tabulation by one of the authors, continued to teach until they reached the then mandatory age of seventy. (The obvious inference as to teachers' motivation is not a cheering one.) A side effect of the teacher shortage had been the recruitment of older women and some older men into teaching; in Buffalo the median age of beginning years had been in some years as high as thirty-one. Career patterns and demography had resulted in a relatively old teaching force. Its age, and to some extent decreasing satisfaction with teaching, made it highly probable that the schools would make far more appointments of new teachers.

Of course, some vacancies would be filled by those who had been unable to enter public school teaching because of the surplus, and some part-time, substitute, and parochial school teachers would be appointed to regular positions. But most of those who had not begun to teach shortly after their graduation would no longer be interested in becoming public school teachers. A dissertation seemed to show that in western New York state only one is six of those who had been unable to secure teaching positions when they had graduated would be interested about ten years later in entering public school teaching.

After the teacher surplus had developed, enrollments in teaching programs had fallen. The number of students in one rather large program fell in three or four years by 90 percent, and some small programs were closed. When the teacher surplus ended, the number of graduates from teacher education sequences increased very slowly at first. The number of students preparing to be teachers again "lagged," changed more slowly than demand. Many high school students make occupational choices, and, naturally, after high school four years pass before they have completed course requirements and graduated from college.

As Donald Warren has pointed out, historically, when the need for teachers has been greater than the number of teachers available, qualifications for new teachers have been reduced. The temporary certificates, emergency appointments, and the use of substitutes during the teacher shortage beginning in the 1950s were only the most recent instances of that. If teaching seemed a not particularly satisfying career, less capable men and women would be admitted to teacher education programs and teaching.

Many parts of the alternatives proposed by the Holmes Group and a Carnegie report, *A Nation Prepared: Teachers for the Twentieth Century*, appeared in the 1987 contract of the AFT in Rochester, New York. There would be increases until starting salaries reached $29,835. If high salaries would attract able new teachers, Rochester would attract them. There would be a "career pattern" for teachers. A chronic and justified complaint had been that the only promotion was out of the classroom into administration or perhaps into guidance. A new teacher would be an "intern," and there would be "resident" and "professional" teachers. "Lead" teachers, with at least ten years of experience, would earn up to $70,000 a year. They would spend half their time as "instructional leaders," developing curricula and being mentors to interns, first-year teachers, who had gotten too little help, had too often been left to sink or swim. Lead teachers would take part in local teacher education programs, which critics had said were too often out of touch with life in the classroom. The teachers' work year would be a week longer, for planning and inservice days. The Rochester plan seemed to offer a chance for better teachers, better teaching, and better schooling.

EDUCATION "R&D"

The most general purpose of educational research is the improvement of schooling. Therefore, at best it serves the purposes of criticism of schooling. The ways in which it criticizes vary, but research that does not imply ways of thinking about schools or schooling is not educational research.

Educational research had begun as far back as the 1880s and 1890s, when Hall and Rice had searched for answers to "why" and "how" questions. Thorndike had developed statistical methods, Terman and others had designed tests of achievement and ability, and George Strayer and others had introduced quantitative methods in the study of school finance. Educational research, which had often served business management in the schools had received less attention and support during the 1930s, when business management was in disgrace, but there was greater confidence in research beginning in the 1950s.

The supporters of research in the 1950s would have agreed that much that had been called "research" was no longer research. The construction of the first achievement tests, for example, had been pioneering in new territory, but developing a test had become nearly routine. Routine census taking and status studies had not been true research, at least after problems of methods had been solved.

There had been many—a hundred thousand, someone guessed—educational studies. But compared with the volume of research in other fields, research in education had been a minor contribution by a few professors, fewer school system directors of research, and many more doctoral candidates. The doctoral candidates were, naturally, beginners and often carried out their research without knowledgeable advice or supervision. Research designs were often flawed, and research led too often to no conclusion, or false conclusion. Doctoral candidates too often looked for easy nontheoretical problems (as they sometimes still do). Mundane questions led at best to mundane answers. Educational research was not cumulative; research was not based upon research. With a very few exceptions, it had little effect upon learning, teaching, or the schools.

But science had made great contributions. In wartime, scientists had made radar invaluable, had created other weapons, and, above all, produced the atom bomb. Research had perfected television, even color television, and led to the development of high-speed electronic computers. Medical research had resulted in cures, of tuberculosis, for instance, and Jonas Salk's polio vaccine offered children protection. If scientific research had been successful in wartime, in industry, in medicine, and other fields, research should be successful in improving schooling.

If research was to be successful in education it was necessary for it to resemble more closely research by engineers and medical researchers. It must, in the first place, rest upon a sound theoretical base, so that it would provide systematic knowledge. It must have been knowledgeably performed by professional researchers, not by inexperienced doctoral candidates. It must match the sophistication of research in other fields.

Beginning the upgrading of educational research was difficult. The U.S. Office of Education staff had experience only in gathering data of generally ordinary and routine sorts, data that were useful for describing or providing examples but that provided few insights. Only a few university schools of education had traditions of competent research and almost none of the teachers colleges did. A few scattered pockets of research skill provided the first researchers for the new, improved theoretically oriented research.

A second difficulty was securing sufficient funding. University contributions were limited. One of the first sources of substantial funding was the W. W. Kellogg Foundation, which, starting in 1950, contributed $6 million to eight universities for the improvement of training of school administrators. The project, called the Cooperative Program in Educational Administration, did produce some changes in administrator training programs. Funds from the training programs were also channeled into research on administration: the project resulted in a new scientific line of approach to school administration. In 1955, Congress passed the Cooperative Research Act and in 1956, appropriated $1 million for research programs to be carried on outside the U.S. Office of Education.

From 1956 to 1960, appropriations for research increased tenfold, to $10 million, and research grants relevant to education were also being made by the National Institute of Mental Health, the Office of Naval Research, and the National Science Foundation. In 1966, appropriations for the U.S. Office of Education were more than $100 million.

At the beginning the U.S. Office of Education distributed most research funds by asking researchers to propose projects, to justify their questions and hypotheses, and to describe their research procedures. This was less than satisfactory for several reasons. Initially, most research proposals were for routine and familiar kinds of research. Proposed and funded projects were small and were not cumulative. Detailed history does not belong here, but the general change by the U.S. Office of Education was from "unsolicited proposals," by which researchers propose their own questions and hypotheses, to "requests for proposals," "RFPs," in which problems were outlined and researchers asked to describe methods of solving them. That seemed to make it more likely that solutions would be more useful in schools and that they would be cumulative. Admitting the advantages, critics felt that if problems and questions were dictated, answers would be dictated, and that the admittedly rare question of great merit would not be forthcoming. There were some later funds for unsolicited research; critics say they are too small.

After the first impulse the most important precedent for the organization of educational research was the private enterprise pattern of "R&D," research and development, that had spread from the General Electric laboratory in Schnectady, where it had first appeared. When he was in charge of U.S. Office of Education-funded research, R. Louis Bright thought of educational research as educational development, to be conducted as private enterprise R&D was. Outside review committees became less important, staff more important. There was more applied research, and theoretical research was more often undertaken by researchers from outside education. To disseminate findings, the Educational Resources Information Center, ERIC, was set up, computer-accessible indexes were developed, and research reports were mass photoreduced. The first of ten "R&D centers was established in 1962. The practical value of research was emphasized, and research programs were planned and analyzed by Program Planning and Budget Systems. Researchers constructed elaborate "PERT," program planning and review charts. All this was most businesslike and impressive.

One standard by which educational research and development can be judged is by its funding. Research and development was not heavily funded, and some years was not successful in maintaining funding levels. Appropriations for the R&D centers fell from $12,400,000 in 1968 to $7,200,000 in 1971, because research and development had not captured the imagination or confidence of budget makers or the public.

A 1987 report by the General Accounting Office (GAO) documents the further decline of support for educational research and development:

> During the past decade, the production of federally sponsored research, statistical, and evaluative information on education has declined notably. . . . The number of grants awarded for research decreased 65 percent from 476

in 1980 and progressively dropped 79 percent to 25 in 1985. . . . Only 11 percent of 1985 awards were for new data collection. . . . Support for research has *decreased* since the early 1970s by more than 70 percent in constant dollars, despite the fact that the federal investment in education *increased* by 38 percent and federal support for research in general increased by about 4 percent in constant dollars between 1980 and 1984 [italics in source].

Confidence in research in education, if federal appropriations were a yardstick, had continued to decrease.

Second, educational research and development can be judged by the contributions it makes to thought, opinions, and practice. Inquiry in educational administration produced new and quite different insights. Educational administration could be thought of as bureaucratic, with the strengths as well as the weaknesses of bureaucracies. The kinds and limits of educational administrators' control could be described as limited by the autonomy of teachers. The "loose coupled" organization, and the ways in which administrative authority is implemented, were in the late 1980s a promising line of inquiry. One could provide other examples, although contributions to thought were rather rare.

The clearest example of the impact of educational research upon opinions, public and professional, is that of the first Coleman report, *Equality of Educational Opportunity*. It concluded that schools as such did not have much effect upon the achievement of their students, and directed thought, research, and probably resources away from schools for the poor and the black, toward pupils' homes, values, and socioeconomic knowledge. Researchers who for one reason or another doubted that conclusion of Coleman spent years developing counterarguments and ways of finding schools that were at least relatively successful. But research can serve to support opinions as well as to change them. The massive research on the teaching of reading by phonics supported the prevailing opinion rather than changing it.

For those who assume as Ellwood Cubberley had that the schools were destined to improve, any change, any innovation, was presumed to be improving. Since we do not share that ideology, we do not automatically accept all innovations as desirable. Research or evaluation can be useful if it supports usual practice or demonstrates that commonsense beliefs are correct. In the foreword to *What Works: Research About Teaching and Learning* (1986), Secretary of Education William J. Bennett wrote that

Most readers will, I think, judge that most of the evidence of this volume confirms common sense. So be it. Given the abuse common sense has taken in recent decades, particularly in the theory and practice of education, it is no small contribution if research can play a role in bringing more of it to American education.

Change in educational practices is not the only yardstick for measuring the contributions of educational research. But Larry Cuban presented evidence that teaching in classrooms had changed remarkably little for at least a century. If research had any major effects upon teaching in classrooms, they were hard to show, and there is no reason to believe that they were more than minor.

Some research that seemed especially promising seemed to have no effect at all. The "talking typewriter," responding vocally each time a key was pressed, seemed to offer quick, efficient, mechanized teaching, but outside the laboratory, it was not successful. Educational researchers and electronic technologists produced a succession of devices: teaching machines, tape recorders, television, and video cameras, each proclaimed as revolutionary, as cure-all ways of teaching. Perhaps these and other educational fads were a factor in public doubts about schools.

ENTER: THE COMPUTER

Technological changes produce intellectual, social, and economic changes. This is a near-truism and has been amply demonstrated in our past. But no other technological change in this century has effects as great as the introduction of computers and computing. It creates new occupations and threatens to diminish or obliterate others. Large computers have expedited the accumulation of information and accelerated centralization of control. On the other hand newer personal computers have already allowed individuals to apply expert knowledge and skills that were previously unavailable to them.

In general, American educators have given little thought to the intellectual, social, and economic changes that have already appeared. That is understandable, and it is also understandable that appropriate uses of the computer in education are unclear, and that possible benefits and possible dangers have not been fully considered.

The first primitive prototype computer was designed and assembled by Henry Babbage in 1822. A cumbersome assembly of brass cams, gears, and cogs, it was intended to calculate the orbits of astronomical bodies. Babbage would spend the rest of his life attempting to build the enormous machine he envisioned.

The concept had vast attractions, but a brass machine driven by steam engines was a technological impossibility. It became a possibility, although probably not much more than that, when relays replaced gears and cams and electricity replaced steam. The computer became practical, within narrow limits, when electronic tubes, "valves," replaced relays. (The first computer "bug" was an insect ensnared in wires and tubes.) It became attractive after the development of the transistor in Bell Laboratories (one of the most successful R&D centers). Miniaturization, subminiaturization, and design improvements increased its speed of operation; the personal computer of the late 1980s was faster in operation than were the largest mainframe computers of the late 1960s. The first electronic computers had been reprogrammed by rewiring. In the 1960s programs and data were punched into computer cards. (Key punching was a useful skill, and some thought it would be a growing occupation.) In the 1980s programs were on "floppy disks," data could be entered on a keyboard, and some young professional computer programmers had never seen an

IBM punch card. The programming and operation of a computer had at the beginning required specialized knowledge and skill, so rare that programmers and operators became for a time a "computer priesthood," the sole possessors of rare and valuable knowledge, and of access to the mainframe computers. At the end of the 1980s programs were commercial products, and even those not adept could oeprate a personal computer.

The computer was first used for military and scientific purposes. For industry, it became a necessary tool for design and made possible the automation of some manufacturing. It was valuable and then necessary for business, for keeping accounts and then for many other purposes. Computers replaced telephone switchboards and operators, and "modems" made possible quick access to and transmission of information. The time-honored pinball machine was replaced by computer-controlled games. Even the liberal arts scholar found it useful, if for no other purpose than typing manuscripts.

One of the first military uses of the computer was the calculation of the trajectory of a projectile, a process mathematically similar to Babbage's calculation of celestial orbits. A computer could link radar and gun. It could simulate a landing on an aircraft carrier's deck, and for war games could simulate a military campaign. One of the first steps in the development of "star wars," the strategic defense initiative, was the development of the necessary computer programs.

For the scientist the computer could solve equations that, while simple in principle, required repeated, "iterative" computations. Calculations that had been too burdensome to undertake became routine. For the social scientist a set of programs, SPSS, made readily available a variety of statistical treatments, and much greater amounts of data could be analyzed. "Supercomputers," introduced in the early 1970s, made it possible to model, almost recreate, such events as the collision of two galaxies.

For industrial design computers had become essential; aircraft designs were based upon aerodynamic analyses far more detailed than those that had been possible by use of a wind tunnel. New, low-air-resistance, high-fuel-economy automobiles were designed by computer. Computers and supercomputers were used for oil exploration, even to select methods of extinguishing oil well fires. Civil engineers used computers to design buildings less vulnerable to earthquake damage, and computers improved meteorological forecasting.

There had been a time when business financial records had been kept by bookkeepers, thought of as little men wearing green eye shades, hunched over huge double-entry ledgers. They were replaced by bookkeeping machines, and then by computers, which kept accounts, calculated, and printed bills. Computers kept inventories, and at supermarket checkout stands computers read prices and calculated bills. Business managers used computers to project costs and profits. Thousands of copies of a spreadsheet program called "Lotus 1-2-3" were sold.

For the historian and other liberal arts scholars, a personal word processor would end the delay and expense of typing manuscripts. Editing could be done without retyping, or messy, easily misread notes in the margin. To consult the catalogue at the Congressional Library, the user went to a computer terminal instead of to a file drawer. Collaborators separated by thousands of miles could exchange information by use of a modem and a telephone connection. It seemed to be only a matter of time before the contents of an encyclopedia could be stored on a single disk.

Naturally, there were other uses of the computer. In medicine, it could suggest diagnoses and monitor a patient's vital signs. Motion and television images were generated by computer. Composers could create music by use of a computer, even a personal computer, and some personal computers could be used for commercial art. Microprocessors controlled furnaces, automobile speeds, and ovens. The uses of computers, visible and invisible, were countless and rapidly increasing.

The development of computers was also accelerating; costs were falling. Designs, programming languages, and user "interfaces" were all being improved. It was said that even a personal computer would be obsolete in four or five years. New supercomputers would be much faster and have much greater capacities. Computer designers talked of "parallel processing," by which computers could do several parts of a computation at the same time. FORTRAN 8 and other new computer languages would speed operation. The first computers had been programmed in part by "patches," wires plugged into switchboards. Later there had been punch cards, which had been replaced by keyboards and optical scanners. The computer mouse added flexibility and "user friendliness." A computer that followed voice instructions seemed a possibility, although there were still difficulties to be overcome. Computer outputs had at first been by printers that were snail paced and noisy; their speed increased steadily. Computers operated plotters, drew graphs, and displayed results on video screens. Computer voices, although still crude, could be understood. A technological revolution, great as that of the Industrial Revolution, was underway.

Many school uses of the computer were like uses in businesses; accounting and budgeting, and calculating and writing paychecks had become everyday practice in school systems. In Glenview, Illinois, a school system a computer network was also used to compile warehouse inventories and pupil attendance records, some of which were to be transmitted electronically to the state education department.

The use of computers in instruction was more perplexing. A year or two ago we met a young, earnest, harried curriculum coordinator. He had a difficult assignment: his school system had a large storeroom filled with personal computers the system had acquired from a grant and as gifts. Obviously, they could not stand in the storeroom unused. The question he was to answer was how to use the computers. We do not know what answers he found, or even if he found them. His problem, it seemed to us, was one for schools in general. Outside the schools there were a thousand uses for computers, but how to use them in schools was perplexing.

Robert Taylor, in *The Computer in the School*, suggests a useful first distinction. A computer can be used to teach, or as a tool to learn, or it can be taught (that is, programmed). As a teacher or tutor, the computer can direct drills intended to help the pupil memorize, as example, to memorize multiplication tables. As a tool, a word processor can aid in learning composition, in performing otherwise time-consuming computations, producing graphs and graphic designs. As a machine that "learns," the computer can be programmed to carry out new or novel tasks.

The use of a computer as drillmaster is simple and obvious and serves the same purpose as an old-fashioned set of flashcards or of a teaching machine. As an aid in writing it seems to have great potential value, by ridding the student of distracting matters of neat penmanship and allowing easy, quick changes in a letter or essay. The "teaching" or programming of computers by students has been controversial.

In the mid-1980s much was said and written about "computer literacy," but the term seemed to have as many definitions as users. One approach to "computer literacy" was to begin by teaching the student to program. That had been the first step in the beginning, before programs were commercially available. A favorite for this use was Logo, a simple "language" largely developed by Seymour Papert at M.I.T. We have two reservations about this sort of "computer literacy." First, as in conventional and writing, there are various standards of "literacy." If Logo, why not BASIC, or COBOL, or FORTRAN, or for that matter the computer's own binary, on-off "language"? Most users of computers will not program, and computer languages not constantly used are quickly forgotten, as one of us can demonstrate; also, computer languages also become obsolete. Second, admitting that the analogy may be flawed, the invention of movable type did not make it desirable for most or all students to become printers. What did become more valuable was knowing how to read. Perhaps instead of "computer literacy" a better term might have been "computer competence."

Although the schools' transition to computer use had just begun, some conclusions could be reached. If computers were simply to be additional instructional aids, they would not have great effect or value. At least since the phonograph record, other instructional aids have had minor effects and benefits. If computers were to be used effectively in schools, it would be necessary to spend time and money training teachers in their use. A computer in the classroom of a teacher who was frightened of it and uninformed about its uses would not be utilized well. If students were to learn with the use of computers, it would be necessary to reoganize curricula. A one-semester course, elective or required, would have only narrow usefulness.

CONCLUSION

Americans had turned from public concerns to private ones, to privatism, to seeking personal gain and pleasure. There had been conservative criticisms of the schools in the 1950s, and in another conservative time, they were again louder and more influential.

One strand of criticism was that the schools taught and students learned too little of the old, conventional subject matter: mathematics, science, history, foreign languages. Critics said that the schools expected too little of students, too little learning, too little effort, too little homework.

Other critics said that the schools (like other public institutions) had betrayed the public interest and the public trust. Their remedy was testing. It would help guarantee, they argued, that a high school diploma ensured at least literacy. The school and the public were to be protected against teachers who were inadequate because of their own (relative) illiteracy or too-limited knowledge of what was to be taught. "Competency" testing was intended to assure quality control, in schools as in factories.

A third concern of critics was the increasing cost of schooling. School budgets were carefully examined and wherever possible reduced. If not reduced, increases in budgets were held to a minimum. These critics, the Secretary of Education among them, talked of "cost effectiveness" and the "bottom line."

Demography had produced the teacher surplus, and it was to be expected that demography would bring it to an end. Historically, the hazard had been to reduce qualifications for teaching when more teachers were needed. What is already needed, of course, is not only more teachers, but more competent teachers. New, more rigorous, teacher education sequences had been proposed, and changes in school organization to keep skilled teachers in classrooms. The Rochester, New York, teacher contract seemed a step in that direction.

The development of computers, especially personal computers, led to other proposals and to innovations. New technology would call for new learning and new ways of learning, learning about computers and learning with computers. It was not clear in the late 1980s what should be learned about computers, and the use of computers for instruction had only begun to be developed.

Many criticisms were conservative and some were reactionary. Although not explicitly, it was assumed that knowledge rather than student interest was to take precedence. Accountability was more important than autonomy. Efficiency was more important than equality.

But the importance of improving teaching, even as the teacher shortage grew, led to proposals and plans, and even to some promising developments in teacher education and the ways in which teachers' duties were assigned.

CODA

In the briefest form, these have been the most important themes of this book:

Education and schooling have been and are inseparable, integral parts of culture and society, sharing their past and common histories.

The development of our culture and our schools has resulted from many factors, many events. There is no single explanation for the development of culture, education, and schooling as they are now.

American culture, education, and schooling grew from roots in Europe near the ends of the Reformation and Renaissance, and the faith and values of their time.

Although there have been times of "awakening" and "reawakenings," faith and religion have tended to become less important in our culture, and in education and schools.

The growth of democratic thought in the earlier 1800s was accompanied by schooling intended for all, instead of for only the gifted or privileged few. The "teacher," following a humble calling, took the place of the master and the ideal of classical knowledge.

America's earlier cultural values and social organization were greatly modified by urbanization and industrialization. Other modifications accompanied changes in technology and the dispersal of cities' residents into suburbs.

Industrialization was accompanied by rationalization, by the development of organizations of what have been seen as logical and efficient forms. In the process, authority has often been centralized. Owner-operated shops were replaced by management-directed factories, which have often become parts of national corporations.

Schooling was rationalized as industry was. Common schools serving small communities became parts of larger school systems. State control of schools increased, and federal control has become more important. In a way, the counterpart of the national corporation was "the one best system," requiring centralization of authority. Efficiency and business management methods were adapted for schools, although often inappropriate and damaging.

At the same time relations between individuals have become less often personal, more often formal, and often contractual.

The traditional nuclear family of mother and wife, father and husband, and children, has become less nearly universal, and households in other forms more commonplace.

In the years since World War II there have been oscillations in American mood, from conservative to liberal and back to conservative. More recently this has been accompanied by changes in ways of thought and may have been due to shifts in American values. Schools have shared in conservative and liberal moods.

Most recently, the individual and the individual's needs and interests have been seen as less important than the more general needs of society, industry, and business.

Schools, like the culture and society of which they are a part, are being and will be affected by computers and other electronic technology, which may have impacts as great as the development of movable type or the Industrial Revolution. That prospect of a new world holds both threats and promises.

BIBLIOGRAPHY, SOURCES, AND NOTES

Additional readings are suggested for each section, with brief descriptions.

The sources of otherwise unidentified quotations appear in the notes following the last three words of the quotations.

Important sources are cited even though not mentioned in the text.

INTRODUCTION

The Introduction is in part an adaptation of H. Warren Button, "Creating More Useable Pasts: History in the Study of Education," *Educational Researcher*, VIII (June, 1979), pp. 3–9. Robert N. Bellah, et al., *Habits of the Heart: Individualism and Commitment in American Life* (repr. New York: Harper & Row, 1986) is the source of the quoted phrase.

The pattern for most histories of American education written in the last half century was set by Ellwood P. Cubberley, in *Public Education in the United States* (Boston: Houghton-Mifflin, 1919, 1934). Cubberley concentrated on the organization and administration of the schools, seeing them as of greatest value and importance, and their history as leading inevitably toward their perfection. A recent text in that tradition is Harry S. Good and James D. Teller, *A History of American Education* (New York: Macmillan, 1973, 3rd ed.). Criticisms of history of American education in Cubberley's tradition, with which we agree, are by Bernard Bailyn in *Education in the Forming of American Society* (New York: Vintage, 1960) and

Lawrence A. Cremin in *The Wonderful World of Ellwood Patterson Cubberley* (New York: Teachers College, Columbia U., 1965). Of related interest is Colin Greer, *The Great School Legend* (New York: Basic Books, 1972).

A newer approach to history of American education has been to employ constructs which emphasize the function of the schools in the distribution of social rewards and power. This approach was employed by Michael B. Katz in *The Irony of Early School Reform: Educational Innovation in Mid-Nineteenth Century Massachusetts* (Cambridge: Harvard, 1968), and subsequently by a number of others. This has been fruitful, but we have substantial reservations. First, this focus is quite narrow. Even if there were complete information on the distribution of rewards and power at a given time and place (which there most certainly is not), history should encompass a great deal more than that. There have been people and thoughts in history, as well as social forces. Second, by unfortunate parallel, the new social history of the schools has had the same air of inevitability as Cubberley's history did. Inevitable is the doom of our culture and society, largely brought on by our schools. There is not much in history, as far as we are concerned, that has dictated the inevitability of events in the past, or that does dictate them in the present or future. Third, some new social historians of education seem as certain of the evilness of schools as Cubberley was of their goodness. We are entitled to value judgments and, as historians, obligated to make them, but the history of our culture and our schools is far too complex for cosmic affirmation, or denial.

The most comprehensive critique of the new educational history—one that we also do not entirely agree with—is found in Diane Ravitch's "The Revisionists Revised: Studies in the Historiography of American Education," *Proceedings of the National Academy of Education*, Vol. 4, 1977, pp. 1–84. An expanded version of this work was published under the title *The Revisionists Revised* (New York: Basic Books, 1978). A response to Ravitch's work can be found in Walter Feinberg, *et al.*, *Revisionists Respond to Ravitch* (Washington, D.C.: The National Academy of Education, 1980).

We have taken the general framework for values from Florence Kluckholn and Fred Strodtbeck, *Variations in Value Orientation* (Evanston, Ill.: Row Peterson, 1961).

General Source Materials: Throughout the section on *Bibliography, Sources and Notes*, there are references to general collections of source materials on the history of American education. The following are some of the more useful sources that can be found in most university and research libraries.

The most extensive collection of general documents on the history of American education is Sol Cohen (ed.), *Education in the United States* (New York: Random House, 1974, 5 vols.); approximately 3,500 pages in length, Cohen's documents are drawn from manuscripts, books, magazines, and other sources, from the sixteenth century to the present.

Numerous American and European sources are in the "Classics in Education" series published by Teachers College Press, Columbia University. Of related interest is Robert H. Bremmer, *et al.*, (eds.), *Children & Youth in America* (Cambridge: Harvard, 1970–71), 3 vols., over 2,000 pages in length. The editors attempted to include documents on all aspects of the welfare of children, including education.

The best general collection of documents of the history of education in the South is still Edgar W. Knight (ed.), *A Documentary History of Education in the South Before 1860* (Chapel Hill: U. N. Carolina, 1953, 5 vols.). No comparable source exists for the period since the Civil War.

Several reprint and microfilm collections are also of particular value to those interested in studying the history of American education. Lawrence A. Cremin, advisory editor, has provided an invaluable service by assembling the 161-volume reprint series titled *American Education: Its Men, Ideas, and Institutions* (New York: Arno/New York Times, 1970–71). Virtually every book published in the United States before 1800 can be obtained on either microprint, microfiche, or microfilm. Clifford K. Shipton, editor, has assembled the microprint collection *Early American Imprints, 1639–1800* (Worcester, Mass.: American Antiquarian Society). For nineteenth century educational sources the microfilm series *American Culture Series* (Ann Arbor, Mich.: University Microfilms) is also extremely useful.

PART ONE:
BEGINNINGS

Readings: The most interesting single volume on pre-Revolutionary history is Daniel J. Boorstin, *The Americans: The Colonial Experience* (New York: Vintage, 1958). Pages 1–69, 97–143, on the beginnings of Massachusetts Bay Colony, Pennsylvania, and Virginia, are especially worth reading. We have read with pleasure J. C. Furnas, *The Americans* (New York: Putnam's, 1969). Pages 13–236 deal with pre-Revolutionary history. Samuel Eliot Morison, *The Puritan Pronaos* (New York: N.Y.U., 1936), republished as *The Intellectual Life of Early New England* (Ithaca, N.Y.: Cornell, 1967) may be overly favorable, but portrays intellectual life generally, rather than that of a few intellectuals exclusively. A general history may be helpful to provide an orderly and relatively succinct overview: Samuel Eliot Morison *et al.*, *Growth of the American Republic*, (New York: Oxford, 1980, 2 vols.) serves that purpose well for this and later sections.

Pre-Revolutionary America has been the subject of some of the most interesting historical writing in the last quarter century; there is almost an overabundance of good scholarship. Among the most interesting works are David Hawke, *The Colonial Experience* (Indianapolis: Bobbs-Merrill, 1966); Max Saville, *Seeds of Liberty* (New York: Knopf, 1948); and Louis Wright, *The Cultural Life of the American Colonies* (New York: Harper and Row, 1957) which are more detailed intellectual histories. Harvey Wish, *Society and Thought in America*, (New York: D. McKay, 1964, 2 vols.) is still worth reading. The best single description of a prototypic New England town, if there was such a thing, is Kenneth A. Lockridge, *A New England Town: Dedham, Massachusetts, 1636–1737* (New York: Norton, 1970), but there are also other studies of individual towns. On education, Lawrence A. Cremin, *American Education: The Colonial Experience, 1607–1783* (New York: Harper & Row, 1970), with much detail, is the best single source. Some of what Robert Middlekauf wrote in *Ancients and Axioms: Secondary Education in the Eighteenth Century* (New Haven: Yale, 1963) also holds for the seventeenth century.

Concerning the distribution of wealth in the colonies, James A. Henretta, "Economic Development and Social Structure in Colonial Boston," *William and Mary Quarterly*, 3rd ser., vol. 22 (1965), pp. 75–92, showing that there was increasing concentration of wealth in Boston, is persuasive. However, Alice Hanson Jones's research, summarized in *Wealth of a Nation to Be: The American Colonies on the Eve of the Revolution* (New York: Columbia U., 1980) indicates that Boston was the exception, and that the rule was that wealth was not more greatly concentrated on the eve of the Revolution. Even so, the wealth of Boston would be important for the development of mercantilism, of shipping, and later of manufacturing. Although the matter can be argued endlessly, we are inclined to accept the argument that industrialization in its earlier stages strongly supported the concentration of wealth, but that in its later stages wealth has been, if anything, dispersed.

CHAPTER ONE:
SOURCES, EUROPEAN AND COLONIAL

The main sources for our description of education in England at the end of the Renaissance were R. L. Clarke, *Classical Education in Britain* (Cambridge: Cambridge U., 1959) and Kenneth Charlton, *Education in Renaissance England* (London: Routledge and Kegan Paul, 1965). An earlier but still useful work is J. W. Baldwin, *William Shakespeare's Small Latin and Lesse Greeke* (Urbana: U. of Ill., 1944), vol. 1. ". . . in the children": Colet quoted in Craig R. Thompson, *Schools in Tudor England* (Washington, D.C.: Folger Shakespeare Library, 1958), p. 11. Our most important source on pre-Revolutionary child rearing is Philip Greven, *The Protestant Temperament* (New York: Knopf, 1977). ". . . face lay hid": Anne Bradstreet quoted in Greven, p. 29. ". . . that doth appear": Adam Winthrop (1620) quoted in Greven, p. 156. ". . . responses for children": Greven, p. 32. "Certain established boundaries": *ibid.*, p. 151. ". . . of this Catechism": *Book of Common Prayer* (Oxford: Thomas Baskett, Printer to the University, 1757), not paginated. ". . . the Puritan creed": Edgar W. Knight, *Education in the United States* (Boston: Ginn, 1929), quoted in Morison, *Puritan Pronaos*, p. 55. ". . . a social obligation": *ibid.*, p. 66. ". . . assisting our endeavours": "Olde Deluder Satan" law, in many sources, including Theodore Rawson Crane (ed.), *Dimensions of Higher Education* (Reading, Mass.: Addison-Wesley, 1974), p. 8. ". . . or in commonwealth": quoted in Bernard C. Steiner, *History of Education in Connecticut* (Washington, D.C.: U.S. Government Printing Office, Bureau Circular of Information No. 2, 1893), p. 17. ". . . to our commonwealth": ". . . societies and republics": quoted in "History of Free Schools in Plymouth Colony. . . ," *Collections of the Massachusetts Historical Society*, 2nd ser., vol. IV (1816), p. 83.

Our information on Enoch Flower is from James Pyle Wickersham, *A History of Education in Pennsylvania* (Lancaster, Pa.: Inquirer, 1885), passim. Pastorius's biography is Marion Dexter Learned, *The Life of Francis Daniel Pastorius* (Philadelphia: Campbell, 1908). ". . . & Young Zealots": Francis Daniel Pastorius, *a New Primer. . .* (New York: William Bradford, 1693), p. 3. ". . . reduced to poverty": *Pennsylvania Gazette*, Nov. 29, 1733, quoted in Wickersham, p. 43. Corlet's biography comes primarily from George E. Littlefield, "Elijah Corlet and the 'Faire Grammar Schoole' at Cambridge," *Colonial Society of Massachusetts Publications*, XVIII (1913-14), pp. 131-40. ". . . youth under him": quoted by Littlefield, p. 134. There are several biographies of Cheever. We used Elizabeth Porter Gould, *Ezekiel Cheever and Some of His Descendants* (Boston: Clapp, 1879). Pauline Holmes, *A Tercentenary History of the Boston Latin School, 1635-1935* (Cambridge: Harvard, 1935) was useful. St. Paul's school, which Cheever had attended, had also been attended by John Milton a few years earlier. It is described in fascinating detail by Harris Francis Fletcher, *The Intellectual Life of John Milton . . . Through Grammar School* (Urbana: U. of Illinois, 1955). ". . . Sycthia [barbaric] grown": Cotton Mather, "An Elegy on Ezekiel Cheever," 1708. Repr. Carl H. Gross and Charles C. Chandler, eds., *History of American Education Through Readings* (Boston: Heath, 1964), p. 39. ". . . me with straw": Metcalf, quoted in Kenneth Lockridge, p. 57. ". . . in New England": Cremin, *Colonial Experience*, p. 212. See George Eliot Morison, *The Founding of Harvard College* (Cambridge: Harvard, 1935) for its beginnings.

Our information about New Netherland schools and Adam Roelansen is primarily from William Heard Kilpatrick, *The Dutch Schools of New Netherland and New York* (Washington, D.C.: U.S. Government Printing Office, 1912). There are many detailed sources, but Wickersham is the starting point in history of schools in Pennsylvania. ". . . worship of God" quoted in Gary B. Nash, *Red, White, and Black* (Englewood Cliffs, N.J.: Prentice Hall, 1974), p. 46.

CHAPTER TWO:
CULTURE AND SCHOOLING BEFORE THE REVOLUTION

The change in thought following the trans-Atlantic passage was noted but not described in Edward Eggleston, *The Transit of Civilization* (Repr. Boston: Beacon, 1959). Douglas Sloan, *The Great Awakening and American Education: A Documentary History* (New York: Teachers College, Columbia U., 1973) documents the Great Awakening well, although it leaves its effect upon schooling problematical.

Several books and articles by Robert Francis Seybolt on colonial and provincial masters and schools provide information. Among them are "The Evening Schools of Colonial New York City. . . ," in Thomas E. Finegan, *Free Schools: A Documentary History . . . Fifteenth Annual Report of the [New York State] Education Department* (Albany: The University of the State of New York, 1910), pp. 630–52; "New York Colonial Schoolmasters," *ibid.*, pp. 653–59; *Public Schools of Colonial Boston, 1635–1775* (Cambridge: Harvard, 1935); "Schoolmasters in Colonial Philadelphia," *Pennsylvania Magazine of History and Biography*, LII (1927–30) (*Transactions*), pp. 130–156. For New York City immediately after the Revolution, see Carl F. Kaestle, *The Evolution of an Urban School System: New York City, 1750–1850* (Cambridge: Harvard, 1973). For Boston, see Stanley K. Schultz, *The Culture Factory: Boston Public Schools, 1789–1860* (New York: Oxford, 1973). Much recent history of education has concerned the cities. Aside from that, their importance is suggested by Richard C. Wade, *The Urban Frontier: The Rise of the Cities, 1790–1830* (Cambridge: Harvard, 1959).

There have been several book-length biographies of the venerated Christopher Dock. As far as we know, the most recent is Gerald C. Studer, *Christopher Dock: Colonial Schoolmaster* (Scottsdale, Pa.: Herald Press, 1967). The fate of Enoch Brown is from Wickersham, p. 109. Several sources remove it from pure legend. Our information on the schools and school masters of Dedham is from Carlos Slafter, *A Record of Education: The Schools and Teachers of Dedham, 1644–1904* (Dedham, Mass.: Dedham Transcript, 1905) ". . . troubling the master" ". . . coxcombs, chimney sweepers" quoted in Page Smith, *John Adams* (Garden City, N.Y.: Doubleday, 1962), p. 25. ". . . came by it" is from Devereux Jarratt, "Autobiography, 1732–63," ed. by Douglas Adair, *William and Mary Quarterly*, 3rd ser., 9 (1952), p. 367. Robertson's accounts were printed in part as "Donald Robertson's School," *Virginia Magazine of History and Biography*, XXIII (1935), pp. 194–98, 288–92; XXIV (1926), pp. 141–48, 232–36; XXV (1927), pp. 55–56. One of the most interesting documents in the history of education in Virginia in the 1700s is *The Journal of John Harrower*, Edward Miles Riley, ed. (Williamsburg, Va.: Colonial Williamsburg, 1963). ". . . know the letters"; *ibid.*, p. 42. *Journals & Letters of Philip Vickers Fithian*, ed. by Hunter Dickinson Farish (Charlottesville, Va.: U. of Va., 1957) is as interesting. ". . . man in Virginia"; *ibid.*, p. 26. Boucher left an autobiography, *Reminiscences of an American Loyalist* (Boston: Houghton Mifflin, 1925). A recent biography, Anne Y. Zimmer, *Jonathan Boucher: Loyalist in Exile* (Detroit: Wayne State, 1978) adds little for our purposes. Carl Bridenbaugh, *The Colonial Craftsman* (Chicago: U. Chicago, 1971) is a good source. The relatively recent biography of Benezet is George S. Brookes, *Friend Anthony Benezet* (Philadelphia: U. of Pennsylvania, 1937).

For Franklin's papers on the academy, see Albert Henry Smith, ed., *The Writ-*

ings of Benjamin Franklin (New York: Macmillan, 1904–1907), III, pp. 395–421. "... they are intended": *ibid.*, p. 404. "... part of learning": *ibid.* "... useful practical knowledge": James Maury, "A Dissertation on Education in the form of a letter from James Maury to Robert Jackson, July 17, 1762," ed. by Helen Duprey Bullock, *Albemarle County [Va.] Historical Society Bulletin*, II (1941–42), p. 47. Dove was the subject of a biographical sketch, Joseph Jackson, "A Philadelphia Schoolmaster of the Eighteenth Century," *Pennsylvania Magazine of History and Biography*, XXXV (1911), pp. 315–32. "... upon his prey": Dove's contemporary, *ibid.*, p. 332. The by-now classical source for information on the development of the colleges is Frederick Rudolph, *The American University and College* (New York: Random House, 1962), which, however, deals briefly, pp. 3–22, with the pre-Revolutionary colleges.

John Lovell appears in Clifford K. Shipton, ed., *Sibley's Harvard Graduates: Biographical Sketches. . .* (Boston: Mass. Historical Society, 1968), vol. viii, pp. 31–48. Other details are in James Speare Loring, *Hundred Boston Orators. . .* (Boston: Jewett, 1852), pp. 29–33. His estate inventory, dated 1781, is the better indicator of the time of his death. Lovell's estate inventory is in the office of the Registrar of Probate, Halifax County, Nova Scotia. James Lovell appears in Shipton, vol. xiv (1968), pp. 31–48, and in Loring, pp. 32–37. "... china punch bowls," "... tea kettle (old)" are from John Lovell's estate inventory.

PART TWO:
AGE OF THE COMMON MAN

Readings: Although many details are inaccurate, John Bach McMaster, *A History of the People of the United States* (New York: Appleton, 1883), Vol. I, pp. 1–102, catches the feeling of the times admirably. It served as one of the exemplars for this book. Ulysses Prentiss Hedrick, *A History of Agriculture in the State of New York* (n.p.: New York State Agricultural Society, 1933) is in part informative about early farming and transportation. For a concise general account, see Samuel Eliot Morison, *et al.*, *The Growth of the American Republic*, Vol. I. George Rogers Taylor, *The Transportation Revolution, 1815-1860*, Vol. IV: *The Economic History of the United States* (New York: Harper & Row, 1951) describes the antecedents of industrialization. Maxine Seller, *To Seek America* (n.p.: Ozer, 1977), pp. 58–197, describes immigrants and immigration and this and subsequent periods.

Concerning education somewhat more narrowly, the best single treatment, though not reaching the excellence of the earlier volume, is Lawrence A. Cremin, *American Education: The National Experience: 1783-1876* (New York: Harper & Row, 1980). Michael B. Katz, *Class, Bureaucracy, and Schools*, 2nd ed. (New York: Praeger, 1975) is an effective and influential "revisionist" statement. As an example of academy education at its best, Julia Ann Hieronymous Tevis, *Sixty Years in a School-Room: An Autobiography. . .* (Cincinnati: Western Methodist, 1878) is informative. For parallel treatments, see Davis L. Tyack, *The One Best System*, (Cambridge: Harvard, 1974) pp. 13–125, and Robert L. Church and Michael W. Sedlak, *Education in the United States* (New York: Free Press, 1976), pp. 3–113, and Davis Madsen, *Early National Education: 1776-1830*, Studies in the History of American Education Series (New York: Wiley, 1974).

In fiction, Washington Irving, *The Legend of Sleepy Hollow* (many editions) is still a telling satire. D[aniel] P. Thompson, *Locke Amsden; or the Schoolmaster, a Tale* (Boston: Mussey, 1847, and later editions), although long out of print, was popular in its day, portraying the common school teacher as hero, the academy master as villain. Edward Eggleston, *The Hoosier Schoolmaster* (several editions), although not written until later, evokes earlier teaching and schooling experience. Ross Ranklin Lockridge, *Raintree County* (Boston: Houghton Mifflin, 1948) has a portrait of an academy master and students on the eve on the Civil War.

Notes: The Corliss engine was famous in its day. One convenient description is James D. McCabe, *The Illustrated History of the Centennial Exposition*, a Collectors Reprint (Philadelphia: National, 1976). The Exhibition is described at length there. Our more general source is Daniel J. Boorstin, *The Americans: The National Experience* (New York: Random House, 1965). An unpublished statistical analysis by Richard A. Zeller, Bowling Green University, shows that the inland port cities grew in a highly coherent collective pattern. Information on immigrants is from Seller, *To Seek America*. Economic and technological growth are described in Stuart Burchey, *The Roots of American Economic Growth* (New York: Harper & Row, 1968), pp. 141-215. More specifically, these were informative: Zadok Cramer, *The Navigator, Containing Directions for Navigating the Monongehela, Ohio, and Mississippi Rivers . . .* (Pittsburgh, 1808, many later editions). Most of the 1814 edition was reprinted in Ethel C. Leahy, *Who's Who on the Ohio River* (Cincinnati: author, 1931). Carter Goodrich *et al., Canals and the American Economic Development* (New York: Columbia U. Press, 1961) was informative, as was Albert Fishlow, *American Railroads and the Transformation of the Antebellum Economy* (Cambridge: Harvard, 1965). Joseph A. Durrenberger, *Turnpikes* (Valdosta, Ga.: Southern Printing, 1931) was less satisfactory because the data available to him were more limited. For this and the following sections, Edward C. Kirtland, *A History of American Economic Life*, 4th ed. (New York: Appleton Century Crofts, 1969) was useful as part of the general background. ". . . will be heard": William Lloyd Garrison, *The Liberator*, Jan. 1, 1831, quoted in Morison *et al., Growth of the American Republic*, Vol. 1, pp. 500-501.

CHAPTER THREE:
SCHOOLING IN THE NEW REPUBLIC

The best single source on history of education for Part Two is Lawrence A. Cremin, *American Education: The National Experience, 1783-1876* (New York: Harper & Row, 1980).

John Davis, *Travels . . . in the United States* (1803, repr. New York: Holt, 1909) is partly description, partly unflattering satire. Abigail Mason's letters, ed. by Bessie M. Henry, appeared as "A Yanke Schoolmistress Discovers Virginia," *Essex Institute Historical Collections*, CI (1965), pp. 121-32. ". . . and domestic economy": Noah Webster, Jr., *American Spelling Book* (Boston: John West, 1810) p. vi.

The most detailed biography of Thomas Jefferson is Dumas Malone, *Jefferson and His Times* (Boston: Little, Brown, 1948-1981, 6 vols.) Jefferson's ideas on education are collected in Gordon C. Lee, ed., *Crusade Against Ignorance: Thomas Jefferson on Education* (New York: Teachers College, Columbia U., 1962). ". . . and liberal mind": *ibid.*, p. xx. ". . . and Mary College": *ibid.*, p. xxx.

The role of education in the philosophies of various theorists is discussed by David Tyack, "Forming the National Character," *Harvard Educational Review*, 26 (1966), pp. 29-41; and Jonathan Messerli, "The Columbian Complex: The Impulse to National Consolidation," *History of Education Quarterly*, 7 (1967), pp. 417-31. For reference to original sources on educational theorists during the republican period, see Frederick Rudolph, ed., *Essays on Education in the Early Republic* (Cambridge: Harvard, 1965). Essays by Webster, Rush, Coram, and others are included. ". . . of our country", ". . . of a court": Rush, *ibid.*, pp. xxx, xxi. On the acquisition of national political symbols, see Provenzo, "Education and the Iconography of the Republic." *Teachers College Record*, Vol. 84, no. 2, Winter 1982.

Owen's educational ideas are discussed in John F. C. Harrison, *Quest for the New Moral World: Robert Owen & the Owenites in Britain and America* (New York: Scribner's, 1969), and A. I. Morton, *The Life and Ideas of Robert Owen* (New York: International, 1969). The most complete collection of Owen's ideas on education are included in Harold Silver's *English Education and the Radicals, 1780-1850* (London: Routledge & Kegan Paul, 1978). ". . . forces of nature": reprinted in Cohen, vol. 2, p. 823. Neef's and Maclure's educational ideas are discussed in detail in Gerald Gutek, *Joseph Neff: The Americanization of Pestalozzianism* (University: U. of Alabama, 1978). ". . . ending in death": Morton, p. 127.

One of the few available accounts of the Sunday schools is Edwin Wilbur Rice, *The Sunday-School Movement (1780-1917) and the American Sunday School Union* (Philadelphia: American Sunday School Union, 1917). Our most important source for biographical information on Andrew Bell is *Dictionary of National Biography* (London: Oxford, 1959-60), Leslie Stephen and Sidney Lee, eds., Vol. II, pp. 149-52. The best biography of Lancaster is David Salmon, *Joseph Lancaster* (London: Longmans, Green, 1904). J. F. Reigart, *The Lancastrian System of Instruction in the Schools of New York City*, Teachers College Contributions to Education No. 81 (New York: Teachers College, Columbia University, 1916) is the best detailed study of the monitorial system in the United States. More recently, Carl F. Kaestle, *Joseph Lancaster and the Monitorial School Movement: A Documentary History* (New York: Teachers College, Columbia University, 1973) is valuable for its documents and for its introductory essay. John M. Griscom, a monitorial school enthusiast who probably deserves more attention than he gets, wrote an autobiography, *Memoirs. . .* (New York: Carter, 1859). ". . . of comfortable fortune" is quoted in Robert H. Potter, *The Stream of American Education* (New York: American, 1967), pp. 143-44. ". . . of his punishment" is from Nathan Hedges, "New Jersey Educational Biography," *American Journal of Education*, XVI (1866), p. 738.

The least unsatisfactory history of American schoolbooks is probably Charles Carpenter, *History of American Schoolbooks* (Philadelphia: U. of Pennsylvania, 1963). Ruth Miller Elson, *Guardians of Tradition: American Schoolbooks in the Nineteenth Century*, (Omaha: U. Nebraska, 1964) struck us as simplistic. ". . . are they called?": Noah Webster, *American Spelling Book* (Concord, N.H.: Jacob Perkins, 1817), p. 56. ". . . more severe manner": *ibid.*, p. 52. ". . . virtue and morality": *Columbian Reader* (Cooperstown, N.Y.: H. & E. Phinney, 1815), p. 3. ". . . thy splendors unfold": Caleb Bingham, *American Reader* (Boston: Manning & Loring, 1799), p. 43. ". . . to his worth" is from *American Biographical and Historical Dictionary*, quoted in Asa Lyman, *American Reader* (Portland, Me.: Author, 1811), p. 65. ". . . name of Americans": Jedidiah Morse, *Geography Made Easy. . .* (Boston: Thomas and Andrews, 1798), p. 97. ". . . years and upwards" and ". . . people in Charlestown": Jedidiah Morse, *Universal American Geography* (Charlestown, Mass.: Lincoln & Edmands, etc., 1819), vol. 1, pp. 285, 473. ". . . the latter severe": Josiah Quincy, *American Journal of Education*, XIII (1863), p. 740.

Miss Pierce's Academy is documented at length in Emily Noyes Vanderpol, *Chronicles of a Pioneer School* (Cambridge: University Press, 1903) and in her subsequent books. ". . . constituted the whole furniture" is by Catherine Beecher, quoted in Vanderpol, p. 79. ". . . in the Scriptures?" and ". . . of immortal beings" *ibid.*, pp. 230-31, 305, 318. ". . . youth was passed": S. H. Dickinson, *Addresses Delivered Before the New England Society in Charleston, S.C.* (Charleston, S.C.: Russell, 1855) quoted in John Hope Franklin, *A Southern Odyssey* (Baton Rouge, La.: State, 1976), pp. 70-71.

CHAPTER FOUR:
THE RISE OF THE COMMON SCHOOLS

Lawrence A. Cremin, *The American Common School, an Historic Conception* (New York: Teachers College, Columbia University, 1951) together with his more recent *American Education: The National Experience, 1783-1876* (New York: Harper & Row, 1980) provide an excellent overview of the Common School Movement and its history. Also useful is Frederick M. Binder's *The Age of the Common School, 1830-65* (New York: Wiley, 1974). Excellent primary sources are included in Rush Welter, ed., *American Writings on Popular Education: The Nineteenth Century* (Indianapolis: Bobbs-Merrill, 1971).

The relationship of economic development and the growth of the Common Schools is discussed at length in a number of studies. An interesting pioneer work is Frank Carlton's *Economic Influences upon Educational Progress in the United States, 1820-1850*. First published in 1908, it was reissued in the "Classics in Education" Series (New York: Teachers College, Columbia U., 1965). Jay M. Pawa, "Workingmen and Free Schools in the Nineteenth Century: A Comment on the Labor Education Thesis," *History of Education Quarterly*, 11 (1971), pp. 287-302, specifically challenges Carlton's argument that labor played a significant role in the establishment of the common schools. Michael B. Katz's *The Irony of Early School Reform: Educational Innovation in Mid-Nineteenth Century Massachusetts* (Cambridge: Harvard, 1968), a key work in the revisionist movement in educational history, argues that the reform movement in Massachusetts was largely supported by—and for the benefit of—the middle class rather than labor. ". . . a reluctant community": *ibid.*, p. 218.

Recent studies of the connection between education and economic expansion include Maris Vinovskis's "Horace Mann on the Economic Productivity of Education," *New England Quarterly*, XLIII (1970), pp. 550-71. Data on the number of individuals attending the Common Schools is provided by Albert Fishlow, "The American Common School Revival: Fact or Fancy?" in Henry Rosovsky, ed., *Industrialization in Two Systems* (New York: Wiley, 1966), and Maris Vinovskis, "Trends in Massachusetts Education, 1826-1860," *History of Education Quarterly*, XII, (1972), pp. 501-30.

Arguments against the Common Schools Movement as a force promoting greater equality in American culture can be found in Samuel Bowles and Herbert Gintis, *Schooling in Capitalist America* (New York: Colophon Books, 1976). In particular see pages 23-29 and 164-79.

The history of the United States Office of Education is described in Donald R. Warren's *To Enforce Education* (Detroit: Wayne State, 1974). ". . . republic's first days": *ibid.*, p. 20.

The differences in role expectations for teachers and masters follows the logic of Peter L. Berger and Thomas Luckman, *The Social Construction of Reality* (Garden City, N.Y.: Doubleday, 1967) ". . . in this respect": quoted in Willard S. Elsbree, *The American Teacher* (New York: American, 1939), p. 300.

William Manning's "The Key to Libberty," ed. by Samuel Eliot Morison, first appeared in print in *William and Mary Quarterly*, 3rd ser., XIII (1956), pp. 202-54. It has been reprinted in part several times. ". . . lucrative as possible": *ibid.*, p. 218. ". . . to hold plow": *ibid.*, p. 232.

Our discussion of the American child draws heavily on Bernard Wishy's *The Child and the Republic* (Philadelphia: University of Pennsylvania, 1972), and Robert Sunled's "Early Nineteenth-Century American Literature on Child Rearing," in Margaret Mead and Martha Wolfenstein, eds., *Childhood in Contemporary Cultures* (Chicago: University of Chicago, 1955), pp. 150-67. English views of

American childhood are interestingly summarized in Richard L. Rapson's "The American Child as Seen by British Travelers, 1845–1935," *American Quarterly*, XVII (1965), pp. 520–34. The classic analysis of American society during this period by a European visitor is found in Alexis de Tocqueville's *Democracy in America* (1835), trans. Henry Reeve, ed. Phillips Bradley, (New York: Knopf, 1945, 2 vols.) Selections from de Tocqueville and Lydia Maria Child's *The Mother's Book* (1835), and Harriet Martineau's work *Society in America* (1837) are included in Robert H. Bremer *et al.*, *Children & Youth in America: A Documentary History*, Vol. 1, 1600–1865. ". . . incontestable superiority warrents": *Democracy in America* (1835), reprinted in Bremer *et al.*, *Children & Youth in America*, Vol. 1, p. 347. ". . . boy's resolute disobedience": *A Diary in America* (1839), quoted by Bremer *et al.*, *Children & Youth in America*, Vol. 1, p. 344. A useful general bibliography on psychohistory that encompasses the history of childhood can be found in Faye Sinofsky *et al.*, "A Bibliography of Psychohistory," *History of Childhood Quarterly*, 2, (1975), pp. 517–62. ". . . the sexual instinct": W. Dewees, *A Treatise on the Physical and Medical Treatment of Children* (Philadelphia: Carey and Lea, 1826), p. 251. ". . . the only good": Lydia Maria Child, *The Mother's Book* (1831), reprinted in Bremer *et al.*, *Children & Youth in America*, Vol. 1, p. 353. There are a number of interesting fictional and eyewitness accounts of district schools during the middle of the nineteenth century.

The South's failure to promote common schools prior to the Civil War is discussed by Irving Gershenberg, "Southern Values and Public Education," *History of Education Quarterly*, X, (1970). James G. Carter's *Essays Upon Popular Education* (Boston: Bowles and Dearborn, 1826; repr. Arno Press, 1970). ". . . become Anglo-Americans": *Transactions of the Fifth Meeting of the Western Literary Institute and College of Professional Teachers* (1936), reprinted in Cohen, *Education in the United States*, Vol. 2, p. 994.

Discussion of the workingman's movement in education is included in Rush Welter, *Popular Education and Democratic Thought in America* (New York: Columbia U., 1962). Sections from *The Working Man's Manual* (1831) are reprinted in Cohen, *Education in the United States*, Vol. 2, pp. 1054–56. ". . . part of government": *ibid.*, p. 1055.

The most convenient introduction to Horace Mann and his work is Lawrence A. Cremin, ed., *The Republic and the School: Horace Mann and the Education of Free Men* (New York: Teachers College, Columbia University, 1951). Additional selections of Mann's writings are included in Louis Filler, ed., *Horace Mann on the Crisis in Education* (Antioch, Ohio: Antioch, 1965). For our interpretation of Mann's life and work we have depended upon the excellent introductory essay by Lawrence Cremin included in *The Republic and the School*, and more specifically on Johnathan Messerli's *Horace Mann: A Biography* (New York: Knopf, 1972). ". . . of amassing property": *Fifth Annual Report* (1842), quoted by Bowles and Gintis, *Schooling in Capitalist America*, p. 164. ". . . distinctions in society": *Twelfth Annual Report* (1848), reprinted in Cremin, *The Republic and the School*, p. 87. ". . . and resistlessly onward": *ibid.*, p. 9.

Our discussion of the importance of phrenology to Horace Mann is based upon Cremin's discussion of the subject in the introduction to *The Republic and the School* and more specifically on John D. Davies, *Phrenology: Fad and Science* (New Haven: Yale, 1955). Also of interest, see Allen S. Horlick, "Phrenology and the Social Education of Young Men," *History of Education Quarterly*, XI (1971), pp. 23–38. ". . . affection is prone": *Seventh Annual Report* (1844), reprinted in Cohen, vol. 2, pp. 1091–92. ". . . fact and form": "Address, August 19, 1846," reprinted in Cohen, vol. 3, p. 1335. ". . . from grown men": *Ninth Annual Report*

(1845), reprinted in Cremin, ed., *The Republic and the School: Horace Mann on the Education of Free Men*, p. 58. ". . . of the state": *Twelfth Annual Report* (1848), *ibid.*, p. 80.

A modern biography of Henry Barnard is needed. Early works on Barnard include Will S. Monroe, *The Educational Labors of Henry Barnard* (Syracuse: C. W. Bardeen, 1893); and Bernard C. Steiner, *Life of Henry Barnard* (Washington, D.C.: Department of the Interior, Bureau of Education, Bulletin No. 8, 1919). For our interpretation of Barnard we have depended upon the documents and introductory essay in Vincent P. Lannie's *Henry Barnard: American Educator* (New York: Teachers College, Columbia U., 1974). Also of use was the chapter on Barnard in Merle Curti, *The Social Ideas of American Educators* (New York: Scribner's, 1935). Most major libraries have bound or microfilm versions of Barnard's *American Journal of Education*. Among the richest sources on the history of American education, Barnard's journal is well worth careful perusal. A reprint of Barnard's *School Architecture* edited by Jean and Robert McClintock is available in the "Classics in Education" series (New York: Teachers College, Columbia U., 1970). ". . . their own grounds": *Connecticut Common School Journal* (August 1839), quoted by Rush Welter, *American Writings on Popular Education*, p. 70.

One biographical sketch of Partridge is Edward J. Durnall, "Alden P. Partridge," in John F. Ohles, ed. *Biographical Dictionary of American Educators* (Westport, Conn.: Greenwood, 1978), vol. ii, pp. 997–99. There is a record of a post-West Point march enjoyed by all in Alden Partridge, *A Record of a Journey Made by the Corps of Cadets of the American Literary, Scientific, and Military Academy. . . June 6, 1822* (Concord [N.H.?]: Hill & Morley, 1822). Henry L. Burr, *Education in the Early Navy* (Philadelphia: n.p., 1939) leaves much to be desired. The voyage of the *U.S.F. Potomac* is described in R. N. Reynolds, *Voyage. . .* (New York: Harper & Brothers, 1835).

There is considerable material on Ticknor, Bancroft and Cogswell, and Round Hill. Our source is James McLachlan, *American Boarding Schools: A Historical Study* (New York: Scribner's, 1970), pp. 71–101. Bruce Catton, *Waiting for the Morning Train: An American Boyhood* (Garden City, N.Y.: Doubleday, 1972) is strongly evocative.

Harriet Webster Marr, *The Old New England Academies* (New York: Comet, 1959) supplied information on Gardiner Academy and on Grant's former students. Orange Park is from a brief account in Arthur O. White, *One Hundred Years of State Leadership in Florida Public-Education* (Tallahassee: U. Florida, 1979), pp. 29–30. Coleman's log cabin academy appears in William Gordon McCabe, *Virginia Schools Before and After the Revolution . . .* (Charlottesville, Va.: Chronical Steam [sic], 1890). Fairfield Academy appears in an unpublished paper by Celia Erlich, "The Education of Asa Gray," SUNYAB. Enrollment figures are from Edgar W. Knight, *The Academy Movement in the South* (no publication data available) and Walter John Gifford, *Historical Development of the New York State High School System* (Albany: Lyon, 1922).

CHAPTER FIVE:
THE GROWTH OF THE COMMON SCHOOLS

For general histories of high schools, see Edward A. Krug, *The Shaping of the American High School 1880-1920* (New York: Harper & Row, 1964) and *The Shaping of the American High School 1920-1941* (Madison: University of Wisconsin, 1972); Krug's views were unfailingly positive. Elmer Ellsworth Brown,

Making of Our Middle Schools (New York: Longmans, Green, 1902 and later editions) is still useful.

". . . tuition and taxes": David Nassau, *Schooled to Order* (New York: Oxford, 1979), p. 83.

Most of the details concerning the Chicago public schools are from Mary J. Herrick, *The Chicago Schools: A Social and Political History* (Beverly Hills, Cal.: Sage, 1971). Chappell's teaching was briefly recounted in Mary H. Porter, *Eliza Chappell Porter: A Memoir* (Chicago: Revell, 1892). Joan K. Smith, *Ella Flagg Young: Portrait of a Leader* (Ames, Ia.: Educational Studies, 1979) is an account of Young's career. Information on the Buffalo schools is primarily from John G. Ramsay, "From Self-Educating Boosters to Stewards of Culture: Buffalo's Friends of Education," dissertation, State U. of N.Y. of Buffalo, 1984. Jack K. Campbell, *Colonel Francis W. Parker, the Children's Crusader* (New York: Teachers College, Columbia U., 1967) is the best source of information on Parker.

There is an almost embarrassing mass of material on *McGuffey's* (or *McGuffey*; both spellings were used), either saccharine sweet or acerbic. The best source is Stanley W. Lindberg, *The Annotated McGuffey: Selections. . .* (New York: Van Nostrand Reinhold, 1976).

". . . overseer, the superintendent": J. L. Pickard, *School Supervision* (New York: Appleton, 1890), pp. 1–2. ". . . and the poor": John Griscom, *A Year in Europe . . . In 1818 and 1819* (New York: Collins, 1923), quoted in McLachlin, p. 58. McLachlin, *Passim*, provided information about von Fellenberg's poor school. The American "manual academies" are described in Knight, *Academy Movement*; the Hawaiian ones, *passim*, in Hiram Bingham, *A Residence of Twenty-one Years in the Sandwich Islands* (Hartford, Conn.: Hezekiah Huntington, 1848). Goodale's "industrial school" for the Sioux was described by her in *Sister to the Sioux: The Memoirs of Elaine Goodale Eastman, 1885–91*, ed. by Kay Graber (Lincoln: U. Nebraska, 1978), pp. 30 ff.

The most nearly complete history of Catholic education in the United States is Harold A. Buetow, *Of Singular Benefit: The Story of U.S. Catholic Education* (New York: Macmillan, 1970). An excellent documentary source is Neil G. McCluskey, ed., *Catholic Education in America* (New York: Teachers College, Columbia U., 1964). ". . . the social order": "Report of the First Plenary Council of Baltimore," reprinted in Cohen, *Education in the United States*, Vol. 2, p. 1162.

The best source on Nativism and one of which we have made extensive use is Roy Allen Billington, *The Protestant Crusade, 1800–1860* (New York: Macmillan, 1938). A discussion of anti-Catholic sentiments in textbooks can be found in Marie Lenore Fell, *The Foundations of Nativism in American Textbooks* (Washington, D.C.: Catholic University of America, 1941).

The work of Bishop Hughes in New York is discussed in both Billington's *The Protestant Crusade* and in Diane Ravitch, *The Great School Wars* (New York: Basic Books, 1974) pp. 46–76. ". . . us with error": McCluskey, *Catholic Education in America*, p. 61. For background on the Protestant response to the Catholics' demands for school support in New York City, see Provenzo, "Thomas Nast and the Church/State Controversy in Education (1870–1876)," *Educational Studies* Vol. 12, no. 4, Winter 1981–1982, pp. 359–379.

Our analysis of black education has depended heavily on Henry Allen Bullock's *A History of Negro Education in the South: From 1619 to the Present* (Cambridge: Harvard, 1967). ". . . than twelve months": *A New Digest of the Statute Laws of Louisiana* (1844), reprinted in Cohen, *ibid.*, p. 1621.

Crandall's school in Canterbury has been a matter of intense and lasting interest. She has been portrayed as near-martyr and as agent provocateur. Our discussion is based on Leon Litwak, *North of Slavery: The Negro in the Free States, 1790-1860* (Chicago: U. Chicago, 1961).

CHAPTER SIX:
SCHOOLING AND INDUSTRIALIZATION

Our discussion of Buisson is drawn from M. Ferdinand Buisson, *Rapport Sur l'instruction primaire a l'exposition univierselle de Philadelphia en 1876* (Paris: Imprimiree Nationale, 1878). Sections of this report were translated and reprinted as "American Education as Described by the French Commissioner to the International Exposition of 1876," *Circular of Information #5-1879, Bureau of Education* (Washington, D.C.: Government Printing Office, 1879). ". . . returned a hundredfold": *ibid.*, pp. 12-13.

Our discussion of the Land Grant College Act is largely based upon Frederick Rudolph's *The American College and University: A History* (New York: Vintage Books, 1962). Other secondary sources on the Land Grant College Act include Edward D. Eddy's *Colleges for Our Land and Time: The Land Grant Idea in American Education* (New York: Harper & Row, 1957), and John H. Florer, "Major Issues in the Congressional Debate of the Morrill Act of 1863," *History of Education Quarterly*, 8, (1968), pp. 459-78.

The history of early art instruction and its relationship to industrialization needs to be more carefully examined. Our source for the subject is I. Edwards Clarke, *Industrial and High Art Education in the United States, Part I, Drawing in the Public Schools* (Washington, D.C.: Government Printing Office, 1885). ". . . from such accomplishments": *ibid.*, p. 49.

Background on early industrial education in the United States is included in Bernice Fisher's *Industrial Education: American Ideals and Institutions* (Madison, Wis.: U. Wisconsin, 1967), and Charles A. Bennett's *History of Manual and Industrial Education up to 1870* (Peoria, Ill.: Manual Arts Press, 1926). Lawrence A. Cremin's *The Transformation of the Schools: Progressivism in American Education, 1876-1957* (New York: Vintage, 1961) provides an excellent introduction to manual training and vocational training during the last quarter of the nineteenth century.

Our discussion of the Della Vos method and Calvin Woodward is based upon several sources. Historical background and documents are included in Charles A. Bennett's *History of Manual and Industrial Education, 1870 to 1917* (Peoria, Ill.: Manual Arts Press, 1937). ". . . trade became apparent": *ibid.*, p. 320. Background on Calvin Woodward and the Manual Training School is included in Charles Dye's "Calvin Woodward and Manual Training: The Man, The Idea and the School," *The Bulletin* (Missouri Historical Society), XXXII, (1976), pp. 75-98. Of particular interest as a source is Calvin M. Woodward's *The Manual Training School* (New York: Arno, 1969, reprint of 1887 edition). A useful documentary collection is Marvin Larzerson and Norton Grubb's *American Education and Vocationalism: A Documentary History* (New York: Teachers College, Columbia U., 1974). ". . . a new tool": *The Manual Training School* (1887), reprinted in Cohen, *Education in the United States*, Vol. 3, p. 1865. ". . . of intellectual improvement": "Manual vs. Technical Training," reprinted in Cohen, *ibid.*, p. 1871.

William Torrey Harris is briefly discussed by Cremin in *The Transformation of the Schools* (New York: Knopf, 1957, repr. Vintage, 1964). A general biography of Harris, which needs to be revised, is Kurt F. Leidecker's, *Yankee Teacher: The Life of William Torrey Harris* (New York: Philosophical Library, 1946).

Lazerson's ideas concerning Manual Training are discussed in *Origins of the Urban School: Public Education in Massachusetts, 1870-1915* (Cambridge: Harvard, 1971). For background on the conditions of child labor and juvenile reform see Joseph M. Hawes, *Children in Urban Society: Juvenile Delinquency in Nineteenth-Century America* (New York: Oxford, 1971), and Walter Trattner, *Crusade for the Children* (Chicago: Quadrangle Books, 1970). The history of the New York Association for Improving the Condition of the Poor can be found in Roy Lubove's *The Progressives and the Slums* (Pittsburgh: U. of Pittsburgh, 1962). ". . . so at home": *A New England Girlhood* (1889), reprinted in Bremer, *et al., Children & Youth in America*, Vol. I, p. 604. ". . . low-respecting community": *The Dangerous Classes of New York* (1880), reprinted in Bremer, et al., *ibid.*, p. 742. ". . . afterwards to fill": Enoch C. Wines and Theodore W. Dwight, "Report on the Prisons and Reformatories in the United States and Canada," (1867). Reprinted in Bremer, *ibid.*, p. 752. Durkheim's writings on education have been republished in recent years. See *Durkheim, Emile, Education and Sociology*, translated and with an introduction by Sherwood P. Fox (Glencoe, Ill.: Free Press, 1956).

The most complete treatment of the Lyceum Movement in America is found in Carl Bode, *The American Lyceum: Town Meeting of the Mind* (New York: Oxford, 1956).

Our interpretation of the history of libraries is drawn from the United States Bureau of Education's *Public Libraries in the United States* (Washington, D.C.: U.S. Government Printing Office, 1876), and Dee Carrison's *Apostles of Culture* (New York: Free Press, 1979). ". . . of public education"; United States Bureau of Education, *Public Libraries in the United States*, p. xi. ". . . to something better": *ibid.*, p. 410. For the early history of libraries in the United States also see Jesse H. Shera, *Foundation of the Public Library: The Origins of the Public Library Movement in New England, 1629-1855* (Chicago: U. Chicago, 1949), and Seymour C. Thompson, *Evolution of the American Public Library, 1653-1876* (Metuchen, N.J.: Scarecrow, 1952).

Several general histories have been helpful in our interpretation of the kindergarten movement in America, including Evelyn Weber's *The Kindergarten: Its Encounter with Educational Thought in America* (New York: Teachers College, Columbia U., 1969) and Elizabeth Dale Ross, *The Kindergarten Crusade: The Establishment of Preschool Education in the United States* (Athens, Ohio: Ohio University, 1976). The kindergarten movement and its relationship to industrialization is dealt with most thoroughly by Marvin Lazerson, *Origins of the Urban School: Public Education in Massachusetts, 1870-1915* (Cambridge: Harvard, 1971), and Marvin Lazerson, "Urban Reform and the Schools: Kindergartens in Massachusetts, 1870-1915," *History of Education Quarterly*, Vol. II (1971), pp. 115-42, and by Dominick Cavallo, "Kindergarten Pedagogy: A Review Essay," *History of Education Quarterly*, XVIII (1978), 365-68. ". . . use to create": Frank Lloyd Wright, *An Autobiography* (New York: Duell, Sloan and Pearce, 1943), p. 14. ". . . wanted to design": Frank Lloyd Wright, *A Testament* (New York: Brahmall House, 1957), p. 20. The impact of the Froebelian materials on Frank Lloyd Wright's work as an architect is discussed by Grant Carpenter Menson, *Frank Lloyd Wright to 1910* (New York: Reinhold, 1958), pp. 5-10. ". . . our Public schools": Letter to Susan Blow to William Torrey Harris, Manuscript Collection, Missouri Historical Society. ". . . as domestic markets": *Twenty First Annual Report, St. Louis Public Schools, 1876* (St. Louis, 1877), p. 11. ". . . place of society": *ibid.*, p. 81. ". . . citizens of them": "The Kindergarten: An Uplifting Social Influence in the Home and District," *NEA Proceedings* (1903), reprinted in Cohen, *Education in the United States*, Vol. 4, p. 2160.

PART THREE:
FROM FARM TO CITY TO SUBURB

Readings: The most respected foreign commentator on the United States in the later 1800s was James Lord Bryce. In *The American Commonwealth* (2 vol., New York: Macmillan, 1888. Abridged ed., New York: Putnam, 1959) he condemned American politics and politicians, admired some other aspects of American life. A short but insightful treatment of urbanization is Blake McKelvey's *The City in American History* (New York: Barnes & Noble, 1969). There are informative histories of many individual cities. Frederick Lewis Allen, *Only Yesterday* (New York: Harpers, 1931) catches effectively the surface details of life in the 1920s. Seller, *To Seek America*, pp. 104–219, describes the immigrants of the time and their institutions. Morison *et al.* provides a general historical background. Dee Brown, *The Year of the Century* (New York: Scribner's, 1976), describes the importance and Americans' spirit of the Centennial. An interesting pictorial treatment of the same subject is Lally Weymouth, *1876: The Way We Were* (New York: Vintage, 1976). A recent and to us most plausable theory concerning the sources and multiple goals of Progressivism is John David Hogan's in *Class and Reform: School and Society in Chicago, 1880–1930* (Philadelphia: U. of Pennsylvania, 1985).

The information on Buffalo's Polonia is from unpublished papers by Thomas A. Michalski. ". . . $1.50 a week": Maxine Seller, *To Seek America* (Philadelphia: Ozer, 1977). Seller is a good introduction to the history of immigrants.

As one deals with the more recent past, preparing a historical account becomes more like constructing a mosaic, of fitting together disparate works, and disparate ways of life. There are many interesting details in Mark Sullivan's rambling *Our Times* (New York: Scribner's, 1926–35). A few others come from Furnas. Ray Ginger, *Age of Excess: United States from 1877 to 1914* (New York: Macmillan, 1965) suggests a general view. Edward C. Kirkland, *A History of American Economic Life* (New York: Appleton-Century-Croft, 1969), provided information on economic change and growth. Ray Ginger, *Six Days or Forever?* (repr. Chicago: Quadrangle, 1969) is not only a vivid account of the Scopes "monkey" trial, but provides backgrounds on the importance of Darwinism and fundamentalism in early twentieth century thought. The conventional view of social Darwinism in the thought of American capitalists is explored by Robert C. Bannister in *Social Darwinism: Science and Myth in Anglo-American Social Thought* (Philadelphia: Temple, 1979). Daniel J. Kelves, *The Physicists: The History of a Scientific Community in Modern America* (New York: Knopg, 1978) is in most ways exemplary and a valuable guide in the development of science.

For feelings and concerns during the Depression, 1929–1939, perhaps the most readable source is Frederick Lewis Allen, *Since Yesterday* (New York: Harper & Row, 1940, 1972). Allen's *The Big Change: America Transforms Itself* (New York: Simon & Schuster, 1952) summarizes his earlier books, but may be most interesting as implying the ways in which America saw itself in the early 1950s. William Manchester, *The Glory and the Dream: A Narrative History of America, 1932–1972* (Boston: Little, Brown, 1973, 1974) is a colorful account of the Depression and subsequent eras and has provided us with a few details. For an informal but informative history, see Eric F. Goldman, *The Crucial Decade and After: America, 1945–1960* (New York: Vintage, 1960). John Brooks, *The Fate of the Edsel and Other Business Ventures* (New York: Harper & Row, 1963) is the most engaging of several books by business journalists. Of social and sociological treatments, perhaps the most interesting are Vance Packard, *The Status Seekers*

(New York: D. McKay, 1959); William H. Whyte, *The Organization Man* (New York: Simon & Schuster, 1956); and C. Wright Mills, *White Collar: The American Middle Class* (New York: Oxford, 1951).

Some of the most lasting impressions of the Depression, World War II, and after are from fiction. John Steinbeck, *Grapes of Wrath* (several editions), captures the feel of rural poverty. Among novels of World War II, Normal Mailer, *The Naked and the Dead* (New York: Rinehart, 1948), about infantry soldiers in the Pacific theater, and Herman Wouk, *Caine Mutiny* (several editions), an account of naval officers aboard a destroyer, were popular in their time and perhaps representative. Sloan Wilson, *The Man in the Gray Flannel Suit* (New York: Simon & Schuster, 1955) seemed to catch a mood of its time.

The third volume of Lawrence A. Cremin's history, *American Education: The Metropolitan Experience, 1876--1980* (New York: Harper & Row, 1988), had not appeared when this revision was prepared. It is informative on many aspects of its period. His earlier *Transformation of the Schools*, was a school-limited account of Progressivism broadly defined and naturally does not include the most recent history. It has been the most important conceptualization of history of American education in the early twentieth century. The most important and most interesting monograph on efficiency in the schools is Raymond E. Callahan, *Education and the Cult of Efficiency* (Chicago: U. of Chicago, 1962). In other texts, see Robert L. Church and Michael W. Sedlak, *Education in the United States* (New York; Free Press, 1976), pp. 251-97, and David B. Tyack, *The One Best System* (Cambridge, Mass.: Harvard, 1974), pp. 126-268.

CHAPTER SEVEN:
PROGRESSIVE REFORM

Social Darwinism is discussed in a number of sources. Richard Hofstader's *Social Darwinism in American Thought* (Philadelphia: U. of Pennsylvania, 1945) has come under increasing criticism in recent years. Our interpretation has drawn heavily from Robert C. Bannister, *Social Darwinism*.

The myth of the "self-made man" is discussed in Irvin G. Wyllie *The Self-Made Man in America* (New Brunswick, N.J.: Rutgers, 1954 repr. New York: Free Press, 1966) and John G. Cawelti's *Apostle of the Self-Made Man* (Chicago: U. of Chicago, 1965). Background on Lester F. Ward and William Graham Sumner can be found in Clifford H. Scott, *Lester Frank Ward* (Boston: Twayne Publishers, 1976), and Robert G. McGloskey, *American Conservatism in the Age of Enterprise; a Study of William Graham Sumner, Stephen J. Field, and Andrew Carnegie* (Cambridge: Harvard, 1951).

Our discussion of the Settlement House Movement in the United States is based upon Cremin's *Transformation of the Schools* and Allen F. Davis's *Spearheads for Reform: The Social Settlements and the Progressive Movement, 1890-1914* (New York: Oxford, 1967). ". . . last analysis education": Cremin, *Transformation of the Schools*, p. 59.

For background on the origins of Jane Addams's idea as a reformer see Franklin Parker's "Jane Addams—Lady Who Cared," *Tradition*, 4 (1961), pp. 43–47. Also see John P. Rousmanière, "Cultural Hybrid in the Slums: The College Woman and the Settlement House, 1889-94," *American Quarterly*, 22, (1970), pp. 45–66. Biographical sources on Addams include Allen Freeman Davis's *American Heroine: The Life and Legend of Jane Addams* (New York: Oxford, 1973). Christopher Lasch's *The New Radicalism in America (1889-1963): The Intellectual As A Social Type* (New York: Vintage Books, 1965), combined with his anthology

The Social Thought of Jane Addams (Indianapolis: Bobbs-Merrill, 1965) are an excellent introduction to Addams and her ideas. A critical and controversial interpretation of Addams is Paul Violas's "Jane Addams and the New Liberalism," in Clarence Karier *et al., Roots of Crisis* (Chicago: Rand McNally, 1973), pp. 66–83.

Our interpretation of Jacob Riis is based upon Alexander Alland's *Jacob A. Riis: Photographer and Citizen* (New York: Aperture, 1974) and James B. Lane's *Jacob A. Riis and the American City* (New York: Kennikat Press, 1974). Several reprints of Riis's work are particularly useful. See, for example, Jacob A. Riis *The Making of an American* (New York: Macmillan, 1970), edited by Jacob Riis Owre and Jacob Riis, *How the Other Half Lives* (Repr. New York: Dover Books, 1971). A limited but useful discussion of Riis is included in Sol Cohen's *Progressives and Urban Reform* (New York: Teachers College, Columbia U., 1964). ". . . do not come": Jacob Riis, "The Making of Thieves in New York," *The Century*, Vol. XLIX (November 1894), pp. 115–16. ". . . one educational thought": Jacob A. Riis, *The Peril and Preservation of the Home* (Philadelphia: George W. Jacobs and Co., 1903), p. 77.

Our interpretation of Rice is drawn in part from Cremin, *The Transformation of the School*. ". . . sensibilities, no soul": *The Public School System in the United States*, reprinted in Cohen, *Education in the United States*, Vol. 3, p. 1893. Our interpretation of the work of the Committee of Ten is based upon Krug's *The Shaping of the American High School: 1880–1920*. The interpretation of the Committee of Fifteen is primarily that of Button, "Committee of Fifteen," *History of Education Quarterly*, V (1965), pp. 253–63. The Herbartian Movement in Europe and America is most thoroughly dealt with in Harold Dunekill, *Herbart and Education* (New York: Random House, 1969) and *Herbart and Herbartianism: An Educational Ghost Story* (Chicago: U. Chicago, 1970).

The foremost biography of G. Stanley Hall is Dorothy Ross's, *G. Stanley Hall: The Psychologist as Prophet* (Chicago: U. Chicago, 1972). Selections of Hall's work appear in Charles E. Strickland and Charles Burgess, eds., *Health, Growth, and Heredity: G. Stanley Hall on Natural Education* (New York: Teachers College, Columbia, 1965). Hall's autobiography, *Life and Confessions of a Psychologist* (New York: Appleton, 1925) is in some ways disarmingly frank and revealing. ". . . twentieth century totalitarianism": Strickland and Burgess, introduction, pp. 25–26.

The sources available on Dewey are innumerable. An excellent starting point is George Dykhuizen's biography, *The Life and Mind of John Dewey* (Carbondale, Ill: Southern Illinois U., 1973). Dewey's collected works are being republished by Southern Illinois U. Our description of Dewey's work at the Laboratory School is based upon Arthur Wirth, *John Dewey as Educator: His Design for Work in Education (1894–1904)* (New York: John Wiley and Sons, 1966); Katherine C. Mayhew and Anna C. Edward, *The Dewey School* (New York: Appleton Century Crofts, 1936); and Provenzo, "History as Experiment: The Role of the Laboratory School in the Development of John Dewey's Philosophy of History," *The History Teacher*, XII (1979), pp. 373–81. Dewey's place in intellectual history is discussed by Morton White in *Social Thought in America: The Revolt Against Formalism* (New York: Viking, 1949). A recent critical examination of Dewey is Clarence Karier's "Liberal Ideology and the Quest for Orderly Change," in Karier, *et al., Roots of Crisis*, pp. 84–107. ". . . its special line": John Dewey, "The University School," *University Record* I (November 6, 1896), p. 417. ". . . and growing experience": John Dewey, *The Child and the Curriculum and The School and Society* (Chicago: U. Chicago, 1971), p. 23.

There is no really good history of the museum movement in the United States. Our interpretation of the Brooklyn Children's Museum is part of ongoing research concerning the origins of children's museums in the United States. For background on the Educational Museum of the St. Louis Public Schools, see Provenzo. "The Educational Museum of the St. Louis Public Schools," *The Bulletin* (Missouri Historical Society), XXXV, (April, 1979), pp. 147-53.

For an introduction to the role of the international expositions and American education see Provenzo, "Education and the Louisiana Purchase Exposition," *The Bulletin* (Missouri Historical Society), XXXII, (January, 1976), pp. 99-109. ". . . the elementary schools": "The Children's Museum of the Brooklyn Institute," *Scientific American*, LXXXIX (1900), p. 296. ". . . on about them": *ibid.* ". . . soap are made": C. G. Rathmann, "Report of the First Year's Work of the Educational Museum, 1905-1906," manuscript included in the historical file of the Audio-Visual Department of the St. Louis Public Schools, p. 1.

Our interpretation of the Youth Movement in the United States has drawn heavily on Selwyn K. Troen's essay, "The Discovery of the Adolescent by American Educational Reformers, 1900-1920: An Economic Perspective," in Laurence Stone, ed., *Schooling and Society: Studies in the History of Education* (Baltimore: Johns Hopkins U., 1976), and Joel Spring's "Youth Culture in the United States," in Clarence Karrier *et al.*, *Roots of Crisis.* Spring's ideas on Youth Culture are also included in his book, *American Education: An Introduction to Social and Political Aspects* (New York: Longman, 1978). ". . . with its problems": *Adolescence* (1905), reprinted in Cohen, *Education in the United States*, Vol. 4, p. 2206.

Lewis Hine's background and significance as a documentary photographer is best described in Judith Mara Gutman's *Lewis Hine, Two Perspectives* (New York: Grossman Publishers, 1974). For background on National Child Labor Committee see Walter I. Trattner's *Crusade for the Children: A History of the National Child Labor Committee and Child Labor Reform in America* (Chicago: Quadrangle Books, 1970). ". . . for any child": Lewis W. Hine, "Baltimore to Biloxi and Back—The Children's Burden in Oyster and Shrimp Canneries," *The Survey*, 30 (May 3, 1913), p. 170. An analysis of Hine as a visual propagandist of education is included in Provenzo, "The Photographer as Educator: The Photo-Stories of Lewis Hine," *Teachers College Record*, Vol. 83, no. 4, Summer 1982.

CHAPTER EIGHT:
EFFICIENCY AND MANAGEMENT

This chapter is based on Callahan's *Cult of Efficiency,* Twenty-five years after its publication, it is possible to add some contextual details from a new biography of Frederick Taylor, a biography of Louis Brandeis, and further historical research on production considerations and engineering history.

That centralization and standardization had begun before the school efficiency movement is stressed by Tyack, *The One Best System*, pp. 126-76. ". . . his entire service": Franklin Bobbitt, *Some General Principles of Management Applied to the Problems of City-School Systems*, Part I of the 12th Yearbook of the National Society for the Study of Education (Bloomington, Ill.: n.p., 1911), pp. 11, 79. Samuel Haber, *Efficiency and Uplift* (Chicago: U. Chicago, 1964), handles the efficiency movement generally as a rationale of social reform—by the efficiency experts. S. Chester Parker's "revisionist" view; "Free Schools and the Lancastrian System," *Elementary School Teacher*, 10 (1910), pp. 388-400.

Sudhir Kakar, *Frederick Taylor: A Study of Personality and Innovation* (Cambridge, Mass.: M.I.T., 1970) suggests that Taylor's eye strain was psychogenic. Taylor's employer at Midvale, William Sellers, had also started his career with an apprenticeship. That had not been unusual in Philadelphia, as Bruce Sinclair points out in "At the Turn of the Screw: William Sellers, the Franklin Institute, and a Standard American Thread," *Technology and Culture*, 10 (1969), p. 25. Sellers was more important for Taylor's success than previously thought.

". . . or monthly installments": Irving A. Berndt, "The Value of a Dollar's Worth of Labor," *Efficiency* (Sept., 1913), p. 13. "Schmidt" appeared in an example of Taylor's methods, in Frederick W. Taylor, *The Principles of Scientific Management* (New York: Harper & Brothers, 1913). The quoted passages appear in Callahan, pp. 37–38. Spaulding, with what strikes us as misplaced pride, wrote two autobiographical volumes: Frank E. Spaulding, *One School Administrator's Philosophy: Its Development* (New York: Exposition, 1952) and *School Superintendent in Action in Five Cities* (Rindge, N.H.: Smith, 1955). Together they are revealing of the man and his views. ". . . recitations in art", ". . . in something else": F. E. Spaulding, "The Applications of Principles of School Management," *NEA Proceedings*, 1913, p. 263. Information on early railroad management patterns is from Alfred D. Chandler, Jr., "The Railroads: Pioneers in Modern Corporate Management," *History of American Management* (Englewood Cliffs, N.J.: Prentice-Hall, 1969) ed. by James P. Paughman.

Most of our information on measurement in the physical sciences comes from Kevles, *The Physicists . . . passim*. ". . . business and industry": Sears, quoted in Callahan, p. 118. ". . . and field efficiency": Sara Helena Fahey, "Moral Education: What the School Can Do," *NEA Proceedings*, 1916, p. 641. ". . . as a monarch": A. W. Rankin, "Who Shall Administer Our Schools," *NEA Proceedings*, 1914, p. 915. ". . . the factory plan": W. C. Bagley, "The Status of the Classroom Teachers," *NEA Proceedings*, 1915, p. 1162. Dewey's misgivings were in "Professional Experience Among Teachers," *American Teacher*, IV (1913), pp. 115–16. Maxwell dissented in "On a Certain Arrogance in Educational Theorists," *Educational Review*, XLVII (1914), pp. 165–82.

CHAPTER NINE:
SCIENTIFIC PEDAGOGY, TEACHERS, CURRICULUM, DEPRESSION AND WAR

There is a considerable literature on the Gary Plan. The essays of Randolph Bourne, liberal journalist, have been reprinted in *The Gary Schools* (Cambridge, Mass.: M.I.T., 1970), edited by Adeline and Murray Levine, who also supplied a helpful introduction. Some recent studies appear in Ronald D. Cohen and Raymond A. Mohl, *The Paradox of Progressive Education* (Port Washington, N.Y.: Kennikat, 1979).

For his formulation of the science of education, see Charles Hubbard Judd, *Introduction to the Scientific Study of Education* (New York: Ginn, 1918) pp. 299–307. Lawrence A. Cremin, David A. Shannon, and Mary Evelyn Townsend, *A History of Teachers College, Columbia University* is less than satisfactory. There are some additional details about the founding of Teachers College in Nicholas Murray Butler, *Across the Busy Years* (New York: Scribner's, 1939, 2 vols.) and about its early years in James Earl Russell, *Founding Teachers College* (New York: Teachers College, Columbia U., 1937).

Our impression of Galton comes from D. W. Forrest, *Francis Galton: The Life and Work of a Victorian Genius* (New York: Taplinger, 1974). Robert I. Watson, *The Great Psychologists* (Philadelphia: Lippincott, several editions) has brief sketches of the life and work of Galton, and also of Binet. ". . . she committed suicide": quoted in Guy Montrose Whipple, *Manual of Mental and Physical Tests* (Baltimore: Warwick & York, 1910), p. 508. Steven Jay Gould, *The Mismeasure of*

Man (New York: W. W. Norton, 1981) is an unsparing critique of IQ measures and their underlying assumptions. Walter S. Monroe, *Ten Years of Educational Research*, U. of Illinois Bulletin No. 51 (Urbana: U. of Illinois, 1928) is a useful source on early educational research. ". . . Now, go ahead": quoted in Whipple, p. 500. ". . . Army and Navy": quoted in Robert M. Yerkes (ed.), *Psychological Examining in the United States Army*, Vol. XV, Memoirs of the National Academy of Science (Washington, D.C.: U.S. Government Printing Office, 1921), p. 7. Cremin's analysis of Thorndike's psychology is in *Transformation*, pp. 111–12. As part of his multi-volume study of genius (that is, those with high IQ scores), Terman's colleagues estimated the IQs of famous men. George Washington as a boy had an estimated IQ of 125. Lewis B. Terman, ed., *Genetic Studies of Genius*, vol. 2 (Stanford: Stanford U., 1926), pp. 345–46. "Philoprogenitiveness," "vitativeness," "consciententiousness," O. S. Fowler, *Self-Culture and Perfection of Character* (New York: Fowlers and Wells, 1854), *passim.* In other books Fowler assigned the faculties other names.

The Thorndike and Woodworth experiments were reported in E. L. Thorndike and R. S. Woodworth, "The Influence of Improvement in One Mental Function Upon the Efficiency of Other Functions," *Psychological Review*, VII (1901), pp. 247–61, 384–95, 553–64. ". . . matter how similar" *ibid.*, p. 250. Lotus Delta Coffman's study, a doctoral dissertation, was *The Social Composition of the Teaching Population*, Teachers College, Columbia U. Contributions to Education No. 41 (New York: Teachers College, Columbia U., 1911).

Beatrice Stephens Nathan, *Tales of a Teacher* (Chicago: Regnery, 1956) is one of the few recent volumes of teacher reminiscences. Francis R. Donovan, *The Schoolm'am* (New York: Stokes, 1938) provided information but did not attempt serious analysis. Willard Waller, *The Sociology of Teaching* (repr. New York: Wiley, 1967) is still seen as an important sociological work. ". . . a Baptist accent": Donovan, p. 178. ". . . their social philosophies", ". . . regulation of authority", ". . . comes to pass": George S. Counts, *School and Society in Chicago* (New York: Harcourt Brace, 1928), pp. 77, 79, 85. Coggin, Haley, and the Chicago Teachers Federation are a subject of William Edward Eaton, *The American Federation of Teachers, 1916–1941* (Carbondale, Ill.: Southern Illinois U., 1975), pp. 5 ff.

There is a brief critique of activity analysis in Cremin, *Transformation*, pp. 198–200. The *Commonwealth Teacher-Training Study* was W. W. Charters and Douglas Waples (Chicago: U. Chicago, 1929). Walter S. Monroe provides more specific information and a guarded criticism. ". . . and sometimes absurd" and ". . . ordinary good breeding": Abraham Flexner, *Universities, American, British, German* (repr. New York: Teachers College, Columbia U., 1967), pp. 97, 104. ". . . is concerned with": Bobbitt, quoted in Monroe, p. 126.

William H. Kilpatrick, "The Project Method," *Teachers College Record*, XIX (1918), pp. 319–25, is a succinct statement of his view. His *Foundations of Method* (New York: Macmillan, 1925) adds little. Julia Weber Gordon, *My Country School Diary* has been reprinted (New York: Dell, 1970) with an introduction by John Holt.

Alice Barrows' perpetuation of the Gary Plan is described in Cohen and Mohl, pp. 10–34. A shorter version by Mohl is "Urban Education in the Twentieth Century: Alice Barrows and the Platoon School Plan," *Urban Education*, IX (1974), pp. 213–37. ". . . meaning to them": Barrows, "A Brief Statement. . . ." unpublished, quoted in Cohen and Mohl, p. 192.

". . . purpose of education": Jesse H. Newlon, *Education for Democracy in Our Time* (New York: McGraw-Hill, 1939), p. 129. ". . . to participate effectively": Grayson N. Kefauver, "Reorientation of School Administration," in *Changing Concepts in School Administration*, Part II, Forty-fifth Yearbook of the National

Society for the Study of Education (Chicago: U. Chicago, 1946), p. 3. David Tyack and Elisabeth Hansot, *Managers of Virtue* (New York: Basic, 1982) provides a good general view of the history of school administrators. Ronald Campbell, et al., *A History of Thought and Practice in Education* (New York: Teachers College, Columbia, 1987) describes the development of scholarship and thought on school administration. The relationship between what was advocated and what was done in practice has been limited and complex.

The results of Lewin's experiment were published in several forms. The first was Kurt Lewin, Ronald Lippitt, and R. K. White, "Patterns of Aggressive Behavior in Experimentally Created Social Climates," *Journal of Social Psychology*, X (1939), pp. 271–99. The Western Electric studies were also influential. They first appeared as F. J. Roethlisberger and W. J. Dickson, *Management and the Worker* (Cambridge: Harvard, 1939).

Many details in this chapter come from Cremin, *Transformation*. The most detailed description of schooling in the Depression is in David Tyack, et al., *Public Schools in Hard Times: The Great Depression and Recent Years* (Cambridge, Mass.: Harvard, 1984). In contrast with the school crises of the 1980s, they point out, there were increasing rather than decreasing numbers of pupils during the Depression, and public confidence in the schools was unshaken. Information on Chicago in the Depression is from Herrick, pp. 209–28. Teachers in Oklahoma recorded their Depression experiences in James Smallwood (ed.), *And Gladly Teach: Reminicences of Teachers from Frontier Dugout to Modern Module* (Norman, Okla.: U. of Oklahoma, 1976), pp. 138–79.

". . . imposition and indoctrination": George S. Counts, "Dare Progressive Education be Progressive," quoted in Cremin, *Transformation*, p. 259. The political statements of Counts and other social reform educators come in large part from C. A. Bowers, *The Progressive Educator and the Depression: The Radical Years* (New York: Random House, 1969). ". . . the status quo": Agnes de Lima, "Education for What?" *New Republic*, LXXI (1932), p. 317, quoted in Bowers, p. 38. ". . . other relevant findings": Augusta Alpert, *New Republic*, LXXII (1932), p. 317, quoted in Cremin, *Transformation*, p. 259. I. L. Kandell, *The Impact of the War on American Education* (Charlotte: U. N. Carolina, 1949) provides some factual information on the immediate effects of the war.

PART FOUR:
YEARS OF TURMOIL

Some details here are from Manchester, although particularly in later passages his interpretations are questionable and over-irate. Much of our information is from a variety of news sources. We have followed Lester B. Thurow's review of recent economic history as it appeared in "A Surge in Inequality," *Scientific American*, 256, no. 30 (1987), pp. 256 ff. Our interpretation of individualism is from Bellah, et al., passim. Some information has come from the files of *Urban Education*.

For additional reading: J. Anthony Lukas, *Common Ground* (New York: Vintage, 1986) is an impressive day-to-day account of school desegregation and other reforms and reformers in Boston in the 1970s. It is an effective reminder that school desegregation was not an effort in isolation. On school history, Cremin, *Transformation*, has much information on the early post-World War II years. Diane Ravitch, *The Troubled Crusade: American Education, 1945-1980* (New York: Basic, 1983) is an interesting generally conservative account of recent history of education. Tyack, et al., *Public Schools in Hard Times*, describes the pressures to which the public schools were subjected in the 1970s and 1980s. Martin Mayer, *The Schools* (New York: Harper, 1961) was enormously popular for nearly a decade. A. S. Neill, *Summerhill: A Radical Approach to Child Rearing* (New York: Hart, 1960) was nearly obligatory reading for aspiring educationists. James Simon Kunen, *The Strawberry Statement* (New York: Random House, 1969) is the most striking account of campus uprisings at the end of the 1960s. Kunen was a student at Columbia University. Edgar Z. Friedenberg, *The Vanishing Adolescent* (Boston: Beacon, 1959) was the first and in many ways the best critique of schools and society. Two novels, Evan Hunter, *The Blackboard Jungle* (several editions) and Bel Kaufman, *Up the Down Staircase* (Englewood Cliffs, N.J.: Prentice-Hall, 1964) now seem encumbered with faulty plots, but do catch the grim aspect of city schools. J. D. Salinger, *Catcher in the Rye* (several editions) was seen as the essence of the plight of the adolescent in the 1950s; reread, it is still of interest, but faulty in execution. John Knowles, *A Separate Peace* (several editions) caught the dilemma of the adolescent boy on the eve of hostilities.

CHAPTER TEN:
EQUALITY IN SCHOOLS

Our analysis of black education has depended heavily on Henry Allen Bullock's *A History of Negro Education in the South: From 1619 to the Present* (Cambridge: Harvard, 1967). ". . . than twelve months": *A New Digest of the Statute Laws of Louisiana* (1844), reprinted in Cohen, *ibid.*, p. 1621.

Crandall's school in Canterbury has been a matter of intense and lasting interest. She has been portrayed as near-martyr and as agent provocateur. Our discussion is based on Leon Litwak, *North of Slavery: The Nego in the Free States, 1790-1860* (Chicago: U. Chicago, 1961).

For background on the history of Hampton Institute, see Francis Peabody, *Education for Life* (New York: Doubleday, 1904). Photographs of Hampton taken in 1900 for the Paris International Exposition were republished in Frances Benjamin Johnston, *The Hampton Album* (New York: Doubleday, 1966).

White Northern teachers in the South after the Civil War have received much attention, and the others little. One might suspect chauvinism; too, the Northern teachers, perhaps particularly the ones on Sea Islands, were prolific letter writers, which provided materials for historians. J. W. Alvard's semiannual reports, *Schools and Finances of Freedmen* (Washington, D.C.: Government Printing Office, 1868-70), reprinted as *Freedmen's Schools and Textbooks*, Vol. I (New York: AMS, 1980), Robert C. Morris, ed., show that more blacks than whites taught in Freedmen's schools, and that some white teachers were Southerners. Booker T. Washington's first schooling and first teaching is from Louis R. Harlan, *Booker T. Washington, The Making of a Black Leader, 1856-1901* (New York: Oxford, 1972), passim. ". . . of the Freedmen": "The Founding of the Hampton Institute," (1904), reprinted in Cohen, *Education in the United States*, Vol. 3, p. 1653. ". . . men and women": "Tuskegee and Its People," reprinted in Cohen, *ibid.*, p. 1674. The first volume of Booker T. Washington's biography cited above and Louis R. Harlan, *Booker T. Washington, The Wizard of Tuskegee, 1901-1915* (New York: Oxford, 1983) demonstrate the complexities of Washington and his political talent.

Biographies of W. E. B. DuBois include Francis Broderick, *W. E. B. DuBois, Negro Leader in a Time of Crisis* (Stanford: Stanford University Press, 1959); Alexander Lacy, *Cheer for Lonesome Traveler: The Life of W. E. B. DuBois* (New York: Dial Press, 1970); and Arnold Rampersad, *The Art and Imagination of W. E. B. DuBois* (Cambridge: Harvard, 1976). A general selection of his work is found in Meyer Weinberg, ed., *W. E. B. DuBois: A Reader* (New York: Harper & Row, 1970).

A collective noun for "Indians" is vexing. "Indians" is a misnomer, of course. But how could one have been a "Native American" before the invention of America, and "native" only in the sense that one's ancestors were the most remote immigrants? George Pierre Castile, in *North American Indians: An Introduction to the Chichimeca* (New York: McGraw-Hill, 1979), uses "Chichimeca," but a word used by the Aztecs is not an ideal solution. Castile's book is a readable and informative one. Although the thesis of Winthrop D. Jordan, *White Over Black*, (Chapel Hill: U. North Carolina, 1968), apparent in the title, seems powerful, first impressions of American Indians as "noble savages" did not result in great subsequent advantage for them.

Background on Pratt and the Carlisle Indian Barracks School is provided by Richard Pratt, *Battlefield and Classroom: Four Decades with the American Indian, 1867-1904* (New Haven: Yale, 1964). ". . . in their hearts": *ibid.*, p. 163. General sources dealing with the history of education of Indians include Estelle Fuchs and Robert J. Havinhurst, *To Live on This Earth: American Indian Education* (Garden City, N.Y.: Doubleday, 1974) and Margaret Szasz, *Education and the American Indian: The Road to Self-Determination, 1928-1973* (Albuquerque: U. New Mexico, 1974).

R. Freeman Butts, *Public Education in the United States* (New York: Holt, Rinehart and Winston, 1978), pp. 326-40, provides a brief resume of desegregation until 1976. Meyer Weinberg, *A Chance to Learn: The History of Race and Education in the United States* (London: Cambridge U., 1977) is useful although it is a wholly pessimistic account. Richard Kluger, *Simple Justice* (New York: Knopf, 1975, 2 vol.) is a painstaking and often absorbing account of *Brown* v. *Board of Education* and related events. ". . . the Fourteenth Amendment": Earl Warren, *Brown* v. *Board of Education of Topeka*, often printed, quoted in Kluger, pp. 890-93. ". . . and poor children": Weinberg, p. 134. Raymond Wolters, *The Burden of Brown* (Knoxville, Tenn.: U. of Tennessee, 1984), argues that subsequent court decisions, especially *Green* v. *New Kent County*, had costly adverse effects upon schooling. A more general and more positive view of the effects of liberal policy after 1960 is Sar A. Levitan, et al., *Still a Dream* (Cambridge, Mass.: Harvard, 1975). Diane Ravitch, *The Great School Wars* is the source of most of our information about the New York City controversies. A late defense of the pursuit of equality is Ann Bastian et al., *Choosing Equality* (Philadelphia: Temple, 1986).

R. Rosenthal and L. Jacobson, *Pygmalion in the Classroom* (New York: Holt, Rinehart and Winston, 1968) is the original account of the Pygmalion experiment. Ray T. Rist's classroom research was described in several articles, probably the most influential of which was "Student Social Class and Teacher Expectations: The Self Fulfilling Prophecy in Ghetto Education," *Harvard Educational Review*, 40 (1970), pp. 411-56. There has been much controversy about both pieces of research. One more recent discussion is Samuel S. Wineberg, "The Self-Fulfillment of the Self-Fulling Prophecy," with rejoinders, *Educational Researcher*, 16, No. 9 (Dec., 1987), pp. 28-44.

CHAPTER ELEVEN:
IN PURSUIT OF FREEDOM

For our interpretation of the youth movement we have depended heavily on Joel Spring, *American Education: An Introduction to Social and Political Aspects* (New York: Longman, 1978). There are numerous sources on the youth culture and education in the 1960s. Theodore Roszak, *The Making of the Counter Culture* (New York: Anchor, 1969) was among the most prominent. Works on the alienation of youth in the 1950s and 1960s include David Riesman, et al., *The Lonely Crowd* (New Haven: Yale, 1950); Friedenberg, *Vanishing Adolescent*; and Paul Goodman, *Growing Up Absurd* (New York: Vintage, 1960). ". . . source of alienation": Friedenberg, pp. 218–19. Jules Henry, in *Culture Against Man* (New York: Random House, 1963) and *Essays on Education* (New York: Vintage, 1972) provides a perceptive analysis of schooling in American society in the 1960s. ". . . jail the child": Henry, *Culture Against Man*, p. 12.

As this revision was being completed, James Miller, *Democracy in the Streets* (New York: Simon & Schuster, 1987) was the best single account of youth activism, SDS, and the New Left in the 1960s. Earlier sources are Louis F. Feuer, *The Conflict of Generations* (New York: Basic, 1969) and Joseph Califano, Jr., *The Student Revolution: A Global Confrontation* (New York: Norton, 1969). *The Port Huron Statement*, until now rather difficult to locate, is reprinted in Miller, pp. 329–74. Allan Bloom, *Closing of the American Mind* (New York: Simon & Schuster, 1987) written a quarter century after events, seems to us to be a reactionary analysis. There are several sources on the student movement at Columbia University. ". . . alone and lost": Kunen p. 11.

There are numerous discussions in the 1960s of new approaches to schooling. Most interesting are: A. S. Niel, *Summerhill*; Joseph Featherstone's articles on schools in *The New Republic* in August and September, 1967; John Holt, *How Children Fail* (New York: Pittman, 1964); Herbert Kohl, *36 Children* (New York: American Library, 1967); and Nat Hentoff, *Our Children Are Dying* (New York: Viking, 1966).

The history of Parkway School is described in John Bremer, *The School Without Walls* (New York: Holt, Rinehart and Winston, 1971). Probably the best introduction to the alternative school is A. Graubard, *Free the Children: Radical Reform and the Free School Movement* (New York: Pantheon, 1972). ". . . the high school" and ". . . the next month": interview conducted by Provenzo, fall, 1974.

CHAPTER TWELVE:
SCHOOL CRISIS, SCHOOL RESPONSES

Many of our sources are identified in the text. ". . . + PC/2 [PL + 55:100])": Albert Lynd, *Quackery in the Public Schools* (Boston: Little Brown, 1973), p. 14. Lynd might have consulted the further elaboration of the formula, which appeared in Harl R. Douglass, "The 1950 Revision of the Douglass High School Teaching Load Formula," *Bulletin of the National Association of Secondary-School Principals*, XXXV, No. 179 (May, 1951). We agree with Lynd that it was a "prodigious triviality." Callahan points out, p. 240, that principals found it "extremely useful." ". . . reduced to nonissues": Nathan Glazer, "Responses," *Harvard Educational Review* (Nov., 1982), quoted in Beatrice and Ronald Gross, eds., *Great School Debate* (New York: Simon & Schuster, 1985), p. 337. The Gross and Gross collection of criticisms, proposals for reform, and rejoinders is useful. ". . . unilateral educational disarmament": National Commission on Excellence in Education, "A Nation at Risk," repr. Gross and Gross, p. 23. ". . . the same track": Mortimer J. Adler, *Paideia: Problems and Possibilities* (New York: Macmillan, 1983), repr. Gross and Gross, p. 189.

Lorrie A. Shapiro and Amelia E. Kreitzer, "The Texas Teacher Test," *Educational Researcher*, 16 (Aug.–Sept., 1917), pp. 22–31, is a summary of the evaluation of the 1986 Texas teacher tests.

Our understanding of the demographics of teaching and of teacher careers has as its most recent origin W. W. Charters, Jr., "The Social Background of Teaching," *Handbook of Research on Teaching*, N. L. Gage, ed. (Chicago: Rand McNally, 1963), pp. 715-813. We have also been influenced by Everett C. Hughes, *Men and Their Work* (Glencoe, Ill.: Free Press, 1958). Information on Buffalo "out of certificate" teachers was compiled from the Buffalo Public School personnel records.

The earlier part of our account of the American Federation of Teachers (AFT) is drawn from William Edward Eaton, *The American Federation of Teachers, 1916-1961* (Carbondale, Ill.: Southern Illinois U., 1975). For the development of the UFT in New York City, see Ravitch, *Great School Wars*. Diane Ravitch and Ronald K. Goodenow, eds., *Educating an Urban People* (New York: Teachers College, Columbia U., 1981) provides additional information and a bibliography. An interesting if somewhat disjointed account of the organization of the UFT, AFT affiliate, in New York City and its recognition as bargaining agent is David Selden, *The Teacher Rebellion* (Washington, D.C.: Howard U., 1985). Seldon also describes failed efforts to combine the AFT and the NEA. ". . . private manufacturing firms": Seldon, p. 55. Many articles describe the UFT affiliate contract with the Rochester schools. One of the first, and the one drawn upon here, appeared in *New York Teacher*, XXIX, No. 2 (Sept. 24, 1987).

The appearance of the first R & D center is described in David F. Noble, *America by Design* (New York: Knopf, 1977). Information on education R & D and subsequent funding of research, although not on substantive matters, appears in Richard A. Dershimer, *The Federal Government and Educational R & D* (Lexington, Mass.: Lexington Books, 1976). ". . . 1980 and 1984": U.S. General Accounting Office, "Education Information: Changes in Funds and Priorities Have Affected Production and Quality" (1987), Executive Summary, pp. 2-4. ". . . to American Education": William J. Bennett, in U.S. Department of Education, *What Works: Research about Teaching and Learning* (1986), pp. v-vi.

For a more detailed view of computers in schools, see Eugene F. Provenzo, Jr., *Beyond the Gutenberg Galaxy* (New York: Teachers College, Columbia U., 1986). Other sources are cited there. ". . . has no parallel" and "beneficial or harmful" *ibid.* A review of the uses of computers and other electronic technology in schools in 1987 appears in "The Electronic School," *American School Board Journal*, 174, No. 7 (July, 1987), pp. A1-A30.

INDEX

and black education, 45
schools of, colonial era, 45
Quincy System, 129
Quintilian, 16

R

Raikes, Robert, 75
Rate-bill, 102
Rathman, Carl, 202, 204
Rationalism, colonial era, 34
Reading:
colonial era, 22
England, 13
Reagan, Ronald, 263
Reeve, Judge Tapping, 87-88
Reform schools, 160
Renaissance, 5
England, 16-18
Republicanism:
classical education and, 96-97
Jefferson, Thomas, 65-68
post-Revolutionary era, 63, 66
Revisionism, and Common School
Movement, 94
Revolution:
and college campuses, 48, 90
effects on education, 51
See also Post-Revolutionary era.
Rice, Joseph Mayer, 194-95, 224
and science of education, 236-37
style of research, 236
Rickover, Admiral Hyman G., 311-12
Rigg, Edward, 85
Riis, Jacob, 191-94
Robbins, Jane, 189
Robertson, Donald, 42
Roberts v. Boston, 278
Roelansen, Adam, 29
Rollin, Charles, 47
Romanticism, America, 57
Roosevelt, Franklin D., 182, 254-55
Roosevelt, Theodore, 179-80
Round Hill School, 117, 136
Rousseau, Jean-Jacques, 69, 71, 100, 291
Rudd, Augustin G., 312
Runkle, John D., 153
Rush, Benjamin, 68-70
on education of women, 69
Russell, James Earl, 234, 236
Rutgers University, establishment of, 50

S

St. Pauls Cathedral School, England, 16-17
School Architecture (Barnard), 114-15
School boards, Progressive era, reducing
size, 212, 214
School control, 212-15
Progressive era:
decision-making in schools, 214-15
politics and schools, view of, 214
school boards, 212, 214
School efficiency, 214-15, 218-19
Bobbitt, Franklin, influence of, 215, 218
educational measurement, 224-27

Gary Plan, 230-31
measurement of industrial costs, 218-19
"minimum essentials,' concept, 216
origins of, 215-16
popularity of, 215-16
school management, 219-20, 222-23
Schooling in Capitalist America (Bowles and
Gintis), 162
Schoolman, 127
School management, 219-20, 222-23
administration texts used, 222, 223
scientific management principle, 222-23
Spaulding's principles, 222-23
Schoolmaster's Assistant (Dilworth), 83
School and Society, The (Dewey), 187, 200,
202, 291-92
Schools and Society in Chicago (Counts),
244, 247
School surveys, 225-26
Schulordnung (Dock), 40
Schurz, Margarethe, 168
Science of education, 233-42
founders of:
Hall, G. Stanley, 236, 237
Rice, Joseph Mayer, 236-37
Thorndike, Edward L., 237-38
Teachers College, influence of, 234, 236
Scientific knowledge, changing view of, 176
Scientific management, 216-18
applied to schools, 222-23
contributions of, 222
Scott, Sir Walter, 57
Sedwick, Theodore, 144
Segregation, blacks, 1840s, 146
Seward, William H., 143, 145
Shakers, 59
Sheldon, Edward A., 129
Simon, Theodore, 238
Simon-Binet intelligence test, 238-39, 240
Slaves:
abolitionism, 58
colonial education of, 44-45
lack of education for, 1800s, 146-47
slave artisans, 45
Small, William, 50, 66
Smith, Patty Hill, 234
*Social Composition of the Teaching
Population* (Coffman), 242-43
Socialization, primary socialization, 19
Scoial settlement movement, 189-91
Society for the Propagation of the Gospel,
38, 39, 44
Sociology of Teaching (Waller), 244
Sophia (Rousseau), 69
South, education in:
colonial era, 23, 24, 41-44
nineteenth century, 102-3
Spaulding, Frank, 219, 222-23
Spirit of Man, The (Froebel), 166
Spring, Joel, 94, 205
Sputnik I, 310-11, 312
Stanford-Binet Intelligence Test, 240
Starr, Ellen Gates, 190
Steele, Oliver, 127
Stone, William J., 145

122574

370.973   B86   122574

Button, H. Warren.

History of education and
  culture in America